The Elements
of Public Speaking

The Elements of Public Speaking

FIFTH EDITION

Joseph A. DeVito

Hunter College of the City University of New York

HarperCollins College Publishers

To Russel R. Windes
for his wise and creative leadership in the study of communication
and for introducing me to the art of writing a textbook.

Acquisitions Editor: Daniel F. Pipp
Project Editor: Thomas R. Farrell
Text and Cover Design: Wendy A. Fredericks
Cover Photos: *(top left)* © General Electric/PhotoEdit, *(top right)* © Daemmrich/Stock Boston, *(center)* © David Young-Wolff/PhotoEdit, *(bottom left)* © 1991 Bill Clark/Stock South, *(bottom right)* © Daemmrich/Stock Boston.
Photo Researcher: Mira Schachne
Production Manager: Willie Lane
Compositor: Black Dot, Inc.
Printer and Binder: R. R. Donnelley & Sons Company
Cover Printer: The Lehigh Press, Inc.

For permission to use copyrighted material, grateful acknowledgement is made to the copyright holders on page C-1, which is hereby made part of this copyright page.

The Elements of Public Speaking, **Fifth Edition**

Library of Congress Cataloging-in-Publication Data

DeVito, Joseph A., (date)–
    The elements of pulbic speaking / Jospeh A. DeVito. — 5th ed.
        p. cm.
    Includes bibliographical references and index.
    ISBN 0-06-501732-3
    1. Public speaking.   I. Title.
PN4121.D389   1994
a808.5'1—dc20   93-23509
                                                                          CIP

94   95   96   97   9   8   7   6   5   4   3   2

Contents

PART ONE
■ ■ ■ ■
Elements of Public Speaking   1

UNIT 1   The Nature of Public Speaking   3

WHY STUDY PUBLIC SPEAKING?   4

Increase Personal and Social Abilities 4 / Enhance Your Academic and Career Skills 4 / Refine Your General Communication Abilities 4 / Increase Your Public Speaking Abilities 5

WHAT IS PUBLIC SPEAKING?   6

Public Speaking and Conversation 6 / A Definition of Public Speaking 8

HOW PUBLIC SPEAKING WORKS   9

Speaker 9 / Listeners 10 / Noise 11 / Effect 11 / Context 12 / Messages and Channels 12 / A Transactional Process 13

CRITICAL THINKING AND PUBLIC SPEAKING   14

CRITICALLY SPEAKING   15

PRACTICALLY SPEAKING   17

UNIT 2   Preparing a Public Speech: An Overview   19

SELECT THE TOPIC AND PURPOSE   22

The Topic 22 / The Purpose 24

ANALYZE THE AUDIENCE   24

Age 24 / Gender 25

RESEARCH THE TOPIC   25

PART TWO
■ ■ ■ ■
Elements of Subjects and Audiences   97

PART THREE
■ ■ ■ ■
Elements of Organization   189

PART FOUR
■ ■ ■ ■
Elements of Public Speeches   251

PART FIVE

■ ■ ■ ■

Elements of Style and Delivery   407

APPENDIX   Thinking Critically About Speeches   475

Speeches and Outlines

SPEECHES
■ ■ ■ ■

OUTLINES
■ ■ ■ ■

Preface

It is a real pleasure to write a preface to a book in its fifth edition. This revision builds on those features that teachers and students found effective. It improves those features that worked less effectively and introduces a great deal that is new.

Elements continues to be a serious, in-depth study of public speaking designed for the beginning college student. It is not a text that glosses over the very real difficulties in preparing and presenting a public speech. *Elements* is, however, easily accessible to the beginning public speaker who is willing to work, and it is easily adapted to a variety of course structures.

The point of view remains pragmatic and practical. The book's major aim is to develop and improve the student's public speaking skills—as speaker, as listener, and as critic.

Elements continues to present public speaking as a transactional process. Each person influences each other person; audience and speaker interact, each responding to and influencing the other.

The book contains 24 short units (rather than traditional long chapters). The 24 units are organized into 5 major parts:

1. Elements of Public Speaking (Units 1–5)

Covers the material needed to start speaking right away. Unit 2, for example, summarizes the entire public speaking process so students can begin to give speeches immediately. This part also addresses the central concerns of public speaking: the nature of public speaking, speaker apprehension, and listening. New to this edition is Unit 5, which deals with speech criticism in the classroom; it presents the standards of evaluation and guidelines for expressing criticism.

2. Elements of Subjects and Audiences (Units 6–9)

Focuses on selecting topics and purposes, researching the speech topic, and analyzing and adapting to the audience.

3. Elements of Organization (Units 10–12)

Looks at the ways to organize a speech into a meaningful whole and the types and structures of outlines.

4. Elements of Public Speeches (Units 13–20)

Discusses the various types of speeches: informative (Units 13, 14, 15), persuasive (Units 16, 17, 18, 19), and special occasion (Unit 20) and their supporting materials: amplifying materials, argument and evidence, motivational appeals, and credibility appeals.

5. Elements of Style and Delivery (Units 21–24)

Focuses on the qualities of effective language, voice, and bodily action and offers suggestions for rehearsing the speech.

Appendix

Features four speeches with questions to guide your critical analysis of public speeches.

Major Features

This text provides a thorough introduction to public speaking. Its major features include the following:

1. Twenty-four brief units instead of the traditional long chapters. This makes for greater learning ease and enjoyment and maximum flexibility for arranging topics.
2. An introductory unit (2) covering the entire public speaking process so students can begin speaking immediately.
3. A strong focus on critical thinking appears throughout the text (see more under "What's New").
4. An entire unit on speech criticism in the classroom (Unit 5).
5. A thorough discussion of persuasion, the types of speeches, and the logical, emotional, and ethical appeals (Units 16, 17, 18, and 19).
6. Frequent speech excerpts, complete speeches (some with traditional annotations and some with critical thinking guidelines), and sample outlines provide concrete illustrations for the various principles. A list of speeches and outlines follows the table of contents.

What's New

Among the features new or substantially improved in this edition are the following:

1. The entire book has been given a "critical thinking" focus. Numerous sections of the text address critical thinking directly, for example, critical thinking and public speaking in Unit 1, listening critically in Unit 4, criticizing the speech in

Unit 5, discovering information in Unit 7, evaluating visual aids in Unit 15, analyzing arguments in Unit 18, evaluating credibility in Unit 19, and accuracy in language in Unit 21. "Critically Speaking" questions appear at the end of each unit and focus on such critical thinking skills as self-analysis, discovery, application, and evaluation. "Critical Thinking Checklists" (at the end of each of the text's five parts) review the critical thinking skills covered in that part. Five complete speeches are presented with critical thinking analysis guidelines.

2. Consistent with this critical thinking emphasis, a new unit, "Speech Criticism in the Classroom" (Unit 5), has been added and focuses on the values and standards for evaluating a speech, why we find it difficult to express criticism, and the guidelines for effectively expressing and receiving classroom criticism.

3. Unit 2—which presents a capsule summary of all the principles of public speaking so students can begin their speeches as early as possible—has been further clarified to provide more practical advice for the early speeches. It also now includes a discussion of delivery.

4. Unit 6 ("Topic, Purpose, and Thesis") is new to this edition and brings these topics together from several units in the last edition and adds new material on how to find topics.

5. "Critically Speaking" sections present questions for class discussion and appear at the end of each unit.

6. End-of-part sections now include two checklists: (1) a "Performance Checklist" to review your speech preparation for topics covered in that part and (2) a "Critical Thinking Checklist," which identifies the skills covered in the preceding units.

Additional Changes

■ The discussion of listening (Unit 4) now includes an in-depth examination of the listening process and listening guidelines for each of its five stages; in addition, the major obstacles to effective listening are considered.

■ Additional organizational patterns for structuring the body of the speech are included in Unit 10.

■ New "Tips from Professional Speakers" have been added; the best from the previous edition have been retained. These "TIPS" continue to provide insight gained from the experience of professional speakers and underscore the very practical value of public speaking training.

■ The unit on research (6) has been thoroughly revised to keep pace with new developments in computer research.

■ The organization has been changed slightly. The unit on credibility and ethics has been moved to the persuasion section to reflect their close connection; the units on topic, research, and audiences have been grouped together to reinforce their interrelatedness. The annotated speeches have been integrated into the text. Additional speeches for analysis are now included in the Appendix. APA style references are used throughout; a bibliography appears at the end of the text.

- The Remember summaries throughout each unit have been sharpened and made more useful; they help the reader review the essence of the material just read before moving on to the next section.
- New or greatly expanded sections also include ethics (Units 1 and 19), listening to your first speeches (Unit 2), shyness (Unit 3), confidence (Unit 3), a bad speech for criticism (Unit 5), analyzing and adapting to your audience during the speech (Unit 9), transitions (Unit 11), and cultural differences (throughout the text).

Supplements

The fifth edition is accompanied by the following supplements:

Instructor's Manual with Test Bank by Eija Ayravainen of Hunter College. This manual includes sample syllabi, speech assignments, a complete lecture outline, unit outlines, classroom activities, and discussion topics. A bibliography includes a list of audiovisual materials. In addition, there are over 1000 true-false, multiple-choice, short-answer, and essay questions.

TestMaster. The test-bank portion of the *Instructor's Manual* is also available on *TestMaster*, a computerized test-generation system that can be used on most IBM and IBM-compatible systems.

From Paper to Podium: The Elements of Public Speaking Video. A state-of-the-art supplement, this video contains over 15 speeches by both students and professional speakers. They illustrate a wide variety of speech types and techniques at different levels of expertise.

A *Video Guide* accompanies the *Public Speaking Video*. It contains suggestions for incorporating the video into classroom situations and evaluation forms for student use.

The HarperCollins Public Speaking Video Library.

Acknowledgments

It is a pleasure for me to express my appreciation to the many people who influenced the development and production of this text. The first and most obvious debt is to those who have contributed to the research and theory in public speaking that I have reported in this volume. Without them, this book could not have been written. Second, I want to thank those who read the manuscript at various stages of development (or who commented on the previous edition) and who offered criticism, suggestions for improvement, and the feedback so important to turning a manuscript into a useful and relevant textbook. The following were most helpful:

Suzanne Lindsey, Belmont University
Peter O'Rourke, Daytona Beach Community College
James Carlsen, Corpus Christi State University
Vincenne Waxwood, University of Pittsburgh
Gloria Kellum, University of Mississippi
Lisa Merrill, Hofstra University
Gaut Ragsdale, Northern Kentucky University

I also wish to thank those colleagues who reviewed earlier manuscripts and editions of this text and whose insights and suggestions I return to repeatedly. Thank you:

Conrad Awtrey, University of Wisconsin, LaCrosse
John E. Baird, Jr. Modern Management Methods
Michael Bartanen, Pacific Lutheran University
John D. Bee, University of Akron
Park G. Burgess, Queens College
James Chesebro, Indiana State Universtiy
Stephen Coletti, Ithaca College
Catherine R. Cowell, Angelo State University
Kathleen German, Miami University of Ohio
Joseph Giordano, University of Wisconsin, Eau Claire
Jeffrey Hahner, Pace University
Richard Jensen, University of New Mexico
Larry Judd, University of Houston
Bradford L. Kinney, Wilkes College
Cal M. Logue, University of Georgia
Joseph M Mazza, Central Missouri State University
Kevin E. McCleary, Southern Illinois Universtiy at Edwardsville
Constance Morris, Wichita State University
Elizabeth Norwood, Loyola University of Chicago
Janice Peterson, University of California, Santa Barbara
Bennett Raforth, University of Illinois, Urbana
Ellen Ritter, University of Missouri
Susan M. Ross, Clarkson University
John R. Schedel, Medaille College
Roselyn Schiff, Loop College
Curt Siemers, University of Nebraska, Omaha
Malcolm O. Sillars, University of Utah
Mary Ann Smith, University of Vermont
Ralph R. Smith, Southwest Missouri State University
Debra Stenger, Mississippi State University
David E. Walker, Jr. Middle Tennessee State University
William E. Wiethoff, Indiana University
Russel R. Windes, Queens College

JOSEPH A. DeVITO

To the Student

Fair questions to ask before beginning this book are "What will I get out of this?," "What will I be able to do after reading this book that I cannot do well now?" Here are some general payoffs or objectives that you should be able to meet after reading this text.

The Payoffs

1. Analyze a wide variety of audiences and effectively adapt your speeches to their unique characteristics and attitudes.
2. Research a wide variety of topics effectively and efficiently, using traditional resources as well as the newest computerized databases.
3. Organize materials into a meaningful and coherent public speech.
4. Support your ideas so that these ideas are understandable and persuasive.
5. Listen more effectively and efficiently.
6. Critically evaluate public speeches—their arguments, their appeals, their impact.
7. Give criticism to others that is constructive and supportive and receive criticism with openness.
8. Develop your own credibility (believability) and express your competence, character, and charisma in your speeches.
9. Word messages so they are clear, persuasive, and easily remembered by the audience.
10. Deliver public speeches to a wide variety of audiences with effective voice and bodily action.
11. Improve your critical thinking abilities, especially your abilities to analyze yourself, to discover significant concepts and relationships, to apply the concepts and principles of public speaking to other forms of communication, and to evaluate and judge with insight and discrimination.
12. Increase your resistance to unfair or unethical persuasive appeals.

In short, you should be able to construct and deliver informative, persuasive, and special occasion speeches to widely different audiences with effectiveness. You should significantly improve your listening and your ability to assess public speeches critically and to express those assessments constructively.

P A R T   O N E

Elements of Public Speaking

This first part covers the fundamentals of public speaking: what public speaking is and how it is similar to and different from everyday conversation (Unit 1); an overview of the entire public speaking process so that you will be able to begin giving speeches immediately and thus learn by doing (Unit 2); speaker apprehension, the normal fear that most people feel when giving speeches and how to control it (Unit 3); how to improve your listening effectiveness (Unit 4); and speech criticism, how to look at and evaluate the speeches you will hear in this class as well as in your personal and professional life (Unit 5).

The checklists at the end of Part One (and for each of the remaining parts) provide a convenient means for evaluating your **performance** in preparing your speech and for reviewing essential **critical thinking skills.**

In **thinking critically** about the elements of public speaking, try to:

- analyze yourself as a public speaker; consider the value of viewing yourself as an effective and accomplished public speaker and ridding yourself of any competing negative images you may have
- listen to (and watch) public speeches on television and on campus and read them in the newspapers: What can you learn about effective speeches and effective speakers from them?
- apply the principles of public speaking to other forms of communication and to interactions in your social and professional life
- apply the principles flexibly; each situation is different and especially each cultural group is different

U N I T 1

The Nature of Public Speaking

■ ■ ■ ■

UNIT OBJECTIVES

After completing this unit, you should be able to:

1. Describe the benefits from studying public speaking

2. Define *public speaking* and explain how it differs from conversation

3. Diagram and explain the process of public speaking

4. Define each of the following aspects of public speaking: speaker, listeners (audience), noise, effect, context, messages and channels, and the transactional process

5. Explain the relationship between critical thinking and public speaking

---

*O*f all the courses you will take in college, public speaking will surely be the most demanding, satisfying, frustrating, stimulating, ego-involving, and useful now and throughout your professional life. In this first unit the study of public speaking is introduced.

■■■■ WHY STUDY PUBLIC SPEAKING?

What benefits will you derive from the time and effort you invest in studying public speaking? Here are just a few.

Increase Personal and Social Abilities

Public speaking provides training in a variety of personal and social competencies. For example, in the pages that follow we cover such skills as self-awareness, self-confidence, and dealing with the fear of communicating. These are skills that you will apply in public speaking, but will also prove valuable in all of your social interactions.

Enhance Your Academic and Career Skills

As you learn public speaking, you also will learn a wide variety of academic and career skills. These skills are central, but not limited, to public speaking. For example, the ability to do the research will be useful throughout college and in most professional careers. A few additional abilities that you should refine during this course that will help you throughout your career are the abilities to:

- explain complex concepts clearly
- support an argument with all the available means of persuasion
- understand human motivation and be able to use your insights in persuasive encounters
- organize a variety of messages for clarity and persuasiveness
- present yourself to others with confidence and self-assurance
- analyze and evaluate the validity of arguments and persuasive appeals

Refine Your General Communication Abilities

Public speaking also will develop and refine your general communication abilities by helping you to improve competencies such as:

- developing a more effective communication style
- enhancing your self-concept and self-esteem
- adjusting messages to specific listeners

- detecting and responding to feedback
- developing logical and emotional appeals
- building and communicating your credibility
- enhancing assertiveness
- improving listening skills
- organizing extended messages
- refining your delivery skills

Increase Your Public Speaking Abilities

Speakers are not born; they are made. Through instruction, exposure to different speeches, feedback, and your individual learning experiences, you can become an effective speaker. Regardless of your present level of competence, you can improve through proper training—hence this course and this book.

At the end of this book and this course you, unlike the cartoon character on page 6, should be a more competent, confident, and effective public speaker. You should also be a more effective listener—more open yet more critical, more discriminating yet more empathic. And you should emerge a more competent and discerning critic of public communication.

As leaders (and in many ways you can look at this course as one in leadership training skills) you will need the skills of effective communication so you can help preserve a free and open society. These skills apply to you as a speaker who wants your message understood and accepted, as a listener who needs to evaluate and critically analyze ideas and arguments before making decisions, and as a critic who needs to evaluate and judge the thousands of public communications you hear.

TIPS FROM PROFESSIONAL SPEAKERS

When we consider candidates for promotion in management, much of our impression comes from the time those candidates have spoken in officer meetings.

Or from the memos or letters they've prepared.

When we consider candidates for a state vice presidency, we think about their primary role:

—communicating with employees, customers, and regulators.

When we promote people to our holding company, U.S. West in Denver, we think about their primary role:

—communicating with shareowners, stock analysts, and subsidiaries.

Without a doubt, communication skills continue to grow more important.

Richard D. McCormick, president, Northwestern Bell. "Business Loves English," *Vital Speeches of the Day* 51(November 1, 1984):53.

"At that point, I leaped to my feet and in a ringing voice cried, 'Ladies and gentlemen of the jury, if I am guilty, then we are all guilty!'"

Reprinted by permission of The General Media Publishing Group.

REMEMBER: **The study of public speaking leads to important benefits:**

1. **The increase in your personal and social abilities**
2. **The enhancement of related academic and professional skills in organization, research, style, and the like**
3. **The refinement of general communication competencies**
4. **The improvement of public speaking abilities—as speaker, as listener, and as critic—which result in personal benefits as well as benefits to society**

WHAT IS PUBLIC SPEAKING?

The best way to introduce public speaking is to compare it to a form of communication you use daily—conversation. Using this comparison, we can examine some of the major similarities and differences.

Public Speaking and Conversation

We can compare public speaking and conversation in purpose, audience, feedback, supporting materials, organization, language, and delivery (DeVito, 1992, 1993; Knapp and Miller, 1985).

Purpose In both conversation and public speaking you communicate with some purpose in mind. For example, in conversation you might want to tell a friend about what happened at a basketball game last night. In this case your purpose is informative. Or you might want to convince your parents to let you use the car over the weekend. Here your purpose is persuasive. In public speaking, you also communicate with a purpose clearly in mind. The two major types of public speeches are speeches to inform and speeches to persuade.

Audience In both conversation and public speaking, your listeners will influence what you say and how you say it. You would not try to convince your friend to go to the football game with the same arguments you would use to convince your teacher to accept a late paper. In conversation, you usually know your listeners so well that you don't even think about adjusting your messages to them. But you do. Think, for example, of how differently you would relay the events of the day to your parents, friends, employer, and children.

In public speaking, you usually do not know your audience quite so well, so you have to make guesses about what they already know (so you don't repeat what they've heard before), what their attitudes are (so you don't waste time persuading them of something they already believe), and so on. In public speaking you need to analyze your audience more thoroughly than in conversation. You need to plan more carefully the adjustments or adaptations you make.

Feedback In conversation you get immediate verbal and nonverbal feedback from the person you're talking with. In fact, as you speak, the other person will react nonverbally (for example, with eye movements, gestures, and facial expressions) and will frequently interrupt to ask questions or make comments. The entire conversational act consists of short messages from one person and then from the other. In public speaking, the speaker does most of the speaking and the listeners do most of the listening. The listeners do send feedback during the speech but this is largely nonverbal. Rarely does the audience speak back to the speaker, except perhaps in a question-and-answer period following the speech.

Supporting Materials If you wanted to convince your friend to go to the football game with you, you would not simply say, "Come to the football game with me." More likely, you would offer some reasons, some inducements: "It's going to be a really exciting game" or "It's the last game of the season." The number of arguments or reasons you offer will depend on how resistant you think your friend might be. The same is true in public speaking. You don't simply say, "Vote for Johnson." Rather, you would give your listeners reasons why they should vote for Johnson and perhaps reasons why they should not vote for Johnson's opponent.

Organization In explaining how to bake a cake or in giving directions to a stranger, you would organize your message so that it follows a logical order. For example, you would start with the cake's ingredients and their quantities, then explain how they are combined, and finally how they are cooked. Organization is even more important in public speaking because listeners can't stop you during a public speech and ask you to fill in the missing parts. You will have to predict what organizational pattern will best help listeners to understand your message.

Language In conversation you vary your language on the basis of the person with whom you are speaking. When talking with children, you might use easier words and shorter sentences than you would with friends. If you were trying to impress someone, you might use a still different style. In public speaking you adjust your language to your audience in the same way as in conversation. In public speaking, however, your listeners cannot interrupt you to ask, for example, what a particular word means, so your language must be instantly intelligible.

Delivery In conversation you wouldn't even think of delivery; you wouldn't concern yourself with how to sit or stand or gesture. Because public speaking is a relatively new experience and you will probably feel uncomfortable at first, you may find yourself wondering what to do with your hands or whether or not you should move about. With time and experience, you will find that your delivery will follow naturally from what you are saying, just as it does in conversation. Perhaps the best advice to give you now is to view public speaking as "enlarged" conversation (we will review delivery in detail in Units 23 and 24. Deliver your speech as if you were conversing with a large group.

Ethics Both conversation and public speaking, and in fact all forms of communication, have an ethical dimension, a topic considered in depth in Unit 19 (Jaksa and Pritchard 1994; Johannesen 1990; Bok 1978). Yet, for many communications, it is not easy to agree on what is and what is not unethical. Consider, for example:

- Is it ethical to exaggerate your virtues in a job interview? On a first date?
- Is it ethical to tell voters what they want to hear just to get elected? To tell your grandmother she is getting well when you know she is terminally ill?
- Is it ethical to use personal attacks to defeat an opponent?
- Is it ethical to persuade an audience to do something by scaring them? By threatening them? By making them feel guilty?

A Definition of Public Speaking

In *public speaking* a speaker addresses a relatively large audience with a relatively continuous discourse. Usually, it takes place in a face-to-face situation: you deliver an oral report in your economics class, you ask your co-workers to elect you as shop steward, you try to convince your neighbors to clean up the streets or other students to donate blood. These are all public speaking situations.

Unlike conversation, where the "audience" is one listener, the public speaking audience is relatively "large," from groups of perhaps 10 or 12 to audiences of hundreds of thousands. During conversation, the role of speaker shifts repeatedly from one person to another. In public speaking, the speaker gives a relatively continuous talk. This does not mean that only the speaker communicates. Both speaker and audience communicate throughout the public speaking situation; the speaker communicates by delivering the speech and the audience by responding to the speech with feedback. Throughout the public speaking transaction there is mutual and simultaneous exchange of messages between speaker and audience.

"Have you noticed ethics creeping into some of these deals lately?"

Drawing by H. Martin; © 1992 The New Yorker Magazine, Inc. Reprinted by permission.

REMEMBER: **Public speaking is a distinctive form of communication, and:**

1. **is similar and yet different from conversation in purpose, audience, feedback, supporting materials, organization, language, delivery, and ethics**

2. **may be defined as a form of communication in which (a) a speaker, (b) addresses, (c) a relatively large audience with (d) a relatively continuous discourse that is (e) usually in a face-to-face situation**

HOW PUBLIC SPEAKING WORKS

Figure 1.1 shows public speaking's major elements: speaker, listeners, noise, effects, context, messages, and channels.

Speaker

As a public speaker you bring to the public speaking situation all that you are and all that you know. Further, you bring with you all that the audience *thinks* you are and

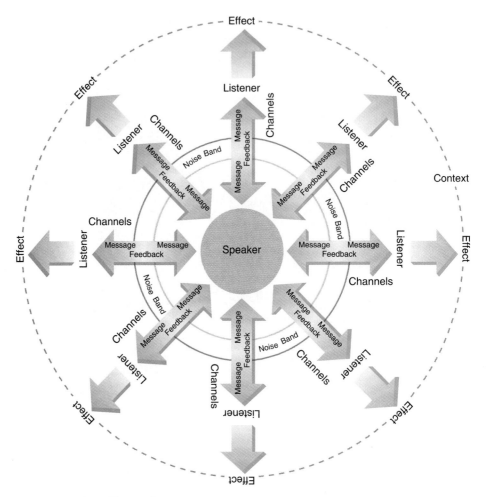

FIGURE 1.1   The public speaking transaction.

thinks you know. Everything about you becomes significant and contributes to the total effect of your speech. Your knowledge, your speech purpose, your speaking ability, your attitudes toward your audience, and other factors tell the audience who you are. These factors interact both during and after the public speaking event.

As the public speaker you are the center of the transaction. Although a speaker faces the audience physically, the speaker appears in the center of the model to illustrate that psychologically the speaker is central. The audience members look to you as the speaker; you and your speech are the reason for the gathering.

Listeners

The listeners are symbolized as separate individuals to emphasize that each is unique. Although we often speak of "the audience" as a collective body, it actually consists of separate and often very different individuals. Each of these listeners comes to the public speaking situation with different purposes, motives, expectations, attitudes, beliefs, and values; therefore each listener is going to respond differently to you and to the entire public speaking process.

Noise

Noise is interference. Noise is anything—audible or not—that interferes with your listeners receiving the messages you are sending. The circle between the speaker and listeners (Figure 1.1), the "noise band," shows that noise interferes with your messages. Noise may be physical (visual), psychological, or semantic. Table 1.1 presents examples of such noise and the effects it has on both speaker and listeners.

As a speaker you may reduce the sources of some noises or lessen their effects, but you cannot eliminate all noise completely. Therefore, learn to combat its effects by, for example, speaking louder, repeating important assertions, organizing your ideas so they are easy to follow, gesturing to reinforce your spoken messages, or defining technical and complex terms.

Effects

As a public speaker, you design and deliver your speeches to influence your listeners: politicians give campaign speeches to secure your vote; advertisers and salespersons give sales pitches to get you to buy their products; teachers give lectures to influence your thinking about history, psychology, or communication.

The model of public speaking in Figure 1.1 shows each effect separately to emphasize that as each listener is unique, each effect is also unique. Reacting to the very

TABLE 1–1 TYPES OF NOISE

TYPE OF NOISE	WHAT IT DOES	EXAMPLE
Physical	Distracts listener, interferes with the transmission or reception of the signal or message	Microphone static, sunglasses, rustling of notes, whispering of listeners
Psychological	Distorts information, prevents ideas from getting through	Prejudices, biases, stereotypes, closed-mindedness
Semantic	Creates misunderstanding when the speaker and listener have different meanings for the same word	Speaker using a non-native language, technical or complex terms, jargon

same speech, one listener may agree completely, another may disagree, and still another may misunderstand the entire message.

Context

The speaker and listeners in Figure 1.1 operate in a physical, sociopsychological, and cultural context. The context influences you as the speaker, the audience, the speech, and the effects of the speech. Therefore, analyze the context with care and prepare your speech with this specific context in mind. The *physical context* is the actual place in which you will give your speech (the room, hallway, park, or auditorium). Treat your presentation of a speech in a small intimate room and one in a sports arena very differently. The *sociopsychological context* includes the relationship between the speaker and audience, and the audience's attitudes toward and knowledge of the speaker and subject. You cannot, for example, treat a supportive and a hostile audience similarly. The *cultural context* refers to the beliefs, lifestyles, values, and ways of behaving that the speaker and the audience bring with them and that bear on the topic and purpose of the speech. Appealing to the "competitive spirit" and "financial gain" may prove effective with Wall Street executives but may insult Buddhist missionaries.

Messages and Channels

Messages are the signals sent by the speaker and received by the listener. These signals pass through one or more channels on their way from speaker to listener and from listener to speaker. The channel is the medium that carries the message signals from sender to receiver. Both the auditory and the visual channels are significant in public speaking. Through the auditory channel you send your spoken messages—your words and your sentences. At the same time, you also send messages through the visual chan-

This woman is giving a talk at a Native American festival, celebrating the Southwest heritage. In what ways would her speech be similar to a two-person conversation? In what ways would it be different?

nel, through eye contact (and the lack of it), body movement, hand and facial gestures, and clothing.

Transactional Process

Public speaking, like all forms of communication, is a transactional process (Watzlawick, Beavin, and Jackson, 1967; Watzlawick, 1978). A "transactional process" is one in which (1) all elements are *inter*dependent, (2) there is mutual influence between speaker and listener, and (3) listeners respond to the speech as a whole. Let's examine each of these characteristics briefly.

All elements of the public speaking process are interdependent. Each element connects with every other element. Each element of the public speaking process depends on and interacts with all other elements. The message, speaker, speech organization, listener, and context all interact. Each depends on each of the others. For example, the way in which you organize your speech will depend on such factors as the speech topic, the specific audience, the purpose you hope to achieve, and a host of other variables—all of which are explained in the units to follow. Keep this interrelatedness clearly in mind. In preparing your speeches, always look to the speech as a whole.

Public speaking involves a mutual influence between speaker and audience. True, when you give a public speech you will do most of the speaking and the listeners will do most of the listening. The listeners, however, also send messages in the form of feedback, for example, applause, bored looks, nods of agreement or disagreement, and attentive glances. To be an effective public speaker, you must attend to these feedback messages and make the appropriate adjustments.

The audience also influences how you will prepare and present your speech. It influences (or should influence) the arguments you select, the language you use, the method of organization you employ, and, in fact, every choice you make. You could not, for example, present the same speech on saving money to high school students and senior citizens.

Listeners respond to the speech as a whole. They do not respond to each part of the speech separately. For example, members of an audience may respond negatively to a speech in which they feel the speaker insulted them (perhaps in one brief remark). Even though the rest of the speech has all those characteristics that would normally lead to success, the speaker may fail. Audiences do not respond to organization, style, or evidence separately, they respond to the speech as a whole.

Because listeners react to the whole speech, the effects of a public speech do not depend only on what occurs during the speech. The effects depend on much more. The experiences of the audience, their opinions, and everything else that influences people's attitudes will influence how they receive your speech.

REMEMBER: Public speaking involves at least the following elements:
1. speaker: the source or originator of the message
2. listeners: each of whom receives a somewhat different message and responds in a unique way
3. noise (physical, psychological, and semantic): interference with the listeners' reception of the speaker's intended messages
4. effects: some immediate and some delayed; some overt and some covert
5. context: the physical, sociopsychological, and cultural setting
6. messages and channels: the verbal and nonverbal signals and the media through which they pass, sent by the speaker to listeners and by listeners to the speaker
7. and is a transactional process: (a) each element is interrelated, (b) speaker and audience influence each other, and (c) participants react to the speech as a whole

■■■■■ CRITICAL THINKING AND PUBLIC SPEAKING

Throughout this book you will cover a wide variety of skills that educators now group under the topic of "critical thinking." The objective of critical thinking training is to foster more reasoned and more reasonable decision making. It is the process of analyzing and evaluating logically what you say and hear. Here are just a few skills that critical thinking theorists have identified (Ennis 1987; Nickerson 1987; McCarthy 1991; Adams and Hamm 1991; and Bransford, Sherwood, and Sturdevant 1987):

- to evaluate and use evidence
- to organize thoughts clearly and logically
- to define concepts and problems specifically and unambiguously
- to discover valid and relevant information
- to distinguish between logical and illogical assumptions and inferences
- to evaluate the validity of an argument
- to judge critically and with good reasons

In great part the principles of public speaking are also the principles of critical thinking. It is impossible to be an effective speaker (or listener or critic) without also being an effective critical thinker. So, this is a particularly good opportunity to learn the skills of critical thinking as you learn public speaking. The two will work together; each will reinforce the other.

To best achieve this blend, numerous sections of this text cover critical thinking skills explicitly (for example, listening critically in Unit 4, criticizing the speech in Unit 5, discovering information in Unit 7, analyzing arguments in Unit 18, evaluating credibility in Unit 19, and accuracy in language in Unit 21). In addition, "Critically Speaking" questions appear at the end of each unit. These questions focus on **self-analysis, discovery, application,** and **evaluation**—four of the most essential critical thinking skills.

At the end of each part of the text, two checklists are provided. The first is a "Performance Checklist," which asks you to review and evaluate your speech preparation. The second is a "Critical Thinking Checklist," which highlights some of the critical thinking skills covered in the units contained in that part. In examining these critical thinking skills, look for ways you might transfer these skills to other areas (Sternberg 1987). Research shows that such transfers will be more efficient if you:

- think about the principles flexibly and recognize exceptions to the rule.
- seek analogies between the situation you are now in and previous experiences. What are the similarities? Differences?
- look for situations at home, at work, and at school where you might transfer the critical thinking skills. For example, might the skills of effective listening also prove valuable in listening to your friends, family, or romantic partner?

The four speeches appearing in the Appendix are annotated with questions suggesting areas to explore in thinking critically about speeches.

CRITICALLY SPEAKING

Each unit of the text ends with a section called "Critically Speaking." These sections contain questions designed to encourage you to think critically about the entire public speaking process. These questions focus on four essential critical thinking skills:

- **Self-analysis** questions ask you to analyze yourself as a public speaker (What are your major strengths and weaknesses? How does communication apprehension influence your willingness to give a speech?) and to consider ways of increasing your skills (How might you increase the audience's perception of your credibility?).

■ **Discovery** questions ask you to examine situations to identify pertinent concepts and relationships (How will you analyze your audience? What strategies will work best with an educated audience?).

■ **Application** questions ask you to apply the concepts and principles of public speaking to other forms of communication (for example, interpersonal, interviewing, or small group) and to other contexts (for example, family, work, or school).

■ **Evaluation** questions ask that you make a judgment about the principles presented (Are the principles of motivation ethical? Are the principles for communicating information useful?) and about their application in specific contexts (Did the speaker effectively gain attention? Was the speech organized so listeners would be able to follow it easily?).

1. How might the skills of public speaking prove useful in other communication situations, for example, interviewing for a job? Meeting a group of new people? Asking someone for a date?

2. Are there elements that are important to public speaking that are not covered here and that should be added to the model of the public speaking transaction?

3. What do you see as the most important benefit of public speaking to you?

4. What personal and social abilities would you like to improve? How might these be cultivated through public speaking training?

5. What is the most important asset that you bring to the public speaking situation? How can you make your listeners aware of it?

6. What type of person would be the ideal listener for your classroom speeches?

7. What kinds of noise do you anticipate in your class speeches? How will you deal with this noise?

8. Do you see yourself as more adept in communicating verbally or nonverbally? Why?

9. What ethical standards or principles do you feel should govern your own public speaking? Would you apply these same standards to contemporary political or religious speaking?

10. Do you think you will change any of your attitudes or beliefs as a result of the speeches you will hear in this class? Can you think of attitudes or beliefs that you would never even consider changing? Why?

11. What would be appropriate headings to cover the various terms in each of these four groups: (a) personal and social abilities, academic and career skills, general communication abilities, and public speaking abilities; (b) **purpose, audience, feedback, supporting materials, organization, language, and delivery**; (c) **speaker, listeners, noise, effect, context, messages, and channels;** and (d) interdependency of elements, mutual in-

fluence between speaker and audience, and responding as a whole? Define each of the boldfaced terms.

1.1 MODELING THE ELEMENTS OF PUBLIC SPEAKING

This exercise introduces some significant issues that will be considered throughout the course. The questions should stimulate you to think of the public speaking situation and of yourself as a public speaker–listener–critic.

Construct a diagrammatic model of the public speaking transaction as you see it taking place in this class. Incorporate the following elements and processes: speaker, speech, communication channel, listeners, feedback, critics, context, effect, and noise. After you have constructed this model, respond to the following questions:

1. How would you characterize yourself as a public speaker? As a listener? As a critic? How would you characterize the others in your class as speakers? As listeners? As critics? On what do you base these conclusions?
2. How would you define a public speech? What communication channels would be involved in the speeches to be given in this class?
3. What are some topics on which you would like to speak? What are some topics you would like to hear others speak on? What topics would turn you off?
4. What form can feedback take? What functions may feedback serve?
5. What do you see to be the function of the critics?
6. How will the context influence the public speaking transaction? How might the context be changed to make it more conducive to effective public speaking?
7. What type of effects do you think can be achieved in the speeches that you will deliver and hear in this class? Why?
8. How might noise enter the public speaking transaction? What might be done about it?

UNIT 2

Preparing a Public Speech: An Overview

■ ■ ■ ■

UNIT OBJECTIVES

After completing this unit, you should be able to:

1. Identify the three major types of speeches

2. Explain the major differences between informative and persuasive speeches

3. Explain the nine steps for preparing a public speech

Y ou're going to give a speech and you're anxious and unsure of what to say. What do you do? What do you speak about? How do you decide what to include in the speech? How should a speech be organized? At this point you probably have a lot more questions than answers but that is the way it should be. The purpose of this unit is to start stimulating answers to your questions. In this way you'll be able to begin public speaking almost immediately. By following the nine steps outlined in this unit, you will be able to prepare and present effective first speeches. The following presentation will help you put the theories and principles of public speaking into practice as soon as possible. These theories and principles, by the way, come from a wide variety of sources, only some of which are given in Table 2.1.

The nine steps for preparing a public speech will also provide you with a frame-work for structuring all of the remaining information in the text. Look at the rest of the text as an elaboration of these nine steps. As the course progresses and as you con-tinue reading, we will return to these principles and further clarify them. This will help you gradually perfect and improve the public speaking skills outlined here. For each of the nine steps, we note where in the text you may find additional information.

Figure 2.1 presents these nine steps in a linear fashion. The process of construct-ing a public speech, however, often does not follow a logical and linear sequence. That is, you will probably not progress simply from Step 1, to 2, to 3, and so on. Instead, your progression might go more like this: Step 1, Step 2, back again to Step 1, Step 3, back again to Step 2, and so on throughout the preparation of your speech. For exam-ple, after selecting your subject and purpose (Step 1), you may progress to Step 2 and analyze your audience. On the basis of this analysis, however, you may wish to go back and modify your subject, your purpose, or both. Similarly, after you research the topic (Step 3), you may want more information on your audience. You may, therefore, return to Step 2.

TIPS FROM PROFESSIONAL SPEAKERS

Most of us are mean to ourselves. We constantly tell ourselves that we are not good enough. We tell ourselves how dumb we are, how stupid we are, that we forgot to do this or forgot to do that. We do it so often that we begin to believe it! In fact, it's like what the prophets have said in the Bible, "What things you say and believe in your heart all come to pass."

The negative public relations we put out reaps negative public relations from others. You don't have to say "I'm so great" to everyone you meet, but you need to put across some self-confidence.

Muhammad Ali told us he was great. He knew he was the greatest before we did, and he was. He put out positive public relations about himself and we bought it. He complimented himself (why not?) and we followed.

Lillian Glass, a vocal image consultant and frequent lecturer. *How to Win: Six Steps to a Successful Vocal Image* (New York: Putnam [Perigee Books], 1987), pp. 161–163.

TABLE 2-1 THE GROWTH AND DEVELOPMENT OF PUBLIC SPEAKING

FROM:	COME:
Classical rhetoric	the emphasis on substance; on the ethical responsibilities of the speaker; on using a combination of logical, ethical, and emotional appeals; and on the strategies of organization
Literary and rhetorical criticism	the approaches to and the standards for evaluation and insights into style and language
Philosophy	the emphasis on the logical validity of arguments and a continuing contribution to ethics
Public address	the insights of how famous speakers dealt with varied purposes and audiences to achieve desired effects
Social psychology	the theories and findings on attitude and attitudinal change, and the emphasis on speech effects
General semantics	the emphasis on using language to describe reality accurately, and the techniques for avoiding common thinking errors that faulty language usage creates
Communication theory	the insights on information transmission; the importance of viewing the whole of the communication act; and the clarification of such concepts as feedback, noise, channel, and message
Psycholinguistics	how language is encoded and decoded, and the research for making language easier to understand and remember
Interpersonal communication	the concepts of transactionalism, and the emphasis on speaker and audience influencing each other
Sociology	data on audiences, their attitudes, values, opinions, and beliefs, and how these influence people's exposure to and responses to a variety of messages

In some situations you will begin with your audience. For example, let's say you're invited to speak to a group of high school seniors. They probably will want you to address a specific topic which is why they have asked you to speak. In this case you would begin your process by asking, What does this audience want? What do they need to know or do? For your classroom speeches you may also wish to focus first on your audience. In other cases you may wish to examine your own feelings about what is especially important. For example, you may feel strongly about the importance of recycling,

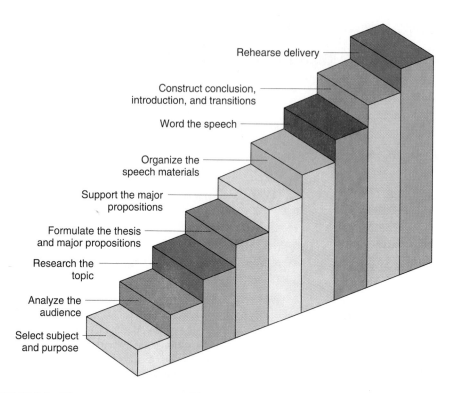

FIGURE 2.1   The steps in preparing a public speech.

amnesty, gay-lesbian rights, or abortion—issues about which you may feel it is important to instruct or convince others. Here you would begin with your own convictions
and ask how you might adapt or relate this topic to your specific audience.

All this back-and-forth should not throw you off track. This is the way most people
prepare speeches and written communications. So, although we present the steps in
the order a speaker normally follows, remember that you are in charge of the process.
Use the order of these steps as guidelines but break the sequence as you need to. As
long as you cover all nine steps thoroughly, you should accomplish your goal.

SELECT TOPIC AND PURPOSE

The first step in preparing a public speech is to select the topic (or subject) and the
purposes you hope to achieve. Let's look first at the topic; initially it will be your major
concern.

The Topic

Perhaps the question students in a public speaking class most often ask is, "What do I
speak about?" For your classroom speeches—where the objective is to learn the skills

of public speaking—there are hundreds of things to talk about. Suggestions are to be found everywhere and anywhere. In Unit 6 this topic is pursued in depth and many suggestions are offered; suggestions also appear in the Practically Speaking exercises at the end of this unit.

The topics of a public speech should be *worthwhile*. Such topics should address issues that have significant implications for the audience. Topics should also be *appropriate* to both you as the speaker and to your audience. Select a topic that you are interested in and that you feel is important to you and to your audience. Try not to select a topic merely because it will fulfill the requirements of an assignment. Try to select a topic about which you know something and would like to learn more. You will not only acquire new knowledge but also will discover how to learn more about the topic, for example, the relevant journals, the noted authorities, and so on. Unless you are a very accomplished speaker, your enthusiasm or lack of it will show during the speech. If you select a topic you are not interested in, you will have an extremely difficult time concealing this from the audience.

Like the penguin in the cartoon, each person sees the world from a unique point of view, so look at your topic from the audience's perspective. What are they interested in? What would they like to learn more about? On what topics would they find the time listening to your speech well spent? It is a lot easier to please an audience when you speak on a topic that interests them.

A suitable topic for a public speech is one that is limited in scope. Probably the major problem for beginning speakers is that they attempt to cover a huge topic in five minutes: the history of Egypt, why our tax structure should be changed, or the sociolo-

Drawing by Leo Cullum; © 1992 The New Yorker Magazine, Inc. Reprinted by permission.

gy of film—such topics are too broad and attempt to cover too much. The inevitable result is that nothing specific is covered—everything is touched on but only superficially. No depth is achieved when the topic is too broad, and all the speaker succeeds in doing is telling the audience what it already knows. Invariably your listeners will go away with the feeling that they have gained nothing as a result of listening to your speech.

The Purpose

The three major purposes of public speeches are to inform, to persuade, and to serve some ceremonial or special occasion function:

- the *informative speech* seeks to create understanding; the speaker clarifies, enlightens, corrects misunderstandings, demonstrates how something works
- the *persuasive speech* seeks to influence attitudes or behaviors; the speaker strengthens or changes the existing attitudes or gets the audience to take action
- the *special occasion speech,* containing elements of information and persuasion, serves varied purposes; for example, the speaker might introduce another speaker or a group of speakers, present a tribute, secure the goodwill of the listeners, or entertain the audience

ANALYZE THE AUDIENCE

In public speaking, your audience is central to your topic and purpose. In fact, Robert L. Montgomery, in the accompanying "TIP," advises you to consider your audience before you select a topic.

In most cases, and especially in a public speaking class, you will be thinking of both your audience and your topic at the same time; it is difficult to focus on one without also focusing on the other. Your success in informing or persuading your audience rests largely on the extent to which you know them and to which you have adapted your speech to them. Ask yourself, Who are they? What do they already know? What would they want to know more about? What special competencies do they have? What opinions, attitudes, and beliefs do they have? Where do they stand on the issues you wish to address? What needs do they have? To illustrate this process of audience analysis (a topic discussed in depth in Units 8 and 9), consider age and gender as just two factors that need to be analyzed.

Age

If you are going to speak on social security and health care for the elderly or the importance of the job interview, it is obvious that the age of your listeners should influence how you develop your speech. But age is always an important, if not so obvious, factor. Ask yourself some questions about the age of your listeners. What is the general age of the audience? How wide is the range? Are there different age groups that you

■ ■ ■

TIPS FROM PROFESSIONAL SPEAKERS

Even before you pick a topic you should analyze the audience you'll be influencing. You can't tailor your communication until you know precisely who you'll be talking to. Some questions the professionals ask include:

What does my audience have in common?
Is the audience made up of men or women, or both?
How many people are in the audience?
What is the average age?
What is their background: education, religion, special interests?
Why are they coming to listen to me?
How much do they know already about the topic I have chosen?
How much more do they need to know about this topic?
What attitudes will they bring with them?
What do I want to accomplish?

Robert L. Montgomery, consultant, speaker, and trainer specializing in communication and president of R. L. Montgomery & Associates. *A Master Guide to Public Speaking* (New York: Harper & Row, 1979), pp. 9–10. Reprinted by permission.

should address? Does the age of the audience impose any limitations on the topic? On the language you will use? On the examples and illustrations you will select?

Gender

Men and women view a variety of topics differently. Each has special knowledge and special interests as a result of their socialization. Ask yourself how the gender of the audience might influence your speech development. What is the predominant gender of your listeners? Do men and women view the topic differently? If so, how? Do men and women have different backgrounds, experiences, and knowledge concerning the topic? How will this influence the way you will develop the topic?

For example, if you plan to speak on caring for a newborn baby, you would approach an audience of men very differently from an audience of women. With an audience of women, you could probably assume a much greater knowledge of the subject and a greater degree of comfort in dealing with the topic. With an audience of men, you might have to cover such elementary topics as the type of powder to use, how to test the temperature of a bottle, and the way to prepare a formula.

RESEARCH THE TOPIC   ■ ■ ■

If the speech is to be worthwhile and if you and the audience are to profit from it, you must research the topic. For your first speeches, this will probably entail research in the library. First read some general source—an encyclopedia article or a general article in a journal or magazine. You might pursue some of the references in the article or seek out a book or two in the library catalog. You might also consult one or more of the guides to periodical literature for recent articles in journals, magazines, and newspapers. For some topics, you might want to consult individuals: professors, politicians, physicians, or people with specialized information are useful sources. See unit 7 for in-depth coverage of research.

■■■■ FORMULATE THE THESIS AND MAJOR PROPOSITIONS

What do you want your audience to get out of your speech? What single idea do you want them to retain? This single idea is the thesis of your speech. It is the essence of what you want your audience to get out of your speech. If your speech is an informative one, then your thesis is the main idea that you want your audience to understand. Examples of such theses would be: "Human blood consists of four major elements" or "The new computerized billing system has three components."

If your speech is to be a persuasive one, then your thesis is the central idea that you wish your audience to accept or act on. Examples of such theses would be: "We should support Grace Moore for Union Representative" or "We should contribute to the college athletic fund."

Once you word the thesis statement, ask yourself—as would an audience—questions about the thesis in order to identify its major components. For an informative speech, the most helpful questions are **What?** or **How?** So, to the thesis "Human blood consists of four major elements," the logical question seems to be, *What are they?* To the thesis "The new computerized billing system has three components," the logical question seems to be, *What are they?* The answers to these questions identify the major propositions that you should cover in your speech. The answer to the question, *What are the major elements of human blood?*, in the form of a brief speech outline, would look like this:

> ***Thesis:*** "There are four major elements in human blood." *(What are they?)*
>
> I. Plasma
> II. Red blood cells (erythrocytes)
> III. White blood cells (leukocytes)
> IV. Platelets (thrombocytes)

In a persuasive speech, the question an audience would ask would be more often of the **Why?** type. If your thesis is "We should support Grace Moore for Union Representative," then the inevitable question is *Why should we support Grace Moore?* Your answers to this question will then enable you to identify the major parts of the speech, which might look like this:

> ***Thesis:*** "We should support Grace Moore." *(Why should we support Grace Moore?)*

I. Grace Moore is honest.

II. Grace Moore is knowledgeable.

III. Grace Moore is an effective negotiator.

SUPPORT THE MAJOR PROPOSITIONS

Now that you have identified your thesis and your major propositions, turn your attention to how you will support each of them. You must tell the audience what it needs to know about the elements in human blood. You need to convince the audience that Grace Moore is in fact honest, knowledgeable, and an effective negotiator.

In the informative speech, your support primarily amplifies—describes, illustrates, defines—the various concepts you discuss. You want the "causes of inflation" to come alive for the audience. You want them to see and feel the drug problem, the crime, or the economic hardships of the people you are talking about. Amplification accomplishes this. Specifically, you might use *examples* and *illustrations* and the *testimony* of others to explain a concept or issue. Presenting *definitions* helps the audience to understand specialized terms. Definitions breath life into concepts that may otherwise be too abstract or vague. *Statistics* (summary figures that explain various trends) are essential for certain topics. *Audiovisual aids*—charts, maps, actual objects, slides, films, audiotapes, records, and so on—enliven normally vague concepts.

In a persuasive speech, your support is proof—material that offers evidence, argument, and motivational appeal and that establishes your credibility. Proof helps you convince the audience to agree with you. Let us say, for example, that you want to persuade the audience to support Grace Moore. To do this you might want to demonstrate that Grace Moore is an effective negotiator. To demonstrate this you would have to give your audience good reasons for believing that this is true. For example, you might present a speech whose major propositions would look like this:

I. Grace Moore is an effective negotiator.

II. Grace Moore knows the company from top to bottom.

III. Grace's Moore opposition has no experience in the field.

Support your propositions with reasoning from *specific instances,* from *general principles,* from *analogy,* and from *causes and effects.* These are *logical* supports. You can also support your position with *motivational appeals.* For example, you might appeal to the audience's desire for status, for financial gain, or for increased self-esteem. You also add persuasive force through your own personal reputation or *credibility.* If the audience sees you as competent, of high moral character, and as charismatic, they are likely to believe what you say. Units 13–19 cover ways of supporting your ideas.

ORGANIZE THE SPEECH MATERIALS

Organize your materials to help your audience understand and retain what you say. You might, for example, select a simple *topical pattern.* This involves dividing your topic into its logical subdivisions or subtopics. Each subtopic becomes a main point (a major proposition) of your speech and each is treated approximately equally. You would then organize the supporting materials under each of the appropriate points. The body of the speech, then, might look like this:

 I. Main point I

  A. Supporting material for I

  B. Supporting material for I

 II. Main point II

  A. Supporting material for II

  B. Supporting material for II

  C. Supporting material for II

 III. Main point III

  A. Supporting material for III

  B. Supporting material for III

For a persuasive speech you may wish to consider other organizational patterns. For example, a *problem-solution pattern* might be effective for a number of topics. Let us say you want to persuade your listeners that medical schools should require communication courses. You might use a problem-solution pattern. Your speech in outline form might look like this:

 I. Doctors cannot communicate. (problem)

  A. They are inarticulate in expressing ideas. (problem 1)

  B. They are ineffective listeners. (problem 2)

  C. They do not see beyond the literal meaning. (problem 3)

 II. Medical schools should require communication courses. (solution)

  A. Communication courses will train doctors to express themselves. (solution 1)

  B. Communication courses will train doctors in listening skills. (solution 2)

  C. Communication courses will train doctors to listen for meaning beyond the literal. (solution 3)

In general, the pattern for a persuasive speech looks like this:

 I. Assertion 1

  A. First reason for accepting I

     B. Second reason for accepting I

        1. First reason for accepting B

        2. Second reason for accepting B

  II. Assertion 2

     A. First reason for accepting II

        1. First reason for accepting A

        2. Second reason for accepting A

     B. Second reason for accepting II

The two assertions (I and II) support the general purpose of the speech. Thus, for example, your specific purpose might be to persuade the audience that they should invest in real estate. Assertions I and II would be reasons why people should invest in real estate. Supports A and B would be reasons why the audience should accept assertions I and II. In short, each item should persuade the audience to accept the item it supports. Units 10 and 12 cover organization in depth.

WORD THE SPEECH

The audience will hear your speech only once. Make sure that your listeners readily understand everything you say by being instantly intelligible. Do not speak down to your audience, but do make your ideas, even complex ones, easy to understand at one hearing.

Use words that are simple rather than complex, concrete rather than abstract. Use personal and informal rather than impersonal and formal language. For example, use lots of pronouns (*I, me, you, our*) and contractions (*can't* rather than *cannot*, *I'll* rather than *I will*). Use simple and direct rather than complex and indirect sentences. Say, "Vote in the next election" instead of "It is important that everyone vote in the next election."

In wording the speech, be careful not to offend members of your audience. Remember that not all doctors are men. Not all secretaries are women. Not all persons are or want to be married. Not all persons love parents, dogs, and children. The hypothetical person does not have to be male.

Perhaps the most important advice to give is this: do *not* write out your speech word-for-word. This will only make you sound like you're reading a text to your audience. You will thus lose the conversational quality that is so important in public speaking. Instead, outline your speech and speak *with* your audience, using this outline to remind yourself of your main ideas and the order in which you want to present them. Units 21 and 22 offer more extensive style suggestions.

Title the Speech

In some ways the title of a speech is a kind of frill. On the other hand, the title may be effective in gaining the interest of the audience and, perhaps, stimulating them to listen. In more formal public speech presentations, the title helps to gain audience attention and interest in announcements advertising the speech.

Titles should be relatively short, attract the attention and arouse the interest of the potential listener, and be integral to the speech.

Short titles are usually easier to remember than long ones. Titles of top television shows, movies, books, and record albums are usually short and easily recalled. A title that is easy to remember will help your listeners remember your speech. A speech title should be integral to the speech. Develop a title that bears a close relationship to the major purpose of the speech. Then rework it so it may be easily remembered and arouses interest. Do not mislead the potential audience to expect something they are not going to get.

One last suggestion: title the speech after you have finished the entire speech. The title—like the frosting on the cake—goes on last.

CONSTRUCT THE CONCLUSION, INTRODUCTION, AND TRANSITIONS

The last items to consider are the conclusion, introduction, and transitions, topics covered in depth in Unit 11.

Conclusion

In concluding your speech, do at least two things. First, summarize the speech. Identify the main points again and sum up what you have told the audience.

Second, wrap up your speech. Develop an appropriate closure, a crisp ending. Do not let the speech hang. End the speech clearly and distinctly.

I hope then that when you vote on Tuesday, you'll vote the straight "Students for Change" ticket. It's the only real choice we have.

Introduction

Because you must know in detail all you are going to say before you prepare the introduction, construct your introduction last. Your introduction should immediately gain the attention of the audience. Most often, your coming to the front of the room will attract their attention. However, as you start to speak, you may lose them if you do not make a special effort to hold their attention. A provocative statistic, a little-known fact, an interesting story, or a statement explaining the topic's significance will help secure this initial attention.

Second, establish a relationship among yourself, the topic, and the audience. Tell the audience why you are speaking on this topic. Tell them why you are concerned

With which of the nine steps covered in this unit do you anticipate having the least difficulty?

with the topic and why you are competent to address them. These are questions that most audiences will automatically ask themselves. Tell them before they need to ask you. Here is one example of how this might be done.

> *I am the mother of a child with AIDS and I'm addressing the Hudson District PTA to talk about my child's experience in class.*

Third, orient the audience. Tell them what you are going to say in the order you are going to say it.

> *I'm going to explain the ways in which war movies have changed through the years. I'm going to discuss examples of movies depicting World War II, the Korean War, and Vietnam.*

Transitions

After you have completed the introduction, review the entire speech to make sure that the pieces flow into one another and that the movement from one part to another (say, from the introduction to the first major proposition) will be clear to the audience. Transitional words, phrases, and sentences will help you achieve this smoothness of movement. Here are a few suggestions:

- Connect your introduction's orientation to your first major proposition: "*Let's now look at the first of these three elements, the central processing unit, in detail.* The CPU is the heart of the computer. It consists of. . . . "

■ Connect your major propositions to each other:"*But, not only is cigarette smoking dangerous to the smoker, it is also dangerous to the nonsmoker.* Passive smoking is harmful to everyone. . . ."

■ Connect your last major proposition to your conclusion: "*As we saw, there were three sources of evidence against the butler:* he had a motive; he had no alibi; he had the opportunity."

■■■■ REHEARSE DELIVERY

You've prepared your speech to be delivered to an audience, so your last step is to practice delivery. Rehearse your speech, from start to finish, at least four times before delivering it in class. During these rehearsals, time your speech so that you stay within the specified time limits.

In your rehearsal and in your actual delivery, your aim should be to use your voice and bodily action to reinforce your message, to make it easier for your listeners to understand your speech. Any vocal or body movements that draw attention to themselves (and away from what you are saying) obviously should be avoided. Here are a few major guidelines that will prove helpful. Units 23 and 24 offer more suggestions.

■ When called on to speak, approach the front of the room with enthusiasm; even if, as do most speakers, you feel nervous, show your desire to speak with your listeners

■ when at the front of the room, don't begin immediately; instead, pause, engage your audience eye to eye for a few brief moments

■ talk directly to the audience; talk in a volume that can be easily heard without straining

■ maintain eye contact with your entire audience; avoid concentrating on only a few members or looking out of the window or at the floor

■ practice any terms that you may have difficulty with; consult a dictionary to clarify any doubts about pronunciation

REMEMBER: **Elements of an effective speech:**

1. a worthwhile and limited *topic* and a clearly defined *purpose*
2. a focus on a specific and clearly defined *audience*
3. a thoroughly *researched topic*
4. a clearly defined *thesis* supported by relevant *propositions*
5. *propositions supported by amplifying materials, evidence, argument, and motivational and ethical appeals*
6. a clear and easily understood *organizational pattern*
7. *wording* that is clear, personal, and direct
8. a *conclusion* that summarizes the speech and achieves closure; an *introduction* that gains audience attention, establishes a relationship among speaker, topic,

and audience, and orients the listeners; and *transitions* that connect the major parts of the speech

9. a delivery that reinforces your message

LISTENING TO YOUR FIRST SPEECHES

Although we have concentrated in this unit on the speaker preparing the speech, we cannot neglect the listeners' role. As a listener you can do a great deal to help the speaker and to improve your own public speaking skills. Perhaps the most important, from the speaker's point of view, is for you to express supportiveness for the speaker. Express your support nonverbally by looking at the speaker attentively and with positive expressions. If there is a question period, ask questions in a supportive manner rather than in a manner that attacks or finds fault with something the speaker says.

If there is an evaluation period, start by saying something positive about the speaker or speech. Help the speaker to improve by offering one or perhaps two suggestions for improvement. Be as specific as possible so that the speaker knows exactly what changes you would make. Avoid the overly general, "I liked your introduction" or "Your conclusion was weak." Instead, be specific: "You really gained my attention when you said . . . " or "I thought your conclusion was too long; it might have been more powerful if you didn't repeat the examples you used in your speech." You may find it helpful to focus your questions on those included in the Part One Performance Checklist at the end of Unit 5.

Listen with an open mind. For informative speeches, assume the speech—whatever it is—has some value for you. Resist the temptation to assume you know all there is to know about the topic or that the topic is irrelevant to your needs. For persuasive speeches, listen with an open mind even to positions that may challenge your current beliefs and opinions.

Listen for both content and form. Listen not only to what the speaker says but also to how he or she says it. Identify the thesis and the major propositions that support the thesis. How are the major propositions supported, for example, with examples, testimony, definitions? Are these forms of support appropriate and sufficient? Ask yourself what works, what doesn't work, and why? In this way you'll see the principles of public speaking in concrete application.

A SAMPLE SPEECH WITH ANNOTATIONS

The following speech is presented as a summary of the major parts of a public speech. The annotations will guide you through the speech and will illustrate the principles considered in this unit. This speech is a particularly good one. It was given by Jay Lane, a student at Southern Utah State College, and won the award for the best informative speech at the 1987 National Individual Events Tournament.

Jay Lane, *Southern Utah State College*

The attention-getting device used here is to arouse curiosity. We wonder what the speech will be on and so we listen to get the answer to our question. The speaker also maintains our attention throughout the speech with humor and with little-known facts.

The topic was itself interesting because dust is something we all experience but few of us really know anything about it.

The purpose of the speech is clearly stated. We know the speech is an informative one by the way the topics are identified in the opening paragraph and in the first two sentences of the second paragraph.

Note the clear orientation. He orients the audience in two ways. First, he represents a general idea of his speech topic when he discusses dust in the introduction and when he says "It [dust] is also the thesis of a speech." Second, he orients us in more detail by identifying the three major points he will cover: "And so, with your kind permission, I present dust: [1] What it is, [2] where it comes from, and [3] how on earth it can affect us." The audience is thus set up to hear these three aspect of dust.

The thesis of the speech is that dust is a significant topic. This he repeats throughout the speech in a variety of ways. For example, "The dust is more than the mystical substance that makes up daydreams," "a subject which 'touches us' literally every day of our lives," and in the final sentence "an entire world of fascination."

Throughout the introduction the author directly involves the audience. For example, he says, "We rarely think about it," "in this room," and "I know what *you're* thinking, but *wait*." Also he relates the experience of Penny Mosier to the audience members: "The experience . . . is *shared by us all.*"

The speaker neatly establishes his credibility by his references to his thorough research.

Webster says it's fine, dry, and pulverized. We rarely think about it. Strange, really. For there's twice as much in this room as there is anywhere outside. And those who study it tell us that 43 million tons will fall on the United States alone. What is it, in a word, dust. And I know what you're thinking, but wait. For there is an inspiration in the examination of such a microscopic phenomena. The November 1986 issue of *Discover* magazine relates the account of author Penny Ward Mosier and the coming of age of Dust. In that article she writes, "I only noticed the dust because my mind was desperately seeking a diversion. That happens during tax time. And so it was one day that I found myself pushing around little clumps of dust, and then it happened, from behind the corner of my desk there appeared a giant dust ball, piloted by my big toe. I picked it up. Intrigued, "What is this dust ball?" I wondered. The experience of the author is one that is shared by us all at one time or another. How many times have you sat and watched the lazy, floating particles falling slowly in the sunlight. The dust is more than the mystical substance that makes up daydreams. It is also the thesis of a speech. One that deals with a subject which "touches us" literally every day of our lives.

And so, with your kind permission, I present dust. What it is, where it comes from, and how on earth it can affect us. Now, I have to admit that until fairly recently, I had never given dust more than a speck of thought. But as my understanding has increased, so has my appreciation. You see what we often think of as, well, as dust, blossoms under a microscope, becoming what some might even consider to be exotic. But, I should slow myself down before my story loses its structure. According to the Library of Congress, there are 322 books that have been published on the subject of dust. Let's see what information they can provide.

In his book entitled *The Secret House* author David Bodine provides a great deal of information. It seems that the principal element that makes up what we refer to as dust is soil. That's a fancy word for dirt. Followed closely by of all things, salt. That's right. These tiny crystals dance out of our oceans at a rate of 300 million tons every year. In addition you will find fabric fibers, fungi, pollens, and a variety of things that quite frankly, you don't want to hear about. But don't worry, I am merely saving the best part for last. Now I realize that at times dust can be a hard sell. Still, I press boldly forward. For dust is becoming a serious business. For this reason, the Maryland Medical Laboratories donated several of their shelves, taking them away from growing cultures of new biotechnologies and bacteria in order to grow samples of Mrs. Mosier's dust balls. They immediately blossomed into a collage, warranting closer examination. Of the experience she wrote, "Everyone came by to stare at my dust, oohed and ahhed over the slides that we had made. Under a microscope my stained dust was a work of art. I now understood that not only could dust be anything, it could be everything."

She also notes that in addition to being everything, it also comes from everything. For example, forest fires. In a good year, for dust, seven percent of the world's total comes from forest fires. In addition, much of it comes from our oceans, as mentioned earlier. And, of course we can't forget man-made pollutants, industrial dust. But, the single largest contributors to the world supply of dust are volcanoes. In fact, the infamous eruption of Krakatoa in 1883 was the dust event of recorded history. But, you know, that happened a long time ago. So the dust that you see must come from some place else. But where? How about Africa. Seriously, *Nature* magazine in November of 1986 notes that the winds that blow across the African deserts carry with them so much dust that in times it falls as a light pink rain on Miami. But is it possible that the dust carries all the way across the country, that the dust here in San Diego is from Africa, that the dust in your home has an international flavor. Yes. Says dust buster, John Ferguson, who last year helped sell some 750 thousand gallons of Endust! He knows. It is not only possible that the dust in your homes comes from all over the world, it does. What's more, much of it comes from outer space. Extra-terrestrial dust. Coming principally from comets and disintegrating meteorites, at a rate of 10,000 tons every year. Well, with so many things coming from so many places, it's not surprising that everything you own is covered by that fine, thin layer, and you don't know half the story yet. Again, according to *Discover* magazine, the average six room city or urban dwelling takes in 40 pounds of dust every year, 40 pounds. And a single cubic inch of air space can contain 1,600,000 tiny

In this section, the speaker covers his first point, namely, the nature of dust ("what it is").

Throughout the speech, the speaker reminds the audience that he appreciates their feelings about dust but that they should continue listening because he will tell them something new and useful.

A neat transition connects the first topic, what dust is, to the second topic, where dust comes from.

Note how the speaker uses a conversational style that engages and involves the listener.

Note how the use of specific numbers communicates about the speaker research efforts and concern for accuracy.

particles. (Cough) Sorry, it got just a little difficult to breathe.

Lane again introduces his next point with a transition: "With so much dust in the air [covered just previously], it seems like it should have some kind of impact on your life, shouldn't it [the third part of the speech: how it can affect us]?" This he covers in two parts: the negative aspects of dust and the more positive side. The transition could have been clearer and it might have summarized both his previous points and previewed his third point.

The significance of the topic and the speech was most clearly established in the coverage of the third point, how dust affects us. Some additional attempt earlier in the speech to establish the significance of the topic might have helped. The speaker might have answered our inevitable question, "Why should we listen?" with reasons other than curiosity (which he did use effectively).

With so much dust in the air, it seems like it should have some kind of impact on your life, shouldn't it? Good point. Let's see. Now you've already heard about dust and how it affects us through hay fever. Of course, that's pollen, a significant source of dust. And I know you've seen a cobweb at one time or another. But there was something else, something significant, that I wanted to share. Now, I don't want to be the cause of anyone's nightmares, and I don't want to keep you awake tonight, but this is the point where I recreate all of your childhood fears. You know, as kids it's fairly easy for us to handle dirt. We roll around with the fungi and the fabric fibers and never really give it a second thought, but it's the monsters, do you remember, the ones under your bed. Well, I'm here today to tell you that those childhood foes are very real in a sense. For this was discovered by the Maryland Medical Laboratories in the research they did for Mrs. Mosier. Dr. and Scientist Charles McCloud discovered under the microscope something he said that he had never seen before. He said it had mouth parts on its legs, and described it as an angry rhinoceros with crustation appendages. In short he said, it's the ugliest thing you have ever seen. So go ahead. Even that tough group of scientists uttered their share of icks and uggs when they saw this little guy. He is a member of a family of house mites. The scientific name is am-uh-huh, I wrote it down. Dermitoffaginous-sparnine, I think. Personally, I just write dust. There are fifteen species of these little guys that live in various parts around the world. They live in your pillows, in your mattresses, in your sheets, and in your dust balls. They eat the 50 million or so skin scales that your body sheds every day. Don't worry, they can't eat anything if it's still attached. Although they will chew on your toenail dirt if you give them half a chance.

Usually a speaker is advised not to emphasize any inadequacies or lack of knowledge. Does the speaker's mentioning his difficulty with technical term work for him or against him?

But now I don't want you to leave with the idea that this isn't really a significant problem. According to Ian Fielding in his book entitled *Dust* there are about two million of these dust mites in every twin sized bed. Kind of makes you want to wrap your body in Saran Wrap, doesn't it? Well that was the response of Mrs. Mosier, but don't worry, even after finding all this out, she, her husband, and their two million tiny pets have learned to share the bed just fine. Of course, that was before she found out her air conditioner had gangrene. Yet another element, that simple term that we call dust.

But I don't want to leave you with a negative impression. Like everything that has to do with dust is bad. For there are many benefits from dust as well. Consider as you would a *Forbes* magazine article of August 12, 1985 entitled "A Handful of Dust." The article relates a revolution in scientific research. It seems that Dr. Von Bryant, a pollentologist, that's a term for someone who studies dust, and Texas A&M University are conducting a group of experiments that they call "chomap." The purpose of the project is to recreate environmental conditions over the past ten thousand years by using dust. According to Dr. Von Bryant, they have already discovered some pollen samples as old as 2.5 billion years. Talk about a direct link to your past, AT&T has nothing on these guys in terms of long-distance communication. But, seriously, Dr. Bryant notes that there is some information that we get from dust we simply cannot get anywhere else. There are also some implications and impacts of dust that are a little bit closer to home. It seems that dust has an interesting effect on light waves. It breaks up the blues and the purples at the short end of the spectrum, but leaves the reds and oranges untouched. The result, beautiful red, orange, yellow in the sunset you saw last night. Oh, yes, there was one more thing. According to the *American Academic Encyclopedia* of 1983, dust serves as an interesting tricha, and essential foundation. It seems that as the dust floats around in the atmosphere and allows water molecules to bond, the result, condensation and precipitation. In case you're wondering if dust has any social significance, try getting a drink of water without it. Dust, what a simple term. But it is anything and everything. It is a glass of water, a sunset, a very ugly bug. But whatever dust may be, the dust ball discovered by Mrs. Mosier was more than just a word, rather an entire world of fascination.

Speech by Jay Lane in *1987 Championship Debates and Speeches*. Copyright © 1987 by the American Forensic Association. Reprinted by permission.

He concludes the speech by referring back to the term itself and the fact that it is anything and everything. After hearing (or reading) the last sentence, we know the speech is over and that closure has been neatly achieved.

Lane uses a variety of supporting materials that help to make the speech interesting and the speaker's major propositions clear to the audience. Little-known statistics ("43 million tons will fall on the United States alone"), personal experiences (Penny Mosier and her dust ball), examples (dust balls, pollen), testimony (from dustbuster John Ferguson), definitions (Webster says . . .), and humor (throughout the speech).

Lane follows the principles of informative speaking. He limits the amount of information communicated. You don't get the feeling that the speaker is trying to cover everything. He has clearly mapped out a small area and covers this in some detail. He demonstrates the relevance and usefulness of his speech especially in the last section where he talks about how dust can affect us. He presents information that can be understood by everyone and yet we do not get the feeling that the speaker is talking down to the audience or is straining to reach their level. He also relates the new information to what the audience is already familiar with, for example, dust balls and pollen.

The sources (*Discover*, *The Secret House*, *Nature*, *Forbes*, *Dust*, and the *American Academic Encyclopedia*) are all cited in the speech without being intrusive. We don't get the feeling that the speaker is shoving these in to establish his credibility. He might have more clearly identified David Bodine, author of *The Secret House* and Ian Fielding, author of *Dust*.

Lane's language is appropriate to the subject and to the audience. He creates images (Penny Mosier with her dust ball, looking at the sunset, wrapping your body in Saran Wrap), involves the audience through questions ("But where?" "Do you remember the ones under your bed?"), uses language that is easily understood and that is personal (there are numerous personal pronouns and direct references to the speaker and to the audience members), and uses concrete rather than abstract language.

CRITICALLY SPEAKING

1. What topics would you like to hear students speak on?
2. How would you analyze this class in terms of the characteristics noted in this unit?

3. Visit the library and select one research source that you think would be useful to students preparing speeches for this class. What types of information does this reference source contain? Why do you think this would prove useful?

4. Select a recent television show or movie and identify its thesis. Are there subordinate theses?

5. What types of supporting materials would you find most useful in explaining the nature of advertising that is addressed to children? In persuading your audience to contribute blood?

6. What thought pattern would you use to describe your college campus to a group of high school students who have never seen a college campus? To persuade your audience to eat a healthy diet?

7. What suggestions for using language more effectively would you offer your typical college instructor? Are these suggestions useful to students preparing public speeches?

8. What problems do speakers often create when they conclude their speeches? How might these problems be avoided?

9. How might a speaker gain attention in the introduction? How might these same techniques be used throughout the speech?

10. What one delivery suggestion would you offer the beginning speaker?

11. As a speaker delivering your first speech, how would your ideal listener behave?

PRACTICALLY SPEAKING

2.1 THINKING CRITICALLY ABOUT INFORMATIVE SPEAKING

Here are suggestions for informative speech topics built around the three types of informative speaking to be discussed in detail in Unit 13: definition, description, and demonstration. Select one topic from each of the three types of speeches, then:

A. formulate a specific thesis

B. formulate a specific purpose suitable for an informative speech of approximately 5 minutes

C. analyze this class as your potential audience and identify ways that you can relate this topic to their interests and needs

D. generate at least two major propositions from your thesis

E. support these propositions with examples, illustrations, definitions, and so on

F. construct a conclusion that summarizes your main ideas and brings the speech to a definite close

G. construct an introduction that gains attention and orients your audience

Discuss these outlines in small groups or with the class as a whole. Try to secure feedback from other members on how you can improve these outlines.

Topics for Speeches of Definition

artificial intelligence	propaganda	cognitive therapy
assault and battery	feminism	Marxism
sexual harassment	counterfeiting	discrimination
felony and misdemeanor	cartel	religion
censorship	violence	atheism
free speech	etiquette	alcoholism
mysticism	prejudice	co-dependency
id, ego, superego	culture	drug abuse
ESP	primitivism	sexual ethics
ethics	a specific type of music	neurosis and psychosis
friendship	a particular sport's rules	creative thinking
love	art and science	libel and slander
infallibility	happiness	love and sex
truth	Freudian theory	fear and jealousy

Topics for Speeches of Description

the computer department of an ad agency	a weather bureau
a courtroom	nuclear power plant
the college hierarchy	a specific country's government
a TV station (studio)	monetary systems
a photography darkroom	academic garb
the types of paintbrushes	time management techniques
a shopping center	Fort Knox
the operation of the heart	a stock exchange
how cholesterol works in the body	a publishing company
weight control techniques	a college newspaper office
exercise guidelines	the structure of an airplane, boat, car
a bee colony	a houseboat
a computer	a rental lease
the skeletal structure of the body	an insurance policy
a lie detector	the library
	Buckingham Palace

Topics for Speeches of Demonstration

how television is censored
how advertising influences the media
how graduate and professional schools select students

how a magazine or newspaper is put together
how to conduct an interview
how to form a campus organization or club
how to complain
how advertisers choose where to place ads
how to lessen guilt
how the brain works
how radar works
how to organize your time
how nicotine effects the body
how steroids work
how sound is produced
how clothing communicates status
how to buy insurance
how to save for retirement
how to apply for student loans, social security, graduate school, life experience credits
how a jury is selected
how to write a will
how to adopt a child
how a bill becomes law
how political candidates raise money
how to organize a protest
how power works in an organization
how to publicize your ideas
how an experiment is conducted
how IQ is measured
how dreams reveal the subconscious
how satellite TV works

2.2   THINKING CRITICALLY ABOUT PERSUASIVE SPEAKING

Here are 20 topics for persuasive speeches. Select any one topic then:

   A. formulate a specific thesis
   B. formulate a specific purpose suitable for a persuasive speech of approximately 5 minutes in length
   C. analyze this class as your potential audience; try to predict their relevant attitudes and beliefs; and identify ways that you can relate this topic to their interests and needs
   D. generate at least two major propositions from your thesis
   E. support these propositions with examples, illustrations, definitions, facts, opinions, and so on
   F. construct a conclusion that summarizes your main ideas and brings the speech to a definite close
   G. construct an introduction that gains attention and orients your audience

Share your outline in small groups or with the class as a whole. Try to secure feedback from other members on how you can improve these outlines.

1. Vote in the next election (college, city, state, national).
2. Capital punishment should be abolished (extended).
3. Support (Do not support) college athletics.
4. Gay men and lesbians should (not) be permitted to adopt children.
5. Military recruitment should (not) be allowed on college campuses.
6. Join the Peace Corps.
7. Sex education in elementary schools should be expanded (eliminated).
8. Volunteer to read for the blind.
9. Teachers, police, and firefighters should (not) be permitted to strike.
10. Personal firearms should be prohibited (permitted).
11. Alcohol should be prohibited (permitted) on college campuses.
12. Marijuana should (not) be legalized.
13. Marriage licenses should be denied to any couple who has not known each other for at least one year.
14. Nuclear plants should be abolished (expanded).
15. The government should (not) support the expansion of solar energy.
16. Required college courses should be eliminated.
17. The military ban on gay men and lesbians should (not) be reversed.
18. Cheating on an examination should (not) result in automatic dismissal from college.
19. This country should (not) establish a system of free legal services for all of its citizens.
20. Church property should (not) be taxed.

From Apprehension to Confidence

■ ■ ■ ■

UNIT OBJECTIVES

After completing this unit, you should be able to:

1. Define *speaker apprehension*

2. Identify the suggestions for dealing with speaker apprehension

3. Identify three suggestions listeners might follow to help the speaker deal with apprehension

4. Identify at least four suggestions for increasing self-confidence as a public speaker

---

*I*f you are like most students, your first concern is not with organization or audience analysis; rather, it is with stage fright or what we call **speaker apprehension.** Apprehension is experienced not only by the beginning public speaker; it is also felt by even the most experienced speakers. Most public speakers don't eliminate apprehension, they learn to deal with and control it.

"Communication apprehension," note researchers James McCroskey and Lawrence Wheeless (1976), "is probably the most common handicap that is suffered by people in contemporary American society." According to a nationwide survey conducted by Bruskin Associates, speaking in public ranked as the number one fear of adult men and women. It ranks above fear of heights and even fear of snakes. According to college students surveyed by McCroskey and Wheeless, between 10 and 20 percent suffer "severe, debilitating communication apprehension." Another 20 percent "suffers from communication apprehension to a degree substantial enough to interfere to some extent with their normal functioning."

You may wish to pause here and take the Apprehension Test on the facing page.

■■■■ WHAT IS SPEAKER APPREHENSION?

Speaker apprehension affects the way you feel and the way you act. Many people develop negative feelings about their ability to communicate orally. They predict that their communication efforts will fail. They feel that whatever gain they would make as a result of engaging in communication is not worth the fear they would experience. As a result, apprehensive speakers avoid communication situations and, when forced to participate, participate as little as possible.

General and Specific Apprehension

Some people have a general speaker apprehension that manifests itself in all communication situations. These people suffer from *trait apprehension*—a fear of communication generally, regardless of the specific situation. Their fear appears in conversations, small group settings, and public speaking situations.

Other people experience speaker apprehension in only certain communication situations. These people suffer from *state apprehension*—a fear that is specific to a given communication situation. For example, a speaker may fear public speaking but have no difficulty in talking with two or three other people. Or, a speaker may fear job interviews but have no fear of public speaking. State apprehension is extremely common. Most people experience it for some situations. As already mentioned, public speaking is the state that provokes the most apprehension.

Degrees of Apprehension

Speaker apprehension exists on a continuum. Some people are so apprehensive that they are unable to function in any communication situation. They suffer greatly in a so-

TEST YOURSELF: HOW APPREHENSIVE ARE YOU?*

Instructions:

This questionnaire is composed of six statements concerning your feelings about public speaking. Indicate in the space provided the degree to which each statement applies to you by marking whether you

1 = strongly agree
2 = agree
3 = are undecided
4 = disagree
5 = strongly disagree

There are no right or wrong answers. Many of the statements are similar to other statements; do not be concerned about this. Work quickly; record your first impression.

____ 1. I have no fear of giving a speech.
____ 2. Certain parts of my body feel very tense and rigid while giving a speech.
____ 3. I feel relaxed while giving a speech.
____ 4. My thoughts become confused and jumbled when I am giving a speech.
____ 5. I face the prospect of giving a speech with confidence.
____ 6. While giving a speech, I get so nervous that I forget facts I really know.

Scoring:

To compute your score, merely add or subtract your scores for each item as indicated below. The number 18 is used here so that your score comes out positive.

Scoring Formula:

18 plus the scores for items 1, 3, and 5, minus the scores for items 2, 4, and 6.

Your score should range from 6 to 30; the higher the score, the greater the apprehension. Any score above 18 indicates some degree of apprehension. Most people score above 18 on this test, so if you scored relatively high, you are among the vast majority of people.

*From An Introduction to Rhetorical Communication, 4th ed., by James C. McCroskey. Reprinted by permission of the author.

ciety oriented around communication since success often depends on the ability to communicate effectively. Other people are so mildly apprehensive that they appear to experience no fear at all. They actively seek out a wide variety of communication experiences. Most of us fall between these two extremes.

For some people, apprehension is debilitating and hinders personal effectiveness in professional and social relationships. For others, apprehension is motivating and may actually help in achieving one's goals. By the end of this course, you should be in this second category.

Positive Apprehension

Apprehension in public speaking is normal. Everyone experiences some degree of fear in the relatively formal public speaking situation. In public speaking you are the sole focus of attention and are usually being evaluated for your performance. Therefore, experiencing fear or anxiety is not strange or unique.

Although you may at first view apprehension as harmful, it is not necessarily so—as the "TIP" from Dorothy Leeds makes clear. In fact, apprehension can work for you. Fear can energize you. It may motivate you to work a little harder to produce a speech that will be better than it might have been. Further, the audience cannot see the apprehension that you might be experiencing. Even though you may think that the audience can hear your heart beat faster and faster, they cannot. They cannot see your knees tremble. They cannot sense your dry throat—at least not most of the time.

REMEMBER: Speaker apprehension:
1. can be distinguished on the basis of its being trait apprehension (fear of communication generally) or state apprehension (fear of a specific communication situation)
2. can vary in degree from extreme through moderate to mild, and can debilitate and hinder personal effectiveness but also can energize and make you more alert and responsive

---

TIPS FROM PROFESSIONAL SPEAKERS

Whether you face real or imaginary fear, physical danger, or emotional stress, the reaction is the same. And speakers benefit: The adrenaline becomes energy; their minds seem more alert; new thoughts, facts, and ideas arise. In fact, some of my best ad libs come to me in front of my toughest audiences; it's yet another gift from the adrenaline.

Nervousness can give your speech the edge—and the passion—all good speeches need. It has always been so; two thousand years ago Cicero said all public speaking of real merit was characterized by nervousness.

Dorothy Leeds, president, Organizational Technologies, Inc., a management and sales consulting firm. *Powerspeak: The Complete Guide to Persuasive Public Speaking and Presenting* (New York: Prentice-Hall, 1988), pp. 9–10.

DEALING WITH SPEAKER APPREHENSION

What should you do about your apprehension? What should you do as a listener-critic when dealing with people who experience high apprehension? You may lessen it, you may control it, but you probably cannot eliminate it totally. The suggestions offered here will help you to lessen and manage apprehension.

If you experience some apprehension and would like to acquire more control over it, the following guidelines should help you feel more comfortable giving speeches (Richmond and McCroskey 1992; Cheek 1989). If you continue to experience extremely high levels of speaker apprehension or if you are so fearful of the speaking situation that you simply cannot function, talk with your instructor after completing this unit.

Speaker Guidelines

A great deal of research has been conducted on speaker apprehension and on ways to reduce or control it (Richmond and McCroskey 1992; Cheek 1989). Here are some of these findings.

Understand (Control) the Influences on Apprehension The first step is to understand apprehension, especially the factors that influence it. Communication researcher Michael Beatty (1988), for example, has found that five factors influence students' public speaking anxiety. Understanding these factors will help you control them and, therefore, your fear of speaking.

1. *Perceived novelty.* Situations that are new and different contribute to anxiety. As the novelty of the situation is reduced (as you gain experience in public speaking), your anxiety is also reduced.

2. *Subordinate status.* When you feel that others are better speakers than you or that they know more about the topic than you do, anxiety increases. Thinking more positively about yourself and being thorough in your preparation are helpful techniques for reducing this particular cause of anxiety.

3. *Conspicuousness.* When you feel you are the center of attention, as you normally do in public speaking, your anxiety may increase. Thinking of public speaking as a type of conversation may help reduce this feeling of conspicuousness.

4. *Dissimilarity.* When you feel you have little in common with your listeners, you may feel anxious. The more different you feel from your listeners, the more apt you are to experience fear in public speaking. Therefore, emphasize your similarity with your listeners whenever you think of your speech as well as during its presentation.

5. *Prior history.* A prior history of apprehension is likely to increase anxiety. Your positive public speaking experiences will help reduce this cause of anxiety.

Prepare and Practice Thoroughly Much of the fear you experience is a fear of failure. Adequate and even extra preparation will lessen the possibility of failure and the accompanying apprehension. Jack Valenti (1982), president of the Motion Picture Association of America and speechwriter for Lyndon Johnson, put it this way: "The most effective antidote to stage fright and other calamities of speechmaking is total, slavish, monkish preparation."

Gain Experience Learning to speak in public is similar to learning to drive a car or ski down a mountain. With experience, the initial fears and anxieties give way to feelings of control, comfort, and pleasure. Experience will prove to you that a public speech can be effective despite your fears and anxieties. It will show you that the feelings of accomplishment in public speaking are rewarding and will outweigh the initial anxiety.

Put Apprehension in Perspective Maintain realistic expectations for yourself and your audience. You do not have to be perfect. Be the best you can be—whatever that is. Compete with yourself. Your second speech does not have to be better than the speech of the previous speaker. It should, however, be better than your own first speech.

Recognize, too, that even if you give six 10-minute speeches in this class, you will only have spoken for 60 minutes . . . one hour . . . 1/24th of a day . . . 1/35,064th of your four-year college life. Let your apprehension motivate you to produce a more thoroughly prepared and rehearsed speech. Let it not, however, upset you to the point where it harms your other activities.

Move About and Breathe Deeply Physical activity—gross bodily movements as well as the small movements of the hands, face, and head—eases or lessens apprehension. If you are apprehensive, work into your speech some writing on the blackboard or some demonstration that requires movement. Using a visual aid, for example, will temporarily divert attention from you and will allow you to get rid of your excess energy.

Deep breathing relaxes the body. By breathing deeply a few times before getting up to speak, you will sense your body relax. This will help you overcome your initial fear of getting out of your seat and walking to the front of the room. If you find yourself getting a bit more nervous than you'd hoped during your speech, just breathe deeply during a pause.

Listener Guidelines

Listeners can do a great deal to assist speakers with their apprehension. Here are just a few suggestions.

Positively Reinforce the Speaker A nod, a pleasant smile, an attentive appearance throughout the speech will help put the speaker at ease. Resist the temptation to pick up a newspaper or talk with a friend. Try to make it as easy as possible for the speaker.

Ask Questions in a Supportive Manner If there is a question period after the speech, ask information-seeking questions rather than fire critical challenges. Instead of saying "Your criticism of heavy metal music is absurd," say "Why do you find the lyrics of heavy metal harmful?" or "What is there about the beat of disco music that you find offensive?" Ask questions in a tone and a manner that do not make the speaker defensive.

Do Not Focus on Errors If the speaker fumbles in some way, do not focus on it. Do not put your head down, cover your eyes, or otherwise nonverbally communicate your intense awareness of the fumble. Instead, continue listening to the content of the speech. Nonverbally, try to communicate to the speaker that you are concerned with what is being said.

REMEMBER: Guidelines in dealing with speaker apprehension:

As a speaker:

1. Understand (and control) the influences on apprehension: perceived novelty of the situation, subordinate status, conspicuousness, dissimilarity, and prior history of apprehension.
2. Prepare and practice thoroughly.
3. Gain experience.
4. Put apprehension in perspective.
5. Engage in physical activity and deep breathing.

As a listener:

6. Positively reinforce the speaker.
7. Ask questions in a supportive manner.
8. Do not focus on errors.

DEVELOPING CONFIDENCE

Confidence separates the effective from the ineffective public speaker. Confidence also seems to separate the speaker who experiences enjoyment from the speaker who feels only pain and anxiety. Fortunately, confidence is a quality that everyone can develop and improve. A few suggestions for developing your self-confidence as a public speaker should help.

Prepare Thoroughly Preparation is probably the major factor in instilling confidence in a speaker, as it is in reducing apprehension. Preparation includes everything you do from the time you begin thinking about your speech to the time you deliver it. The more you know about your topic, the more confident you will feel and the more confidence you will project. Thorough rehearsal will lessen any fears of forgetting.

Familiarize Yourself with the Public Speaking Situation Familiarize yourself with the arrangement of the room in which you will speak, the type of audience you will address, and so on. Familiarity with any situation increases your ability to control it. The public speaking situation is no exception. Perhaps a day or two before you are to speak, stand in front of the room. Look it over. Try to imagine the entire speaking situation as it will be when you deliver your speech. Then, when you do go to the front of the room to give your first speech, you will face the familiar instead of the unexpected.

Develop the Desire to Communicate Avoid rehearsing fear responses. Replace any thoughts of fear with thoughts of control. Avoid self-critical statements; replace these with thoughts of confidence—substitute positive "scripts." Tell yourself that the

Thorough preparation is one of the major ways to reduce anxiety and develop confidence in a public speaking situation. What other advice would you give to a speaker on the path from apprehension to confidence?

experience can be an enjoyable one—it really can be! With time, you will find that you are operating with a more positive and confident view of the entire public speaking experience.

Rehearse Rehearsing your speech and its presentation—and thus sensing your control over it—is essential for increasing self-confidence. Rehearse your speech often. Rehearse out loud. If possible, rehearse your speech in front of a few supportive listeners. Rehearsals that approximate the actual speaking situation will especially help reduce the novelty of the situation and will help build your confidence as a public speaker.

Rehearse your speech as a confident, fully-in-control public speaker. Rehearse with a positive attitude and perspective. When you then present the actual speech, you will find that you can present the speech as you rehearsed it, with confidence.

Each public speaking experience—like each rehearsal—should add to your self-confidence. After five or six speeches, you should be looking forward to future speaking engagements.

Develop a Communicator Self-Image A "communicator self-image" implies a view of yourself as a capable, proficient, and confident communicator. See yourself as an advocate who is effective in getting her or his message across to others. Think of yourself as a confident speaker. Act like a confident speaker. For example, maintain eye contact with your listeners; stand tall as would a leader. Acting confidently will go a

■-■-■-

TIPS FROM PROFESSIONAL SPEAKERS

Shortly before you get up to make your remarks is the time to visualize yourself delivering a confident, well-received speech. It works—if you've done your homework well and have earned the right to psych yourself up.

Think of times you've succeeded at your endeavors in any field rather than the times you've failed. Think in terms of how good it'll be to succeed rather than how bad it'll be to fail. Think about your purpose in delivering the speech.

Concentrate on what you want to do. Concentrate on the emotions you want to spread outward, not on the emotions you want to keep inside. Concentrate on what you're saying, not how you're saying it or how you look.

Ed McMahon, television emcee and frequent public speaker. *The Art of Public Speaking* (New York: Ballantine, 1986), pp. 101–102.

long way toward actually increasing your confidence. This process occurs in three steps:

You act as if you are confident.

⬇

You come to think of yourself as confident.

⬇

You become confident.

Build your positive qualities by acting as if you already have them. This "acting as if" will help you make these positive qualities a more integral part of your thinking and your behaviors.

REMEMBER: **To develop confidence:**
1. **prepare thoroughly**
2. **familiar yourself with the public speaking situation**
3. **develop the desire to communicate**
4. **rehearse often and with a positive attitude**
5. **develop an image of yourself as a successful speaker**

CRITICALLY SPEAKING

1. In what situations do you experience the greatest communication anxiety? What do these situations have in common?
2. How accurately do you feel the communication Apprehension Test identified your apprehension in public speaking?
3. How closely do your scores on the communication Apprehension Test and the Shyness Test (see Practically Speaking exercise 3.1) match? Do the scores and their degree of similarity seem reasonable?

4. Of the five influences on apprehension discussed here, which do you feel is the most important to you as a public speaker?

5. What kinds of listening behaviors help to lessen your anxiety when you are speaking?

6. What other suggestions might you offer for helping speakers to manage their apprehension in public speaking?

7. In what ways is interpersonal confidence similar to confidence in public speaking? How are they different?

8. What well-known celebrity do you feel displays confidence most effectively? What is there about this person's behaviors that led you to this judgment?

9. What other suggestions might you offer for developing self-confidence?

10. Are the methods for increasing self-confidence the same for men and women? For members of different cultures?

11. What would be appropriate headings to cover the various terms in each of these five groups: (a) *trait* and *state;* (b) *perceived novelty, subordinate status, conspicuousness, dissimilarity,* and *prior history;* (c) *understand the influences on apprehension, prepare and practice thoroughly, gain experience, put apprehension in perspective,* and *move about and breathe deeply;* (d) *positively reinforce the speaker, ask questions supportively,* and *avoid focusing on errors;* (e) *prepare thoroughly, familiarize yourself with the speech situation, develop the desire to communicate, rehearse,* and *develop an image of yourself as a competent, confident speaker.*

PRACTICALLY SPEAKING

3.1   SHYNESS

Earlier you assessed your own communication apprehension in a variety of communication contexts. Often, but not always, communication apprehension results from a general shyness*. Here is a shyness scale that will enable you to measure your own degree of shyness. Respond to these statements, as noted in the directions, and then consider the questions presented after the test.

Directions

The following 14 statements refer to talking with other people. If the statement describes you very well, circle "YES." If it somewhat describes you, circle "yes." If you are not sure whether it describes you or not, or if you do not understand the statement, circle "?" If the statement is a poor description of you, circle "no." If the state-

*From "Communication Apprehension of Elementary and Secondary Students and Teachers" by James C. McCroskey, J. F. Andersen, Virginia Richmond, and L. R. Wheeless in *Communication Education* 30:122–132. Reprinted by permission of James C. McCroskey.

ment is a very poor description of you, circle "NO." There are no right or wrong answers. Work quickly; record your first impression.

1.	I am a shy person.	YES	yes	?	no	NO
2.	Other people think I talk a lot.	YES	yes	?	no	NO
3.	I am a very talkative person.	YES	yes	?	no	NO
4.	Other people think I am shy.	YES	yes	?	no	NO
5.	I talk a lot.	YES	yes	?	no	NO
6.	I tend to be very quiet in class.	YES	yes	?	no	NO
7.	I don't talk much.	YES	yes	?	no	NO
8.	I talk more than most people.	YES	yes	?	no	NO
9.	I am a quiet person.	YES	yes	?	no	NO
10.	I talk more in a small group (3–6) than others do.	YES	yes	?	no	NO
11.	Most people talk more than I do.	YES	yes	?	no	NO
13.	Other people think I am very quiet.	YES	yes	?	no	NO
14.	I talk more in class than most people do.	YES	yes	?	no	NO
15.	Most people are more shy than I am.	YES	yes	?	no	NO

Scoring

YES = 1; yes = 2; ? = 3; no = 4; NO = 5.
Please score your responses as follows:

1. Add the scores for items 1, 4, 6, 7, 9, 11, and 12.
2. Add the scores for items 2, 3, 5, 8, 10, 13, and 14.
3. Complete the following formula: Shyness = 42 *plus* the total from Step 1 *minus* the total from Step 2.

You may interpret your score as follows:

Above 52 = a high level of shyness
Below 32 = a low level of shyness
Between 32 and 52 = a moderate level of shyness

Questions to Consider

1. In what situations are you most shy? Least shy? Why?
2. Can you think of early experiences that contributed to your level of shyness?
3. How does your level of shyness impact on your meeting other people? Your work relationships? Your classroom behavior? Your interactions with other students? Your interactions with your instructors?
4. How do you respond to shy people as potential relationship partners? As other students? As colleagues at work? As your public speaking instructor?
5. Would you like to change your degree of shyness? How might you use the suggestions for managing communication apprehension to alter your shyness behavior?

U N I T 4

Listening

■ ■ ■ ■

UNIT OBJECTIVES

After completing this unit, you should be able to:

1. Describe the process of listening and the five-stage model

2. Explain the major obstacles to effective listening

3. Explain the principles for effective listening

4. Explain the nature of critical listening and the seven propaganda devices

*P*reparing and presenting a public speech is the task you are most concerned with and most anxious about. But that is really only half the process of public speaking. The other half is critical listening. Before reading about this area of human communication, examine your own listening habits by taking the Listening Test.

▣▪▪▪▣ THE LISTENING PROCESS

The process of listening can be described as a series of five steps: receiving, understanding, remembering, evaluating, and responding. The process is represented in Figure 4.1.

Receiving

Unlike listening, hearing begins and ends with this first stage of receiving. *Hearing* is something that just happens when you get within earshot of some auditory stimuli. *Listening* is quite different; it begins (but does not end) with receiving the messages the speaker sends. The messages are both verbal and nonverbal; they consist of words as well as gestures, facial expressions, variations in volume and rate, and lots more as we will see throughout this text.

At this stage you recognize not only what is said (verbally and nonverbally) but also what is omitted. The politician's summary of accomplishments in education as well as the omission of the failures in improved health care programs are both received at this stage.

FIGURE 4.1   A five-step model of the listening process. This five-step model draws on a variety of previous models that listening researchers have developed (for example, Barker, 1990; Steil, Barker, and Watson, 1983; Brownell, 1987; Alessandra, 1986).

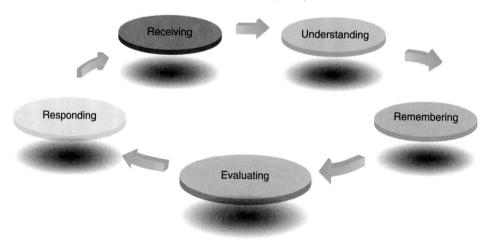

■ ■ ■

TEST YOURSELF: HOW GOOD A LISTENER ARE YOU?

Instructions:

Respond to each question using the following scale:

1 = always
2 = frequently
3 = sometimes
4 = seldom
5 = never

_____ 1. I consider listening and hearing to be essentially the same and so I listen by simply keeping my ears open.

_____ 2. I allow my mind to wander away from what the speaker is talking about.

_____ 3. I simplify messages I hear by omitting details.

_____ 4. I focus on a particular detail of what the speaker is saying instead of the general meanings the speaker wishes to communicate.

_____ 5. I allow my attitudes toward the topic or speaker to influence my evaluation of the message.

_____ 6. I assume that what I expect to hear is what is actually said.

_____ 7. I stop listening when the speaker attacks my personal beliefs.

_____ 8. I listen to what others say but I don't feel what they are feeling.

_____ 9. I judge and evaluate what the speaker is saying before I fully understand the meanings intended.

_____ 10. I rehearse my questions and responses while the speaker is speaking.

Scoring the Listening Effectiveness Test

All statements describe ineffective listening tendencies. High scores, therefore, reflect effective listening and low scores reflect ineffective listening. If you scored significantly higher than 30, then you probably have better-than-average listening skills. Scores significantly below 30 represent lower-than-average listening skills. Regardless of your score, however, most people can significantly improve their listening skills. Each of the questions in this listening test refers to an obstacle or effectiveness principle discussed in this unit.

Receiving messages is a highly selective process. You do not listen to all the available auditory stimuli. Rather, you selectively tune in to certain messages and tune others out. Generally, you listen carefully to messages that you feel will prove of value to you or that you feel are particularly interesting. At the same time you give less attention to messages that have less value or interest. Thus, you may, for example, listen carefully when your instructor tells you what will appear on the examination but will listen less carefully to an extended story or to routine announcements. When receiving:

- focus your attention on the speaker's verbal and nonverbal messages, on what is said and on what is not said
- avoid focusing your attention on distractions in the environment
- focus your attention on what the speaker is saying rather than on any questions you may wish to ask later

Understanding

Understanding is the stage at which you learn what the speaker means. This understanding includes both the thoughts that are expressed as well as the emotional tone that accompanies these thoughts, for example, the urgency or the joy or sorrow expressed in the message. To enhance understanding:

- relate the new information the speaker is giving to what you already know (In what way will this new proposal change our present health care?)
- see the speaker's messages from the speaker's point of view; avoid judging the message until you fully understand it as the speaker intended it
- rephrase (paraphrase) the speaker's ideas into your own words as you continue to listen

Remembering

Messages that you receive and understand need to be retained at least for some period of time. In public speaking situations you can augment your memory by taking notes or by taping the messages.

What you remember is actually not what was said, but what you think (or remember) was said. Memory for speech is not *reproductive;* you don't simply reproduce in your memory what the speaker said. Rather, memory is *reconstructive;* you actually reconstruct the messages you hear into a system that seems to make sense to you. To illustrate this important concept, try to memorize the following list of 12 words (Glucksberg and Danks, 1975). Don't worry about the order of the words. Only the number remembered counts. Take about 20 seconds to memorize as many words as possible. Don't read any further until you have tried to memorize the list of words.

Word List

bed	dream	comfort
rest	wake	sound
awake	night	slumber
tired	eat	snore

Now close the book and write down as many of the words from this list as you can remember.

How did you do? If you are like my students, you not only remembered a good number of the words on the list but you also "remembered" at least one word that was not on the list: *sleep*. You did not simply reproduce the list; you reconstructed it. In this case you gave the list a meaning and part of that meaning included the word *sleep*. This happens with all types of messages; the messages are reconstructed into a meaningful whole and in the process a distorted version of what was said is often "remembered." In remembering:

- identify the thesis or central idea and the major propositions
- summarize the message in a more easily retained form, being careful not to ignore crucial details or qualifications
- repeat names and key concepts to yourself
- identify the organizational pattern and use it (visualize it) to organize what the speaker is saying

Evaluating

Evaluating consists of judging the messages' and the speaker's credibility (Unit 19), truthfulness, or usefulness in some way. At this stage your own biases and prejudices become especially influential. These will influence what you single out for evaluation and what you will just let pass. They will influence what you judge good and what you judge bad. In some situations, the evaluation is more in the nature of critical analysis, a topic we explore in detail in Unit 5. When evaluating:

- resist evaluation until you fully understand the speaker's point of view
- distinguish facts from inferences (see Unit 5), opinions, and personal interpretations that you are making as well as those made by the speaker
- identify any biases, self-interests, or prejudices that may lead the speaker to slant unfairly what is presented or lead you to remember what supports your biases and to forget what contradicts them

Responding

Responding occurs in two phases: (1) nonverbal (and occasionally verbal) responses you make while the speaker is talking and (2) responses you make after the speaker has stopped talking. Responses made while the speaker is talking should support the speaker and show that you are listening. These include what nonverbal researchers call **backchanneling cues** (Burgoon, Buller, and Woodall 1989) such as nodding your head, smiling, leaning forward, and similar signals that let the speaker know that you are attending to the message.

Responses made after the speaker has stopped talking are generally more elaborate and might include questions of clarification ("I wasn't sure what you meant by *reclassification*"); expressions of agreement ("You're absolutely right on this and I'll support your proposal when it comes up for a vote"); and expressions of disagreement ("I disagree that Japanese products are superior to those produced in the United States"). When responding:

- support the speaker throughout the talk by using a variety of backchanneling cues; using only one backchanneling cue—for example, nodding constantly—will make it appear that you are not listening but are on automatic pilot
- support the speaker in your final responses by saying something positive
- own your own responses; state your thoughts and feelings as your own; use I-messages (for example, say "I think the new proposal will entail greater expense than you outlined" rather than "Everyone will object to the plan for costing too much")

In the "Hagar the Horrible" cartoon there is a communication failure that the tax collector attributes to poor listening. Can you trace what is happening in this cartoon through the five stages of the listening process?

REMEMBER: Listening can be viewed as a five-step process:

1. receiving or hearing what is said (verbally and nonverbally) as well as what is omitted
2. understanding the thoughts and the emotions that the speaker conveys
3. remembering the messages and retaining them for some time
4. evaluating or judging the messages in some way
5. responding or reacting to the messages

■■■■ OBSTACLES TO EFFECTIVE LISTENING

The first step in improving listening abilities is to recognize and combat the various obstacles to effective listening (Nichols and Stevens 1957; Nichols 1961; Murphy 1987; Roach and Wyatt 1988).

Hagar the Horrible. Copyright © by King Features Syndicate, Inc. Reprinted with special permission of King Features Syndicate.

Preoccupation with Other Issues

Probably the most serious and most damaging obstacle to effective listening is the *tendency to become preoccupied with yourself.* For example, if you have an examination the next period, you might focus on yourself, on whether you will do well on the exam.

Sometimes the preoccupation with yourself centers on assuming the role of speaker. You begin to rehearse your responses, to think of what you will say to answer the speaker or perhaps a question you want to ask the public speaker. While focusing on yourself, you inevitably miss what the speaker is saying.

In a similar way, you may become *preoccupied with external issues* that are irrelevant to what is being said. You think about what you did last Saturday or your plans for the evening or a movie you saw. Of course, the more you entertain thoughts of external matters, the less effectively you listen.

Assimilation

Another obstacle to listening is *assimilation:* the tendency to reconstruct messages so they reflect your own attitudes, prejudices, needs, and values. It is the tendency to hear relatively neutral messages ("Management plans to institute drastic changes in scheduling") as supporting your own attitudes and beliefs ("Management is going to screw up our schedules again").

Friend-or-Foe Factor

You may also distort messages because of the *friend-or-foe factor,* the tendency to listen for positive qualities about friends and negative qualities about enemies. For example, if you dislike Freddy, then it will take added effort to listen objectively to Freddy's speeches or to criticism that might reflect positively on Freddy.

Hearing What You Expect to Hear

Another obstacle is the failure to hear what the speaker is saying and instead *hear what you expect.* You know that your history instructor frequently intersperses lectures with long personal stories and so when she says, "I can remember . . . ," you automatically hear a personal story and perhaps tune out.

Prejudging the Speech or Speaker

Whether in a lecture auditorium or in a small group, avoid the tendency to prejudge some speeches as uninteresting or irrelevant. All speeches are, at least potentially, interesting and useful. If you prejudge them and tune them out, you will never be proven wrong; at the same time, however, you close yourself off from potentially useful information. Most important, perhaps, is that you are not giving the other person a fair hearing. Avoid jumping to conclusions before you've heard the speaker; the conclusions

What obstacles to effective listening might be present in this type of communication situation?

that you reach may in reality be quite different from the conclusions the speaker draws.

Rehearsing Your Responses

Often a speaker may say something with which you disagree. Then, during the remainder of the speech, you rehearse your response or question, you then imagine the speaker's reply to your response, and then your response to the speaker's response. The dialogue goes back and forth in your mind. Meanwhile, you miss whatever else the speaker said. You may even miss the very part that would answer your question.

If the speech is long, jot down the point or question and go back to listening. If the situation makes this impossible, simply make mental note of what you want to say. You might try to keep this in mind by relating it to the remainder of what the individual is saying. In either event, get back to listening.

Filtering Out Unpleasant Messages

Resist the temptation to filter out difficult or unpleasant messages: you don't want to hear that something you believe in is untrue or that people you care for are unpleasant, and yet these are the very messages you need to listen to with great care. These are the messages that will lead you to examine and reexamine your implicit and unconscious assumptions. If you filter out this kind of information, you risk failing to correct misinformation. You risk losing new and important insights.

REMEMBER: **To avoid these obstacles to listening:**
1. being preoccupied with oneself or with external issues
2. assimilation
3. the friend-or-foe factor
4. hearing what you expect to hear and not hearing what you do not expect to hear
5. prejudging the speech or speaker
6. rehearsing your responses
7. filtering out unpleasant messages

PRINCIPLES OF EFFECTIVE LISTENING

Effective listening is extremely important because you spend so much time listening. In fact, if you measured importance by the time you spend on an activity, listening would be your most important communication activity. Most of your communication time is spent in listening. You will improve your listening if you listen actively, for total meaning, with empathy, and with an open mind.

Listen Actively

The first step in listening improvement is to recognize that it is not a passive activity. You cannot listen without effort. Listening is a difficult process. In many ways it is more demanding than speaking. In speaking you control the situation; you can talk about what you like in the way you like. In listening, however, you have to follow the pace, the content, and the language of the speaker.

The best preparation for active listening is to act like an active listener. Recall, for example, how your body almost automatically reacts to important news. Almost immediately you sit up straighter, cock your head toward the speaker, and remain relatively still and quiet. You do this almost reflexively because this is how you listen most effectively. This is not to say that you should be tense and uncomfortable, but only that your body should reflect your active mind. In listening actively:

- Use the thought-speech time differential effectively. Because your mind can process information faster than the average rate of speech, there is often a time lag. Use this time to summarize the speaker's thoughts, formulate questions, draw connections between what the speaker says and what you already know.
- Work at listening. Listening is hard work so be prepared to participate actively. Avoid what James Floyd (1985) calls "the entertainment syndrome," the expectation to be amused and entertained by a speaker. Combat sources of "noise" as much as possible. Remove distractions or other interferences (newspapers, magazines, stereos) so that your listening task will have less competition.
- Assume there is value in what the speaker is saying. Resist assuming that what you have to say is more valuable than the speaker's remarks.

■■■■

TIPS FROM PROFESSIONAL SPEAKERS

Be a responsive listener. Be responsive in your demeanor, posture, and facial expression. Let your whole being show you are interested in other people and their ideas.

As you listen, look at the other person and show some signs of hearing and understanding. Nod your head occasionally—gently, not vigorously. Nod slightly with a *yes* for agreement or a *no* when it's something sad or unhappy. Show through your posture, whether seated or standing, that you are concentrating on listening totally. . . .

To understand this important principle of being responsive, it helps to ask, "How do we turn people off?" The answers come quickly: by not looking at them, not asking questions, not showing any positive response, by looking at our watch or out the window, shuffling papers, interrupting, and giving other negative types of feedback.

Robert L. Montgomery, professional speaker, trainer, author, and president of his own consulting firm. *Listening Made Easy* (New York: American Management Associations, 1981), pp. 75–76.

Listen for Total Meaning

The meaning of a message is not only in the words used, it is also in the speaker's nonverbal behavior. Sweating hands and shaking knees communicate as surely as do words.

The meanings communicated in a speech will also depend on what the speaker does not say. For example, the speaker who omits references to the homeless or to drugs in a speech on contemporary social problems communicates meaning by these very omissions. Exactly what inferences listeners will draw from such omissions will depend on a variety of factors. Some possible inferences might be:

- the speaker is poorly prepared
- the speaker's research was inadequate
- the speaker forgot part of the speech
- the speaker is trying to fool the audience by not mentioning this
- the speaker is trying to cover up certain issues and thinks we won't notice
- the speaker thinks we are uninformed, stupid, or both

As a listener, therefore, be particularly sensitive to the meanings that significant omissions may communicate. As a speaker, recognize that most inferences that audiences draw from omissions are negative. Most such inferences will reflect negatively on your credibility and on the total impact of the speech. Be careful, therefore, to mention significant issues that the audience expects to be discussed. In listening for total meaning:

- Focus on both verbal and nonverbal messages. Recognize both consistent and inconsistent "packages" of messages and take these cues as guides for drawing inferences about the meaning the speaker is trying to communicate. Ask questions when in doubt. Listen also to what is omitted.

- See the forest, then the trees. Connect the specifics to the speaker's general theme rather than merely remembering isolated facts and figures.

- Balance your attention between the surface and the underlying meanings. Do not disregard the literal (surface) meaning of the speech in your attempt to uncover the more hidden (deep) meanings.

Listen with Empathy

Try to *feel* what the speaker feels—empathize with the speaker. To empathize with others is to feel what they feel, to see the world they see, to walk in their shoes. Only when you achieve this will you be able to understand fully another's meaning (Eisenberg and Strayer 1987). Listen to feelings as well as to thoughts and ideas; listen to what the speaker is feeling and thinking. To listen with empathy:

- see the speaker's message from the speaker's point of view; ask yourself how this might influence what the speaker says and does

- understand both thoughts and feelings; do not consider your listening task complete until you have understood what the speaker is feeling as well as thinking

- avoid "offensive listening," the tendency to listen to bits and pieces of information that will enable you to attack the speaker or find fault with something the speaker has said

Listen with an Open Mind

Listening with an open mind is difficult. It is not easy to listen to arguments attacking your cherished beliefs. It is not easy to listen to statements condemning what you fervently believe. Listening often stops when such remarks are made. Yet it is in these situations that it is particularly important to continue listening openly and fairly. In listening with an open mind:

- Avoid prejudging. Delay both positive and negative evaluation until you have fully understood the intention and the content of the message being communicated.

- Avoid filtering out difficult, unpleasant, or undesirable messages. Avoid distorting messages through oversimplification or leveling, the tendency to eliminate details and to simplify complex messages to make them easier to remember.

- Recognize your own biases; they may interfere with accurate listening and cause you to distort message reception through *assimilation,* the tendency to interpret what you hear (or think you hear) in terms of your own biases, preju-dices, and expectations. Biases may also lead to *sharpening*—when an item of information takes on increased importance because it seems to confirm your stereotypes or prejudices.

REMEMBER: **These principles of effective listening:**
1. listen actively
2. listen for total meaning
3. listen with empathy
4. listen with an open mind

■■■■ CRITICAL LISTENING

Throughout this discussion of listening we have emphasized listening for understand-ing. There is also, however, critical listening. Critical listening depends on the skills al-ready noted but also demands focused attention to the truth and accuracy of the infor-mation and to the honesty and motivation of the speaker. Thus, in addition to keeping an open mind and delaying judgments, for example, it is necessary to focus on other is-sues as well: Is what the speaker says the truth as far as you understand it? For exam-ple, is this car really that great? Are there any disadvantages to this particular car? Has the speaker presented the information in enough detail? Have crucial parts been left out? For example, has the speaker identified all the costs?

In addition, pay special attention to the following distortions that speakers may in-troduce. These distortions were first introduced in *The Fine Art of Propaganda,* pre-pared for the Institute for Propaganda Analysis (Lee and Lee 1972). The propagandist (one who distorts the truth, an unethical persuader) uses these seven techniques to gain our compliance without logic or evidence. These devices are as important today as they were in the 1940s when they were first developed. They appear in public mes-sages of all sorts, most notably in speeches and in the appeals of advertisers. They also appear in our own thinking as we try to evaluate the messages we hear and as we try to make important decisions. Learn to identify these devices so that you will not be fooled by them.

Name-Calling and Personal Attacks

Here the speaker gives an idea, a group of people, or a political philosophy a bad name ("atheist," "Neo-Nazi"). In this way, the persuader tries to make you condemn the idea without analyzing the argument and evidence.

Some speakers, instead of arguing against the issue and disputing the evidence, at-tack the character of its supporters. For example, a speaker might say, "You know she's an atheist. What can you expect from an atheist?" when one's religious beliefs have nothing at all to do with the issue at hand. The purpose here is to give listeners a negative impression of the person or the person's proposal and to turn their attention away from the issues being disputed.

Glittering Generality

This is the opposite of name-calling. Here the speaker tries to make you accept some idea by associating it with things you value highly ("democracy," "free speech," "academic freedom"). By using "virtue words," the speaker tries to get you to ignore the evidence and simply approve of the idea.

Transfer

Here the speaker associates her or his idea with something you respect (to gain your approval) or with something you detest (to gain your rejection). Television commercials that use highly regarded personalities to sell their products are using the transfer device. Jell-O, for example, tries to get you to buy their products by associating them with Bill Cosby. Mouthwash commercials try to get you to buy their products so as to avoid bad breath or "medicine mouth."

Testimonial

This device involves using the image associated with some person to gain your approval (if you respect the person) or your rejection (if you do not respect the person). This is the technique of advertisers who use people dressed up to look like doctors or plumbers or chefs to sell their products. And, it seems, the technique works.

Sometimes this technique takes the form of using only vague and general "authorities." For example, we frequently hear such appeals as "experts agree," "scientists say," "good cooks know," or "dentists advise." Exactly who these experts are or how many of them have agreed is seldom made clear. The advertisers hope, however, that we will simply remember that "experts agree" (with the commercial).

Sometimes the testimonials are from people who have no recognizable authority in the field in which they are speaking. Does Bill Cosby have a specialized knowledge of Jell-O or of photography? Does Angela Lansbury have specialized knowledge of painkillers?

Plain Folks

Using this device, the speaker identifies himself or herself and the proposition with the audience. The speaker and the proposition are good—the "reasoning" goes—because they are one of the people. They are just "plain folks" like the rest of you. Consider, for example, the following excerpt for a hypothetical proposal. Notice that it provides absolutely no evidence. Instead, it seeks to associate the proposal with "plain folks."

This bill will benefit the small farmers and small businesses—the backbone of this country. Let's give the average person a break, the person who struggles to make a living for his or her family, the person like you and like me. Let's respond to their needs and give people like us a break.

Card-Stacking

The speaker here selects only the evidence and arguments that support the case. The speaker might even falsify evidence and distort the facts to better fit the case. Despite these lies, the speaker presents the supporting materials as "fair" and "impartial." For example, when advertisers say, "90 percent of the dentists surveyed endorse WhiterWhite Toothpaste as an effective cleansing agent," what are they really saying? Are they saying that WhiterWhite is better than any other toothpaste on the market? Or, are they saying that 90 percent of the dentists endorse WhiterWhite compared to not brushing your teeth at all?

Bandwagon

Using this method, the speaker persuades the audience to accept or reject an idea or proposal because "everybody is doing it." The persuader might also try to show that the "right" people are doing it. The propagandist persuades by convincing you to jump on this large and popular bandwagon.

This is a popular technique in political elections where results of polls are used to get undecided voters to jump on the bandwagon with the candidate leading in the polls. After all, the implication goes, we don't want to vote for a loser.

"Once we know these devices well enough to spot examples of their use," say Lee and Lee (1972), "we have taken a great and long step towards freeing our minds from control by propagandists. It is not the only step necessary, but it is certainly the most important."

REMEMBER: **These seven devices:**
1. **Name-calling and personal attacks:** attacking the character of the speaker
2. **Glittering generality:** associating a proposal with things we value highly
3. **Transfer:** associating ideas with what we respect (to gain our approval) or with what we detest (to gain our rejection)
4. **Testimonial:** using an image or authority to gain our approval
5. **Plain folks:** identifying oneself with the audience of "plain folks"
6. **Card-stacking:** selecting only what supports one's case and ignoring what is not supportive
7. **Bandwagon:** claiming that one's proposal is good because everyone believes it is

CRITICALLY SPEAKING

1. How would you describe the listening process? Does the five-step model presented here adequately describe listening as you understand it? How might you improve on this model?

2. How would you describe yourself as a listener in a public speaking situation? What is your greatest weakness? Your greatest strength?

3. Are you a better listener in interpersonal situations? If so, why do you behave differently in the two types of situations?

4. What obstacle to effective listening do you think occurs most often? How might these obstacles be related to interpersonal listening?

5. What principle of effective listening do you think is the most important? Why? What other principles would you suggest to make the listening process more effective?

6. Can you supply specific examples from advertising that illustrate the seven distortions discussed under critical listening?

7. What other distortions do you see in the various persuasive messages that you hear?

PRACTICALLY SPEAKING

4.1   IDENTIFYING LISTENING PROBLEMS

This exercise provides convincing support for the proposition that listening is difficult and requires a considerable expenditure of energy. It also enables students to focus on some of the changes that result when messages travel from source to source. The procedure is as follows.

Six students participate as subjects; the remaining students serve as observers. Five of the subjects leave the room while a brief verbal message* is read to the one remaining subject. This subject tries to retain as much of the message as possible and repeats it as accurately as possible to the next person who enters the room after the message has been read to the first subject. The third subject then enters the room and

---

*A message that works particularly well is the following, taken from William Haney's "Serial Communication of Information in Organizations," in Joseph A. DeVito, *Communication: Conceptions and Processes*, 3rd ed. (Englewood Cliffs, NJ: Prentice-Hall, 1981):

Every year at State University, the eagles in front of the Psi Gamma fraternity house were mysteriously sprayed during the night. Whenever this happened, it cost the Psi Gams from $75 to $100 to have the eagles cleaned. The Psi Gams complained to officials and were promised by the president that if ever any students were caught painting the eagles, they would be expelled from school.

hears the second subject's version of the message, tries to retain as much as possible, and repeats it to the fourth subject. The process continues until all six subjects have had an opportunity to hear and repeat the message. The sixth subject should repeat the message to the class as a whole. After this sixth reproduction, focus on some of the following processes that are normally considered in the passage of messages from source to source.:

1. What was omitted? Can you describe the specific omissions that were made? Why do you suppose such omissions were made?

2. What was distorted? Can you describe the specific distortions that were made? Why do you suppose they were made?

3. What was added? Describe the specific additions that were made. Why do you suppose they were made?

What are the implications of this experience for the public speaker? For the listener? That is, what specific recommendations would you be willing to advance for the public speaker and for the listener as a result of this exercise?

4.2   YOUR OWN LISTENING BARRIERS

Most people put on blinders when they come upon particular topics or particular spokespersons. Sometimes these blinders prevent information from getting through fairly and objectively. For example, you may avoid listening to certain people or reading certain newspapers because they frequently contradict your beliefs. Sometimes these blinders color the information you take in, influencing you to take a positive view of some information (because it may support one of your deeply held beliefs) and a negative view of other information (because it may contradict such beliefs). Read over the following situations and identify any barriers that may get in the way of your listening to these people and these messages fairly and objectively. Some situations may seem likely and others extremely unlikely. For this exercise, however, assume that all speakers are speaking on the topic indicated and that you are in the audience. Ask yourself the following questions about each of the 20 situations presented below.

- What are your initial expectations?
- How credible do you find the speaker—even before he or she begins to speak?
- Will you begin listening with a positive, a negative, or a neutral attitude? How will these attitudes influence your listening?
- What will you be saying to yourself as you begin listening to the speaker? Will this influence what you receive, understand, and remember of the speech? Will this influence how you evelute and respond to the speech?
- What do you think your final assessment of the speech will be? On a 10-point scale (10=extremely sure; 1=extremely unsure) how sure are you that this will be your assessment?
- Can you identify at least one barrier that you (or someone else) might set up for each of these speech situations?

1. Elizabeth Taylor on the need to contribute to AIDS research.

2. Gloria Steinem criticizing (or praising) the contemporary women's movement.

3. Former Vice-President Dan Quayle (or President Bill Clinton) speaking on the role of the military in defending American democracy.

4. A noted and successful business leader on the futility of a college education in today's economy.

5. Edward Kennedy on the importance of moderation.

6. Spike Lee on race relations.

7. Ross Perot on financial mistakes the government must avoid.

8. A Mexican business leader urging American businesses to consider relocating to Mexico.

9. Oprah Winfrey on the mistakes of modern psychology.

10. A representative from General Motors, Ford, and Chrysler urging greater restrictions on foreign imports.

11. A catholic priest on why you should remain a virgin until marriage.

12. A homeless person petitioning to be allowed to sleep in the local public library.

13. A representative of the leading tobacco companies voicing opposition to (or support for) the legalization of marijuana.

14. An Iranian couple talking about the need to return to fundamentalist values.

15. A person with AIDS speaking in favor of lower drug prices.

16. A successful Japanese business leader talking about the mistakes of contemporary American businesses.

17. A lesbian mother speaking against lesbians being granted custody of their children.

18. A person without sight or hearing speaking in favor of including the handicapped in the definition of multiculturalism used on campus.

19. A man (or woman) speaking on the failings of the opposite sex and how to tolerate them without going crazy.

20. An 85-year old multi-millionaire speaking on why social security must be given to everyone regardless of income or need.

U N I T 5

Speech Criticism in the Classroom

■ ■ ■ ■

UNIT OBJECTIVES

After completing this unit, you should be able to:

1. Define *criticism* and explain its values

2. Explain effectiveness and conformity to the principles of the art as standards of criticism

3. Explain the principles of giving and receiving criticism

4. Identify the guidelines for speech criticism

*I*n learning the art of public speaking, much insight will come from the criticism of others as well as from your criticism of others. This unit will address some of the values of criticism, the standards for evaluating a speech, and some of the ways to make criticism easier and more effective.

■■■■ CRITICISM AND ITS VALUES

Critics and criticism are essential parts of any art. The term *criticism* comes from the Latin *criticus*, which means "able to discern," "to judge." There is nothing inherently negative about criticism; it is a process of judging and evaluating—a work of art, a movie, or a public speech.

The major purpose of criticism in the classroom is to improve your public speaking abilities. Through constructive criticism you will learn the principles of public speaking more effectively. You will be shown what you do well and what you could improve.

As a listener-critic you will also learn the principles of public speaking through assessing the speeches of others and applying these principles to them. Just as you learn when you teach, you also learn when you criticize.

Criticism also helps identify standards for evaluating the wide variety of speeches you'll hear throughout your life. This critical frame of mind and the guidelines for critical evaluation will prove useful in assessing all communications: the salesperson's pitch to buy a new car, the advertiser's plea to buy Tylenol rather than Excedrin, and the newspaper's or network's editorial.

When you give criticism—as you do in a public speaking class—you are telling the speaker that you have listened carefully and that you care enough about the speech and the speaker to offer suggestions for improvement.

■■■■ THE DIFFICULTY OF CRITICISM

Criticism is difficult for the critic as well as for the person criticized (Weisinger 1989; Heldmann 1988). As a critic, you may feel embarrassed or uncomfortable to offer criticism— after all, you might think, "Who am I to criticize another person's speech; my own speech won't be any better." Or you may be reluctant to offend anyone and fear that your criticism may make the speaker feel badly. Or you may view criticism as a confrontation that will do more harm than good. Still another obstacle is that in offering criticism, you put yourself on the line; you state a position with which others may disagree and which you may be called upon to defend. Considering these difficulties, you may conclude that the process is not worth the effort and may decide to leave the criticism to others.

But, reconsider. By offering criticism you are helping the speaker; you are giving the speaker another perspective for viewing her or his speech and which will prove valuable to the speaker in future speeches. When you offer criticism, you do not claim to be a better speaker. Again, you are simply offering another perspective. It is true that by stating your criticism you put yourself in a position with which others may disagree. But, that is what will make this class and the learning of the principles exciting and challenging.

Criticism is also difficult to receive. After working on a speech for a week or two or three and dealing with the normal anxiety that comes with delivering a speech, the last thing you want is to stand in front of the class and hear others say what you did wrong. Public speaking is ego-involving and it is normal to personalize criticism. If you learn how to give and how to receive criticism, it will become an effective teaching and learning tool and will help you sharpen your skills and improve every aspect of the public speaking process. It will also serve as an important support mechanism for the developing public speaker, as a way of patting the speaker on the back for all the positive effort.

STANDARDS OF CRITICISM

What standards do you use when you criticize a speech? How do you measure the excellence of a speech? On what basis do you say that one speech is weak, another is good, and still another is great? Two major standards quickly suggest themselves: effectiveness and conformity to the principles of the art.

Effectiveness

The *effectiveness* standard judges the speech in terms of whether or not it achieves its purpose. If the purpose is to sell soap, then the speech is effective if it sells soap and is ineffective if it fails to sell soap. Increased sophistication in measuring communication effects makes this standard tempting to apply.

There are, however, problems with this approach. In many instances—in the classroom, for example—the effects of a speech cannot always be measured. Sometimes the effect of a speech is long term and you may not be present to see it take hold. Also, some effects are simply not measurable; you cannot always measure changes in attitude and belief. Sometimes audiences may be so opposed to a speaker's position that even the greatest speech will have no observable effect. It may take an entire campaign to get such an audience to change its position even slightly. At other times audiences may agree with the speaker and even the weakest speech will secure their compliance. In situations like these, the effectiveness standard will lead to inaccurate and inappropriate judgments.

Furthermore, a speech interacts with so many other factors that it is difficult to attribute a change in behavior to it. The change may have been caused by something that happened on the way to the speech or after the speech or by a host of other factors. To isolate the effects of the speech is extremely difficult, often impossible. But, perhaps more important is that there is more to a speech than its effect; for example, there are ethical obligations. A speech that violates ethical standards may be effective but doesn't deserve a positive evaluation.

Conformity to the Principles of the Art

A more useful standard (and one which I use in my own public speaking classes) is to evaluate the speech on the basis of its *conformity to the principles of the art*. With this standard a speech is positively evaluated when it follows the principles of public speaking established by the critics, theorists, and practitioners of public speaking (and as described in this text) and negatively evaluated as it deviates from these principles.

This standard is of course not totally separate from the effectiveness standard since the principles of the art of public speaking are largely principles of effectiveness. When you follow the principles of the art, your speech will in all likelihood be effective.

The great advantage of this standard (especially in a learning situation such as this) is that it will help you master the principles of public speaking. When your speech is measured by its adherence to these principles, you will be learning the principles by applying them to your unique situation and through the critic's feedback.

The principles of public speaking are presented throughout this book, and it is by these principles—supplemented by whatever principles your instructor adds—that your public speech efforts will be evaluated. In your early speeches, follow the principles as closely as you can, even if their application seems mechanical and unimaginative. After you have mastered their application, then begin to play with the principles, altering them to suit your own personality, the uniqueness of the situation, and your specific goals.

Additional Standards

Of course there are other standards that critics have applied. The *universality* standard (Murphy 1957) asks to what extent does the speech address values and issues that have significance for all people in all times. This standard is often the one used in evaluating literature. By this standard Martin Luther King, Jr.'s "I Have a Dream" (see Appendix for the complete text) would be judged positively because it argues for beliefs, values, and actions that most of the civilized world view positively.

The *historical justification* standard asks to what extent was the speech's thesis and purpose justified by subsequent historical events. By this standard William Jennings Bryan's famous "Cross of Gold" speech (delivered in 1896)—although it won Bryan the Democratic nomination for president—would be judged negatively because it argued for a rejected monetary standard and against a monetary standard (gold) that the entire world had accepted.

The *ethical merit* standard asks to what extent does the speech argue for what is true, moral, humane, or good. By this standard the speeches of Adolf Hitler would be judged negatively because they supported ideas most people find repugnant.

REMEMBER: Criticism is valuable because it:
1. helps to identify strengths and weaknesses and thereby helps you improve as a public speaker
2. helps to identify standards for evaluating all sorts of public speeches

3. shows that the audience is listening and is concerned about the speaker's progress

and may use the standards of

4. effectiveness (How effectively did the speaker accomplish the purpose?)
5. conformity to the principles of the art (How effectively did the speaker apply the principles of public speaking?)
6. universality (Does the speech have application to all people in all times?), historical justification (Is the speech's thesis justified by history?), and ethical merit (Does the speech defend what is moral or good?)

EXPRESSING CRITICISM

Before reading the specific suggestions for expressing criticism, take the following test, which asks you to identify what's wrong with selected critical comments.

Here are a few suggestions for making critical evaluations a more effective part of the total learning process and for avoiding some of the potentially negative aspects of criticism.

TEST YOURSELF: WHAT'S WRONG WITH THESE COMMENTS?
Instructions:

Examine each of the following critical comments. For the purposes of this exercise, assume that each comment represents the critic's complete criticism. What's wrong with each?

1. I loved the speech. It was great. Really great.
2. The introduction didn't gain my attention.
3. You weren't interested in your own topic. How do you expect us to be interested?
4. Nobody was able to understand you.
5. The speech was weak.
6. The speech didn't do anything for me.
7. Your position was unfair to those of us on athletic scholarships; we earned those scholarships.
8. I found four things wrong with your speech. First, . . .
9. You needed better research.
10. I liked the speech; we need more police on campus.

The following discussion will identify how to express your criticism effectively and will illustrate why each of these 10 comments is ineffective.

Say Something Positive

Egos are fragile and public speaking is extremely personal. Speakers are all like Noël Coward when he said, "I love criticism just as long as it's unqualified praise." Recall that part of your function as a critic is to strengthen the already positive aspects of someone's public speaking performance. Positive criticism is particularly important in itself, but it is almost essential as a preface to negative comments. There are always positive characteristics, and it is more productive to concentrate on these first. Thus, instead of saying (as in the self-test) "The speech didn't do anything for me," tell the speaker what you liked first, then bring up some weakness and suggest how it might be corrected.

When criticizing a person's second or third speech, it is especially helpful if you can point out specific improvements ("You really held my attention in this speech," "I felt you were much more in control of the public speaking today than in your first speech").

Be Specific

Criticism is most effective when it is specific. Statements such as "I thought your delivery was bad," "I thought your examples were good," or, as in the self-test, "I loved the speech . . . Really great" and "The speech was weak" are poorly expressed criticisms. These statements do not specify what the speaker might do to improve delivery or to capitalize on the examples used. In commenting on delivery, refer to such specifics as eye contact, vocal volume, or whatever else is of consequence. In commenting on the examples, tell the speaker why they were good. Were they realistic? Were they especially interesting? Were they presented dramatically?

In giving negative criticism, specify and justify—to the extent that you can—positive alternatives. Here is an example.

> I thought the way in which you introduced your statistics was vague. I wasn't sure where the statistics came from or how recent or reliable they were. It might have been better to say something like "The 1990 U.S. Census figures show that. . . ." In this way we would know that the statistics were recent and the most reliable available.

Be Objective

In criticizing a speech, transcend your own biases as best you can, unlike our earlier example, "Your position was unfair . . . ; we earned those scholarships." See the speech as objectively as possible. Assume, for example, that you are strongly for women's rights to abortion and you encounter a speech diametrically opposed to your position. In this situation, you would need to take special care not to dismiss the speech because of your own bias. Examine the speech from the point of view of a detached critic, and evaluate, for example, the validity of the arguments and their suitability to the audience, the language, the supporting materials.

Conversely, take special care not to evaluate a speech positively *because* it presents a position with which you agree, as in "I liked the speech; we need more police on

"We liked your novel very much. Yes, very much. Very very much indeed. We liked it. We liked it indeed very much. Yes, indeed. But—"

Courtesy of Catherine O'Neill.

campus." Similarly, when evaluating a speech by a speaker you feel strongly about—whether positively or negatively—be equally vigilant. A disliked speaker may give an effective, well-constructed, well-delivered speech, and a well-liked speaker may give an ineffective, poorly constructed, poorly delivered speech. Keep in mind Matthew Arnold's definition of *criticism:* a "disinterested endeavour to learn and propagate the best that is known and thought in the world."

Limit Criticism

Cataloging a speaker's weak points, as in "I found four things wrong with your speech," will overwhelm, not help, the speaker. If you are the sole critic, your criticism naturally will need to be more extensive. If you are one of many critics, limit your criticism to one or perhaps two points. In all cases, your guide should be the value your comments will have for the speaker.

Be Constructive

Your primary goal should be to provide the speaker with insight that you feel will prove useful in future public speaking transactions, a point that Ron Hoff makes clear in the accompanying "TIP." For example, to say "The introduction didn't gain my at-

■ ■ ■

TIPS FROM PROFESSIONAL SPEAKERS

Keep the focus of your critique clearly on the future. "We're talking about your *next* presentation, and how we can help you make it the best one of your life." Presentation style is hard to change. It becomes ingrained, a part of behavior, as habit-forming as a golf swing that has stroked some very good hits. By critiquing the presentation *now*, you aren't knocking what has worked in the past, you are simply offering suggestions for the future. Keep the emphasis of your critique where it does the most good—on "the next presentation."

Ron Hoff, speaker, writer, and advertising director. *"I Can See You Naked,"* A Fearless *Guide to Making Great Presentations* (New York: Andrews and McMeel, 1988), p. 238.

tention" doesn't tell the speaker how he or she might have gained your attention. Instead, you might say "the example about the computer crash would have more effectively gained my attention in the introduction."

Focus on Behavior

Focus criticism on what the speaker said and did during the actual speech. Try to avoid the very natural tendency to mindread the speaker, to assume that you know why the speaker did one thing rather than another. Compare the critical comments presented in Table 5.1. Note that those in the first column, "Criticism as Attack," try to identify the reasons the speaker did as he or she did; they try to mindread the speaker. At the same time, they blame the speaker for what happened. Those in the second column, "Criticism as Support," focus on the specific behavior. Note, too, that those in the first column are likely to engender defensiveness; you can almost hear the speaker saying "I

TABLE 5-1 CRITICISM AS ATTACK AND AS SUPPORT

CRITICISM AS ATTACK	CRITICISM AS SUPPORT
"You weren't interested in your topic."	"I would have liked to see greater variety in your delivery. It would have made me feel that you were more interested."
"You should have put more time into the speech."	"I think it would have been more effective if you looked at your notes less."
"You didn't care about your audience."	"I would have liked it if you looked more directly at us while speaking."

was so interested in the topic . . . " or "How do you know I didn't work on my speech; I sure did." Those in the second column are unlikely to create defensiveness and are likely to be appreciated as honest reflections of how the critic perceived the speech. In short, instead of stating *why* you think the speaker did what he or she did, state *what* the speaker did and *what* you think the speaker should have done differently.

Own Your Own Criticism

In giving criticism own your comments; take responsibility for your criticism. The best way to express this ownership is to use "I-messages" rather than "you-messages." Instead of saying "You needed better research," say "I would have been more persuaded if you used more recent research."

Avoid attributing what you found wrong to others. Instead of saying "Nobody was able to understand you," say "I had difficulty understanding you. It would have helped me if you spoke more slowly." Remember that your criticism is important precisely because it is *your* perception of what the speaker did and what the speaker could have done more effectively. Speaking for the entire audience ("We couldn't hear you clearly" or "No one was convinced by your arguments") is neither your right nor will it help the speaker, and it is likely to prove demoralizing.

I-messages will also prevent you from using "should messages," a type of expression that almost invariably creates defensiveness and resentment. When you say "you should have done this" or "you shouldn't have done that," you assume a superior position and imply that what you are saying is correct and that what the speaker did was incorrect. On the other hand, when you own your evaluations and use I-messages, you are giving your perception; it is then up to the speaker to accept or reject them.

Remember the Irreversibility of Communication

Communication is irreversible. Once something is said, it cannot be unsaid. Remember this when offering criticism, especially criticism that may be too negative. If in doubt, err on the side of gentleness, a lesson the parents in the cartoon on page 82 seem not to have learned.

REMEMBER: **When giving criticism:**
1. say something positive
2. be specific
3. be objective
4. limit criticism
5. be constructive
6. focus on behavior
7. own your own criticism
8. remember the irreversibility of communication

"Frankly, your mother and I think you did better work when you were two."

Drawing by Koren; © 1991 The New Yorker Magazine, Inc. Reprinted by permission.

RECEIVING CRITICISM

Receiving criticism, although a valuable part of public speaking and of life in general, is one of the most difficult experiences we have to deal with. Here are some suggestions for receiving criticism and using it to improve your skills.

Accept the Critic's Viewpoint

When the critic offers a comment, it is simply the critic's perception and because it is, the critic is always right. If the critic says that he or she wasn't convinced by the evidence, it doesn't help to identify the 10 or 12 references that you used in your speech—this critic was simply not convinced. Instead, consider why these references were not convincing to your critic. Perhaps you didn't emphasize the credibility of the source or didn't stress their recency or didn't emphasize their connection to your proposition.

Listen Openly

Because public speaking is so ego-involving, it is tempting to block out criticism. The problem with this is that if you do block it out, you will lose out on potentially useful suggestions for improvement.

Respond Without Defensiveness

Whenever people are evaluated, especially when negatively, they tend to become defensive. Perhaps they try to protect their self-esteem. Defensiveness, however, seals off effective communication and prevents you from receiving the very information that may prove helpful to your future efforts. The more you defend yourself, the less attention you can give to the critic's comments.

Separate Speech-Criticism from Self-Criticism

If you are to improve your skills and yet not be psychologically crushed by negative evaluations, separate any criticism of your speech from criticism of yourself. Recognize that when some aspect of your speech is criticized, your personality or your worth as an individual is not being criticized. Externalize critical evaluations so that you view them dispassionately.

Seek Clarification

Ask for clarification if you do not understand the criticism or if you don't understand how you would apply the criticism to improve your future efforts. Thus, for example, if it is unclear when you are told that your specific purpose was too broad, ask how you

---

TIPS FROM PROFESSIONAL SPEAKERS

For self-criticism to work, you have to be gentle with yourself and learn from feedback: If people say you were good, why not believe them? Coaching is criticism, but it is also developing your confidence by ignoring your insecurities and accepting positive comments. You have to be able to pick out critically the *good* things about your performance, the things you improved since the last speech. Be gentle with yourself and make self-evaluation an uplifting not a negative experience.

Dorothy Leeds, president, Organization Technologies, Inc., a management and sales consulting firm. *Powerspeak: The Complete Guide to Persuasive Public Speaking and Presenting* (New York: Prentice-Hall, 1988), p. 182.

might narrow the specific purpose. Your critics—instructor and students—should welcome such attempts to seek clarification.

Try also to understand the reasons for the criticism. Ask yourself why certain aspects of the speech or its presentation were criticized. Ask why the suggested alterations would make a more effective speech. Once you understand the *basis* for the criticism, you will be in a better position to incorporate these suggestions into future public speaking efforts.

Support the Critic

Critics will be more likely to offer their views and suggestions if they feel their efforts are appreciated. Since what the critic has to say is often vital to self-improvement, express support for the critic and the critic's comments. Demonstrate an openness in hearing the criticism; make the critic know that you are hearing and really listening to what the critic has to say. Also, express positive reactions (nonverbally and verbally) to the critic; make the critic know that you appreciate his or her careful listening and evaluation.

REMEMBER: **When receiving criticism:**
1. **accept the critic's viewpoint**
2. **listen openly**
3. **respond without defensiveness**
4. **separate speech from self-criticism**
5. **seek clarification**
6. **be supportive of the critic; respond positively to criticism**

▧■■■ GUIDELINES FOR SPEECH CRITICISM

The following serles of questions are in the nature of a beginner's guide to speech criticism. These questions come from the topics in Unit 2 and are discussed in greater detail in the units to follow. Throughout the text additional principles will be introduced; those covered in Unit 2 and identified here will be amplified. So, view the following questions as a preliminary guide to some of the issues to come. You will also find it helpful to use these questions as a checklist for your own speeches. They will help you make sure that you have followed the principles of public speaking.

The Subject and Purpose   The speech subject should be worthwhile, relevant, and interesting to the audience. The speech purpose should be clear and sufficiently narrow so that it can be achieved in the allotted time. Here are some questions to guide your criticism:

1. Is the subject a worthwhile one?
2. Is the subject relevant and interesting to the audience and to the speaker?
3. Is the information presented of benefit to the audience in some way?

4. What is the general purpose of the speech (to inform, to persuade, to secure goodwill, etc.)? Is this clear to the audience?

5. Is the specific topic narrow enough to be covered in some depth in the time allotted?

The Audience, Occasion, and Context A public speech is designed for a specific audience and occasion and takes into account the characteristics of the audience.

6. Has the speaker taken into consideration the age; sex; cultural factors; occupation, income, and status; and religion and religiousness of the audience? How are these factors dealt with in the speech?

7. Is the speech topic appropriate to the specific occasion and the general context?

Research A public speech needs to be based on accurate and reliable information. The topic needs to be thoroughly researched and the speaker needs to demonstrate a command of the subject matter.

8. Is the speech adequately researched? Do the sources appear reliable and up-to-date?

9. Does the speaker have a thorough understanding of the subject?

10. Is the speaker's competence communicated in some way to the audience?

The Thesis and Major Propositions The public speech should have one clear thesis to which the major propositions in the speech are clearly related.

11. Is the thesis of the speech clear and limited to one central idea?

12. Are the main propositions of the speech clearly related to the thesis? Are there an appropriate number of major propositions in the speech (not too many, not too few)?

Supporting Materials The speech's propositions need to be supported by a variety of appropriate supporting materials that explain or prove their validity.

13. Is each major proposition adequately supported? Are the supporting materials varied and appropriate to the speech and to the propositions?

14. Do the supporting materials amplify what they purport to amplify? Do they prove what they purport to prove?

Organization The speech materials need to be organized into a meaningful whole to facilitate the audience's comprehending the speaker's message.

15. Is the body of the speech organized in a pattern that is appropriate to the speech topic? To the audience?

16. Is the pattern of organization clear to the audience? Does it help the audience follow the speech?

Style and Language The language and style of the speech should help the audience understand the speaker's message. It should be consistent in tone with the speech topic and purpose.

17. Does the language help the audience to understand clearly and immediately what the speaker is saying? For example, are simple rather than complex, concrete rather than abstract, words used? Is personal and informal language used? Are simple and active sentences used?

18. Is the language offensive to any person or group of persons?

The Conclusion, Introduction, and Transitions The conclusion should summarize the major points raised in the speech and should provide clear and crisp closure. The introduction should gain attention and orient the audience. Transitions should connect the various parts of the speech so that they flow into one another and should provide guideposts for the audience to help them follow the speaker's train of thought.

19. Does the conclusion effectively summarize the main points identified in the speech and effectively wrap up the speech, providing recognizable closure?

20. Does the introduction gain the attention of the audience and provide a clear orientation to the subject matter of the speech?

21. Are there adequate transitions? Do the transitions help the audience to better understand the development of the speech?

Delivery Effective delivery should help maintain audience attention and help the speaker to emphasize the ideas in the speech.

22. Does the speaker maintain eye contact with the audience?

23. Are there any distractions (of mannerism, dress, or vocal characteristics) that will divert attention from the speech?

24. Can the speaker be easily heard? Are the volume and rate of speech appropriate?

THE SPEECH CRITIQUE

It is often helpful to have a form for recording your evaluation of a particular speech. This critique form is organized around the steps identified for preparing a speech and highlights just some of the important characteristics to look for. As you progress through this course, you will focus on a larger number of characteristics and on their greater refinement.

A SAMPLE SPEECH WITH CRITICAL THINKING QUESTIONS

This speech (pp.88–92), given by William Fort, a student from California State University at Chico, is presented here as a kind of summary of the basic elements of public speaking.* Read the speech all the way through first. Then glance over the questions

---

* Speech by William Fort in *1989 Championship Debates and Speeches.* Copyright © 1989 by the American Forensic Association. Reprinted by permission.

PUBLIC SPEAKING CRITIQUE FORM

Evaluation key: 1 = excellent; 2 = good; 3 = fair; 4 = needs improvement; 5 = needs lots of improvement. *Circle or underscore* items that the speaker needs to "*Work on*"; write in additional items requiring attention.

Speaker _____ Date _____
Speech _____

_____ **Subject and Purpose**
Work on: selecting more worthwhile subject; making subject relevant and interesting to audience; clarifying purpose; narrowing purpose

_____ **Audience, Occasion, Context**
Work on: relating topic and supporting materials to specific audience, occasion, and context

_____ **Research**
Work on: doing more extensive research; using more reliable sources; stressing your command of the subject

_____ **Thesis and Major Propositions**
Work on: clarifying thesis; limiting thesis to one central idea; relating propositions to thesis

_____ **Supporting Materials**
Work on: using more support; using more varied and appropriate support; relating support more directly to the propositions

_____ **Organization**
Work on: using a clear thought pattern; making pattern clear to audience

_____ **Style and Language**
Work on: clarity, vividness, appropriateness, personal style, forcefulness/power

_____ **Conclusion, Introduction, Transitions**
Work on: conclusion's summary, closure; introduction's attention, orientation; using more transitions

_____ **Delivery**
Work on: eye contact, eliminating distracting mannerisms, gestures, volume, rate

_____ **General Evaluation**

How is criticism in the classroom different from the criticism that accompanies a presentation in business? In what ways are they the same?

to get a general idea of the areas highlighted. Then, reread the speech while considering each of the questions on the right. These questions should help you review the principles of public speaking and also provide experience in formulating and expressing criticism.

How effective was the opening quotation? Did it gain attention? Did it introduce the importance of the topic?

How would members of your class respond to this topic? Would they see it as important? As relevant to their everyday lives?

"What is so terrible as war? I will tell you what is ten times and ten thousand times more terrible than war—outraged nature. I see that three persons out of every four are utterly unaware of the general causes of their own ill-health, and that is to stupid neglect, or what is just bad, stupid ignorance."

In 1859, Reverend Charles Kingsley used these powerful words to address the cholera epidemic. Which created a 40 percent infant mortality rate in England, simply because of a lack of sanitation. Today we face a similar situation. There is a problem that most are unaware of, which is causing influenza, smallpox, pneumonia, tuberculosis, meningitis, airborne lead poisoning, and most fatally, legionnaire's disease. This problem? Sick Building Syndrome. Sick Building Syndrome describes any building with actual or potential health hazards due to conta-

minated air. The incidence of SBS is rising, partially because buildings have been planned with maximum energy
savings in mind since the energy crisis of the 1970s. Dr.
Tony Pickering, who is currently studying SBS, states in
the May 1987 issue of *World Press Review* that "SBS affects 90 percent of supersealed buildings, and in some
cases sickens up to 70 percent of the building occupants."
Supersealed buildings describe any building which uses
mechanical ventilation. In basic terms, a building whose
windows cannot open or close.

SBS is a serious problem that we need to become
aware of, because if we don't do something to cure this
disease today, then like England in the 1860s, thousands
of Americans will die in the 1990s. So today we will investigate SBS by first examining the general causes of the
problem, then looking at the symptoms of SBS, and finally, we will find ways to end the outraged nature of SBS.

There are three majors causes of SBS. The first is
that buildings are using ineffective heating, ventilation,
and air conditioning systems, also known as HVAC systems. Architect William Heineman describes these systems in the December 1985 issue of *National Safety and
Health News:* "Once we enter these air-tight buildings, we
are completely dependent upon its support systems for
survival. The quality and quantity of air we breathe are
totally contained within the system."

Not only do these systems pick up fungus and bacteria and recirculate it throughout a system, but also airborne viruses, germs from co-workers, and cigarette
smoke. "Microbiological health hazards are the most
widespread of the many hazards in mechanically ventilated buildings," declares environmentalist Sandy Moretz in
the February 1988 issue of *Occupational Hazards* magazine. Ms. Moretz goes on to state, "The vast majority of
this microbial growth is caused by stagnant water and dirt
build-up in air filters, and condensation drainage trays
that are not regularly cleaned." Or, in Kingsley's words,
"stupid neglect and stupid ignorance."

The third major cause of SBS is the lack of governmental support. The Environmental Protection Agency's
Eileen Claussen states in the June 6, 1988, issue of *Time*
magazine that "Some Americans spend an estimated 90
percent of their time indoors, however no specific federal
regulations have been adopted for control of air in offices,
even though the air in some buildings is 100 times as pol-
luted as the air outside the buildings."

How might you relate this topic to members of your class?

What method did Fort use to orient his listeners? How effective was this?

What is the thesis? How would members of your class respond to this thesis?

What is the specific purpose? Was the purpose sufficiently limited?

Did the speaker effectively weave in relevant research? Was the research appropriate? Sufficient? What additional research would you have wanted to be convinced of the importance of this topic?

Does the speaker use sufficient guide phrases or transitions to help listeners follow his development? How effective is this internal summary?

Ineffective HVAC systems, lack of maintenance on existing systems, and no governmental support all perpetuate the problems associated with Sick Building Syndrome. And those problems are significant. The symptoms of SBS don't start out with our building throwing up or your elevator doors getting a fever, rather as minor annoyances such as a dry throat, headaches, or drowsiness. In fact, the May 1987 issue of *Occupational Health and Safety* printed a survey of over 1,000 office workers, half of which worked in naturally ventilated buildings, and half worked in mechanically ventilated buildings. The results showed that while only 15.7 percent of those in naturally ventilated buildings had frequent headaches, 37.4 percent of those in mechanically ventilated buildings did. When it comes to drowsiness, 13.8 percent in naturally ventilated buildings, and 51.4 percent, four times as many in mechanically ventilated buildings were frequently drowsy on the job.

Are these statistics convincing to you? Would you want additional information before accepting the importance of SBS?

These lopsided figures translate into a monetary loss by building owners. James Repace, an indoor air specialist with the EPA, states in the January 1989 issue of *Discover* magazine, "The millions of workdays lost each year (due to SBS) translate into billions of dollars in medical expense, diminished productivity, and compensation claims." In May 1988, 70 workers boycotted their office building, claiming that the air inside the building was so contaminated it caused frequent headaches, dizziness, eye irritation, chest pains, and breathing difficulties. The Washington, D.C. building is the National Headquarters of the Environmental Protection Agency.

How important would this argument be to members of your class?

Although usually the symptoms of SBS are the ones I've previously mentioned, sometimes just one visit into any supersealed building can be fatal. In May 1985, 37 men, women and children who stayed on the fourth floor of Stafford General Hospital mysteriously died. Later the cause was found to be Legionnaires' disease, a harmful bacterium which originated in an air conditioning system which blew the deadly disease through the air ducts right into the unsuspecting patients' rooms. The HVAC system hadn't been cleaned in over a year. This incident outlined in the *Air Conditioning, Heating and Refrigeration News* is not an isolated one. In fact, the September 2, 1985, issue of *U.S. News & World Report* says "Legionnaires' disease strikes 25 to 50,000 Americans a year, and about 15 percent of the victims die." Translating these figures,

How might the speaker have made these deaths more dramatic?

we can see that the outraged nature of SBS causes around 5,000 deaths annually.

Hospitals, hotels, the Environmental Protection Agency, and school buildings are places where we should be able to go and feel safe and secure. However until we, as individuals and as a nation, do something to stop the enraged nature of Sick Building Syndrome, then each and every trip into a supersealed building will be potentially life threatening.

On an individual level, the one sure-fire way to prevent becoming a victim of SBS is to wear a gas mask at all times. But since gas masks are uncomfortable, hard to find—and let's face it—unattractive, I'll recommend other means of survival. First, we need to become aware of general causes of our own ill health in these buildings. Realize that if you have frequent headaches, dry throat, drowsiness, eye irritation, chest pains, or breathing difficulties inside a building, that it probably is a sick building.

Once this awareness is achieved, please act. Pick up the phone and call your local building inspector and ask him or her to examine your sick building, and let you and the building owner know what actual or potential health hazards are there due to contaminated air. Another practical step we can all take is to tell others about the problem so they can also help find these sick buildings and pressure building owners to start a preventative program against SBS.

On a larger level, we can see the need to attack the number one cause of SBS, which is microbial growth in HVAC systems. David Custer, the Vice President of Environmental Management Systems, says in the February 1987 issue of *Buildings*, "Microbiological health hazards are the most preventable of the many hazards in supersealed buildings. They can be virtually eliminated through simple maintenance." The types of simple maintenance which Mr. Custer speaks of include replacing all dirty air filters, emptying all condensation drainage trays, and treating the entire system with an inexpensive antimicrobial solution. By spending a few dollars today, they can save millions tomorrow, and end their stupid neglect. This is a simple, and logical solution which will be easy and inexpensive to implement.

Finally, federal legislation which a) requires building owners to use certain types of tested, effective HVAC systems, and b) which requires them to clean and maintain

How effectively did the speaker use humor? Was this appropriate?

Note that the speaker discussed the causes of SBS before identifying the problems it creates. Was this pattern effective? How would you have arranged this speech?

Are these calls to action effective? Should the speaker have been more specific (less specific) in his recommendations? If you heard this speech would you be willing to do as requested? Why?

What organizational pattern did the speaker use? Was this pattern effective given the speaker's specific purpose?

Do you believe that "Sick Building Syndrome will be one of the major problems in the 1990s" and that we can "save thousands of lives lost each year to SBS"?

If not, what might the speaker have done to make you believe these statements?

How effective was the conclusion? Did the speaker summarize his major points? Did he bring the speech to a definite close?

their existing systems, would be a great help in calming the outraged nature of SBS.

In 1859, one of England's major problems was a cholera epidemic which created a 40 percent infant mortality rate. This could have been solved by taking simple preventative measures and being more sanitary. Unfortunately, most ignored Reverend Kingsley, and because of it, hundreds of thousands needlessly died. Research scientist Michael McCawley said in the June 6, 1988, issue of *Time* that "unless we realize the severity of the problem today, Sick Building Syndrome will be one of the major problems in the 1990s." If we follow the simple steps which I've outlined, we can learn from the English mistakes of the 1860s, and end the stupid neglect, stupid ignorance, and outraged nature associated with SBS, and in the process we can all play doctor and save the thousands of lives lost each year to SBS.

CRITICALLY SPEAKING

1. Do you agree with the conformity-to-the-principles-of-the-art standard for evaluating a public speech? Can you identify disadvantages of this standard?

2. Lincoln's "Gettysburg Address" was negatively evaluated when it was delivered in 1863. Today, it is regarded as one of the greatest speeches of all time. What problems does this present for evaluating speeches with the effectiveness standard?

3. Are there standards other than conformity and effectiveness that you might apply to evaluating a public speech? What are the advantages and disadvantages of these other standards?

4. How do you feel about serving as a critic for your classmates? How do you feel about others criticizing your speeches?

5. How is criticism in a public speaking class similar or different from interpersonal criticism? For example, criticism of your parenting behavior? Your friendship behavior? Your behavior as a lover?

6. Which of the suggestions for giving criticism do you think is the most important? What other suggestions would you add to this list?

7. Which of the suggestions for receiving criticism do you think is the most important? What other suggestions would you add to this list?

8. Critically evaluate the Public Speaking Critique Form presented. How would you revise it so that it becomes a more useful tool in your learning the art of public speaking?

PRACTICALLY SPEAKING

5.1   CRITICIZING A GOOD SPEECH

Read one of the speeches contained in the Appendix and respond to the critical thinking questions. Then complete the Public Speaking Critique Form presented in this
unit. In small groups or with the class as a whole compare and discuss your evaluations. This exercise should help you identify the qualities that make an effective
speech and will illustrate that different people will see the same speech very differently.

5.2   CRITICIZING A BAD SPEECH

The sample speeches presented throughout this book are good ones and are designed
to illustrate the effective application of the principles of public speaking. Here, however, is an especially poor speech, constructed to illustrate clearly and briefly some of the
major faults with public speeches. This exercise can be returned to several times
throughout the course. As the course progresses, the responses will become more
complete, more insightful, and more effective.

Review the speech and think critically about the following:

■ What specific errors can you find?
■ How would you state your advice for avoiding such errors?
■ What specific comments would you make to the speaker so that he or she might
   avoid such errors in the future? In phrasing your comments, apply the principles for expressing criticism covered in the unit.
■ Assume that this is the student's first speech and that you are the public speaking instructor. How would you communicate your general evaluation to the student? Phrase your evaluation as if you are speaking directly to the student several minutes after the student spoke.
■ How would you introduce this speech? Why is your way better than the way
   presented here?
■ How would you introduce each of the three jobs? Why is your way better than
   the way presented here?
■ How would you amplify each of the three jobs?
■ How yould you better adapt this speech to the specific audience (assume that
   your class is the audience)?
■ How would you conclude this speech? Why is your way better than the way
   presented here?

Three Jobs

Well, I mean, hello. Er . . . I'm new at public speaking so I'm a little nervous. I've always been shy. So, don't watch my knees shake. Ehm, let me see my notes here. [Mumbles to self while shuffling notes: One, two, three, four, five, -oh, they're all here.] Okay, here goes.

Three jobs. That's my title and I'm going to talk about three jobs.

The Health Care Field. This is the fastest growing job in the country, one of the fastest, I guess I mean. I know that you're not interested in this topic and that you're all studying accounting. But, there are a lot of new jobs in the health care field. The Star *had an article on health care and said that health care will be needed more in the future than it is now. And now, you know, like they need a lot of health care people. In the hospital where I work—on the West side, uptown—they never have enough health aides and they always tell me to become a health aide, like you know, to enter the health care field. To become a nurse. Or maybe a dental technician. But I hate going to the dentist. Maybe I will.*

The Robotics Field. This includes things like artificial intelligence. I don't really know what that is but its like growing real fast. They use this in making automobiles and planes and I think in computers. Japan is a leading country in this field.

The Computer Graphics Field. This field has a lot to do with designing and making lots of different products—CAD/CAM. This field also includes computer-aided imagery—CAI. And in movies, I think. Like Star Wars *and* Terminator 2. *I saw* Terminator 2 *four times. I didn't see* Star Wars *but I'm gonna rent the video.*

I got my information from a book that Carol Kleiman wrote, The 100 Best Jobs for the 1990s and Beyond. *It was summarized in last Sunday's* News.

My conclusion. These are three of the fastest growing fields in the U.S. and in the world I think—not in third world countries, I don't think. China and India and Africa. More like Europe and Germany. And the U.S.—the U.S. is the big one. I hope you enjoyed my speech. Thank you.

I wasn't as nervous as I thought I'd be. Are there any questions?

■ PART ONE CHECKLISTS

Performance Checklist: Evaluating Your Preliminary Speech Preparations

These questions—and similar ones presented at the ends of the remaining four parts of the text—will help you review your public speaking performance on topics covered in that part.

YES	NO	Have you:
☐	☐	1. Selected a speech topic and purpose that is worthwhile and sufficiently limited?
☐	☐	2. Analyzed and adapted to your audience?
☐	☐	3. Researched the topic appropriately?
☐	☐	4. Clearly identified your thesis and major propositions?
☐	☐	5. Supported these propositions?
☐	☐	6. Organized your materials into an easily identifiable pattern to help the audience follow your ideas?
☐	☐	7. Worded the speech with simple, personal, and informal words?
☐	☐	8. Composed an introduction to gain attention? To orient your audience? Composed a conclusion to summarize? To close?
☐	☐	9. Rehearsed your speech for effective delivery?

Critical Thinking Checklist: Thinking Critically About the Elements of Public Speaking

Throughout Part One we have covered a wide variety of critical thinking skills. Some of these are presented in brief here (and in the remaining Part Checklists). In all, 36 critical thinking skills are reviewed in these checklists. Review and reflect on them as skills that have applications not only to public speaking but also to all forms of communication and interaction. You may find it useful to think of other specific situations in which these critical thinking skills will prove relevant.

YES	NO	Do you:
☐	☐	1. Listen critically to (analyze and evaluate and not just accept) what others say (Unit 4)?

☐   ☐   2. Listen with an open mind and without prejudging ideas and positions that may contradict existing beliefs and attitudes (Unit 4)?

☐   ☐   3. Identify such illogical appeals as name-calling, glittering generality, transfer, testimonial, plain folks, card-stacking, and bandwagon techniques (Unit 4)?.

☐   ☐   4. Evaluate the speeches of others according to the standards established for effective public speaking (Unit 5)?

☐   ☐   5. Express critical evaluations logically and with evidence (Unit 5)?

☐   ☐   6. Maintain an open mind in receiving criticism and try to use others' suggestions for improving your efforts (Unit 5)?

P A R T   T W O

Elements of Subjects and Audiences

Part Two examines the subjects and purposes of speeches—how to find, develop, and research them (Units 6 and 7)—as well as how to analyze your audience (Units 8 and 9). These two elements (subject and audience) cannot be separated. Your audience will influence the topics you choose and how you develop and adapt them. Public speeches do not exist without audiences.

In this part you will learn how to analyze your audience and how you might adapt your speech to them. Most of this analysis and adaptation takes place during the speech preparation process. Some analysis and adaptation, however, must take place during the actual delivery of the speech. Suggestions are offered for this essential but often neglected aspect of audience analysis.

In **thinking critically** about topic, research, and audience try to:

- view each audience as unique; beware of stereotyping; test what is presented here against what you know of specific audiences—there are exceptions to every rule
- keep up with changing research methods, it is a skill you will always use; learn to use the available research sources effectively and efficiently
- evaluate information as you locate it: its validity (Is it true?) and its application to your purpose (Is this useful and directly related to this particular issue?)
- pay special attention to intercultural differences in audiences and how your cultural identity will interact with the audiences' identities

U N I T **6**

Topic, Purpose, and Thesis

■ ■ ■ ■

UNIT OBJECTIVES

After completing this unit, you should be able to:

1. Identify the characteristics of an effective speech topic

2. Explain the principles of brainstorming and use it to generate speech topics

3. By using tree diagrams describe how a topic may be limited

4. Explain the system of *topoi* and use it to generate appropriate speech topics

5. Identify the three general speech purposes and distinguish these from specific speech purposes

6. Define *thesis* and explain its major uses

*I*n this unit we explain how you can find a suitable topic and how to limit it to manageable proportions, how to establish your purpose, and how to develop your thesis.

■■■■■ SELECTING A TOPIC

Perhaps the question students in a public speaking class most often ask is, "What will I talk about?" "I'm not knowlegdgeable about international affairs, the Middle East, or environmental issues." "I don't know much about social and political problems such as abortion, Somalia, Bosnia, or church-state relations." "I'm not up on issues such as mass transit, national health insurance, or gay rights." This situation is not uncommon; many, if not most, college students feel the same way. This need not lead to despair; all is not lost.

The answer to "What do I speak about?" will change as your life situations change. For your classroom speeches—where the objective is to learn the skills of public speaking—there are hundreds of things to talk about. Throughout this unit many suggestions for suitable speech topics are offered. But, before identifying specific suggestions, you need to distinguish between topics that are suitable and topics that are not.

What Is a Suitable Speech Topic?

A suitable speech topic should be (1) worthwhile and deal with matters of substance; (2) appropriate to the speaker, audience, and occasion; and (3) limited in scope.

Worthwhile Some topics are best reserved for the cafeteria, for parties, or for filling in periods of silence. As illustrated in the cartoon, not all topics are worth our attention. The topics for a speech in a public speaking class should be *worthwhile*. Such topics must address issues that have significant implications for the audience. Topics that are worthwhile have consequences that are significant for your listeners. The consequences may be educational, social, religious, political, economic, relational, medical, or so on, but they must be significant. In short, the topic must be important enough to merit the time and attention of a group of intelligent and educated persons.

Appropriate To be suitable a speech must be *appropriate* to you as the speaker, to the audience you will address, and to the occasion. The best way to ensure that your topic is appropriate to you as the **speaker** is to select a topic about which you know something and would like to learn more. You will not only acquire new knowledge but also will discover how to learn more about the topic, for example, the major books, the relevant journals, and the noted authorities. You will also be more interested in and enthusiastic about the topic and this will be noted and appreciated by your audience.

Look also at your topic in terms of its appropriateness to the **audience.** What are they interested in? What would they like to learn more about? On what topics would

"That was not an important message!"

Drawing by Chon Day. Copyright © 1977 The New Yorker Magazine, Inc. Reprinted by permission.

they find the time listening to your speech well spent? It is a lot easier to please an audience when the topic interests them. Speaking in a class situation makes this potentially difficult decision a lot easier since you can assume that your classmates are interested in many of the same things that you are.

The topic should also be appropriate for the **occasion.** For example, time limitations will exclude certain topics because they are too complex. You could not explain
the problems with our educational system or solutions to the drug problem in a five-
minute speech. While a classroom offers few problems created by the "occasion," it
imposes a number of serious restrictions outside the classroom. Some occasions call for
humorous subjects that would be out of place in other contexts. Speeches of personal
experience may be appropriate in one context but inappropriate in another.

Limited in Scope   A suitable topic for a public speech is limited in scope. Probably
the major problem for beginning speakers is that they attempt to cover a huge topic in
too short a time; the inevitable result is that nothing specific is covered—everything is
touched on but only superficially. No depth is achieved with a broad topic, so all you
can succeed in doing is telling the audience what it already knows.

Let's look at how you might go about narrowing and limiting your topic. The
process is simple and consists of repeatedly dividing the topic into its significant parts.

Using the criteria suggested here (worthwhile, appropriate, and limited in scope), how would you evaluate the following topics: (1) Buy American-made cars. (2) Resolve the Middle East conflict. (3) The field of biology. (4) Take the HIV AIDS test. (5) Happiness: How to get there.

For example, divide your general topic into its component parts. Then, take one of these parts and divide it into its parts. Continue with this process until the topic seems manageable, one that you can reasonably cover in some depth in the allotted time.

For example, take the topic of *television programs* as the first general topic area. You might divide this topic into such subtopics as *comedy, children's programs, educational programs, news, movies, soap operas, quiz shows,* and *sports.* You might then take one of these topics, say *comedy,* and divide it into subtopics. Perhaps you might consider it on a time basis and divide television comedy into its significant time periods: *pre-1960, 1961–1979, 1980 to the present.* Or, you might focus on *situation comedies.* Here you might examine a topic such as *women in television comedy, race relations in situation comedy,* or *family relationships in television comedies.* The resultant topic is at least beginning to look manageable. *Television programs,* without some limitation, would take a lifetime to cover adequately.

The construction of tree diagrams (actually, they resemble upside down trees) might clarify the process of narrowing a topic. Let us say, for example, that you want to do a speech on mass communication. You might develop a tree diagram with branches for the division that interests you most, as shown in Figure 6.1. Thus you can divide *mass communication* into *film, television, radio, newspapers,* and *magazines.* If *television* interests you most, then develop branches from *television. Comedy, news, soaps, sports,* and *quiz shows* would be appropriate. Now, let us say that it is the *soaps* that most interest you. In this case you would create branches from *soaps,* perhaps

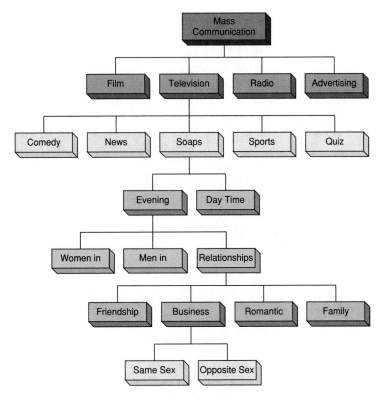

FIGURE 6.1   A tree diagram for limiting speech topics.

primetime and *daytime*. Keep dividing the topic until you get something that is significant, appropriate to you and your audience, and manageable in the allotted time.

Searching for Topics

Searching for speech topics is a relatively easy process. Here are four ways to generate topics: surveys, news items, brainstorming, and the idea generator.

Surveys   Look at some of the national and regional polls concerning what people think is important—the significant issues, the urgent problems. For example, a survey conducted by the Roper organization for H&R Block, in *The American Public and the Income Tax System,* found that Americans felt the following were among the most significant issues: lowering the crime rate, making the tax system fair, improving the educational system, improving the nation's defense capabilities, setting up a program to provide national health insurance for everyone, lowering unemployment, improving and protecting the environment, lowering Social Security taxes, and improving public transportation.

In a survey conducted by Public Research, the following issues were among the major problems confronting our country that the respondents themselves worried about: crime and lawlessness, the tax burden of the working American, the rising costs of hospital and health care, unemployment, energy, the condition of older people, the declining quality of education, the pollution of air and water, and the condition of minorities in our society.

A study conducted by *Psychology Today* identified the 10 top "hassles and uplifts" of Americans. The 10 greatest hassles were concern about weight; health of a family member; rising prices of common goods; home maintenance; too many things to do; misplacing or losing things; yard work or outside home maintenance; property, investment, or taxes; crime; and physical appearance. The 10 greatest uplifts were relating well with your spouse or lover; relating well with friends; completing a task; feeling healthy; getting enough sleep; eating out; meeting responsibilities; visiting, phoning, or writing someone; spending time with family; and a pleasing home.

Naturally, all audiences are different. Yet, such surveys are useful starting points for giving you some insight into what others think is important and, hence, what should be of interest to them.

News Items Another useful starting point is a good newspaper or magazine. Here you will find the important international and domestic issues, the financial issues, and the social issues all conveniently packaged in one place. The editorial page and the letters to the editor are also useful in learning what people are concerned about.

News magazines like *Time* and *Newsweek*, and financial magazines such as *Forbes, Money,* and *Fortune* will provide a wealth of suggestions. Similarly, news shows like *20/20, 60 Minutes, Meet the Press,* and even the ubiquitous talk shows often identify the very issues that people are concerned with and on which there are conflicting points of view.

Brainstorming Another useful method is to brainstorm (Osborn, 1957; Beebe and Masterson, 1990). *Brainstorming* is a technique for bombarding a problem and generating as many ideas as possible. In this system the process occurs in two phases. The first is the actual brainstorming period. The second is the evaluation period.

The procedures are simple. You begin with your "problem," which in this case is "What will I talk about?" You then record any idea that occurs to you. The following four rules will help you get the most out of your brainstorming session.

Withhold any criticism of your ideas. Record all ideas. Do not evaluate them. You may have to fight a normal tendency to censor ideas that may seem outlandish or too far-fetched. Try to resist this very natural temptation; an outlandish idea may suggest a much more reasonable idea. If you censor the original idea, the new idea might never occur to you.

Generate as many ideas as possible. The more ideas you think of, the better. Somewhere in a large pile of ideas will be one or two good ones. The more ideas you generate, the more effective your brainstorming session will be.

Combine and extend ideas. Although you should not criticize a particular idea, do try to extend or combine it in some way. The value of a particular idea may well be in the way it stimulates another idea.

Encourage freewheeling. The wilder the idea, the better. It is easier to tone down an idea than to spice it up. A wild idea can easily be tempered, but it is not as easy to elaborate on a simple or conservative idea.

At times, your brainstorming will break down. You will find that no new ideas occur to you. Don't get discouraged and don't abandon the process until you have tried to restimulate yourself. Prod yourself by agreeing to stay with the process for another five minutes or so. Ask yourself if you can piggyback any other ideas or extend any of the ideas already generated. Reread the list you have generated and see if your ideas will stimulate additional ones.

After you have generated a sizeable list, a period that should not take more than about 15 minutes, review the list and begin to evaluate the suggestions. Cross off the ones that are unworkable or that do not meet the criteria identified earlier.

The Idea Generator This system consists of using a dictionary of general topics and a series of questions that you can ask of any subject. "Ideas: The Dictionary of Topics," consists of a dictionarylike listing of subjects within which each topic is broken down into several subtopics. These subtopics should begin to suggest potential subjects for your informative and persuasive speeches (Table 6.1, pp. 107–112). The questions come from the system of *topoi* used in the classical rhetorics of Ancient Greece and Rome.

The method consists of asking a series of questions about your general subject. In the following listing, the columns on the left contain seven general questions (*Who? What? Why? When? Where? How?* and *So?*) and a series of more specific questions. The right column illustrates how *some* of the questions on the left might suggest *some* of the specific aspects of the general subject of "dictionary." Not all the questions on the left will apply to every topic. However, by asking these general and specific questions about your subject, you will see how you can divide and analyze a topic into its significant parts.

TOPOI: THE SYSTEM OF TOPICS

Who?	
Who is he or she?	Who are the people responsible for making dictionaries?
Who is responsible?	
Who did it?	What is the role of the linguist? The lexicographer? The grammarian?
To whom was it done?	
Who is in favor of (against) this?	Who was Noah Webster? Who was Samuel Johnson?

What?	
What is it?	What is a dictionary?
What are its parts?	What does a dictionary contain?
What is it like?	What are other dictionarylike works?

What is it different from?

What does it do?

What are its functions?

What are some examples?

What should we do?

What is a thesaurus?

What are some different types of dictionaries?

What is a dictionary used for?

What is the difference between an abridged and an unabridged dictionary?

Why?

Why use it?

Why do it?

Why did it happen?

Why did it not happen?

Why were dictionaries developed?

Why were specialized dictionaries developed?

When?

When did it happen?

When will it occur?

When should it be done?

When did it begin?

When did (will) it end?

When were dictionaries developed?

When should students learn about dictionaries?

When will dictionaries be computerized for everyday use?

Where?

Where did it come from?

Where is it going?

Where is it now?

What is the history of the dictionary?

What were early dictionaries like?

What is the state of the art?

What will the dictionary of the future look like?

How?

How does it work?

How is it used?

How do you do it?

How do you operate it?

How is it organized?

How do you use a dictionary?

What do you look for in a dictionary?

What questions are better answered by other reference books?

So?

What does it mean?

What is important about it?

Why should I be concerned with this?

Who cares?

Why should I be concerned with dictionaries?

What is the value of a dictionary?

What kind of dictionary should I use?

Let's take another idea: You want to give a speech on "homelessness." Applying the system of *topoi*, you would ask such questions as:

- *Who* are the homeless?
- *Who* is the typical homeless person?
- *Who* is responsible for the increase in homelessness?
- *What* does it mean to be homeless?
- *What* does homelessness do to the people themselves?
- *What* does homelessness do to the society in general?
- *What* does homelessness mean to you and me?
- *Why* are there so many homeless people?
- *Why* did this happen?
- *When* did homelessness become so prevalent?
- *Where* is homelessness most prevalent?
- *Where* is there an absence of homelessness?
- *How* does someone become homeless?
- *How* can we help the homeless?
- *How* can we prevent others from becoming homeless?
- *Why* is homelessness such an important social problem?
- *Why* must we be concerned with homelessness?

Such questions should be helpful to you in using general topics to generate more specific ideas for your speeches. Try this system on any one of the topic listed in the dictionary in Table 6.1. You'll be amazed at how many topics you will generate. Your problem will quickly change from "What can I speak on?" to "Which one of these should I speak on?"

TABLE 6–1 IDEAS: THE DICTIONARY OF TOPICS

Presented here are ideas for speech topics. This list is not intended to provide specific topics for any of your speeches; it should, however, alleviate any anxiety over "having nothing to talk about" and should stimulate you to develop speech subjects and purposes suitable to you and to your specific audience. Each topic is broken down into several subtopics that should stimulate you to see these as potential ideas for your informative and persuasive speeches.

Abortion arguments for and against; techniques of; religious dimension; legal views; differing views of
Academic freedom nature of; censorship; teachers' role in curriculum development; and government; and research; restrictions on
Acupuncture nature of; development of; current practices in; effectiveness of; dangers of

Adoption agencies for; procedures; difficulties in; illegal; concealment of biological parents; search for birthparents.
Advertising techniques; expenditures; ethical; unethical; subliminal; leading agencies; history of; slogans
Age agism; aging processes; aid to the aged; discrimination against the aged; treat-

ment of the aged; different cultural views of aging; sex differences
Aggression aggressive behavior in animals; in humans; as innate; as learned; and territoriality
Agriculture science of; history of; in ancient societies; technology of; theories of
Air pollution; travel; embolism; law; navigation; power; raids

Alcoholism nature of; Alcoholics Anonymous; Al Anon; abstinence; among the young; treatment of

Amnesty in draft evasion; in criminal law; and pardons; in Civil War; in Vietnam War; conditions of

Animals experimentation; intelligence of; aggression in; ethology; and communication

Arts theater; dance; film; painting; support for; apathy; social aspects of; economic aspects of; styles in the arts

Athletics professional; Little League; college; support for; corruption in; benefits of; little-known sports; records; Olympics

Automobiles development of; economics of; advances in; new developments; mass production

Awards Academy; sports; Tony; Cleo; Emmy; scholarship; athletic

Bermuda Triangle nature of; myths; structure of; losses

Bicycling as exercise; as transportation; touring; Olympic; development and types of cycles; social aspects; ecological aspects

Birth defects; control; rites; racial differences; natural

Blind number of blind persons; training of the blind; Braille; communication and the blind; prejudice against; adjustment of; famous blind persons

Books binding; burning; collecting; rare; making; publishing; writing

Boxing professional; amateur; great fights; styles of; famous fighters; economics of

Brain trust; washing; damage; genius; intelligence; aphasia

Business cycles; associations; laws; in performing arts; finance

Cable television; underground; development of; economics of

Calorie nature of; and exercise; and diets; and weight gain

Capitalism nature of; economics of; development of; depression and inflation; philosophy; alternatives to

Cards playing; tarot; fortune telling; development of games; rules for games

Censorship arguments for and against; and violence; and sex; television; literacy

Chauvinism and patriotism; and sexism; and learning; changing conceptions of

Cities problems of; population patterns; and tourism; crime; government of

Citizenship different conceptions of; acquiring; loss of; naturalization; tests; in different countries

College functions of; economics of; differences among; historical development of; and job training; and education

Communication public; media; intrapersonal; interpersonal; satellite

Computer memory; music; programming; and communication; chess; personal; and education

Copyright laws; infringements; rules; practices

Credit nature of; public; agricultural; card use; unions; bureau

Crime prevention; types of; and law; and punishment

Cults types of; programming; deprogramming; influences of; power of

Culture cultural relativism; lag; drift; diffusion; change; shock

Death legal aspects of; and religion; and suicide; and life; reincarnation

Debt management; retirement; limit; and credit cards

Defense national; mechanisms; self; techniques; karate

Depression nature of; and suicide; among college students; dealing with

Diet water; Scarsdale; dangers of; alternatives to; fasting; Cambridge

Disasters natural; wartime; prevention of; famous; economics of

Discrimination sensory; and prejudice; racial; religious

Diseases major diseases of college students; prevention; detection; treatment; recovery

Divorce rate; throughout world; causes of; advantages of; disadvantages of; proceedings

Drugs addiction; treatment; allergies; poisoning; problems; effects; legalizing

Earthquakes nature of; famous; Alaskan; San Francisco; volcanos; seismic readings

Ecology nature of; approaches of; applications of

Economics principles of; macro; micro; schools of; of education; in education

Education system of; social; religious; medical; legal; economics of; segregation; desegregation

Emigration migration; changing population patterns; uses of; problems with

Employment theory; and unemployment; service insurance

Energy conservation; nature of; types of; crisis; sources nuclear; solar; fusion

Entertainment industry; benefits; abuses; tax; functions of; and communication

Environment biological; influences; versus innate factors in learning; pollution of

Ethnicity meaning of; and prejudice; theories of; and culture

Ethology nature of; animal behavior patterns; pioneers; theories of

Evolution philosophical; theological; of human race; theories of; and revolution

Exercise importance of; methods of; dangers of; gymnastics

Farming techniques; government subsidies; equipment; effect of droughts

Federal Communications Commission (FCC) structure of; powers; functions; and television programming; rulings of; licenses

Feminism meaning of; implications of; changing concepts of

Folk literature; medicine; music; poetry; society; tales; wisdom

Food health; preservatives; additives; red dye; and allergies; preparation; stamps

Football rules; college; professional; abuses in; training in

Freedom of speech laws protecting; and Constitution; significance of; abuses of; and censorship; and economics

Freedom of the press and Constitution; revealing sources; importance of; investigative reporting

Gambling types of; legal aspects of; casino; houses; and

chance; legalization of

Game(s) history of; theory; shows; children's; psychological; destructive

Gay rights; lifestyle; laws against; prejudice against; and religion; and lesbian; statistics; relationships

Gender roles; identification; differences

Government federal; state; city; powers of

Guilt causes of; symptoms; dealing with; effects of; and suicide; and religion

Health services; human; education; laws; audiology

Heroes nature of; and adolescence; fictional; social role of; real-life heroes

Hospital(s) structure; function; and preventive medicine; and concern for community; and cost

Housing urban; cost; inflation discrimination in; subsidized; underground

Humor theories of; nature of; situational; verbal; cultural differences

Hypnotism nature of; and memory; and age regression; potentials of; uses of; dangers of; medical uses of

Immigration migration; patterns; laws governing

Imports and exports; laws regulating; and tariffs; and protection of workers

Income personal; national; and employment theory; tax; statement

Industrialization social aspects; economics of; political aspects of; development of; psychological aspects

Infant mortality causes of; prevention of; racial differences; preventive medicine

Intelligence quotient; tests;

theories of; cultural differences

Journalism as profession; investigative; photojournalism; education

Kidnapping nature of; famous; laws governing; penalties; Act; Lindberg

Labor types of; division of; hours; in pregnancy; economics of; and management; unions

Languages artificial; sign; natural; learning of; loss of; pathologies of

Laws international; criminal; of nature

Libraries functions; support; science; design; largest; collections; types of

Life definition of; extraterrestrial; cycle; insurance; support; systems

Literacy rate; world distribution; definition; problems in rising rate of

Love nature of; theories of; romantic; family; and hate; and interpersonal relationships; of self; and materialism

Magic nature of; and religion; significance of; types of; and science; history of; and magicians; and sleight of hand

Marriage and divorce; vows; traditions; open; contracts; bans; changing views of; laws against

Media forms of; contributions of; abuses; regulations; popularity of; influences of; and violence; and censorship

Medicine preventive; forensic; and health insurance; history of; holistic; and poisoning; alchemy; industrial

Men education of; problems of; and women; and chauvinism; changing roles of; and sexism; and prejudice; and homosexuality; in groups; as fathers

Military organizations; preparedness; confrontations and conflicts; governments; law

Morality nature of; cultural variations in views; teaching of; and crime

Music festivals; forms; instruments; compositions; styles; drama

Myth(s) nature of; origin of; symbolism of; and ritual; contemporary significance of

Narcissism nature of; and Narcissus; Freudian view of; and autoeroticism; and love of others

National Organization of Women (NOW) structure of; functions of; influences of; contributions of; beliefs of

Newspapers functions of; advertising; reporters; famous; structure of; economics of

Noise pollution; white; and communication; redundancy and; combating; causes of; types of

Nuclear plants; explosion; family; war; reaction; weapons; arguments for and against nuclear plants

Nutrition nature of; functions of food; essential requirements; animal; human; and starvation; and diet

Obscenity nature of; laws prohibiting; and pornography; effects of; influences on

Occupational diseases; psychology; satisfaction; therapy

Peace Corps; treaty; pipe; economics of

Personality development of; measurement of; theories of; disorders; tests

Photography nature of; types of; art of; color; development of; infrared; technology;

holography

Police functions of; structure of; crime prevention; and education; community relations; civilian review; abuses by

Pollution air; atmospheric research; chemical radiation; water; and food; sources; effects; laws governing

Population(s) beliefs; theories; Malthusianism; Marxism; and education; and elderly; and family size; world; innate factors; racial typing; evolution; mutation

Pornography and censorship; types of; influences of; restrictions on

Prison reform; systems; security; routine; effect on crime; personality; behavior; and sex; and conditioning

Psychic phenomena ESP; psychokinesis; reliability of; and frauds; theories of

Psychoanalysis development of; leaders; impact of; training in; theories of

Public relations in colleges; and propaganda; public opinion; advertising

Public schools support of; changing curriculum; and parochial schools; problems with; PTAs

Publishing economics of; history of; copyright; and media exposure; trade and textbook; magazine and newspapers

Racing auto; dog; horse; corruption in; jockeys; fame

Racism nature of; self-hatred; genetic theory; human rights; education; religious; UN position; in United States

Radio development of; advertising; air traffic control; police; surveillance; radioactivity

Religion different religions;

leaders in; influence of; beliefs of; and agnosticism; and atheism; and God; social dimensions of; and art; and architecture

Salaries minimum wage; professional; white- and blue-collar; racial variation; and unions; and inflation

Sales advertising; methods; forecasting; and excise taxes; effects on consumers

Satellite communication; launchings; research

Sciences history of; procedures in; empirical data; methods of; fiction

Security personal; Social; national

Segregation genetic; racial; leaders in fight against; legal aspects; and legal decisions; effects of; and education

Self-concept meaning of; and communication; and depression; and conditioning

Self-defense in criminal law; international laws; and war; martial arts

Self-disclosure benefits of; cautions in; influences of; influences on; effects of; types of; conditions conducive to

Sex education; roles; therapy; surrogate; change; and love; and the concept of deviation; variations; and learning

Social Security; facilitation; class; control; differentiation; Darwinism; equilibrium; groups; movement; realism

Solar system; wind; radiation; energy; heating

Space exploration; flight; probes; age

Sports nature of; psychology of; fans; in college; professional; records; Little League; figures; salaries; international competition;

Olympics; invention of; stadiums

Strikes famous; violence; unions; essential-service occupations; teacher; causes and effects

Subconscious Freud; development of concept; defense mechanisms

Subversive activities definition of; political; legislation penalties for

Suicide causes; among college students; laws regulating; methods; aiding the suicide of another; philosophical implications; religious dimension

Superstition beliefs; mythology; influences on history

Supreme Court judicial review; decisions; make-up of; chief justices; jurisdiction

Taxation alcohol; cigarette; history of; purposes of; historical methods of; types of; without representation; evasion; tariffs

Teaching methods; teachers; machines; programmed learning; behavioral objectives; and conditioning

Technology benefits of; and undeveloped areas; as threat to workers; and economics; history of

Telepathy nature of; evidence for; tests of; and fraud

Television development of; history of; working of satellite; commercials; propaganda; and leisure time; programming; economics of; effects of; and violence; and radio; and film; producing; Nielsen ratings

Test-tube babies developments in; opposition to; methods; dangers; variations

Theater Greek; Roman; commedia dell'arte; American; British; Eastern; Italian; French; performers; styles of; and television; and film; Broadway; and critics

Theology forms; development of; different religions; education

Therapy physical; psychological; language; techniques of; schools of

Time management; travel; records

Tobacco production of; smoking; effects of; causes of; methods of stopping; nicotine dangers of; economics of

Translation computer; missionary impetus; problems in; history of; kinds of

Transplants nature of; rejection; donor selection; legal aspects; ethical aspects; future of; advances in

Transportation history; urban; water; air; land

Trust nature of; and love; and self-disclosure; types of; and communication

UFOs evidence for; types of; reported sightings; theories of; agencies in charge of

Unemployment urban; seasonal; and violence; insurance; disguised

Unions development of; problems with; advantages of; arguments for and against; unionism

United Nations (UN) development of; functions of; agencies; and League of Nations; structure; veto powers; Security Council; Declaration of Rights

Urban living; problems; benefits; stress; crime; transportation; development; decay

Vaccine nature of; types; vaccination; immunization

Values and attitudes; and communications; social; economic; changing; religious; axiology; sex differences

Vietnam country; people; war; language; rehabilitation

Virtue natural; religious; nature of; changing conceptions of; learning and

Vitamins deficiency; excess; types of

Voice qualities; voiceprints; and personality; training; and persuasion; paralanguage

Wages minimum; and inflation; and fringe benefits; average; differences among cultures

War conduct of; financing; destruction by; causes of; debts; games; casualties; effects of

Weapons hand and missile; firearms artillery; rockets; automatic; nuclear; biological; psychological

Weather forecasting; hurricanes; control of; rain; snow; heat; cold; and population patterns; and health; and psychology; divining

Weightlifting techniques in; as exercise; as sport; leading weightlifters; competition; dangers in; benefits of; societal attitudes toward; and sexual attraction

Witchcraft meaning of; white and black; and magic; structure of; functions of; theories of; in primitive societies; contemporary

Women and sexism; biology; learning and programming; in different societies; accomplishments of; prejudices against; ERA; social roles

Words history; coinage; foreign contributions; semantics; and meaning

Youth problems of; crime; education; hostels; music; communication problems; genera-

tion gap
Zodiac nature of; different conceptions of; constellations;

myths surrounding; and horoscopes

REMEMBER: **Speech topics should be:**

1. **worthwhile**
2. **appropriate to the speaker, audience, and occasion**
3. **limited in scope**

and may be found through

4. **surveys**
5. **news items**
6. **brainstorming**
7. **the idea generator**

▩ ■ ■ ■ ESTABLISHING YOUR PURPOSE

The purpose of your speech is your goal; it is what you hope to achieve during your speech. It identifies the effect that your want your speech to have on your audience. In constructing your speech, first identify your general purpose and second, your specific purpose.

General Purposes

The three major purposes of public speeches are to inform, to persuade, and to serve some ceremonial or special occasion function.

In the *informative speech* you seek to create understanding: to clarify, to enlighten, to correct misunderstandings, to demonstrate how something works. In this type of speech you would rely most heavily on materials that amplify—examples, illustrations, definitions, testimony, audiovisual aids, and the like.

In the *persuasive speech* you try to influence attitudes or behaviors; you seek to strengthen or change existing attitudes or to get the audience to take some action. In this type of speech you would rely heavily on materials that offer proof—on evidence, argument, and psychological appeals, for example.

Any persuasive speech is in part an informative speech and as such contains materials that amplify, illustrate, define, and so on. In its focus on strengthening or changing attitudes and behaviors, however, the persuasive speech must go beyond simply providing information. Logical, motivational, and credibility appeals are essential.

The *special occasion speech* contains elements of information and persuasion. You might, for example, introduce another speaker or a group of speakers, you might present a tribute or try to secure the goodwill of the listeners, or, you might seek to entertain your listeners.

Specific Purposes

After you have established your general purpose, identify your specific purpose, which identifies more precisely what you aim to accomplish. For example, in an informative speech, your specific speech purpose would identify that information you want to convey to your audience. Here are a few examples on the topic of AIDS:

General purpose: to inform
Specific purposes: to inform my audience of the recent
              progress in AIDS research
          to inform my audience of our college's
              plans for AIDS Awareness Day
          to inform my audience of the currently
              used tests for HIV infection

In a persuasive speech, your specific purpose identifies what you want your audience to believe, to think, or perhaps to do. Here are a few examples, again on the topic of AIDS:

General purpose: to persuade
Specific purposes: to persuade my audience to contribute to
              AIDS research
          to persuade my audience that they should
              be tested for HIV infection
          to persuade my audience to become better
              informed about how AIDS can be
              transmitted

In formulating your specific purpose, keep the following four guidelines in mind:

Use an infinitive phrase that elaborates on your general purpose. Both your general and your specific purpose statements should begin with the word *to* followed by *inform, persuade, entertain,* or perhaps *strengthen listeners beliefs* or *change audience's attitudes.*

Limit your specific purpose to one main point. Avoid the common pitfall of trying to accomplish too much in too short a time. For example, "to inform my audience about the development of AIDS and the recent testing procedures for HIV infection" is actually two specific purposes. Select either one and build your speech around it.

Follow the same principle in developing your specific purpose for your persuasive speeches. Thus, for example, "to persuade my audience of the prevalence of AIDS in our community and that they should contribute money for AIDS services" contains

---

two specific purposes. Select either "to persuade my audience of the prevalence of AIDS in our community" or "to persuade my audience to contribute money to services for persons with AIDS." Beware of specific purposes that contain the word *and;* it's almost always a sign that you have more than one purpose.

Phrase your specific purpose with precise terms. The more precise your specific purpose, the more effectively it will guide you in the remaining steps of preparing your speech. Compare, for example, the following specific purpose statements:

A. to persuade my audience to do something about AIDS

B. to persuade my audience to contribute food to homebound persons with AIDS

Note how much more specific the "B" purpose statement is. The "A" statement merely identifies the general topic area; it does not identify what you hope to accomplish in your speech. The "B" statement does.

Limit your specific purpose to what you can reasonably accomplish in the time allotted. Remember that your time limitations mean you can only accomplish so much. Specific purposes that are too broad are useless. Note how broad and overly general the following purposes are:

■ to inform my audience about clothing design

■ to persuade my audience to improve their health

Note how much more reasonable the following restatements are for a relatively short speech:

■ to inform my audience of the importance of color in clothing design

■ to persuade my audience to exercise at least three times a week

REMEMBER: Formulate a clear

1. general purpose, for example, to inform or persuade

2. specific purpose that is phrased as an infinitive phrase, limited to one main point, phrased with precise terms, and limited to what you can reasonably accomplish in the time available

THE THESIS (YOUR MAIN ASSERTION)

The first step in organizing your speech is to write out your thesis statement. This is your main assertion, what you want the audience to absorb from your speech. The thesis of Lincoln's Second Inaugural Address was that Northerners and Southerners should work together for the entire nation's welfare; the thesis of the *Rocky* movies was that the underdog can win. The importance of the thesis is stressed by professional speech writer James Humes in the accompanying tip.

Let us say, for example, that you are planning to deliver a speech supporting Senator Farrington. Your thesis statement might be something like this: "We should support Farrington's candidacy." This is what you want your audience to believe as a result of your speech. In an informative speech the thesis statement focuses on what you want your audience to learn. For example, a suitable thesis for a speech on jealousy might be: "There are two main theories of jealousy." Be sure to limit the thesis statement to one central idea. Statements such as "We should support Farrington and the entire Democratic party" contain not one but two basic ideas.

■■■■

TIPS FROM PROFESSIONAL SPEAKERS

Sir Winston Churchill, while dining at Claridge's, once asked for his favorite dessert, Sherry Trifle. After tasting the first spoonful, he signaled for the waiter. "Pray, take this pudding away—it has no theme."

Well, Churchill liked his puddings as well as his presentations to hold together, to be consistent—to have one theme.

That laudable goal is not as easily achieved as it sounds. The temptation in any speech is to divert and digress. Points which you think have to be mentioned end up deflecting the audience's attention from the central problem.

James C. Humes, speech writer and consultant. *Standing Ovation: How to Be an Effective Speaker and Communicator* (New York: Harper & Row, 1988), p. 28.

Notice that in persuasive speeches, the thesis statement puts forth a point of view, an opinion. The thesis is an arguable, debatable proposition. It is a nonneutral statement. In informative speeches, the thesis appears relatively neutral and objective.

Using Thesis Statements

The thesis statement serves three useful purposes. First, it helps you generate your main ideas or assertions. Second, it suggests suitable organizational patterns and strategies. Third, it focuses the audience's attention on your central idea. Let's look at each of these functions in more detail.

Generating Main Ideas   Once you have phrased your thesis statement, the main divisions of your speech are readily suggested. Let's take an example: "The Hart bill will provide needed services for senior citizens." Once stated in this form, the obvious question to address in preparing a speech with this thesis is: *What are they?* The answer to this question suggests the main parts of your speech, for example, health, food, shelter, and recreational services. These four areas then become the four main points of your speech. An outline of the main ideas would look like this:

I. The Hart bill provides needed health services.
II. The Hart bill provides needed food services.
III. The Hart bill provides needed shelter services.
IV. The Hart bill provides needed recreational services.

The remainder of the speech would then be filled in with supporting materials (covered in Units 14, 15, 17, 18, and 19). Under I, you might identify the several needed health services and explain how the Hart bill provides for these services. This first main division of your speech might, in outline, look something like this:

I. The Hart bill provides needed health services.

   A. Neighborhood clinics will be established.

   B. Medical hotlines for seniors will be established.

In the completed speech, this first major proposition and its two subordinate statements might be spoken like this:

The Hart bill provides senior citizens with the health services they need so badly. Let me give you some examples of these badly needed health services. One of the most important services will be the establishment of neighborhood health clinics. These clinics will help senior citizens get needed health advice and services right in their own neighborhoods.

Another important health service will be the health hotlines. These phone numbers will be for the exclusive use of senior citizens. These hotlines will help senior citizens secure health care quickly and efficiently. The Department of Health estimates that this part of the Hart bill alone will save thousands of lives annually. The Department of Health also estimates that the hotlines will help prevent thousands of more serious illnesses from developing.

Suggesting Organizational Patterns   The thesis provides a useful guideline in selecting your organizational pattern. For example, let's suppose your thesis is: "We can improve our own college educations." Your answer to the inevitable *What can we do?* will suggest a possible organizational pattern. If you identify the remedies in the order in which they should be taken, then a time-order pattern would be appropriate. If you itemize a number of possible solutions, all of which are of about equal importance, then a topical pattern would be appropriate. These and other patterns are explained in detail in the following unit.

In short, the thesis statement will suggest not only the items of information or the main arguments that you will advance, it will also suggest how you might go about structuring these into a meaningful, coherent, and organized whole.

Focusing Audience Attention   The thesis sentence also focuses the audience's attention on your central idea. In some speeches you may wish to state your thesis early in your speech, for example, in the introduction or perhaps early in the body of the speech.

There are instances, however, when you may not want to state your thesis. Or, you may want to state it late in your speech. For example, if your audience is hostile to your thesis, it may be wise to give your evidence and arguments first. In this way you will be able to move them gradually into a more positive frame of mind before stating your thesis.

In other cases, you may want the audience to infer your thesis without actually spelling it out. Beginning speakers especially should be careful in choosing not to state their thesis explicitly. Research shows, for example, that audiences—especially uneducated audiences—are not persuaded by speeches in which the speaker does not explicitly state the thesis. Listeners often fail to grasp what the thesis is and so do not change their attitudes or behaviors.

Make your decision as to when (or if) to state your thesis on the basis of what will be more effective with your specific purpose and your specific audience. Here are a few guidelines to help you make the right decision.

1. In an informative speech, state your thesis early, clearly, and directly.

2. In a persuasive speech where your audience is neutral or positive, state your thesis explicitly and early in your speech.

3. In a persuasive speech where your audience is hostile to your position, delay stating your thesis until you have moved them closer to your position.

Wording the Thesis

State your thesis as a simple declarative sentence. This will help you focus your thinking, your collection of materials, and your organizational pattern (as already noted). You may, however, phrase your thesis in a number of different ways when you present it to your audience. At one extreme, you may state it to your audience as you phrased it for yourself. Here are a few examples:

We should support Farrington.

I want to tell you in this brief speech why we should support Farrington.

Or, you may decide to state your thesis as a question, for example:

Why should we support Farrington?

Are there valid reasons for supporting Farrington? I think so.

In persuasive speeches in which you face a hostile or mildly opposed audience, you may wish to state your thesis in vague and ambiguous terms. Here are some examples:

I want to talk about Farrington's qualifications.

Does Farrington deserve our support? Let's look at the evidence.

In these cases you focus the audience's attention on your central idea, but you delay presenting your specific point of view until a more favorable time.

A Note on Thesis and Purpose

The thesis and the purpose are similar in that they both guide you in selecting and organizing your materials. In some ways, however, they are different.

Thesis and purpose differ in the form of expression. The thesis is phrased as a complete declarative sentence. The purpose is phrased as an infinitive phrase (to inform . . . , to persuade . . .).

A more important difference is that the thesis is message-oriented; the purpose is audience-oriented. The thesis identifies the central idea of your speech; it summarizes—it epitomizes—the speech content. The purpose identifies the change you hope to achieve in your audience, for example, to gain information, to change attitudes, to engage in a certain behavior.

Further, the purpose limits what you hope to achieve given the practical limitations of time and your audience's expectations and attitudes. The thesis, on the other hand, epitomizes the speech without regard to these practical limitations. In one sense, the purpose specifies what you hope to achieve once you have established your thesis. For example, the thesis might be, "Colleges are not educating students for today's world." The purpose of this speech, however, might be (1) to persuade my audience that colleges must change to keep pace with today's world, (2) to persuade my audience to adapt the Illinois Educational Proposal, or (3) to persuade my audience to quit college.

Another distinguishing factor is that the thesis is usually stated somewhere in the speech. Often, for example, the speaker will state the thesis in the introduction or perhaps as a preface to the main ideas. The purpose, however, is rarely stated. You would rarely say, for example, "I want to persuade you to vote for me" or "I'm going to convince you to buy Brand X." However, you might say (in thesis form), "I'm the most qualified candidate" or "Brand X is an excellent product."

Here are a few more examples to clarify further the difference between thesis and purpose:

Thesis: We can reduce our phone bills by following three rules.
Purpose: To inform my audience of three ways to save on their phone bills.

Thesis: Computer science knowledge is essential for all students.
Purpose: To persuade my audience to elect a computer science course.

Especially in these early stages of mastering public speaking, formulate both the thesis statement and the purpose. With both the thesis and the purpose clearly formulated, you should eliminate a great many problems; you will avoid a speech that rambles all over the field and that audiences find difficult to understand and remember.

REMEMBER: **The thesis statement should be:**
1. phrased as a complete declarative sentence
2. clear and specific
3. limited to one central idea or focus

and is especially useful to:
4. generate main ideas
5. suggest suitable organizational patterns
6. focus audience attention

but may in the actual speech:
7. be phrased in various ways (as a statement, as a question, as a relatively ambiguous statement)
8. be stated early or late in the speech (or even only implied)

CRITICALLY SPEAKING

1. What three topics would you like to hear other students speak on? (You may find it helpful to share these topics with others so that a pool of interesting topics may be established.)
2. What three topics would you like to see other students avoid? (Again, you may find it helpful to share these.)
3. What distinguishes the topics that class members want to hear about from topics they do not want to hear about? Do these differences suggest guidelines for suitable public speaking topics?
4. Can you identify one topic that would be inappropriate for every conceivable audience?
5. How would you draw tree diagrams for limiting topics beginning with such general subjects as *immigration, education, sports, transportation,* or *politics?*
6. Are the following purposes appropriate for your class? If not, how might they be rephrased?
   a. to inform my audience of how we can reverse the current economic situation
   b. to inform my audience of why they should take a health education course
   c. to inform my audience of how to use the *Windows* software program
   d. to persuade my audience to change their eating habits
   e. to persuade my audience that street gangs should be government regulated

f. to persuade my audience to buy products with minimal packaging

7. Read through your local newspaper. What topics for public speaking do just one issue suggest? Try the same for *Time*, *Newsweek*, or *U.S. News & World Report*. What topics do these magazines suggest?

8. Are there other questions that you might want to add to the system of *topoi*? Why might these additional questions prove useful?

9. Can you think of a persuasive speech that would not also contain some elements of information?

10. What is the thesis of at least three recent television shows you have watched? What is the thesis of the last novel you read? What is the thesis of the last movie you saw?

11. Do you agree with the suggestions offered here for focusing or not focusing audience attention on your thesis? How would you revise these suggestions? What other suggestions might you offer?

PRACTICALLY SPEAKING

6.1   BRAINSTORMING

Together with a small group of students or with the class as a whole, sitting in a circle, brainstorm for suitable speech topics. Be sure to appoint someone to write down all the contributions or use a recorder.

After this brainstorming session, consider these questions:

1. Did any members give negative criticism (even nonverbally)?
2. Did any members hesitate to contribute really wild ideas? Why?
3. Was it necessary to restimulate the group members at any point? Did this help?
4. Did some useful speech topics emerge in the brainstorming session?

6.2   GENERATING AND EVALUATING TOPICS

A useful way to generate speech topics and at the same time focus on their suitability is for each student to write on an index card a topic for a 5-to-7 minute informative speech. On another card, write a topic for a 5-to-7 minute persuasive speech. Limit the topics in purpose and scope. The cards should be collected and the topics discussed in terms of their being worthwhile, appropriate to the audience, and sufficiently limited in scope. As the topics are read aloud, try to think of other topics that these topics suggest.

6.3   LIMITING THE SPEECH TOPIC

Select one of the following topics. Create a tree diagram with your topic as the beginning point and with at least five layers of division. Select one of these narrowly defined topics and formulate a thesis and a specific purpose. Share your tree, thesis, and specific purpose with others in small groups or with the class as a whole.

1. history
2. emotions
3. family
4. communication
5. psychology
6. education
7. newspapers
8. politics
9. religion
10. economics

U N I T 7

Research

■ ■ ■ ■

UNIT OBJECTIVES

After completing this unit, you should be able to:

1. Identify at least four general principles for conducting research

2. Explain the way your library catalogs its books

3. Identify at least three sources for biographical material

4. Identify at least three newspaper, magazine, and journal indexes

5. Explain the types of information that are available in government publications

6. Define *database* and explain how you would go about doing your research by means of computers

7. Explain the general principles for interviewing

8. Explain the ways to integrate research into your speech

*R*esearch is a formidable sounding term. It conjures up images of scientists working feverishly in their laboratories and of professors in the dusty recesses of the library going over obscure manuscripts. Actually, research today is a lot different. It can be and should be one of the most exciting and enjoyable aspects of your speech preparation.

Say that you are to speak to your class on surrogate motherhood. Where do you go for information? How can you learn about the number of surrogate mothers there are? How do you discover the procedures involved for securing a surrogate mother? What are the legal issues involved? What were the prominent legal battles? Research will enable you to answer these and hundreds of other questions.

In this unit, we examine research and explain how you can go about the process of answering your questions regardless of the topic.

■■■■ GENERAL PRINCIPLES

These general principles will help you throughout your entire college and professional career. You will always need to find information, so here are some ways to handle this task more efficiently and effectively.

TIPS FROM PROFESSIONAL SPEAKERS

One of my "secrets" for doing creative work of any sort is simply to do what I call "getting out of my own way."

I discovered, quite early in life, that there is some strange creative center in my brain that, once stimulated, will give up a considerable volume of whatever I ask it to produce: jokes, stories, philosophical observations, or ideas for essays, newspaper or magazine features, television comedy sketches, plays, songs, and so on. Part of the process involves shutting "me" up, calming myself down, relaxing, and just listening to the ideas as an internal computer cranks them out.

. . . Don't worry if, when you first begin timidly listening to your own creative center, it doesn't immediately begin cranking out ideas that would dazzle Aristotle.

By simply agreeing to give a speech, or by self-generating a plan to do so, you will have stimulated your own mysterious idea center. What you must do next is *listen to its responses*. At this stage don't—whatever you do—serve as a censorious judge, telling yourself, "Oh, that's no good" or "That will never work." Stopping self-criticism at once is part of the process of getting out of your own way.

Steve Allen, writer and performer. *How to Make a Speech* (New York: McGraw-Hill, 1986), pp. 24–25.

"*This is Prentiss J. Parmenter recording. It's eight o'clock, the morning of August 24th. The air is crisp and the sky is clear as I leave for my office. On the way, I shall record my thoughts on business, politics, the parlous state of humanity, and perhaps, should the spirit move me, a word or two of philosophical commentary.*"

Drawing by Stan Hunt; © 1991 The New Yorker Magazine, Inc. Reprinted by permission.

Examine What You Know

Begin your search by examining what you already know, perhaps somewhat less formally than Prentiss J. Parmenter in our cartoon. Before Edward Gibbon, the famed English historian and author of *The History of the Decline and Fall of the Roman Empire*, would begin to write a new book, he would take a long walk or sit alone and try to recall everything he knew about the topic. Only after doing this did he move on to other sources of information. Winston Churchill followed the same procedure when preparing his speeches.

Write down what you know, for example, about books or articles on the topic or persons who might know something about the topic. In this way you can attack the problem systematically and not waste effort and time. Throughout this process, keep your audience clearly in mind. Ask frequently how your audience might influence the information you record and collect.

Work from the General to the Specific

Get a general overview of the topic first. An encyclopedia or journal article will serve this purpose well. This will help you see the topic as a whole and how its various parts fit together. Many of these general articles contain lists of references to direct the next stage of your search for more specific information.

After securing this overview, consult increasingly specific and specialized source materials. For example, when consulting indexes to locate articles, begin with a general index such as *Readers' Guide to Periodical Literature*. Then, depending on your topic, go on to more specific indexes such as *Index to Legal Periodicals, Education Index,* or *Humanities Index*. These and many other indexes are explained later in this unit.

Take Accurate Notes

The more accurate your initial notes are, the less time you will waste going back to sources to check on a date or spelling. Accurate records will also prevent you from going to sources you have already consulted but may have forgotten.

A looseleaf notebook works best to keep everything relating to a speech or article in the same place. For example, you can keep in this looseleaf the sources consulted, quotations, ideas, arguments, suggested references, and preliminary outlines. This way you don't waste time looking in several different places to pull all the material together. Another advantage of the looseleaf notebook is that you can xerox book pages, articles, and the like and insert them in the appropriate places (do not waste time copying long quotations and statistics).

Whether you use a looseleaf notebook or the more common index cards, be sure you record your data accurately and thoroughly. Here are some general principles to keep in mind as you are taking your research notes.

1. Key your notes to the topics in your preliminary speech outline. For example, let us say that your speech is to be on surrogate motherhood. Your preliminary outline looks like this:

Surrogate Motherhood

  I. Legal aspects

 II. Moral aspects

III. Psychological aspects

You might then classify your notes under these three major topics. Simply head the card or page with "legal", "moral," or "psychological."

Because this is a preliminary outline, you will need a large category for miscellaneous information. You will probably come upon interesting information that you are not sure you will use and yet you don't want to lose it, so copy the relevant sections and mark it "MISC."

Taking notes with your preliminary outline will help focus your research and will remind you of those topics for which you need more information.

You may also find it useful to classify your research as to the type of supporting material. For example, you might consider a general classification such as the following:

■ Factual information
■ Opinions and quotations

■ Statistics

■ Examples and illustrations

■ Arguments

2. Make sure your notes are complete (and legible). If you have to err, then err on the side of having notes that are too detailed. You can always cut the quotation or select one example out of the three at a later time. As you take notes, be sure to identify the source so that you can find that reference again should you need it. You might also want to include the catalog number or otherwise indicate where you can find the book or journal again.

3. Use only one side of the card or paper and leave plenty of white space on all sides of your notes. Never write on the back of your notes. One-sided pages are easier to rearrange and to cut in half, if, for example, you decide to divide up a topic. It will also save you lots of time in locating your materials.

By leaving white space on the sides, you'll be able to write in your comments or indicate headings that might be appropriate. The white space gives you a chance to interact with your notes by writing in your comments, questions, ideas.

Use Research Time Effectively

Manage the time you have effectively and efficiently. If you are going to give two speeches on the same topic, do the research for both at the same time. Don't wait until you have finished the first speech to begin researching the second. You might, for example, divide the looseleaf notebook into two sections and insert the material with appropriate cross-references.

Learn the Available Sources of Information

Research is a chore for many people because they are unfamiliar with the available sources of information. Those who have difficulty researching are invariably those who have not learned to do it effectively and efficiently. When you know how to research, it will be easy, pleasant, and rewarding. When you lack this information, research throughout your college and professional career will be understandably stressful and wasteful. Learn what is available, where, and in what form. For example, spend a few hours in the library learning where some of the most useful source materials are located.

■ Where are the encyclopedias? The almanacs? The indexes to the various journals?

■ How are newspapers and journals maintained in your library?

■ What material is on microfilm (reels of film)? What is on microfiche (pieces of film containing perhaps 100 frames on 4 × 6-inch cards)? What is on microcards (printed rather than filmed material)? What is on ultramicrofiche (pieces of film containing up to 1200 pages on a 2 × 2-inch card)? How do you use the machines to read this material?

■ How does your library operate interlibrary loans? How long do such loans take? May you borrow both journals and books? Are there any restrictions?

■ What other libraries are available in your area? Are there municipal libraries that might complement your college library? Do other colleges allow students from your college to use their facilities? Are they better equipped in certain areas?

■ What computer search facilities are available at your library? Most libraries have facilities for accessing various on-line databases (information stored electronically that can be accessed or retrieved by computer).

Critically Evaluate the Research

Collecting research materials is only part of the process; the other part is critically evaluating them. Although evaluating specific amplifying materials and arguments is discussed in later units (see Units 14 and 17, for example), some general questions to ask of all researched information may be suggested here.

1. Is the information recent? Generally, the more recent the material the more useful it will be. With some topics, for example, unemployment statistics, developments in AIDS research, and tuition costs, the recency of the information is crucial to its usefulness.

2. Is the information fair and unbiased? Bias is not easy to determine, but try to examine any sources of potential bias. Obvious examples come quickly to mind: cigarette manufacturers' statements on the health risks from smoking; newspaper and network editorials on the fairness of news reporting; and the National Rifle Association's arguments against gun control. But, other examples are not so easy to see as potentially biased. Consider the potential bias in these few examples from the college environment:

■ the foreign language department's advocacy of foreign language requirements for undergraduate and advanced degrees

■ the department of education's argument for additional education courses for the state's teachers

■ the student association's arguments for mandatory increased student activity fees

3. Is the information directly relevant to your topic and purpose? An interesting quotation or startling statistic is only useful if it relates directly to the point you wish to make. Avoid including information solely because of its interest value; make sure that all your information relates directly to issues you wish to discuss.

4. Is the information sufficient? Ask yourself if the collected information is sufficient to illustrate your point, to prove that one proposal is better than another, or to show why your system will work better than the existing system. The opinion of one dietician is insufficient to support the usefulness of a particular diet; the statistics from five private colleges on tuition increases are insufficient to illustrate national trends in rising tuition costs.

Always ask these questions with your specific audience in mind. Remember that you are collecting, evaluating, and communicating this information because you want to achieve some effect on your audience.

REMEMBER: Follow these general principles in researching your speech topics:

1. Begin by examining what you know.
2. Work from the general to the more specific.
3. Keep an accurate research record.
4. Use your research time effectively.
5. Become familiar with the available sources of information.
6. Critically evaluate the research.

SOURCES FOR RESEARCH

More than 30 million different books have been published since the beginning of printing. Currently, approximately 400,000 titles are published each year. Millions of articles are published each year in thousands of different journals and magazines. There are now more than 100,000 journals and magazines in the area of science alone.

The information currently available on just about any topic is so vast that it is understandably daunting for many people. This unit will make the initial search procedure easier and less forbidding by identifying some significant sources of information.

Experts

The faculty is one of the best, if rarely used, sources of information for almost any speech topic. Regardless of what your topic is, someone on the faculty of some department knows a great deal about the topic. At the least, they will be able to direct you to appropriate sources.

Experts in the community can serve similar functions. Local politicians, religious leaders, doctors, lawyers, museum directors, and the like are often suitable sources of information.

Another obvious expert is the librarian at your college or local library. Librarians know the contents and mechanics of libraries; they are experts in the very issues that may be giving you trouble. Librarians will be able to help you in finding biographical material, indexes of current articles, materials in specialized collections at other libraries, and so on. Your librarian will also help you access the appropriate computerized databases and assist you in identifying the descriptors (the key words) that will help you retrieve the information you need.

Book Catalogs

Each library catalogs its books in a slightly different way, depending on its size and the needs of its users. All, however, make use of some form of catalog. If your library uses the traditional card catalog, you will find three types of cards: title, subject, and author cards. Thus, if you know the title or the author of the book you want, go to these cards to find out where the book is located. If you have just a general subject heading, go to the subject cards. These identify all the books your library has on this subject.

Although computer research is expanding rapidly, the primary source for most speech materials will still be in the library in printed form. How will researching a speech be different for those who take this type of course ten years from now? Thirty years from now?

Some libraries, such as the New York Public Library, have their catalogs in book form. Corresponding to the cards noted above, there are title, author, and subject matter books to help you locate the books you need.

Other libraries have their catalogs "on-line" (computerized), a system most libraries are instituting. A computer terminal is used to find the location of desired books. Usually, you may search the library's contents using title, author, or subject matter identifiers. This system is extremely easy to use. In addition, it tells you the book's present status, for example, if it is on reserve or on loan, and, if so, when it is due.

Encyclopedias

One of the best places to start to investigate your topic is a standard encyclopedia. You will get a general overview of the subject and suggestions for additional reading. The most comprehensive and the most prestigious is the *Encyclopaedia Britannica* (32 volumes). The *Macropaedia* (17 volumes) contain the detailed articles that have made the *Britannica* popular since its publication in Scotland in 1771. The *Micropaedia* (12 volumes) contain short entries that provide general information on the subject and identify the detailed articles in which the topic is covered in the *Macropaedia*. There are also 2 index volumes and a *Propaedia*, which contains an outline of knowledge and general essays on each of the major topics in the *Britannica*. The annual *Britannica Book of the Year* updates the encyclopedia as a whole.

Collier's Encyclopedia, the *Encyclopedia Americana*, and the *Academic American Encyclopedia* are also excellent and comprehensive. These works provide much insight into just about any subject you might look up. The *Americana* consists of 30 volumes and, as its title implies, focuses on American issues. The articles are generally shorter and easier to read than those in the *Britannica. Collier's* consists of 24 volumes; it is less detailed and scholarly than both the *Britannica* and the *Americana*. It is distinguished by its illustrations and attractive format. The *Academic American Encyclopedia* is addressed specifically to high school and college students. It contains many essays on topics frequently discussed in the classroom.

There are also many specialized encyclopedias. *The New Catholic Encyclopedia* (15 volumes) is the best and most scholarly source for general information on the Catholic Church. It contains articles on such topics as philosophy, science, and art as these have been influenced by and have influenced the Church. *Encyclopedia Judaica* (16 volumes plus yearbooks) emphasizes Jewish life and includes biographies and detailed coverage of the Jewish contribution to world culture. *Encyclopedia of Islam* and *Encyclopedia of Buddhism* cover the development, beliefs, institutions, and personalities of Islam and Buddhism, respectively.

For the physical, applied, and natural sciences there is the 20-volume *McGraw-Hill Encyclopedia of Science and Technology*. This is complemented by an annual supplement, the *McGraw-Hill Yearbook of Science and Technology. Our Living World of Nature* is a 14-volume popular encyclopedia dealing with natural history from an ecological point of view. The *International Encyclopedia of the Social Sciences* concentrates on the theory and methods of the social sciences in 17 well-researched volumes. Other widely used encyclopedias include the *Encyclopedia of Bioethics* (4 volumes), the *Encyclopedia of Philosophy* (8 volumes), and the *Encyclopedia of Religion* (16 volumes).

Computerized Encyclopedias Some encyclopedias, such as *Compton's Multimedia Encyclopedia* and *Grolier's* are now available on CD-ROM (compact disk, read-only memory), a computerized database. This system allows you to locate articles, maps, diagrams, and even definitions of difficult terms (through the built-in dictionary) easily and efficiently. For example, you would locate articles simply by typing in terms that describe the topic you want to explore.

Biographical Material

A speaker often needs information about particular individuals. Consult the *Biography Index* first. It contains an index to biographies appearing in various sources—magazines, books, letters, and diaries. This work is particularly useful for locating information on living persons who have not yet been the subject of thorough biographies.

The *Dictionary of National Biography* (DNB) consists of two sets of volumes. The two sets are *From the Earliest Times to 1900* and *The Twentieth-Century Dictionary of National Biography*. Both contain articles on famous deceased British men and women. These volumes are the most authoritative source for such biographical data. *The Dictionary of American Biography* (DAB) is modeled after the DNB. It contains articles on famous deceased Americans from all areas of accomplishment, for example, politics, sports, education, art, and industry. *The Dictionary of Canadian Biography* (DCB), only some volumes of which have been published so far, is arranged chronologically rather than alphabetically. In all three works (DNB, DAB, DCB) the signed articles contain bibliographies to consult for additional information.

For living individuals the best single source is *Current Biography*. This is issued monthly and in cumulative annual volumes. Beginning in 1940 *Current Biography* contains articles of one to two pages in length, most with photographs and brief bibliographies. The essays in *Current Biography* are written by an editorial staff and, therefore, include both favorable and unfavorable comments. *Who's Who in America* also covers living individuals.

In addition, there are a host of other more specialized works whose titles indicate their scope: *Directory of American Scholars, International Who's Who, Who Was Who in America, Who's Who* (primarily British), *Dictionary of Scientific Biography, American Men and Women of Science, Great Lives from History* (25 volumes), *Notable American Women, National Cyclopedia of American Biography* (1888–1984), *Who's Who in the Arab World, Who's Who in the World, Who's Who in Finance and Industry, Who's Who in American Politics, Who's Who Among Black Americans, Who's Who of American Women,* and *Who's Who Among Hispanic Americans*.

Newspaper, Magazine, and Journal Indexes

Indexes to the various newspapers, magazines, and professional journals are extremely useful.

Newspaper Indexes *The New York Times Index,* published since 1913, is important because it indexes one of the leading newspapers in the world. The newspaper is widely available and carefully indexed. The index is published twice a month with cumulative annual issues. It enables you to locate important news stories; book, play, and movie reviews; sports accounts; obituaries; complete texts of important speeches; and political, economic, and social commentaries. It also contains brief summaries of major news items and lists the major events in chronological order. This will help you to get, at a glance, an overview of the major developments of many events. This index is also useful since it enables you to locate the specific dates on which events occurred. This in turn will help you use other materials such as local newspapers.

Also useful is *The Wall Street Journal Index,* published since 1958. This indexes the most important newspaper reporting financial and business news. *The National Newspaper Index,* published since 1972, indexes such newspapers as the Chicago *Tribune,* the Los Angeles *Times,* and the *Washington Post,* each of which also has its own index.

Magazine Indexes The *Readers' Guide to Periodical Literature* covers magazine articles for the period from 1900 to the present. This guide indexes by subject and by author (in one convenient alphabetical index) articles published in about 180 different magazines. The *Abridged Readers' Guide* indexes about 60 publications. This brief version is often more convenient to use, at least in initial searches, than the longer version. *Readers' Guide* is valuable for its broad coverage, but it is limited in that it covers mostly general publications and only a few of the more specialized ones.

For more advanced materials, consult some of the more specific and specialized indexes noted here. Also, consult specialized indexes for other popular but perhaps less conservative periodicals. For example, *Readers' Guide* does not index such publications as *Mother Jones* and *Interview*. The *Popular Periodical Index,* published since 1973, indexes these and similar publications. The *Alternative Press Index,* published since 1970, indexes almost 200 magazines, newspapers, and journals that we might label "radical." This index is valuable for speakers dealing with such issues as the Third World, minority rights, socialism, and the like. *Access,* published since 1975, also indexes publications not covered in *Reader's Guide.*

For the period from 1802 to 1907, see *Poole's Index to Periodical Literature.* This covers both British and American periodicals. The *Education Index,* published since 1929, indexes articles from about 330 journals and magazines relevant to education at all levels. It also indexes most of the speech communication journals and government periodicals.

The Social Sciences Index covers periodicals in such areas as psychology, economics, sociology, and political science. Although more specialized indexes cover these subjects in greater depth, this one is useful for its cross-disciplinary coverage. Among the more specialized indexes that will prove useful to many speakers are the *Business Periodicals Index, Art Index, Applied Science and Technology Index, Biological and Agricultural Index, General Science Index, Index to Legal Periodicals, Humanities Index, Music Index,* and *PAIS* (Public Affairs Information Service).

In addition to indexes to articles appearing in periodicals, there is also a useful index to periodicals. The *Standard Periodical Dictionary,* published since 1970, lists about 70,000 periodicals under both title and subject headings. This directory is particularly useful for locating specialized periodicals that you might not have known existed.

Journal Abstracts   In addition to the cited indexes, which are guides to locating material within a general subject area, there are many helpful abstracts. The most comprehensive is *Psychological Abstracts.* This gives you short summaries of articles that appeared in psychology journals and books. It contains both subject and author indexes. *Sociological Abstracts, Linguistics and Language Behavior Abstracts,* and *Communication Abstracts* are other important abstracts. All of these abstracts devote considerable attention to articles dealing with speech communication in all its forms.

A somewhat different abstract is *Resources in Education,* a monthly journal published by ERIC (Education Resources Information Center). ERIC stores a wide variety of documents on such subjects as communication, language, counseling, testing, handicapped and gifted children, and so on. It publishes abstracts of these in *Resources in Education.* Documents appearing in *Resources* may be obtained from ERIC on microfiche or photocopy. This service is useful for obtaining copies of papers delivered at professional conventions and which are not available in journals and magazines. Thus, ERIC not only informs you of the available resources but also distributes them for a modest fee. For a more extended survey of a particular topic, you can request a computer search of the ERIC documents on a specific subject. This computer printout contains the titles, authors, abstracts, and prices of all the documents on this topic stored in ERIC.

Computerized Indexes and Abstracts If your library has computerized indexes and abstracts, you will find these much easier to use. Many of these are available on CD Rom (see the "Researching On-line" section that follows). For example, *Magazine Index Plus* is a computerized database that indexes over 400 magazines covering a wide variety of topics such as entertainment, travel, and current affairs. *Periodical Abstracts* contains abstracts from over 250 magazines covered by *Reader's Guide to Periodical Literature.*

National Newspaper Index provides indexes to *The New York Times, The Wall Street Journal,* the *Christian Science Monitor,* the *Washington Post,* and the Los Angeles *Times. Newspaper Abstracts* contains indexes to the above papers as well as to the *Atlanta Constitution,* the Chicago *Tribune,* and the *Boston Globe.*

Almanacs

The best single source for information of all kinds is the almanac. Numerous inexpensive versions published annually are perhaps the most up-to-date source on many topics. The most popular are *The World Almanac & Book of Facts* and the *Information Please Almanac. Whitaker's Almanac* is the best of the British almanacs and *Canadian Almanac and Directory* is the best source for Canadian data.

Government Publications

The U.S. government is the country's largest publisher. It prints more pages per year than any other publisher. It publishes materials on government, history, population, law, farming, and many other subjects. Here is just a small sampling of the publications that are available in most libraries or directly from the Government Printing Office (GPO) in Washington, D.C.

The United States Bureau of the Census publishes *Statistical Abstract of the United States* (from 1878 to the present) and *Historical Statistics of the United States, Colonial Times to 1957* (with various supplements). Together these volumes contain the most complete information on immigration, economics, geography, education, population, and various other topics that has been collected during the various census counts. Other valuable statistical sources include *Vital Statistics of the United States* (especially useful for demographic statistics), *Morbidity and Mortality Weekly Report* (useful for health-related issues), and *Employment and Earnings* (useful for labor force statistics). For international statistics see *United Nations Statistical Yearbook, World Statistics in Brief,* and *UNESCO Statistical Yearbook.*

The *Official Congressional Directory* (1809 to date) and the *Biographical Directory of the American Congress* (1774–1961) provide biographical information on government personnel, maps of congressional districts, and various other helpful information to those concerned with the workings of Congress.

The *Congressional Record* (1873 to date) is issued daily when Congress is in session. The *Record* contains all that was said in both houses of Congress. It also contains materials that members of Congress wish inserted.

Government publications originate in the various divisions of its 13 departments, each of which is a prolific publisher. The Departments of Agriculture, Commerce, Defense, Education, Energy, Health and Human Services, Housing and Urban Development, Interior, Justice, Labor, State, Treasury, and Transportation each issue reports, pamphlets, books, and assorted documents dealing with its various concerns. Because of the wealth of published material, you will have to first consult one of the guides to government publications. A few of the more useful ones that should be in your college or local libraries include *Government Reference Books* (1968 to date), *A Bibliography of United States Government Bibliographies,* and *U.S. Government Books: Recent Releases* (published quarterly).

Perhaps the best procedure to follow is to ask your librarian what guides to government documents and actual government publications your library has.

REMEMBER: **Major research sources:**

1. **the faculty and other experts**
2. **book catalogs**
3. **encyclopedias**
4. **biographical material**
5. **newspaper, magazine, and journal indexes**
6. **almanacs**
7. **government publications**

RESEARCHING ON-LINE

As noted, many of the indexes and abstracts formerly available only in print form are now available on-line (you can access an "outside" database) and on CD-ROM (with which you access a database contained on high-density compact disks that have read-only memory). New indexes and journals are being added to these databases regularly. These systems enable you to access many of the indexes and abstracts discussed previously. For example, *Psychological Abstracts, Sociological Abstracts, Humanities Index, Social Science Index,* and *ERIC* are available on-line and on CD-ROM. Some indexes are only available on-line or on CD-ROM, for example, ABI/INFORM and LEXIS/NEXIS discussed later.

One great advantage is that you don't have to copy each reference you find. Instead you can print out your search or download it to your own computer disk.

An even greater advantage of computerized searching is that it enables you to search for two or more concepts at the same time. For example, let's say you are giving a speech on the relationship between crime and drugs. In a manual search, you would have to go through all the entries on crime for those that linked crime with drugs. In some cases the titles of the articles will not be revealing. You would therefore have to get the actual article to discover if it was relevant or not. This would take considerable time. With a computerized search you can specify that you want a search of only those references dealing with both crime *and* drugs. The computer will do the work for you. It will retrieve only those references directly related to your topic of the relationship of crime and drugs.

Cartoon by Bill Maul. Reprinted by permission of the author.

Some computerized searches provide a simple list of references. For example, in preparation for a lecture I wanted to give on the concept of "feedforward"—information that we send prior to our regular messages (for example, "What til you hear this" or "You're not going to believe what happened last night"). I had a computer search done on this concept. A small part of that search appears in Figure 7.1.

Some computer searches provide you with detailed abstracts of the information contained in the book or article. In preparing for a lecture on ways in which we gain compliance from others, I had a computer search done. It yielded 31 references, one of which is reproduced in Figure 7.2 on page 138. From reading this abstract I can now tell if securing and reading the complete article would be worth the effort or not.

Databases

When you do research through a computer, you will be accessing one or more databases. A database is simply information contained in one place. A dictionary, an encyclopedia, and an index to magazines are all examples of databases. A computerized database is the same except that it is accessed through a computer. A number of dealers or vendors now make a variety of databases available. Through them you can avail yourself of a wide variety of reference materials.

For example, Dialog offers nearly 400 databases. One of the databases available from Dialog is *PsycINFO*. This database examines over 1300 periodicals and technical reports each year that deal with just about every psychological issue imaginable. The example of the abstract presented in Figure 7.2 came from the *PsycINFO* database. The *Linguistics and Language Behavior Abstracts* database contains references to

PRINTS   User: 020345 07oct87 P907: PR 1/3/ALL (items 1-19)   PAGE: 63
          DIALOG   Item 1 OF 19

DIALOG File 7: SOCIAL SCISEARCH - 72-87/WK36 (COPR. ISI INC. 1987)

01723965   Genuine Article#: G4020   No. References: 13
  THE LEARNING-PROCESS IN BIOFEEDBACK - IS IT FEEDFORWARD OR
FEEDBACK
    DUNN TG; GILLIG SE; PONSOR SE; WEIL N; UTZ SW
    UNIV TOLEDO, CTR APPL COGNIT SCI/TOLEDO//OH/43606; MED COLL
OHIO/TOLEDO//OH/43699
    BIOFEEDBACK AND SELF-REGULATION, V11, N2, P143-156, 1986
    Language: ENGLISH   Doc Type: ARTICLE

01676559   Genuine Article#: XN702   No. References: 43
  THE ROLE OF FEEDBACK AND FEEDFORWARD IN THE TEACHING OF
PRONUNCIATION - AN OVERVIEW
    DEBOT CLJ
    INST PHONET/NIJMEGEN//NETHERLANDS/
    SYSTEM, V8, N1, P35-45, 1980
    Language: ENGLISH   Doc Type: REVIEW, BIBLIOGRAPHY

01654239   Genuine Article#: E6512   No. References: 0
  LONG-TERM POTENTIATION AND FEEDFORWARD INHIBITION IN THE
DENTATE GYRUS
    KAIRISS EW; GODDARD GV
    UNIV OTAGO, DEPT PSYCHOL/DUNEDIN//NEW ZEALAND/
    NEW ZEALAND JOURNAL OF PSYCHOLOGY, V15, N1, R35, 1986
    Language: ENGLISH   Doc Type: MEETING ABSTRACT

01591177   Genuine Article#: C1737   No. References: 19
  CONTRIBUTION OF VISUAL INFORMATION TO FEEDFORWARD AND
FEEDBACK PROCESSES IN RAPID POINTING MOVEMENTS
    BEAUBATON D; HAY L
    CNRS-INST NEUROPHYSIOL & PSYCHOPHYSIOL 4, 31 CHEMIN JOSEPH
AIGUIER, BP 71/F-13277 MARSEILLE 9//FRANCE/
    HUMAN MOVEMENT SCIENCE, V5, N1, P19-34, 1986
    Language: ENGLISH   Doc Type: ARTICLE

01549186   Genuine Article#: AXA61   No. References: 0
  THE LEARNING-PROCESS IN BIOFEEDBACK-IS IT FEEDFORWARD OR
FEEDBACK
    DUNN T; GILLIG S; PONSOR S; WEIL N; UTZ SW
    UNIV TOLEDO/TOLEDO//OH/43606; MED COLL OHIO, SCH
NURSING/TOLEDO//OH/43699
    BIOFEEDBACK AND SELF-REGULATION, V10, N1, P87, 1985
    Language: ENGLISH   Doc Type: MEETING ABSTRACT

01515249   Genuine Article#: ARU14   No. References: 12
  FEEDFORWARD - FUTURE QUESTIONS, FUTURE MAPS
    PENN P
    ACKERMAN INST FAMILY THERAPY, 149 E 78TH ST/NEW
YORK/NY/10021
    FAMILY PROCESS, V24, N3, P299-310, 1985
    Language: ENGLISH   Doc Type: ARTICLE

01439419   Genuine Article#: ACK29   No. References: 19
  A SYSTEMS-APPROACH TO BANK PRUDENTIAL MANAGEMENT AND
SUPERVISION - THE UTILIZATION OF FEEDFORWARD CONTROL
    GARDENER EPM
    UNIV COLL N WALES, INST EUROPEAN FINANCE/BANGOR LL57
2DG/GWYNEDD/WALES/
    JOURNAL OF MANAGEMENT STUDIES, V22, N1, P1-24, 1985
    Language: ENGLISH   Doc Type: ARTICLE

01258227   Genuine Article#: RF282   No. References: 0
  THE ROLES OF FEEDBACK AND FEEDFORWARD IN PHASIC HR CONTROL
DURING STRESS
    RILEY DM
    ADDICT RES FDN/TORONTO M5S 2S1/ONTARIO/CANADA/; UNIV
TORONTO/ TORONTO M5S 1A1/ONTARIO/CANADA/
    PSYCHOPHYSIOLOGY, V20, N4, P464-465, 1983
    Language: ENGLISH   Doc Type: MEETING ABSTRACT

01133626   Genuine Article#: PF395   No. References: 5
  COMPUTER SYNTHESIZES FEEDFORWARD FEEDBACK-CONTROL
    WU RCT
    CHINESE PETR CORP. KAOHSIUNG REFINERY, CTR COMP, DIV ENGN
APPLICAT/KAOHSIUNG//TAIWAN/
    HYDROCARBON PROCESSING, V61, N8, P77-78, 1982
    Language: ENGLISH   Doc Type: ARTICLE

01128509   Genuine Article#: PC917   No. References: 24
  SELF-CONTROL SYSTEM OF SMALL-GROUPS - EFFECTS OF FEEDFORWARD
AND FEEDBACK
    OHTA M
    UNIV KANAZAWA/KANAZAWA/ISHIKAWA 920/JAPAN/
    PSYCHOLOGIA, V25, N2, P71-80, 1982
    Language: ENGLISH   Doc Type: ARTICLE

00975760   Genuine Article#: L0972   No. References: 20
  FEEDFORWARD AND FEEDBACK IN MULTIPLE-CUE
PROBABILITY-LEARNING - FACILITATING OR DEBILITATING
    HENDRIX WH; DUDYCHA AL
    USAF, INST TECHNOL/WRIGHT PATTERSON AFB//OH/45433; UNIV
WISCONSIN PARKSIDE/KENOSHA//WI/53140
    JOURNAL OF EXPERIMENTAL EDUCATION, V49, N3, P137-146, 1981
    Language: ENGLISH   Doc Type: ARTICLE

00917772   Genuine Article#: KR487   No. References: 5
  ANTICIPATORY REGULATION - A RAINCOAT DOES NOT FEEDFORWARD
MAKE
    BOURBON WT
    STEPHEN F AUSTIN STATE UNIV. DEPT
PSYCHOL/NACOGDOCHES//TX/75962
    BEHAVIORAL AND BRAIN SCIENCES, V3, N3, P465-466, 1980
                                         (cont. next page)

FIGURE 7.1   Output from a computer search.

studies on language. The *Social Scisearch* database covers the social and behavioral sciences. The references on "feedforward" given in Figure 7.1 were from this database. The *Legal Resource Index* covers those periodicals devoted to law. CompuServe (a subsidiary of H&R Block) contains such databases as *Grolier's Encyclopedia* and general and business news services. *The Source* (a subsidiary of Reader's Digest Association) contains, for example, Associated Press and United Press International news services. ABI/INFORM database covers more than 800 periodicals in business.

The LEXIS/NEXIS System allows you to retrieve the complete text of articles from hundreds of newspapers, magazines, journals, and even newsletters in addition to a wide variety of legal and statutory records.

There is probably a vendor and an appropriate database for just about any topic you might think of. Once you have selected your topic, you might wish to consult a directory of the available databases to locate the database that would be most appropri-

```
    Compliance-Gaining Message Strategies: A Typology and Some
Findings Concerning Effects of Situational Differences
    Miller, Gerald; Boster, Frank; Roloff, Michael; Seibold,
David
    Communication Monographs 1977, 44, 1, Mar, 37-51. CODEN:
COMODN
    Pub. Year: 1977
    Country of Publication: United States
    Language: English
    Document Type: Abstract of Journal Article (aja)
    Availability: Hardcopy reproduction available: document not
on microfiche
    Investigated were the possible control strategies a
persuader may use, & determining factors in how situational
differences affect a persuader's strategic choices. By
modifying a study by G.  Marwell & D. R. Schmitt ("Dimensions
of Compliance-Gaining Behavior: An Empirical Analysis."
Sociometry, 1967, 30, 350-364), dimensions of control
strategies were sought in four situations: (1) interpersonal,
long-term consequences, (2) interpersonal, short-term
consequences, (3) noninterpersonal, long-term consequences &
(4) noninterpersonal, short-term consequences. Responses
(Number of cases = 168) were obtained from University
students, community college students, & army recruiter
samplings. Results indicated that situational differences
affected the cluster structures & led to the conclusion that a
general typology of control strategies is improbable. 7
Tables. Modified HA
    Descriptors: Compliance (104775); Control, Controls,
Controlled (114800); Strategy, Strategies, Strategic (446700)
; Situation, Situations, Situational (424500); Difference,
Differences, Differential, Differentials, Differentiation
(132330)
```

FIGURE 7.2   Output from a computer search (with annotations).

ate for you. For example, *The CD-ROM Directory* contains over 1500 databases. The *Directory of Online Databases* identifies about 2500 databases throughout the world. In these directories, you would discover the particular database that would contain the subject area that you wish to research. Your librarians will be familiar with the various databases and you should avail yourself of their expertise.

Computer searches vary in cost. Scientific databases are relatively expensive to access. Social science data bases are relatively inexpensive. Some colleges will perform computer searches for faculty and graduate students but not for undergraduates. In most college libraries CD-ROM searches are free to all students.

Since the information retrieval systems vary so much from one school to another and since they are expanding so rapidly, it is best to ask your librarian about the available computer search facilities.

THE RESEARCH INTERVIEW

Earlier we noted that among the best sources of information are the experts. Here are some suggestions to make your dealing with the experts more productive and efficient.

Select the Person You Wish to Interview

Let us say that you wish to speak on family therapy. You look through your college cat-alog and you find that a course in family communication is offered by Professor Bernard Brommel. You think it might be worthwhile to interview him. You are now on your first step; you've selected one of the people you hope to interview. But, don't stop there. Before you pursue the interview try to learn something about this instructor. Has the instructor written a book in the field? Look at the book catalog. Has he writ-ten articles on the topic? Look in relevant indexes, for example, *Sociological Abstracts* and *Communication Abstracts.*

Secure an Appointment

Phone the instructor or send a letter requesting an interview. In your call or letter, identify the purpose of your request and that you would like a brief interview. For ex-ample, you might say: "I'm preparing a speech on family therapy and I would appreci-ate it if I could interview you to learn more about the subject. The interview would take about 15 minutes." (This time limitation helps since Brommel now knows it will not take very long and is more likely to agree to being interviewed.) Generally, it is best to be available at the interviewee's convenience, so indicate flexibility on your part, for example, "I can interview you any day after 12 p.m."

You may find it necessary to conduct the interview by phone. In this case, you should call to set up a time for a future call. For example, you might say: "I'm prepar-ing a speech on family therapy and I would like to interview you on the role of com-munication in family therapy. I want to ask you four or five questions. If you agree, I can call you back at a time that's convenient for you." In this way, you don't run the risk of asking him to hold still for an interview when he is eating lunch, talking with colleagues, or running to class.

Prepare Your Questions

Prepare the questions you wish to ask in advance. This will ensure that you use the time available to your best advantage. Of course, as the interview progresses other questions will come to mind and should be asked. But, having a prepared list of ques-tions will help you feel more relaxed and will help you obtain the information you need most easily.

Arrive on Time

This will enable you to use the time set aside to your advantage. You don't want the in-terviewer's first 5 minutes to be spent waiting for you. It will also demonstrate your competence and seriousness of purpose. If you are returning the call to conduct the interview by phone, then call at exactly the time agreed.

Establish Rapport with the Interviewee

Open the interview with an expression of thanks for making the time available to you and again state your purpose. Many people receive lots of requests and it helps if you remind the person of your purpose. You might say something like this: "I really appreciate your making time for this interview. As I mentioned, I'm preparing a speech on family therapy and your expertise and experience in this area will help a great deal."

Ask for Permission to Tape the Interview

Generally, it is a good idea to tape the interview, especially since inexpensive cassette recorders are so readily available. But, ask permission first. Some people prefer not to have informal interviews taped. Even if the interview is being conducted by phone, ask permission if you intend to tape the conversation.

Ask Open-ended Questions

Use questions that provide the interviewee with room to discuss the issues you want to raise. Thus, instead of asking "Do you have formal training in the area of family therapy?" (a question which requires a simple "yes" or "no" and will not be very informative), you might ask, "Can you tell me something of your background in this field?" (a question which is open-ended and allows Professor Brommel to tell you about his background).

Close the Interview with a Note of Appreciation

Thank the person for making the time available for the interview. Thank the person for being informative, cooperative, helpful, or whatever. In short, let the person know that you do in fact appreciate the effort made to help you with your speech. On the more practical side, this will also make it a great deal easier if you want to return for a second interview.

Follow up on the Interview

Follow up on the interview with a brief note of thanks. Or, perhaps you might send the person you interviewed a copy of your speech, again with a note of thanks for the help.

REMEMBER: **Steps in conducting the research interview:**
1. **select the person you wish to interview**
2. **secure an appointment**
3. **prepare your questions in advance**
4. **arrive on time**
5. **establish rapport**
6. **ask permission to tape the interview**
7. **ask open-ended questions**
8. **close the interview with an expression of appreciation**
9. **follow up on the interview**

INTEGRATING RESEARCH INTO YOUR SPEECH

Now that you have amassed this wealth of research material, how do you integrate it into your speech? Here are a few suggestions.

Mention the sources in your speech by citing at least the author and, if helpful, the publication and the date. Here is how C. Kenneth Orski (1986) did it:

> *In assessing what the future may hold for transportation, I will lean heavily on a technique pioneered by John Naisbitt, author of* Megatrends. *Naisbitt believes that the most reliable way to anticipate the future is to try to understand the present. To this end he methodologically scans 6000 daily local newspapers from around the country.*

Provide smooth transitions between your words and the words of the author you're citing. In this excerpt, Marilyn Loden (1986) does this most effectively:

> *In this book,* Leadership, *James MacGregor Burns advocates new leadership styles which encourage employees to take more risk, to be more self-reliant and manage more creatively. He calls this new management approach "transformational leadership."*

Avoid such useless expressions as "I have a quote here" or "I want to quote an example." Let the audience know that you are quoting by pausing before the quote, taking a step forward, or referring to your notes to read the extended quotation. Marilyn Loden (1986) again does this effectively:

> *Mary Kay Ash believes in feminine leadership. Recently she said: "A woman can no more duplicate the male style of leadership than an American businessman can exactly reproduce the Japanese style."*

If you feel it is crucial that the audience know you are quoting and you want to state that this is a quotation, you might do it this way:

> *Recently, Mary Kay Ash put this in perspective, and I quote: "A woman can no more duplicate the male style of leadership."*

Deanna Gunderson (Boaz and Brey 1988), a student from the University of Northern Iowa, in a speech entitled "Communication Analysis," gave a detailed account of her sources:

> *My analysis is based on Donald Horton and Richard Wohl's article, "Mass Communication and Para-Social Interaction: Observation on Intimacy at a Distance," which first appeared in the* Journal of Psychiatry, *August 1956, and has since reappeared in Gumpert and Cathcart's text,* Intermedia. *My analysis is extended by an understanding of self-disclosure, as developed in the early work of John Powell, entitled,* Why Am I Afraid to Tell You Who I Am?

By integrating and acknowledging your sources of information in the speech, you will give fair credit to those whose ideas and statements you are using and at the same time you will help establish your own reputation as a responsible researcher.

CRITICALLY SPEAKING

1. How would you describe your current system for doing research? Do you follow a pattern that might prove useful to others?

2. Are there other useful principles of research that might have been included here?

3. In critically evaluating research, what other issues should you consider (in addition to recency, bias, relevance, and sufficiency)?

4. Can you find examples from recent advertising that violate the principles for evaluating research discussed here?

5. If you were researching "recent advances in AIDS education," how would you go about it? What sources would you consult?

6. What three sources might prove useful in your search for information on "abortion"? On "sexual harassment"? On "civil disobedience"?

7. What one computer database would you find especially useful for your next speech? How would you go about accessing this database?

8. Who might you realistically interview (given your present location, resources, time limitations, and so on) on the following topics: marital problems faced by young couples, gay and lesbian rights, bias crimes, modern art, religion and politics?

PRACTICALLY SPEAKING

7.1   ACCESSING INFORMATION

In order to gain some familiarity with the various ways of locating information, each student should select or be assigned one of the following items of information and should report back to the class the answer and the reference work(s) he or she used to find the answer. In reporting how the answer was found, report on unproductive as well as productive sources.

1. The Japanese flag during World War II
2. The ethnic population of Nebraska
3. The age of the author of one of your textbooks
4. The ingredients of a Harvey Wallbanger
5. The first capital of the United States
6. The current president of the Speech Communication Association, The American Psychological Association, or the International Communication Association
7. The world's largest library and the number of volumes it contains
8. The Academy Award winner in 1952 for best actress

9. The literacy rate for China
10. The main languages of Cambodia
11. The prime interest rate for today
12. The faculty-student ratio for Harvard
13. The film grossing the largest amount of money and the amount of money it has grossed to date
14. The profits or losses for IBM last year
15. The author of the quotation: "Though it be honest, it is never good to bring bad news"
16. The birthplace and real name of John Wayne
17. The full name of the journals usually abbreviated QJS, JC, CM, CE
18. The use and origin of the word *meathead*
19. The early years of John Travolta
20. The number of votes received by Stephen Douglas from Illinois in the Lincoln-Douglas presidential election of 1860
21. The text of Winston Churchill's speech "After Dunkirk"
22. The political configuration of Europe in 1942
23. The graduate program in communication at Indiana University
24. The amount of money *Playboy* pays for an article
25. The amount of money charged for a full-page, four-color advertisement in *Reader's Digest*
26. The characteristics of the Hudson River school of painting
27. The rules for playing chess
28. Contemporary speeches on U.S. energy problems
29. The major contributions of psychologist B. F. Skinner
30. The birthplace and political biography of one of your state's senators
31. The principles and beliefs of Islam
32. The history of the Boy Scouts in Canada
33. The author and source of the quotation, "My only love sprung from my only hate!"
34. The title of the Ph.D. dissertation of someone teaching at your school
35. The psychological studies on "learned helplessness"

The Audience: Sociological Analysis and Adaptation

■ ■ ■ ■

UNIT OBJECTIVES

After completing this unit, you should be able to:

1. Define *audience*

2. Define *attitude* and *belief*

3. Identify at least five characteristics that need to be included in an audience analysis and explain why they must be considered in audience adaptation

4. Explain the context characteristics and how they relate to audience analysis and adaptation

*P*ublic speaking audiences vary greatly. Thousands of people at Yankee Stadium listening to Billy Graham, 30 students in a classroom listening to a lecture, and 5 people listening to a street orator are all audiences. The characteristic that seems best to define an audience is *common purpose*. A public speaking *audience* is a group of individuals gathered together to hear a speech.

You deliver a speech to inform or persuade your audience. A teacher lectures on Gestalt psychology to increase understanding; a minister talks against adultery to influence behaviors and attitudes; a football coach gives a pep talk to motivate the team to improve—all of these persons are trying to produce change. If they are to be successful, then they must know their audience. If you are to be successful, you must know your audience. This knowledge will help you in a variety of ways; here are just a few:

- in selecting your topic
- in phrasing your purpose
- in establishing a relationship between yourself and your audience
- in choosing examples and illustrations
- in stating your thesis, whether directly or indirectly
- in the arguments you use and the motives to which you appeal

APPROACHING AUDIENCE ANALYSIS AND ADAPTATION

Your first step in audience analysis is to construct an audience profile in which you analyze the sociological or demographic characteristics of your audience. These characteristics help you to estimate the attitudes, beliefs, and values of your audience. If you want to effect changes in these attitudes and beliefs, you have to know what they are.

Attitudes and Beliefs

Attitude refers to your tendency to act for or against a person, object, or position. If you have a positive attitude toward the death penalty, you are likely to argue or act in favor of instituting the death penalty (for example, vote for a candidate who supports the death penalty). If you have a negative attitude toward the death penalty, then you are likely to argue or act against it. Attitudes influence how favorably or unfavorably listeners will respond to speakers who support or denounce the death penalty.

Belief refers to the confidence or conviction you have in the existence or truth of some proposition. For example, you may believe that there is an afterlife, that education is the best way to rise from poverty, that democracy is the best form of government, or that all people are born equal. If your listeners believe that the death penalty is a deterrent to crime, for example, then they will be more likely to favor arguments for (and speakers who support) the death penalty than would listeners who do not believe in the connection between the death penalty and deterrence.

As you can readily see from this example of the death penalty, the attitudes and beliefs that your listeners have will influence how receptive they will be to your topic,

BOOTH

"You do like octopus?"

Drawing by Booth; © 1991, The New Yorker Magazine, Inc. Reprinted by permission.

your point of view, and your evidence and arguments. It is essential, therefore, that you learn about your listeners' attitudes and beliefs before you prepare your speech, unlike the cartoon character.

Seeking Audience Information

The most effective way to learn about your audience's attitudes and beliefs is to analyze the audience's demographic or sociological characteristics. You can seek out audience information using a variety of methods: observation, data collection, interviewing, and inference (Sprague and Stuart 1992).

Observe. How do they dress? Can you infer their possible economic status from their clothing and jewelry? Might their clothing reveal any conservative or liberal leanings? Might clothing provide clues to attitudes on economics or politics? What do they do in their free time? Where do they live? What do they talk about?

Collect data systematically. Use a questionnaire to collect information before your speech. Let's say you took a course in desktop publishing and were thinking about giving an informative speech on the nature of desktop publishing. One thing you would need to know is how much your audience already knows. This will help you judge the level at which to approach the topic, information that you can assume, terms you need to define, and so on. You might also want to know if the audience has ever seen documents produced by desktop publishing. If they haven't, examples would provide interesting visual aids. To help you answer these and other relevant questions you might compose a questionnaire such as appears in Figure 8.1.

Audience questionnaires are even more useful as background for your persuasive speeches. Let's say you plan to give a speech in favor of allowing single people to adopt children. To develop an effective speech, you need to know your audience's attitudes toward single-parent adoption. Are they in favor? Opposed? If they have reservations, what are they? To help you answer such questions, you might use a questionnaire such as that presented in Figure 8.2.

FIGURE 8.1   Audience questionnaire.

Audience Questionnaire

I'm planning to give my informative speech on desktop publishing, a procedure where printed pages similar to those that would appear in magazines or newspapers are produced with a personal computer.

1. How much do you know about desktop publishing?
   ____ a great deal
   ____ something but not very much
   ____ very little
   ____ virtually nothing
2. Have you ever seen a publication produced by desktop software?
   ____ yes
   ____ no
   ____ not sure
3. How interested are you in learning more about desktop publishing?
   ____ very interested
   ____ neither interested nor uninterested
   ____ uninterested
4. Is there anything special about desktop publishing that you would like to learn?

Audience Questionnaire

1. How do you feel about single people adopting children?

   ___ strongly in favor of it
   ___ in favor of it
   ___ neutral
   ___ opposed to it
   ___ strongly opposed to it

2. Is your attitude the same for interracial adoption? For gays and lesbians adopting? Please explain.

3. What is your main reason for or against single-parent adoption?

FIGURE 8.2   Audience questionnaire.

Interview a few members of your intended audience. In a classroom situation, this is easily accomplished. If you are to speak with an audience you will not meet prior to your speech, you might interview those who know the audience members better than you. For example, you might talk with the person who invited you to speak. The guidelines for interviewing resource people (Unit 7) should prove useful here as well.

If you do survey your audience—with a questionnaire or by interview—be sure to mention this in your speech. It will alert your listeners to your thoroughness and your concern for them. It will also satisfy their curiosity since most people will be interested in how others responded. You might say something like this:

> *I want to thank you all for completing my questionnaire on single-parent adoption. Half of you were neutral; 30 percent were in favor, and 20 percent were opposed. The major reason in favor of single-parent adoption was that it would provide homes for an enormous number of children who would otherwise not be adopted. The major reason against such adoption was the belief that a child needs two parents to grow up emotionally healthy. Let's look more carefully at each of these reasons*

Use "intelligent inference and empathy." Use your knowledge of human behavior and human motivation and try to adopt the perspective of the audience. For example, if you are addressing recovering alcoholics, you might infer that your listeners have known both low and high esteem, that they have had experience in dealing with conflicts, and that they have a determination to take control of their own lives. Of course, you may be wrong about some of your listeners, but you can almost always make some reasonable inferences.

◼◼◼◼ ANALYZING AUDIENCE CHARACTERISTICS

Caution: All generalizations are false. The generalizations inherent in the following characteristics seem true in most cases but may not be valid for any specific audience. *Beware of using these generalizations as stereotypes.* Don't assume that all women or all older people or all highly educated people think or believe the same things. They do not. Nevertheless, there are characteristics that seem to be more common among one group than another, and it is these characteristics that are explored in these generalizations. Use them to stimulate your thinking about your specific and unique audience. Most important, test what is offered here against your own experience.

Let's look at the six major sociological or demographic variables: (1) age; (2) gender; (3) cultural factors; (4) educational and intellectual levels; (5) occupation, income, and status; and (6) religion.

Age

Different age groups have different attitudes and beliefs simply because they have had different experiences. Take these differences into consideration in preparing your speeches.

For example, let us say that you are an investment counselor and you want to persuade your listeners to invest their money to increase their earnings. Your speech would have to be very different if you were addressing an audience of retired people (say in their 60s) and an audience of young executives (say in their 30s). You might, for example, begin your speech to the retired audience as follows:

> *I want to talk with you about investing for your future. Now, I know what you're thinking. You're thinking to yourself, our future is now. You're thinking that you need more income now, not in the future. Well, that is what investing is all about. It's about increasing your income now, tomorrow, and next week and next month. Let me show you what I mean.*

In your speech to the young executives, you might begin with something like this:

> *I want to talk with you about investing for your future. In 20 years—years that will pass very quickly—many of you will be retiring. You quickly will learn that your company pension plan will prove woefully inadequate. Social security will be equally inadequate. With only these sources of income, you will have to lower your standard of living drastically. But, that need not happen. In fact, with extremely small investments made now and throughout your high-income earning years, you will actually be able to live at a much higher standard than you ever thought possible.*

Note that in both of these examples the speaker made inferences about the audience's attitudes toward investments based on their age. The speaker demonstrated a knowledge of the audience and their immediate concerns. As a listener hearing even these brief excerpts, you would feel that the speaker is addressing you directly and specifically. As a result you would probably give this speaker more attention than you'd give to one who spoke in generalities and without any clear idea of who was listening.

Here are some questions about age that you might find helpful in analyzing and adapting to your audience.

1. Do the age groups differ in the goals, interests, and day-to-day concerns that may be related to your topic and purpose? Graduating from college, achieving corporate success, raising a family, and saving for retirement are concerns that differ greatly from one age group to another. Learn your audience's goals. Know what they think about and worry about. Connect your propositions and your supporting materials to these goals and concerns. Show the audience how they can more effectively achieve their goals and you will win a favorable hearing.

2. Do the groups differ in their ability to absorb and process information? Will they differ in their responses to visual cues? With a young audience, it may be best to keep up a steady, even swift pace. If possible use visuals. Make sure their attention doesn't wander. With older persons, you may wish to maintain a more moderate pace.

3. Do the groups differ in their respect for tradition and the past? Is one age group (traditionally the young) more likely to view innovation and change positively? Might appeals to tradition be more appropriate for an older audience? Might appeals to discovery, exploration, newness, and change find a more receptive hearing among the young?

4. Do the groups differ in the degree to which they are motivated by their peer group? Young people have strong needs to be evaluated positively by their peer group; group identification is very important to the young. Use this motive in your speeches. Show a young audience that what you are advocating has the approval of like-minded young people. Show them why agreement with you will result in peer approval.

Gender

Gender is one of the most difficult audience variables to analyze. The rapid social changes taking place today make it difficult to pin down the effects of gender. At one time, researchers focused primarily on biological sex differences. Now, however, many researchers are focusing on psychological sex roles. When we focus on a psychological sex role, we consider a person feminine if that person has internalized those traits (attitudes and behaviors) that society considers feminine and rejected those traits society considers masculine. We consider a person masculine if that person has internalized those traits society considers masculine and rejected those traits society considers feminine. Thus, a biological woman may assume a masculine sex role and a biological man may assume a feminine sex role.

Because of society's training, biological males generally internalize masculine traits and biological females generally internalize feminine traits. So, while there is probably great overlap between biological and psychological sex roles, they are not equivalent. At times, in fact, they may be quite different. Although we use the shorthand "men" and "women," remember that psychological sex roles may be more significant than biological sex in accounting for these differences.

Let's say that you are a counselor and are delivering a speech on how to communicate more effectively in a romantic relationship. Your speech should be very different if delivered to a group of women versus a group of men. Women will probably be more receptive to the topic and more willing to talk about their relationships than men. In your speech to an audience of women, you might say:

Most of you are probably in relationships with men who have difficulty expressing themselves, especially when it comes to romance. Oh, they are good men, of course, but they don't know how to talk romance. They don't know the language of romance. You do; women have been taught this language and feel comfortable with it. And so, you have to assume the role of teacher and teach your partner this new and different language. But you must do it with subtlety; that is what I want to talk about.

To an all-male audience, however, you might introduce your topic very differently. You might, for example, say something like this:

Most of you are probably in relationships with women who do all or most of the talking about the relationship. They are the ones who talk romance. Somehow you're not comfortable talking like this; You have difficulty using the language of romance. You're men of action. But, maybe there are ways of talking this language that will make it less painful. In fact, I'm going to show you how to talk the language of romance so that you'll love each and every syllable.

Note that in these two examples, the speaker begins with and builds on the feelings the audience is assumed to have. The audience is made to see that the speaker knows who they are and does not intend to contradict or criticize these feelings but rather take these feelings into consideration in the speech.

Here are some questions to guide your analysis of this very difficult audience characteristic.

1. Do men and women differ in the values they consider important and that are related to your topic and purpose? Traditionally, men have been found to place greater importance on theoretical, economic, and political values. Traditionally, women have been found to place greater importance on aesthetic, social, and religious values. In framing appeals and in selecting examples, use the values your audience members consider most important.

2. Will your topic be seen as more interesting by men? By women? Will men and women have different attitudes toward the topic? Men and women do not, for example, respond in the same way to such topics as abortion, rape, and equal pay for equal work. Select your topics and supporting materials in light of the sex of your audience members. When your audience is mixed, make a special effort to relate "women's" topics to men and "men's" topics to women.

3. Will men or women feel uncomfortable with your topic or purpose? For example, women are generally more relationally oriented than are men. Women express their feelings more readily than do men. Many men operate with the "cowboy syndrome," the tendency to remain strong and silent regardless of what is happening. Relational topics—for example, friendship, love, and family—are more popular with women than with men. (All you have to do to convince yourself of this is to pick up a

What would be your ideal audience (in terms of age; gender; cultural factors; educational and intellectual levels; occupation, income, and status; and religion) for your next speech? What would be the most difficult audience imaginable?

random selection of magazines addressed to women and magazines addressed to men.) Look at the advertisements, the articles, and even the cartoons.) When speaking on these topics to women, you will probably find a receptive audience. When speaking on such topics to men, draw explicit connections between these topics and their values, needs, and interests.

Cultural Factors

Nationality, race, and cultural identity are crucial in audience analysis. Largely because of different training and experiences, the interests, values, and goals of various cultural groups will also differ.

1. Are the differences within cultures relevant to your topic and purpose? Speakers who fail to demonstrate an understanding of these differences will be distrusted. Speakers, especially those who are seen to be outsiders, who imply that all African-Americans are athletic and all lesbians are masculine will quickly lose credibility. Avoid any implication that you are stereotyping audience members (or the groups to which they belong). It is sure to work against achieving your purpose.

2. Are the attitudes and beliefs held by different cultures relevant to your topic and purpose? Find out what these are. For example, the degree to which listeners are loyal to family members, feel responsibility for the aged, and believe in the value of education will vary from one culture to another. Build your appeals around *your* audience's attitudes and beliefs.

■ ■ ■

TIPS FROM PROFESSIONAL SPEAKERS

Another time, I prepared a speech for a client I hadn't worked with in over seven years. The speech was to be given at the end of a conference of 500 senior managers from around the world. I was not able to get a clear idea of how to focus my speech from discussions with the people who invited me, and other sources were not readily available. I planned my speech based on what I knew about the group seven years ago, but decided to travel to the conference site the evening before in order to gather "intelligence" from participants. I discovered that the group had changed dramatically, and realized that the focus of my speech was inappropriate. I altered my design and began by talking about the changes I'd observed. The audience knew immediately that I was speaking to *them* and this rapport created the context for success.

Whether you are leading a seminar, addressing a group of 500 or talking to your local PTA, it is critically important to know your audience and to *think of them.*

Michael J. Gleb, speaker and author. *Present Yourself* (Rolling Hills Estates, CA: Jalmar Press, 1988), p. 90.

---

3. Will the varied cultures differ in their goals or suggestions to change their lives? For example, groups that have experienced recent oppression may be more concerned with immediate goals and immediate means of affecting change in their lives. Many want revolutionary rather than evolutionary change. They may have little patience with the more conservative posture of the majority that tells them to be content with small gains.

4. Will the cultures have different views toward education, employment, and life in general? Oppressed groups often cannot afford the luxury of idealism. Pragmatic appeals will work best with formerly and currently oppressed members. Some cultures value formal education and take great pride in their members graduating from college and earning advanced degrees. Other cultures may place greater value on practical experience, on hard work, or on living for the pleasure of the moment.

Educational and Intellectual Levels

An educated person may not be very intelligent. Conversely, an intelligent person may not be very well educated. In most cases, however, the two go together. Further, they seem to influence the reception of a speech in similar ways and so are considered together. The shorthand "educated" is used to refer to both qualities.

Let's say you are an advertising executive and are giving a speech on how spokespersons for television commercials are chosen. If your audience is highly educated and knowledgeable, you might say something like this:

The credibility of the spokesperson depends on three essential dimensions. First, it depends on the person's perceived competence. Second, it depends on the person's moral character. Third, it depends on the person's charisma. Rhetorical scholarship and experimental research have found support for these three factors.

If your audience is less educated and less knowledgeable, you might communicate essentially the same information this way:

What makes us believe one person and disbelieve another person? Research tells us that there are three main characteristics. First, we believe someone we think has knowledge or competence. Second, we believe someone who is moral, who is essentially a good person. Third, we believe someone who is dynamic and outgoing.

The first example assumes that the audience knows such technical terms as *credibility, rhetorical, competence,* and *charisma.* The second example does not take this knowledge for granted and instead uses everyday language to explain the same concepts. When a technical vocabulary is used, the terms are explained (as in ". . . we think has knowledge or competence").

In looking at the education and intelligence of your audience, consider asking questions such as the following.

1. Is the educational level related to the audience's level of social or political activism? Generally, the more educated are more responsive to the needs of others. They more actively engage in causes of a social and political nature. Appeals to humanitarianism and broad social motives should work well with an educated audience. However, when speaking to less educated groups, concentrate on the value your speech has to their immediate needs and to the satisfaction of their immediate goals.

2. Will the interests and concerns of the audience differ on the basis of their educational level? Generally, the educated are more concerned with issues outside their immediate field of operation. They are concerned with international affairs, economic issues, and the broader philosophical and sociological issues confronting the nation and the world. The educated recognize that these issues affect them in many ways. Often the uneducated do not see the connection. Therefore, when speaking to a less educated audience, draw the connections explicitly and relate such topics to their more immediate concerns.

Note too that groups from different educational levels will be familiar with different sources of information. Thus, for example, only a relatively educated audience would be familiar with such magazines as *Architectural Digest, Byte,* and *Barron's.* Depending on the city in which you live, the educated and the less educated will probably also read different newspapers and watch different television shows. Recognize these differences and use the relevant sources appropriately.

3. Will the educational levels influence how critical the audience will be of your evidence and argument? The more educated will probably be less swayed by appeals to emotion and to authority. They will be more skeptical of generalizations (as you may and should be of my generalizations in this unit). They will question the validity of statistics and frequently demand better substantiation of your propositions. The educated are more likely to apply the tests of evidence discussed in later units (see

Units 14 and 17). Therefore, pay special attention to the logic of your evidence and arguments in addressing an educated audience.

4. Will the educational level relate to what the audience knows about your topic? As a speaker you will be able to assume more background knowledge when addressing an educated than an uneducated audience. Fill in the necessary background and detail for the less educated.

Occupation, Income, and Status

Occupation, income, and status, although not the same, are most often positively related. Therefore, they can be dealt with together.

1. How will job security and occupational pride be related to your topic and purpose? Appeal to these when appropriate and attack them only with extreme caution. If you can show your audience how your topic will enhance their job, give them greater job security or mobility, or make them more effective and efficient workers, you will have a most attentive and receptive audience.

"O.K., but change 'Her tawny body glistened beneath the azure sky'
to 'National problems demand national solutions.'"

Drawing by Mankoff; © 1982 The New Yorker Magazine, Inc. Reprinted by permission.

2. Will people from different status levels view long-range planning and goals differently? Higher-status people are generally more future-oriented. They train and plan for the future. Their goals are clear and their efforts are directly addressed to achieving these goals. Even their reading matter relates directly to these goals. For example, they read *Forbes, Fortune,* and *The Wall Street Journal* to help them achieve their financial goals. When speaking to a lower-status audience, relate future-oriented issues to their more immediate and demanding situations.

3. Will the different status groups have different time limitations? Higher status, more financially secure people may be more likely to devote their time to social and political issues. Lower-status people may be more concerned with meeting their immediate needs. Time is extremely valuable to the poor. The speaker who asks anything that would take their time is demanding a great deal—perhaps more than many can afford. Relate any request for them to see "the larger picture" to the fulfillment of their present needs.

Religion

Today there is great diversity within each religion. Almost invariably there are conservative, liberal, and middle-of-the-road groups within each. As the differences within each religion widen, the differences between and among religions seem to narrow. Different religions are coming closer together on various social and political, as well as moral, issues. Generalizations here, as with sex, are changing rapidly.

1. Will the religious see your topic or purpose from the point of view of religion? Religion permeates all topics and all issues. On a most obvious level, we know that such issues as birth control, abortion, and divorce are closely connected to religion. Similarly, premarital sex, marriage, child-rearing, money, cohabitation, responsibilities toward parents, and thousands of other issues are clearly impacted by religion.

Religion is also important, however, in areas where its connection is not so obvious. For example, religion influences one's ideas concerning such topics as obedience to authority, responsibility to government, and the usefulness of such qualities as honesty, guilt, and happiness.

2. Does your topic or purpose attack the religious beliefs of any segment of your audience? Even those who claim total alienation from the religion in which they were raised may still have strong emotional (though perhaps subconscious) ties to that religion. These ties may continue to influence their attitudes and beliefs.

When dealing with any religious beliefs (and particularly when disagreeing with them), recognize that you are going to meet stiff opposition. Proceed slowly and inductively. Present your evidence and argument before expressing your disagreement.

3. Do the religious beliefs of your audience differ in any significant ways from the official teachings of their religion? Do not assume that a religious leader's opinion or pronouncement is accepted by the rank-and-file members. Generally, opinion polls demonstrate that official statements by religious leaders take a more conservative position while members are more liberal.

4. Can you make reliable inferences about people's behavior based on their religiousness? One of the common beliefs about religious people is that they are more honest, more charitable, and more likely to reach out to those in need than would the nonreligious. A review of research, however, finds even this seemingly logical connection not true (Kohn 1989). For example, in a study of cheating among college students, religious beliefs bore little relationship to honesty; in fact, atheists were less likely to cheat than those who identified themselves as religious. Other studies have found that religious people were not any more likely to help those in need, for example, to give time to work with retarded children or to comfort someone lying in the street. So, be careful of making assumptions about people's behavior on the basis of their religiousness. You are much more likely to be accurate in judging attitudes than behaviors.

Other Factors

No list of audience characteristics can possibly be complete and the list presented here is no exception. You will need another category—"other factors"—to identify any additional characteristics that might be significant to your particular audience. Such factors might include the following.

Expectations. ***How will your audience's expectations about you influence their reception of your speech?*** These expectations should influence what you will say. This is not to imply that you should simply give the audience what it expects. It is to say, however, that you always need to consider their expectations, whether you intend to fulfill them or explode them. If your audience expects you to be humorous, you must either be humorous or explain why you won't be.

Relational Status. ***Will the relational status of your audience members influence the way in which they view your topic or your purpose?*** Are the audience members married? Single? Divorced? Cohabitors? Widowed? Do the members wish to get married? Are they content in their present state or do they wish to change in some way? Are they without primary relationships?

Special Interests. ***Do the special interests of your audience members relate to your topic or purpose?*** What special interests do the audience members have? Do they have hobbies you might refer to? What occupies their leisure time? Are they interested in films? Television? Community projects? Sports?

Organizational Memberships. ***How might the organizational memberships of your audience influence your topic or purpose? Might you use these organizational memberships in your examples and illustrations?*** Are the members of your audience "joiners"? What organizations do they belong to? How might these organizations' goals influence what you as a speaker might say or expect? Are they members of NRA? AMA? CORE? What does this mean for your speech development?

Political Affiliation. ***Will your audience's political affiliations influence how they view your topic or purpose?*** Are members of the audience identified with any particular political party? Are they politically liberal? Conservative? Are they uninvolved and uninterested? What does this mean to the development of your speech?

REMEMBER: **Consider the following factors in analyzing an audience:**

1. age
2. sex (psychological sex role)
3. cultural factors
4. educational and intellectual levels
5. occupation, income, and status
6. religion and religiousness
7. other factors—expectations, relational status, special interests, organizational memberships, political affiliation

ANALYZING CONTEXT CHARACTERISTICS

In addition to analyzing specific listeners, devote attention to the specific context in which you will speak. Consider the size of the audience, the physical environment, the occasion, the time of your speech, and where your speech fits into the sequence of events.

Size of Audience

How might the size of your audience influence your speech presentation? Generally, the larger the audience, the more formal the speech presentation should be. With a small audience, you may be more casual and informal. Also, the larger the audience, the more differences there will be. In a large audience you will have more variety of religions, a greater range of occupations and income levels, and so on. All the variables noted earlier will be even more intensified in a large audience. Therefore, you will need supporting materials that will appeal to all members.

Physical Environment

How will the physical environment influence your speech presentation? The physical environment—indoors or outdoors, room or auditorium, sitting or standing audience—is important. Take a few minutes to erase or lessen the problem of entering the public speaking environment totally cold. Spend some time in front of the room. See the room from the perspective of the speaker, before you are ready to speak.

Another factor in speech effectiveness is audience density. Whether the listeners are close or far apart will influence their interaction and your persuasiveness. Generally, audiences are easier to persuade if they are sitting close together than if they are spread widely apart. With listeners close together, it is easier to maintain eye contact and to concentrate your focus.

Occasion

How might the occasion influence the nature and the reception of your speech? The occasion greatly influences the nature and the reception of the speech. Whether the speech is a class exercise (as most of your early speeches will be) or some invited address (as most of your professional life speeches will be) will influence much of the speech. When the speech is given as a class assignment, for example, you will probably be operating under a number of restrictions—time limitations, the type of purpose you can employ, the types of supporting materials, and various other matters. When your speech is invited because of who you are, you have a great deal more freedom to talk about what interests you, which by virtue of the invitation will also interest the audience.

The occasion will dictate, in part, the kind of speech required. A wedding speech will differ drastically from a funeral speech, which will differ drastically from one at a political rally. In constructing the speech, focus on each element in relation to the occasion. Ask yourself in what way the particular public speaking variable (language, organization, supporting materials, for example) might be made more responsive to this particular occasion.

Time of the Speech

How might the time during which you are to give your speech influence your presentation? If your speech is to be given in an early morning class, say around 8 AM, then take into consideration that some of your listeners will still be half asleep. Tell them you appreciate their attendance; compliment their attention. If necessary, wake them up with your voice, gestures, attention-gaining materials, visual aids, and the like. If your speech is in the evening when most of your listeners are anxious to get home, recognize this as well.

Sequence of Events

Also consider where your speech fits into the general events of the time. A useful procedure is to scan a recent news magazine as well as the morning newspaper to see if any items relate to what you will say in your speech. If so, you might make reference to the story as a way of gaining attention, adding support to your argument, or stressing the importance of the topic.

Also consider where your speech fits in with the other speeches that will be heard that day or during that class. If you are to speak after one or more other speakers, try especially hard to build in some reference to a previous speech. This will help to stress your similarity with the audience members and will also help you demonstrate important connections between what you are saying and what others have said.

REMEMBER: **Consider the following factors in analyzing the public speaking context:**

1. size of the audience
2. physical environment
3. occasion
4. time
5. sequence of events

CRITICALLY SPEAKING

1. What kind of questionnaire might prove useful in securing information about your audience for your next speech? What questions would you ask?
2. Can you formulate a generalization that is true for all people or for all people from the same culture, occupation, or sex? It might prove interesting to try to develop such a proposition and to test it in class discussions.
3. What evidence can you locate to contradict any of the assumptions made throughout this unit?
4. In what other ways do the young and the old differ? In what other ways do men and women differ?
5. In what ways does your age and your sex influence the way in which you think about contemporary issues?
6. How might the religions of your class members influence the ways they might view two or three of today's news items?
7. If you were writing this textbook, what other audience characteristics would you include? What would you advise the student of public speaking to do on the basis of these characteristics?

8. What is the most important single mistake that a speaker could make in thinking about his or her audience?

PRACTICALLY SPEAKING

8.1   ANALYZING AN UNKNOWN AUDIENCE

This experience should familiarize you with some of the essential steps in analyzing an audience on the basis of relatively little evidence and in predicting their attitudes.

The class should be broken up into small groups of five or six members. Each group will be given a different magazine; their task is to analyze the audience (i.e., the readers or subscribers) of that particular magazine in terms of the characteristics discussed in this unit. The only information the groups will have about their audience is that they are avid and typical readers of the given magazine. Pay particular attention to the types of articles published in the magazine, the advertisements, the photographs or illustrations, the editorial statements, the price of the magazine, and so on.

Appropriate magazines for analysis are *Gentlemen's Quarterly, Movie Life, Ms., Playboy, Playgirl, Scientific American, Field and Stream, Family Circle, Good Housekeeping, Reader's Digest, National Geographic, Modern Bride, Gourmet, Architectural Digest, Christopher Street, Essence, Personal Computing*. Magazines that differ widely from each other are most appropriate for this experience.

After the audience has been analyzed, try to identify at least three favorable and three unfavorable attitudes that they probably hold. On what basis do you make these predictions? If you had to address this audience advocating a position with which they disagreed, what adaptations would you make? That is, what strategies would you use in preparing and presenting this persuasive speech?

Each group should share with the rest of the class the results of their efforts, taking special care to point out not only their conclusions but also the evidence and reasoning they used in arriving at the conclusions.

8.2   ANALYZING YOUR AUDIENCE

Develop an audience analysis questionnaire for your next speech. Specifically, use your questionnaire to secure information about your topic:

1. How much does your audience know about your topic?
2. How interested is your audience in this topic?
3. What are their attitudes or beliefs that may be relevant to your topic?

Well before your next speech, distribute your questionnaire to your future listeners. On the basis of their responses—as well as on the basis of your own analysis of their age; sex; cultural factors; educational and intellectual levels; occupation, income, and status; and religion—identify the ways in which you will adapt your speech to this specific and unique audience.

8.3   ADVISING THE SPEAKER

Imagine yourself a speech advisor to each of the following people who—let's further assume—will address the suudent body of your college on the topics indicated. First, phrase a specific speech purpose on the basis of the topic given here. Second, with that purpose in mind and armed with what you know about the students at your college, what advice would you give the speaker?

1. Dan Quayle on the legacy of the Reagan-Bush administration.
2. Oprah Winfrey on self-esteem.
3. Mel Gibson on the meaning of Shakespeare in today's world.
4. Steven Speilberg on what makes a movie classic.
5. Colin Powell on gays and lesbians in the military.
6. Helen Gurley Brown on your later years.
7. Betty Friedan on the women's movement.
8. Ross Perot on the national economy.
9. Hillary Clinton on the health care system.
10. Janet Reno on crimes against civil rights.

U N I T 9

The Audience: Psychological Analysis and Adaptation

■ ■ ■ ■

UNIT OBJECTIVES

After completing this unit, you should be able to:

1. Explain the five dimensions of an audience

2. Explain how the public speaker might adapt to audiences that differ on the five dimensions

3. Explain at least three guidelines for dealing with a mixed audience

4. Explain the suggestions for analyzing and adapting to the audience during the speech

---

*N*ow that you have a firm grasp on the sociological characteristics of audiences, let's look into some additional ways in which audiences differ. In focusing on these differences, keep in mind the observation of Blaise Pascal: "The more intelligent a man is, the more originality he discovers in men. Ordinary people see no difference between men."

We may view audiences along such scales as those in Figure 9.1. By indicating on each scale where a particular audience is (or where you think it is), you may construct an audience profile. Since each audience is unique, each audience will have a unique profile.

HOW WILLING IS YOUR AUDIENCE?

Audiences gather with varying degrees of willingness to hear a speaker. Some are anxious to hear the speaker and might even pay a substantial admission price. The "lecture circuit," for example, is a most lucrative aspect of public life. Public figures often earn substantially more from speaking than they do from their regular salaries.

While some audiences are willing to pay to hear a speaker, others do not seem to care one way or the other. Still other audiences, not unlike the unwilling guests in the cartoon, need to be persuaded to listen (or at least to sit in the audience). A group of people who gather to hear Shirley MacLaine talk about supernatural experiences are probably there willingly; they want to be there and they want to hear what MacLaine has to say. On the other hand, some groups gather because they have to. For example, the union contract may require members to attend meetings. Administrators may require teachers to attend college and department meetings. These people may not wish to be there, but they do not want to risk losing their jobs or their vote.

Your immediate concern, of course, is with the willingness of your fellow students to listen to your speeches. How willing are they? Do they come to class because they have to or do they come because they are interested in what you'll say? If they are a willing group, then you have few problems. If they are an unwilling group, all is not lost, you just have to work a little harder in adapting your speech.

FIGURE 9.1   The dimensions of an audience.

The Audience

Willing	_____	Unwilling
Favorable	_____	Unfavorable
Passive	_____	Active
Knowledgeable	_____	Not Knowledgeable
Homogeneous	_____	Heterogeneous

**"Now here are some interesting scenes
from my gallbladder operation."**

Courtesy Sieron.

Adapting to the Unwilling Audience

The unwilling audience demands special and delicate handling. Here are a few suggestions to help change your listeners from unwilling to willing.

Secure their interest and attention as early in your speech as possible. Reinforce this throughout the speech by using little-known facts, quotations, startling statistics, examples and illustrations, audiovisual aids, and the like. These devices will help you secure and maintain the attention of an initially unwilling audience. Here, for example, Judith Maxwell (1987), Chair of the Economic Council of Canada, uses humor to gain the interest and attention of her audience. She then quickly connects this humor with the topic of her talk:

> Yogi Berra said something once that's relevant to a discussion of economic forecasting. "If you don't know where you're going, you could wind up somewhere else." Whether we are business economists or economists in the public sector, what society expects from us is advice on how to "know where we are going." Our mission is to help captains of industry or captains of the ship of state plot an orderly path forward. In that sense, we are navigators.

Reward the audience for their attendance and attention. Do this in advance of your main arguments. Let the audience know you are aware they are making a sacrifice in coming to hear you speak. Tell them you appreciate it. One student, giving a speech close to mid-term time, said simply:

> I know how easy it is to cut classes during mid-term time to finish the unread chapters and do everything else you have to do. So I especially appreciate your being here this morning. What I have to say, however, will interest you and will be of direct benefit to all of you.

Once acknowledged, it is difficult for an audience to continue to feel unwilling.

Relate your topic and supporting materials directly to your audience's needs and wants. Show the audience how they can save time, make more money, solve their problems, or become more popular. If you fail to do this, then your audience has a good reason for not listening.

REMEMBER: **If you are faced with an unwilling audience:**
1. **secure their attention as early as possible**
2. **reward the audience for their attendance and attention**
3. **relate your topic and supporting materials to the audience's needs and interests**

▪▪▪▪ HOW FAVORABLE IS YOUR AUDIENCE?

Audiences may or may not agree with your thesis or point of view. One group may be in agreement with your speech advocating comprehensive health insurance while another group may be totally against it. If you intend to change an audience's attitudes, beliefs, or behaviors, you must understand their present position.

Audiences also differ in their attitudes toward you and toward your topic. At times the audience may have no real feeling, positive or negative. At other times they will have very clear feelings that must be confronted. Thus, when Richard Nixon addressed the nation after Watergate, it was impossible to avoid the audience's unfavorable attitude toward him as a person.

Sometimes the degree of favorableness will depend not only on the specific speaker but also on some of the speaker's characteristics. Thus, a group of police officers may resent listening to a convicted felon argue against unlawful search and seizure. On the other hand, they might be quite favorable toward essentially the same speech given by a respected jurist or criminologist.

Similarly, audiences may have favorable or unfavorable responses to you because of your racial or ethnic origin, religion, or social status. Find out, therefore, how the audience sees not only your speech purpose but also you as a speaker. If you conclude that your audience is unfavorable, the following suggestions should help.

Adapting to the Unfavorably Disposed Audience

Build on commonalities; emphasize not the differences but the similarities. Stress what you and the audience share as people, as interested citizens, as fellow students. Theorist and critic Kenneth Burke argues that we achieve persuasion through identification with the audience. Identification involves emphasizing similarities between speaker and audience. When an audience sees similarity or "common ground" between itself and you, it becomes more favorable to both you and your speech.

Here, for example, Alan Nelson (1986) identifies with the city of his audience in his introduction:

> *Returning to the Golden Gate, my home area, reminds me of another harbor and a beautiful statue . . . the Statue of Liberty, which has stood for 100 years in New York Harbor, is being rededicated this year and represents the heritage of America.*

Build your speech from areas of agreement, through areas of slight disagreement, up to the major differences. Always proceed in small steps. Let's say, for example, that you represent management. You wish to persuade employees in your factory to accept a particular wage offer. You might begin with such areas of agreement as the mutual desire for improved working conditions or for economic growth. In any disagreement or argument, there are still areas of agreement; emphasize these.

Strive for small gains. Do not try to convince a pro-life group to contribute money for the new abortion clinic or a pro-choice group to vote against liberalizing abortion laws in a 5-minute speech. Be content to get them to see some validity in your position and to listen fairly. About-face changes take a long time to achieve. To attempt too much persuasion, too much change, can only result in failure or resentment.

REMEMBER: **If you are faced with an unfavorable audience:**
1. build on the similarities you have with the audience
2. build your speech from areas of agreement up to the major differences
3. strive for small gains

HOW ACTIVE IS YOUR AUDIENCE?

Most individuals are active listeners. They do not merely take in the information and use it as we might encourage them. Rather, they work actively with it: they analyze, evaluate, question, and challenge it.

There is, however, another kind of audience—the audience that public speakers dread. This audience simply doesn't care about you, about your speech, or about your position. Its members may be physically present at your speech, but emotionally and intellectually they are somewhere else. These listeners need to be awakened and made to feel concern.

Adapting to the Passive Audience

Show the audience why they should listen to your speech. Show them why they need to be concerned with what you are saying. During your first few minutes, answer your listeners' inevitable questions: Why should I listen? Why should I care about what you are saying? Why should I bother to clutter up my mind with this information, with these arguments? The techniques for gaining attention (Unit 11) and for motivating listeners (Unit 18) should prove helpful with this task.

Involve the audience directly in your speech. Ask questions and pose problems directly to the audience members, pausing so they can consider a response.

Here is how Nadine Jackson-Smith (1988) involved the audience. Notice too how she emphasizes commonalities by identifying with the audience. She began her speech in this way:

> By the power vested in me as your luncheon speaker, I hereby declare each and every one of you to be persons of excellence; persons of high ability, standing conspicuously among the best of your time.
>
> As Oscar Wilde was fond of saying, . . . "I have the simplest of tastes; I am always satisfied with the best."
>
> Good Afternoon.

I am pleased to be here with you today, because it brings back memories of my first real job. I worked as a secretary at the University of Washington and my office was located in the same wing as the Assistant Attorney General for Student Affairs.

Use supporting materials that gain attention and secure interest. Once you get the audience to pay attention, they will begin to listen willingly. They will begin to internalize some of your arguments and information. Be sure to continue to maintain their interest and attention throughout your speech.

Focus on a few (even one) very strong issues. Don't diffuse your energies and time on many issues, none of which may awaken the truly passive audience. You want your audience to stop thinking there is no reason to care, no reason to be concerned. If you give them four or five poorly developed reasons, they may still feel there is no reason to care. If, however, you devote most time to your one strongest argument, it will be difficult for them to continue to be passive.

REMEMBER: **If you are faced with a passive audience:**
1. give your audience reasons why they should listen to your speech
2. involve the audience as directly as possible in your speech
3. use lots of attention-gaining and interest-securing materials
4. focus on the few strongest issues

HOW KNOWLEDGEABLE IS YOUR AUDIENCE?

Listeners differ greatly in the knowledge they have. Some listeners will be quite knowledgeable about the topic, others will be almost totally ignorant. Mixed audiences are the most difficult ones.

If you are unaware of the audience's knowledge level, you will not know what to assume and what to explain. You will not know how much information will overload the channels and how much will bore the audience to sleep.

Perhaps you want to show that their previous knowledge is now inadequate. Perhaps you want to demonstrate a new slant to old issues. Or perhaps you want to show that what you have to say will not repeat but instead will build on the already extensive knowledge of the audience. However you accomplish this, you need to make the audience see that what you have to say is new. Make them realize that you will not simply repeat what they already know.

Adapting to the Knowledgeable and Unknowledgeable Audience

Treat audiences that lack knowledge of the topic very carefully. Never confuse a lack of knowledge with a lack of ability to understand.

Do not talk down to your audience. This is perhaps the greatest communication error that teachers make. After having taught a subject for years, they face, semester after semester, students who have no knowledge of the topic. As a result, many teachers often talk down to the audience and, in the process, lose them. No one wants to listen to a speaker putting them down.

Do not confuse a lack of knowledge with a lack of intelligence. An audience may have no knowledge of your topic but be quite capable of following a clearly presented, logically developed argument. Try especially hard to use concrete examples, audiovisual aids, and simple language. Fill in background details as required. Avoid jargon and specialized terms that may be clear to you but would not be to someone new to the subject.

As a teacher and speaker I find it useful to keep in mind a simple (perhaps overly simple) warning: Never overestimate your audience's knowledge but never underestimate their intelligence.

Let the audience know that you are aware of their knowledge and expertise. Try to do this as early in the speech as possible. Audiences with much knowledge also require special handling because their response may well be, "Why should I listen to this? I already know about this topic." Emphasize that what you have to say will not be redundant. Tell them that you will be presenting recent developments or new approaches. In short, let them know that they will not be wasting their time listening to your speech.

Emphasize your credibility, especially your competence in this general subject area (see Unit 19). Let the audience know that you have earned the right to speak. Let them know that what you have to say is based on a firm grasp of the material.

Here, for example, Richard Colino (1986) establishes his credibility early in his speech:

> *I'm pleased to be here today to discuss the impact of the Information Age on national policies—a subject which merits more analysis and debate than it gets. I'm the Director General and Chief Executive of the International Telecommunications Satellite Organization, better known as INTELSAT. However, my commentary on a series of issues and themes today represents my personal, rather than official IN-TELSAT, views.*

REMEMBER: When adapting to the unknowledgeable audience:
1. avoid talking down to them (or to any audience)
2. do not confuse a lack of knowledge with a lack of intelligence

and when adapting to the knowledgeable audience:
3. let the audience know that you are aware of their expertise
4. emphasize your credibility

HOW HOMOGENEOUS IS YOUR AUDIENCE?

Audiences vary in homogeneity—the degree to which they have similar characteristics, values, attitudes, knowledge, and so on. Homogeneous audiences consist of individuals who are very much alike; heterogeneous audiences consist of widely different individuals.

Obviously, it is easier to address a homogeneous group than a heterogeneous group. If your listeners are alike, your arguments will be as effective for one as for an-

"Eleven hamburgers, one frank. Eleven coffees, one
tea. Eleven apple pies, one chocolate cake. . . . "

Courtesy Sieron.

other. The language appropriate for one will be appropriate for another, and so on, through all the elements of the public speaking transaction.

With a heterogeneous group, however, this does not apply. The argument that works with one subgroup will not necessarily work with another. The language that is appropriate for the educated members will not be appropriate for the uneducated, so when you address a heterogeneous audience you will have to make some tough decisions.

Homogeneity-heterogeneity also relates to the four adapting guidelines just considered. Thus, audience homogeneity-heterogeneity applies to their willingness to listen, their favorableness, their passivity, and their knowledge. For example some audiences will be extremely similar (homogeneous) in their willingness to listen; others may contain members who differ widely in their willingness to listen.

Adapting to the Heterogeneous Audience

The most difficult audience to address is not the unwilling or the unfavorable or the unknowledgeable. It is the mixed audience: the audience consisting of some who care and some who don't, of some who know and some who don't. At times, addressing this type of audience will seem an impossibility. It isn't, so don't despair. Teachers face this type of audience every day, as do politicians and advertisers. Some general principles (rather than specific adaptation guidelines) for dealing with the heterogeneous audience follow. These should help you in this difficult but not impossible task.

The greater the homogeneity of the audience, the easier will be your analysis and adaptation. There will also be less chance of making serious mistakes as a speaker. Consider an audience whose members are all middle-aged men working in nonunion sweat shops, earning the minimum wage. They all share the same religious and cultural backgrounds and they all have less than an eighth-grade education. This audience is homogeneous. The members share a number of important characteristics so it will be relatively easy to analyze and adapt to them.

On the other hand, a heterogeneous audience will require a much more complex audience analysis and a much more careful plan of adaptation. Consider, for example, a PTA audience composed of parents, differing widely in income, education, and cultural background, and teachers, differing widely in background, training, and age. Each of these groups will have different points of view, backgrounds, and expectations. As a speaker you will have to recognize these differences and take special care to appeal to all groups.

When the audience is too heterogeneous, it is sometimes helpful to subdivide it and appeal to each section separately. A common example is the audience consisting of men and women. Say the topic is abortion on demand. To limit yourself to arguments that would appeal equally to men and women might seriously damage your case. Consider, therefore, concentrating first on arguments that women can relate to

Here George Stephanopoulos, President Bill Clinton's first communications director, holds a press conference. How would you characterize the political press conference in terms of willingness, favorableness, activity, knowledge, and homogeneity? Would a type of simulated press conference (in which you answered questions on your topic rather than give a formal speech) be a useful additional educational experience for you? What skills would it enhance?

and then on those to which men can relate. You thus avoid using supporting materials that fall in between the groups and that are effective with neither.

Homogeneity does not equal attitudinal sameness. The audience that is similar in age, sex, educational background, and so on, will probably also share similar attitudes and beliefs. However, this is not always true. Heterogeneity increases with the size of the group. As any group expands in size, its characteristics become more diverse—keep this in mind when you are analyzing your audiences.

REMEMBER: When faced with a heterogeneous audience:

1. give special attention to analyzing the differences among heterogeneous listeners
2. consider appealing to each of the major groups within the audience separately
3. do not assume that homogeneous listeners will all have the same attitudes and values

ANALYSIS AND ADAPTATION DURING THE SPEECH

In your classroom speeches, you will face a known audience, an audience you have already analyzed and for which you have made appropriate adaptations. At other times, however, you may face an audience that you not been able to analyze beforehand or one that differs greatly from the audience you thought you would address. In these cases you will have to analyze and adapt to them as you speak. Here are some suggestions for making this process easy and effective.

Ask "What If" Questions

As you prepare your speech, you will have your anticipated audience clearly in mind. For example, let us say you have been told that you are to explain the opportunities available to the nontraditional student at your college. You have been told that your audience will consist mainly of working women in their 30s and 40s who are just beginning college. As you prepare your speech with this audience in mind, ask yourself, for example:

- what if the audience has a large number of men?
- what if the audience consisted of women much older than 40?
- what if the audience members also came with their spouses or their children?

As you prepare your speech with these "what if" questions in mind, you will force yourself to consider alternatives and will find them readily available when or if you face this new or different audience.

Speak Extemporaneously

As explained in detail in Unit 23, when you speak extemporaneously, you prepare your delivery outline (see Unit 12) to include your main assertions and your supporting materials in the order in which they will be presented. However, avoid memorizing your speech or committing yourself to any exact wording. This method provides you with the flexibility to delete examples that may be inappropriate or to add examples that may be more relevant to this new audience. If you memorize your speech, you will find it impossible to make these essential last-minute adjustments.

Do Extra

The more preparation you put into your speech, the better prepared you will be to make on-the-spot adjustments and adaptations. For example, if you anticipate a knowledgeable audience you may decide not to include background material or definitions in your speech. But, you should have these ready just in case you discover that your listeners are not as knowledgeable as you thought. The more alternatives you consider as you prepare your speech, the more alternatives you will have available as you deliver your speech.

Focus on Listeners as Message Senders

This is an obvious suggestion but one which many speakers ignore. As you are speaking, look at your listeners. Remember that public speaking is a transactional process; just as you are sending messages to your audience, they are also sending messages to you. Just as they are responding to what you are communicating, you need to respond to what they are communicating. Pay attention to these messages and on the basis of what these "tell" you, make the necessary adjustments.

If your listeners are talking among themselves or reading their newspapers, then it should be clear that they are not paying attention and that you have to do something to win them back, but not all audience behaviors are so obvious. Wanda Vassallo, in the accompanying tip, offers a wide variety of suggestions that you may wish to look for. These are more subtle behaviors and their meanings are harder to decode. You may wish to use Vassallo's suggestions as starting points, but remember that any bit of nonverbal behavior may mean many different things. Thus, "folding arms across chest" *may* mean that your listener is closed or hostile, but there are occasions when it may mean something totally different.

There are a wide variety of adjustments that could be made to each type of audience response. A few suggestions are presented to start you thinking. For example, if your audience shows signs of boredom, you might increase your volume, move closer to them, or tell them that what you are going to say will be of value to them. If your audience shows signs of disagreement or hostility, you might stress some similarity or commonality you have with them. If your audience looks puzzled or confused, you might pause a moment and rephrase your ideas, provide necessary definitions, or insert an internal summary. If your audience seems impatient, you might say, for example, "my last argument. . . ," instead of your originally planned "my third argument. . . ."

Address Audience Responses Directly

Another way of dealing with such responses is to confront them directly and say to those who disagree, for example:

TIPS FROM PROFESSIONAL SPEAKERS

These are some generally accepted messages listeners give a speaker by what they do.

Folding arms across chest—closed mind or hostile response
Moving chair forward, leaning forward toward speaker—open-mindedness, interest in message
Crossing legs—competitive attitude, opposition
Stroking chin—undecided, contemplating
Open hands—willingness to listen
Hands behind head—taking it all in
Fidgeting, looking around—bored
Swinging foot in circle, tapping foot—bored, impatient
Wrinkled brow—puzzled, contemplating
Wringing hands—nervous, anxious
Twiddling thumbs—bored
Shrugging shoulders—indifference
Gritting teeth—anger
Rolling eyes—disgust
Dropping mouth open—disbelief
Covering mouth with hand—surprise, shock
Biting lip—concentration, thinking
Looking off in distance—indifference, daydreaming
Touching nose with index finger quickly—doubt
Glancing sideways, drawing back—suspicion
Steepling hands—confidence

Wanda Vassallo, speaker, writer, and minister. From *Speaking With Confidence: A Guide for Public Speakers.* Copyright © 1990 by Wanda Vassallo. Reprinted by permission of Betterway Publications, Inc.

I know you disagree with this position but all I ask is that you hear me out and see if this new way of doing things will not simplify your accounting procedures.

Or, to those who seem puzzled, you might say:

I know this plan may seem confusing, but bear with me; it will become clear in a moment.

Or, to those who seem impatient, you might respond:

I know this has been a long day but give me just a few more minutes and you'll be able to save hours recording your accounts.

By responding to your listeners' responses, you acknowledge your audience's needs. You let them know that you hear them, that you are with them, and that you are responding to their very real needs.

REMEMBER: Because speeches need to be adapted to the audience during the actual presentation, you may find it helpful to:

1. ask "what if" questions
2. speak extemporaneously
3. do more than you anticipate is necessary
4. focus on your audience as message senders, not merely message receivers
5. address audience responses directly

A SAMPLE SPEECH WITH ANNOTATIONS

Black History

Rufus L. Billups

Rufus L. Billups, Major General, United States Air Force, delivered this speech at a Black Heritage Week Banquet at Chanute Air Force Base, Illinois, on February 10, 1979. I include this speech here for a number of reasons. First, it is a particularly clear example of the merging together of information and persuasion; in large part the speech is one of information—informing the audience of many things they probably did not know, and yet it is also persuasive—attempting to reinforce and even change various beliefs and attitudes. Most "real-life" speeches are a blend of information and persuasion. Second, I include it because Billups has so effectively mixed specific instances, examples, and illustrations with broad generalizations—a quality that makes a speech interesting to listen to or read, and also memorable. Third, like so many of the speeches included here, this speech raises issues that are significant to all educated citizens. The text is reprinted from *Vital Speeches of the Day* 45 (September 15, 1979): pp. 712–714.

I am delighted to be here, and I am grateful for your invitation to meet and talk with each of you about Black Americans. We are once again observing our National Afro-American Heritage in these United States for the preservation and promotion of ethnic understanding, and we are celebrating Black Heritage Week here at Chanute Air Force Base as a part of that need for complete and total education in the United States Air Force.

Our National theme is "Black History, Torch for the Future."

This popular observance, which has become a feature of American life, was the design and plan of Dr. Carter G. Woodson, a native of New Canton, Virginia, who is revered as the "Father of Black History" in America.

Even before the speech begins, the speaker starts off with considerable credibility. He is a major general in the United States Air Force. He has risen in the military establishment hierarchy to a level far above 99+ percent of the audience; this is his initial credibility. Further, like most of the audience, he is a military man and black, so he shares two extremely important qualities with the audience and he easily identifies with them. More important, they may easily identify with him. Throughout the speech Billups reinforces his credibility through his knowledge of history in general and black history in particular.

Here the speaker gains attention by complimenting the audience (but not overdoing it) and by relating his speech and his presence here to the specific occasion. He indicates that he is pleased with this speaking encounter: "I am delighted . . . ," "I am grateful. . . ."

In 1915, he founded the Association for the Afro-American Life and History. Later, in 1926, he launched the celebration of Black History Week.

Dr. Woodson wanted more than anything for Black persons to appreciate their heritage. He wanted them to know about Black contributions to the development of America. He wanted all Americans to appreciate the Blacks of our great nation.

His efforts were widely supported by schools, churches, clubs and among Blacks, and the movement gradually found support among institutions of other races in America and abroad. Today, the celebration enjoys widespread participation.

In 1978, Afro-American Black History Month received statements of approval from President Jimmy Carter; Governors of nearly all the States; Mayors and Presidents of City Councils of many larger cities in America; and approval from many of the officials in smaller city governments.

The theme this year, "Torch for the Future," was chosen for the celebration to inspire the search for knowledge about Black accomplishments; to inspire the continued search by many Black citizens for their own ethnic roots; and to encourage a period of introspection about ethnic heritage leading to a fuller participation by all people in the American democracy, and in the American dream.

As I look at the situation in America, today, I could make an assumption that many Black Americans would be surprised and elated to learn of the remarkable achievements by Blacks throughout the history of America, and of the world. I, too, have been enlightened over the years, and, consequently, I want very much to share some of that knowledge of our Black people with you at this most appropriate time.

Our great Blacks, past and present, have a history that truly is fascinating and phenomenal. Out of the mists of time has come evidence that the Blacks were prevalent in all of old world culture, and sailed the Indian Ocean from Africa to Japan.

From prehistoric to medieval times, and even later, Black Africans left their mark in India and Melanesia. Nor was the Black race a stranger to Europe. Their blood flowed in the veins of Frenchmen; in King Alexander de Medici of Italy; in professor John Latino of Spain; in Saint Benedict the Moor of Italy; and in painters, sculp-

---

Notice that the speaker stresses the unity of "all Americans." This is a theme that he will return to throughout the speech. He wants the audience, primarily black military men, to see themselves as an integral part of mainstream America.

Here Billups connects "the establishment" with "Black Heritage," a theme that underlies his thesis that blacks should work for advancement within the system, and especially within the military system.

Billups orients the audience to his thesis and general purpose here. Note that he explicitly states his informative purpose: "to share some of that knowledge of our black people. . . ." But he does not explicitly state his persuasive goal: to persuade the audience to develop more pride in black heritage and to work within the system to achieve what other blacks have achieved. This is probably an appropriate strategy because the audience is a predominantly black one, and its members might well be hostile to a black major general stating at the outset that they should work through the system.

Although there are some deviations, the predominant organizational pattern is a temporal one. Billups begins with the earliest times, works quickly up to the 1500s, spends considerable time in the eighteenth century, moves to the present, and concludes by making predictions about the future. Although other organizational patterns (e.g., a topical one) could have been chosen, this temporal pattern seems most appropriate, given Billups's purpose.

tors, and authors like Alexandre Dumas; and in composers like Samuel Taylor Coleridge of England.

European art from ancient Greece through the Renaissance to the Impressionist period reflects clearly how well Europe knew of Black men and women.

African contributions to the Americas from Canada to Argentina have been relatively recent though some go back beyond 400 years. In the light of these realities, we must view Black people as a powerful influence in world exploration and settlement.

On our own American soil, the first recorded instances of Black settlement in the 1500s were connected with early Spanish explorers, the travels of D'Allyon and DeSoto, and in the old world settlement that became Alabama, and the deep south.

Saint Augustine, Florida, oldest city in the United States, owes much to Black men and women in the early 1500s. The Fort, houses, streets, artillery platforms, and the first Smith's Forge were all built by Black skills and craftmanship.

Blacks were much involved in the history of later Spanish settlements, in Portuguese America, in the Hispanic Americas, in Dutch and English settlements, and in the early American-French colonies.

When British rifles fired in 1770 at the Boston Massacre, a Black man, Crispus Attucks, was the first to die for American independence.

At Bunker Hill, in June 1775, the Black hero was Peter Salem, who had also been a crack rifleman at Lexington and Concord.

And, on Christmas, 1776, Oliver Cromwell crossed the Delaware with General Washington and James Monroe, and became one of the first Blacks to attack the British at Trenton.

For the next 200 years, Blacks in America displayed remarkable talents. From the signing of American Independence to the Bicentennial celebration in 1976, and forward, American Black men and women explored, invented, and contributed immensely to the growth and development of this great land of ours. Some of their names and deeds are familiar to us for they excelled in military service, in science and industry, in business enterprise, as leaders and spokesmen and educators, and as writers, playwrights, actors, musicians, and artists.

Today, historic sites, landmarks, monuments and shrines are scattered throughout this nation to commemo-

After providing some specific instances of black contributions and influence on society in general and on specific fields, Billups becomes a bit more direct in stating his thesis: "We must view black people as a powerful influence in world exploration and settlement." From this statement, he later states his thesis directly, then follows with additional specific instances—the settlement of Alabama, the contributions to St. Augustine, and so on.

Observe how these examples—probably unknown to most listeners—help to establish the speaker's credibility.

Notice how the speaker concentrates on examples from the military. Since his purpose is to persuade the audience to work within the system for advancement, his military examples are particularly appropriate. His examples are also appropriate to his own background. As a major general in the U.S. Air Force, military examples carry a great deal more credibility than any others.

rate Black men and women as they achieved, often against fierce adversity, often against overwhelming odds. But, they achieved, and you can be proud of them.

Let me acquaint you perhaps for the first time with some of our great people who rose above the catastrophe of war and learned to make constructive use of peace.

There was James Fortin in the late 1700s. A Philadelphian, abolitionist, and writer. The tide for the Blacks began to turn as he wrote this:

> *Has the God who made the white man and the black man left any record declaring us a different species?*
>
> *Are we not sustained by the same power, supported by the same food, hurt by the same wounds, wounded by the same wrongs, pleased with the same delights, and propagated by the same means?*
>
> *And should we not enjoy the same liberty and be protected by the same laws?*

Later, the "Golden Voice of Abolition," and one of the greatest spokesmen for the Black people in the 1800s, was Frederick A. Douglass.

Then came Harriet Tubman, "The Black Moses of Her Race." Strong as a man, brave as a lion, cunning as a fox, she led her people to freedom in abolition escapes to the north.

And, in that never-to-be-forgotten war between the North and South, Sgt. William H. Carney became the first Black American to win the Congressional Medal of Honor.

From the Civil War forward, through the turn of the century, until today, the reconstruction periods were always quickly followed by a tremendous increase in the discovery and exploration of our nation's resources. Within a span of some 116 years, an impressive 327 Black American inventors gained patents for their original ideas. Everything, and I mean just about everything that you can think of from folding beds, rotary engines, street sprinklers, railway signals, and horse shoes to lawn mowers were invented by Black men and women seeking the unknown.

The list goes on and on, and is truly fascinating.

Elijah McCoy had 57 patents, mostly for large industry; George Washington Carver, the "Savior of Southern Agriculture," searched and found hundreds of ways to make the soil more productive; and Matthew Hensen,

---

Billups uses quotations five times in the speech. Note that in four of the cases he briefly establishes the credibility of the person he quotes. Note that in the last quotation, he does not "explain" Booker T. Washington, on the probably accurate assumption that the audience is aware of his credentials.

Note the use of simile here; these comparisons make Harriet Tubman's strength, bravery, and cunning most vivid.

Note the simplicity of this transition.

polar explorer with Admiral Peary, placed the American flag on the North Pole, 7 April 1909, and is recognized in history as the indispensable Black man for the success of that expedition.

Many other Blacks made their mark during this historical time in America. Ebenezer Bassett became the first American Black diplomat, representing the United States as Minister to Haiti; Augustus Tolton, first Black American to be ordained a Catholic priest in America; Ida B. Wells, famous anti-lynch crusader and woman journalist; and Booker T. Washington, educator, founder of Tuskegee Institute, Alabama. He carried the "Lamp of Learning," and was the first Black to be honored on a U.S. stamp, July 4th, 1881.

It has been said that "When all men know the truth about all men, they will live together in peace."

This was the world that Dr. Martin Luther King wanted. He stood his ground, and could do no other in the struggle against bigotry, injustice, and immorality. Clear vision, courage, and determination were the hallmarks of his life.

Because of the great work that Dr. King did for the Black people of America, and for the work that so many others before him have done, Black men and women in all walks of life have an opportunity to help themselves as never before in history.

Learn to know your Black ancestors and forefathers, know of their achievements, and you will be amazed and inspired by their deeds and their acts of courage and dedication.

Every field of endeavor has a Black champion. Since the early 1600s until today, Black warriors have excelled in wars on this continent and on foreign soil.

Many Blacks earned medals in World War[s] One and Two, Korea, and Southeast Asia. Some received Medals of Honor, and all were gallant, and gifted Black Americans.

Today, the current situation for Black Americans in the military and in our society is clearly one of total recognition for all. No longer will the successes of many be awarded to only a few. An open door to a future of your own choice has been prepared for you by the personal struggles of Black leaders before you.

In this new year, 1979, our United States Air Force and you can be rightfully proud of retired Lieutenant General Benjamin Davis, Jr.; Major Generals Lucius

---

Another simple but appropriate transition.

Note how effectively a group of specific instances can be used to make a point. It would be difficult to better highlight the point that blacks contributed greatly to science. Through this barrage of specific instances we learn and become quite convinced that blacks contributed greatly to the development of this country.

Note the phrasing Billups uses to describe Martin Luther King: "The struggle against bigotry, injustice, and immorality"; "clear vision, courage, and determination." These word choices and combinations help to further establish the speaker's competence and to show the wide range of King's concerns. Note the following use of the phrases "Black Champion" and "Black Warrior." These are phrases that seem particularly appropriate for reinforcing racial pride.

Note how Billups orients the audience to what is to follow. Note the directness of the language: "Learn to know. . . ."

Here, the speaker returns to the military field, his area of expertise and the field that both he and the audience are most comfortable with.

Here, Billups states one of his most important arguments, namely, that the situation today is one of equality and fairness. Perhaps recognizing that his audience will expect proof of this, Billups provides this proof throughout the speech in the form of examples and quotations from black leaders, especially military leaders.

Theus, and Thomas E. Clifford; and Brigadier General William E. Brown, Jr.

These are the men who have done much to enhance human dignity in our Air Force. Their work is continuing for we are committed to insuring that every Black American in the Air Force has a worthwhile job that is both challenging and rewarding.

In order to achieve this goal for our minorities, every level of command and supervision is totally involved and is aggressively and continually promoting affirmative steps to improve the utilization and dignity of all our people.

What then lies ahead for young Blacks in our country and in our Air Force? This depends upon each of us as individuals, and the social attitudes we develop and perpetuate for the good of our race. No one is going to hand us a thing that we do not deserve. History has revealed that. We will have to earn our future, step by step as others before us have. But, it will be well worth it. The record shows we can meet the challenge, for we have become more and more a successful people.

One of the most inspiring Air Force leaders who believed in the future of young Black Americans was the late General Daniel "Chappie" James, the fourth Black General in American History—and the first to wear four stars.

Listen now to a man who loved America, and his people.

> *This is my country, and I believe in her, and I believe in her flag, and I'll defend her, and I'll fight for her and hold her hand until in God's given time, through her wisdom and consideration for the welfare of the entire nation, she rights the wrongs of the past generations.*

America is a nation of some 25 million Blacks, the third largest number of Blacks within a nation anywhere in the world.

We are also the most highly developed Black people in the world with approximately 7,500 physicians, some 2,700 dentists, over 4,000 attorneys, and thousands of public school teachers. We are an academic, learned, scholarly people, today, in 1979, and we are a family-loving, nation-loving race, a happy people.

Black Americans are the ninth wealthiest race in the noncommunist world. In the early 1970s, for example,

A useful preview sentence that helps to orient the audience to what follows.

Notice how Billups inoculates his audience, answering possible objections that may be raised to his thesis. He provides the audience with appropriate responses to these potential objections: "No one is going to hand us a thing that we do not deserve. . . ." To the potential objections: that blacks have not contributed sufficiently to society, he says: "We are also the most highly developed Black people in the world . . ." and that "Black Americans are the ninth wealthiest race in the noncommunist world . . . ."

Billups does not elaborate on these figures. Is 7,500 physicians a lot? It is difficult to say without knowing what percentage these numbers represent. And although $51.8 billion and $46 billion are impressive figures, their meaning is not clear without comparable figures for other groups. Here, it seems, Billups could have used more supporting materials. It is impossible to determine whether the audience also questioned the meaningfulness of these figures.

Blacks earned $51.8 billion dollars, spent some $46 billion, and generated more than $900 million in advertising and public relations.

These figures are growing each year, and could be staggering by the 1980s.

Another statistic: approximately 50 percent of Black Americans are 20 years old or younger. Now, that condition concerns you and your future. Hear how Air Force General David C. Jones, Chairman of the Joint Chiefs of Staff feels about you:

All our people must have a sense of belonging, and be made aware that they are our most important resource.

Hear, too, how Air Force Major General Lucius Theus feels about your future:

In the Air Force, human goals are established to make the Air Force a model of equitable, fair treatment for all its people. These goals carry the highest priority.

These priorities will succeed for you and for me if we remember our responsibility to our Country—to America. As Black Americans, we must recognize how others are attempting to right the wrongs and improve our way of life. For that we should be grateful and pay our dues, and help make it work. One of the best ways for you to show your goodwill and be an asset to your country is to have faith in your American society, and in your Air Force. Everything and everyone in your life will work out better if you do.

But make no mistake, it has not been easy to reach this time and place in our American way of life. Hard work and determination have preceded you and your place here today. Look around our country and see the changes. Black men and women, alive and prominent in our society are voicing their opinions, are making today's Black history, and are building a better life for you and for all Black Americans.

The world acknowledges these talented people: Andrew Young, Ambassador to the United Nations since 1977; Thurgood Marshall, Associate Justice to the Supreme Court with Honorary Degrees from all over the world; Julian Bond, renowned Georgian Senator; Patricia Harris, Law Professor, Harvard University; Shirley Chisholm, influential Congresswoman; and Coretta King, President of the Martin Luther King Memorial Center,

Notice how Billups identifies with the audience. Throughout his speech he uses "we," "us," and "our," emphasizing his connection with the audience members and the audience's identification with him—a black who has worked his way to the top within the system.

Here, Billups answers the potential objection that the "system" does not work for blacks: "As Black Americans, we must recognize how others are attempting to right the wrongs. . . ." He further supports this contention by noting specific instances of blacks who have made it and who are now influential parts of the system, as is Billups himself.

active in civil rights, and a Black woman of many talents. All are famous Black Americans of our time.

A long time ago, another Black spokesman had this to say to the people of his time, and I feel for your time, and for all time:

> *I believe that you who are heirs of the opportunities, the culture, and the wealth of the ages; you who have humanity and justice; you who love our glorious country will recognize that you have a chance to be trained, a chance to be educated, a chance to be efficient, a chance to be useful to your race and country, a chance to be decent, a chance to serve.*

That was Booker T. Washington.

And, so, I say to all of you fine young people here with me today, have respect for yourselves! Be understanding of others of all races who reach out for your friendship. Maintain integrity, and perform in a professional manner no matter how complex and demanding your career-field in the Air Force.

I want each of you to remember that there is a chance for you. You can earn respect, and the more difficulties you overcome, the greater will be your success.

I say to you the time is now to look ahead, to strive for individual achievement, but to maintain your true identity. You are following in the footsteps of many gone before you who gave much that you might have a chance in your lifetime, and in the lifetime of your children.

I say to you, hold your head high, be proud and confident of your future, try to attain higher educational goals, and make use of your opportunities on behalf of yourselves, your forefathers, and those who will follow you in times to come.

And, I say to you, above all, have pride in your heritage, pride in your country, pride in yourself, and pride in your United States Air Force.

Thank you.

Complimenting the audience ("all of you fine young people") seems to work best when it is not overdone. A simple, honest compliment (as in this Billups example) seems universally appreciated by audiences.

Note the effectiveness of the parallel structure, "I say to you. . . ." in these last few paragraphs. This phrase also signals that the speaker is nearing the conclusion. In these last three paragraphs Billups restates his major thesis and attempts to motivate the audience to act on what he has said.

CRITICALLY SPEAKING

1. What other psychological factors might have been included in this unit?
2. How would you analyze your class in terms of their willingness, favorableness, activity, and knowledge for your next speech? What possible adaptations can you make that will take these factors into consideration?

3. How heterogeneous is your class in terms of age? Sex? Culture? Educational and intellectual levels? Occupation, income, and status? Religion? What problems might this heterogeneity pose for your next speech?

4. How heterogeneous is your class in terms of their willingness to listen? Their favorableness to your topic? To you? Their activity or passivity? Their knowledge of your topic?

5. Can you identify any adaptations that speakers made during the speeches so far this semester? Were they effective? Were there additional opportunities for such adaptations that were not made?

6. How important is adapting to your audience during your speech? How important is this on-the-spot adaptation in teaching?

7. What other suggestions would you offer for during-the-speech analysis and adaptation?

PRACTICALLY SPEAKING

9.1 IDENTIFYING AUDIENCE ATTITUDES

This exercise will enable you to deal with some of the issues involved in audience analysis and adaptation. Try to predict the attitudes of your class members toward each of the following propositions by indicating how you think the majority of the class members feel about each. Record the number of the attitude you predict the majority of the members hold. Use the following scale:

1 = strongly in favor of the proposition as stated
2 = mildly in favor of the proposition as stated
3 = neutral
4 = mildly against the proposition as stated
5 = strongly against the proposition as stated

After you have completed the predictions for all propositions, select one that you predicted the audience to be "strongly against" and indicate what kinds of adaptations you would make to get your audience to accept the proposition or at least to feel more positively toward it than they do now.

After all persons have completed both parts of this experience, the class as a whole or in small groups should discuss the following issues:

■ the accuracy-inaccuracy with which the various attitudes were predicted
■ the possible sources for the inaccurate and the accurate guesses
■ the appropriateness-inappropriateness of the adaptations proposed

1. Marijuana should be legalized for all persons over 18.
2. All required courses (general education requirements) should be abolished.
3. Parochial elementary and high schools should be tax supported.

4. X-rated movies (even XXX movies) should be shown on television without time restrictions.

5. Prostitution (male and female) should be legalized.

6. Puerto Rico should be made the fifty-first state.

7. Members of minority groups that have been discriminated against should be given preferential treatment in entrance into graduate and professional schools.

8. Homosexuals should be allowed to be teachers, fire fighters, and police officers without any restrictions based on affectional preference.

9. Mandatory retirement should be abolished.

10. Tenure for college teachers should be eliminated.

9.2   PREDICTING LISTENERS' ATTITUDES

Described below are six public speaking situations. Each student should analyze the audience based on the five dimensions identified in this unit, then complete a set of scales (such as that presented in Figure 9.1) for each of the six situations. On the basis of this analysis, what one suggestion would you give the speaker to help her or him better adapt the speech to this audience?

In small groups or with the class as a whole, be prepared to give reasons for your decisions and to discuss your one major bit of advice for each of the six speakers.

1. film students listening to George Lucas discuss the filming of the *Star Wars* movies

2. high school athletes listening to a college athletic director speaking against sports scholarships

3. pregnant women listening to an advertising agency executive speak on how advertisers try to protect the consumer

4. office managers listening to an organizational communication consultant speaking on ways to increase employee morale and productivity

5. your class listening to a famous actor speaking in favor of supporting the Will Rogers Institute

6. Chicago high school seniors listening to a college recruiter speak on the advantages of a small rural college

■ PART TWO CHECKLISTS

Performance Checklist: Evaluating Your Subject and Audience Analysis

YES   NO   Have you:

☐   ☐   1. Selected a topic that is worthwhile, appropriate, and limited in scope?

☐   ☐   2. Selected a purpose that is limited to one main issue, phrased in precise terms, and capable of being accomplished?

☐   ☐   3. Selected a thesis that is clear and specific and limited to one central idea?

☐   ☐   4. Thoroughly researched your topic?

☐   ☐   5. Integrated the research into your speech?

☐   ☐   6. Analyzed your audience in terms of its dominant age; sex; cultural factors; education and intellectual levels; occupation, income, and status; religion; and such other factors as expectations, special interests, and organizational memberships?

☐   ☐   7. Built in adjustments on the basis of this analysis?

☐   ☐   8. Analyzed the public speaking context for size, physical environment, occasion, and time?

☐   ☐   9. Built in adjustments on the basis of this context analysis?

☐   ☐   10. Analyzed your audience in terms of its willingness to hear you, favorableness to you and your position, active or passive attitude, knowledge about your topic, and homogeneity?

☐   ☐   11. Built in adjustments on the basis of this analysis?

☐   ☐   12. Considered ways of dealing with any adaptations that would be necessary during the speech, for example, ask "what if" questions, speak extemporaneously, prepare more than usually necessary, focus on your audience as message senders, and consider addressing audience responses directly?

Critical Thinking Checklist: Thinking Critically About Subjects and Audiences

YES   **NO**   Do you:

☐   ☐   1. Distinguish among worthwhile and insignificant topics and issues (Unit 6)?

☐   ☐   2. Analyze a topic into its component parts (Unit 6)?

☐   ☐   3. Generate the major issues from a thesis or assertion by asking strategic questions (Unit 6)?

☐   ☐   4. Research a wide variety of topics, using traditional sources as well as the newest in computer search techniques (Unit 7)?

☐   ☐   5. Evaluate research in terms of its validity and application to a specific issue (Unit 7)?

☐   ☐   6. Analyze an audience in terms of its demographic characteristics such as age, sex, and culture, in order to predict their attitudes and beliefs from this analysis, and to adapt a message to them (Unit 8)?

☐   ☐   7. Analyze the context in which a communication is to take place and to adapt the message on the basis of this analysis (Unit 8)?

☐   ☐   8. Analyze a variety of "what if" situations and plan ahead to deal with these as they arise (Unit 8)?

☐   ☐   9. Analyze an audience in terms of its attitudes and predispositions and make necessary adaptations (Unit 9)?

PART THREE

Elements of Organization

Part Three explores ways of organizing the speech. Much like an essay or composition, the speech has to be organized if it is to communicate your meaning. Useful ways of organizing the body of your speech (Unit 10), constructing the introduction and conclusion (Unit 11), and inserting transitions and internal summaries to hold the speech together (Unit 11) will be explained.

As you develop and organize your speech, you'll be outlining it so that you'll be able to see how the pieces fit together, what needs additional work, and what seems to work well. Also explained is how to write a delivery outline, the brief outline that you use when delivering your speech to your audience (Unit 12).

In **thinking critically** about organization and outlining, try to:

- use organization as a guide for communicating information so that it can be more easily understood and remembered but also as a strategic method for persuasion
- apply the strategies of organization to interpersonal and small group situations as well as in written communications
- view organizational patterns and strategies as heavily influenced by culture; the functions of the introduction and conclusion, for example, will vary from one culture to another

New plant saf
economic impacts
Engineering
Cost analysis
Cost allocat
vironmental
Environmental testing procedures –
1. Air quality
2. Water quality
3. Solid waste

U N I T 10

The Body of the Speech

■ ■ ■ ■

UNIT OBJECTIVES

After completing this unit, you should be able to:

1. Explain how major propositions are selected and worded

2. Distinguish between coordination and subordination

3. Identify the major thought patterns (temporal, spatial, topical, problem-solution, cause-effect, and motivated sequence) and suitable topics for each

4. Explain the suggestions offered concerning climax-anticlimax orders and primacy-recency

---

*I*n developing the body of your speech, you select your major propositions and organize them in some meaningful way.

■■■■ MAJOR PROPOSITIONS

The major propositions are your principal assertions, your main points. If your speech were a play, the propositions would be its acts. Let's consider how to select and word these propositions and how they may be related to each other.

Selecting and Wording Propositions

In discussing the thesis (Unit 6), you saw how you can develop your main points or propositions by asking strategic questions. To see how this works in detail, imagine that you are giving a speech to a group of high school students on the values of a college education. Your thesis is: "A college education is valuable." You then ask, "Why is it valuable?" From this question you generate your major propositions. Your first step might be to brainstorm this question and generate as many answers as possible without evaluating them. You may come up with answers such as the following:

1. It helps you get a good job.
2. It increases your earning potential.
3. It gives you greater job mobility.
4. It helps you secure more creative work.
5. It helps you to appreciate the arts more fully.
6. It helps you to understand an extremely complex world.
7. It helps you understand different cultures.
8. It allows you to avoid taking a regular job for a few years.
9. It helps you meet lots of people and make new friends.
10. It helps you increase your personal effectiveness.

There are, of course, other possibilities, but for purposes of illustration, these 10 possible main points will suffice. But not all 10 are equally valuable or relevant to your audience, so you should look over the list to see how to make it shorter and more meaningful. Try these suggestions:

1. Eliminate those points that seem least important to your thesis. On this basis you might want to eliminate No. 8 since this seems least consistent with your intended emphasis on the positive values of college.

2. Combine those points that have a common focus. Notice, for example, that the first four points all center on the values of college in terms of jobs. You might, therefore, consider grouping these four items into one proposition:

A college education helps you get a good job.

This point might be one of the major propositions that could be developed by defining what you mean by a "good job." This main point or proposition and its elaboration might look like this:

I. A college education helps you get a good job.

    A. College graduates earn higher salaries.

    B. College graduates enter more creative jobs.

    C. College graduates have greater job mobility.

    Note that A, B, and C are all aspects or subdivisions of a "good job."

3. Select points that are most relevant to or that interest your audience. On this basis you might eliminate No. 5 and No. 7 on the assumption that the audience will not see learning about the arts or different cultures as exciting or valuable at the present time. You might also decide that high school students would be more interested in increasing personal effectiveness, so you might select No. 10 for inclusion as a second major proposition:

A college education increases your personal effectiveness.

Earlier you developed the subordinate points in your first proposition (the A, B, and C of I) by defining more clearly what you meant by a "good job." Follow the same process here by defining what you mean by "personal effectiveness." It might look something like this:

I. A college education helps increase your personal effectiveness.

    A. A college education helps you improve your ability to communicate.

    B. A college education helps you acquire the skills for learning how to think.

    C. A college education helps you acquire coping skills.

Follow the same procedure you used to generate the subordinate points (A, B, and C) to develop the subheadings under A, B, and C. For example, point A might be divided into two major subheads:

A. A college education helps improve your ability to communicate.

    1. College improves your writing skills.

    2. College improves your speech skills.

Develop points B and C in essentially the same way by defining more clearly (in B) what you mean by "learning how to think" and (in C) what you mean by "coping skills."

    Some Added Guidelines Now that the general process of identifying and developing your main points is understood, here are a few additional guidelines.

1. Use two, three, or four main points. For your class speeches, which will generally range from 5 to 15 minutes, use two, three, or four main propositions. Too many main points will result in a speech that is confusing, contains too much information and too little amplification, and proves difficult to remember.

2. Word each of your major propositions in the same (parallel) style. Phrase points labeled with Roman numerals in a similar style. Likewise, phrase points labeled with capital letters and subordinate to the same Roman numeral (for example, A, B, and C under point I or A, B, and C under point II) in a similar style. Parallel style is used in the example on college education.

This parallel styling helps the audience follow and remember your speech. Notice in the following that the first outline is more difficult to understand than the second, which is phrased in parallel style.

Not This:

Mass Media Functions

I. The media entertain.

II. The media function to inform their audiences.

III. Creating ties of union is a major media function.

IV. The conferral of status is a function of all media.

This:

Mass Media Functions

I. The media entertain.

II. The media inform.

III. The media create ties of union.

IV. The media confer status.

3. Develop your main points so they are separate and discrete. Do not allow your main points to overlap each other. Each section labeled with a Roman numeral should be a separate entity.

Not This:

I. Color and style are important in clothing selection.

This:

I. Color is important in clothing selection.

II. Style is important in clothing selection.

4. Use the principle of balance. Devote about equal time to each of your main points. A useful rule of thumb is to give about equal time to each item having the same symbol in your outline. Give each Roman numeral about equal time, each item denoted by a capital letter about the same amount of time, and so on. Break this rule only when you have an especially good reason.

REMEMBER: Generate your propositions—your major assertions and ideas—by asking strategic questions of your thesis. In selecting the propositions for development in your speech:

1. select those that are most important to your thesis
2. combine those points that have a common focus
3. select those that are most relevant to your audience

Your speech will be most effective when:

4. propositions are few in number (two, three, or four work best)
5. propositions are phrased in parallel style
6. propositions are separate and discrete items
7. propositions are each developed with about equal emphasis

Coordination and Subordination

Central to a well-organized speech is the logical coordination and subordination of your assertions and supporting materials. Focus on the following partial outline dealing with two areas of study, some specific courses, and some areas covered in these courses (Table 10.1). This outline is *not* intended to illustrate how a speech outline would look, but only to illustrate coordination and subordination.

Coordination Focus first on the two major headings: *psychology* and *sociology*. In the outline in Table 10.1 they are equal and parallel. They are *coordinate* items. Within the *psychology* heading there are other coordinate items. *Learning* and *motivation* are coordinate; they represent two specific courses taught in psychology departments. The course in learning covers *classical conditioning* and *operant conditioning*, again coordinate items. *Development* and *current status* are likewise coordinate; they are two topics covered in each of the different theories. The same is true of the *sociology* outline.

Note that the coordinate items of *psychology* and *sociology* both are given Roman numerals (I and II), the major courses capital letters (A and B), and the specific theories Arabic numerals (1 and 2).

Subordination Two items of information are *subordinate* when they are related in such a way that one item is a part of, supports, or amplifies the other. For example, *learning* and *motivation* are two courses that are part of *psychology* and, hence, are subordinate to *psychology*. *Classical conditioning* and *operant conditioning* are types of *learning* and as such are subordinate to *learning*. Similarly, *cognitive* and *instinct* theories are subordinate to *motivation* in the same way that *prejudice* and *crime* are subordinate to *sociology*.

Note that items that are immediately subordinate to another item are given symbols of one order lower: items subordinate to Roman numeral items are given capital letters; items subordinate to Arabic numeral items are given small letters; and so on. There is nothing magical about the hierarchy of this symbol system; it is simply the customary, agreed-on system.

TABLE 10.1 **AN OUTLINE ILLUSTRATING COORDINATION AND SUBORDINATION**

I. Psychology
   A. Learning
      1. Classical conditioning
         a. Development
         b. Current status
      2. Operant conditioning
         a. Development
         b. Current status
   B. Motivation
      1. Cognitive theories
         a. Development
         b. Current status
      2. Instinct theories
         a. Development
         b. Current status
II. Sociology
   A. Prejudice
      1. Instinct theories
         a. Development
         b. Current status
      2. Learning theories
         a. Development
         b. Current status
   B. Crime
      1. Instinct theories
         a. Development
         b. Current status
      2. Learning theories
         a. Development
         b. Current status

REMEMBER:

1. coordinate items are equal in value and are given the same outline symbol
2. subordinate items are related such that the subordinate item is a part of, supports, or amplifies the other

ORGANIZATIONAL PATTERNS

Once you have identified the major propositions you wish to include in your speech, you need to devote attention to how you will arrange these propositions in the body of your speech. When you follow a clearly identified organizational pattern, your listeners will be able to see your speech as a whole and will be able to see more clearly the connections and relationships among your various pieces of information. Should they have a momentary lapse in attention—as they surely will at some point in just about every

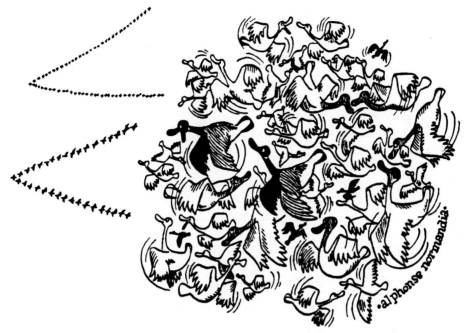

"There are times when I wish we had a somewhat stronger organization."

Courtesy Alphonse Normandia.

speech—they will be able to refocus their attention and not lose your entire train of thought.

Consider each pattern in terms of the topics to which it is most applicable and the ways in which you can arrange your main points and supporting materials. The introduction, conclusion, and transitions are considered in depth in Unit 11. The mechanical aspects of outlining and additional guidance in preparing the outline are presented in Unit 12.

Temporal Pattern

Organizing your propositions on the basis of some temporal (time) relationship is a popular and easy-to-use organizational pattern. It is also a pattern that listeners will find easy to follow. Generally, when you use this pattern, you organize your speech into two, three, or four major parts, beginning with the past and working up to the present or the future, or beginning with the present or the future and working back to the past.

The temporal (sometimes called "chronological") pattern is especially appropriate for informative speeches in which you wish to describe events or processes that occur over time. It is also useful when you wish to demonstrate how something works or how to do something.

A speech on the development of language in the child might be organized in a temporal pattern and could be divided something like this:

■ ■ ■ ■

TIPS FROM PROFESSIONAL SPEAKERS

One of the best-kept secrets of successful professional speakers is this: *Get your speech organized very clearly—in a few very specific, precise points—and it's much more likely that your audience will get your message.*

Failure to know—or use—that secret is usually the main reason so many speeches are forgotten so quickly.

A speech MUST be designed in a structure that's easy-to-follow, *if* it's to achieve its purpose—to get your listeners to accept your ideas, remember what you say, and take the action you want.

Leon Fletcher, teacher, author, and speaker. *How to Speak Like a Pro* (New York: Ballantine, 1983), p. 61.

The Development of Language

   I. Babbling occurs around the fifth month.

  II. Lallation occurs around the sixth month.

 III. Echolalia occurs around the ninth month.

 IV. "Communication" occurs around the twelfth month.

Here you would cover each of the events in a time sequence beginning with the earliest stage and working up to the final stage—in this case the stage of true communication.

Most historical topics lend themselves to organization by time. The events leading up to the Civil War, the steps toward a college education, or the history of writing would all be appropriate for temporal patterning. A time pattern would also be appropriate in describing the essential steps in a multistep process in which temporal order is especially important. The steps involved in making interpersonal contact with another person might look something like this:

Making Interpersonal Contact

   I. Spot the person you want to make contact with.

  II. Make eye contact.

 III. Give some positive nonverbal sign.

 IV. Make verbal contact.

Spatial Pattern

You can also organize your main points on the basis of space. This pattern is especially useful when you wish to describe objects or places. Like the temporal pattern, it is an organizational pattern that listeners will find easy to follow as you progress, from top to bottom, left to right, inside to outside, or from east to west, for example.

Geographical topics generally fit well into organization by spatial patterning. For example, for a speech on places to visit in southern Europe, you might go from west to east, considering the countries to visit and, within these countries, the cities. The main headings of such a speech might look like this:

Touring Southern Europe

  I. Your first stop is Portugal.

 II. Your second stop is Spain.

III. Your third stop is Italy.

IV. Your fourth stop is Greece.

Similarly, the structure of a place, object, or even animal is easily placed into a spatial pattern. You might describe the layout of a hospital, school, skyscraper, or perhaps even the structure of a dinosaur with a spatial pattern of organization.

Topical Pattern

Perhaps the most popular pattern for organizing informative speeches is the topical pattern. When your topic conveniently divides itself into subdivisions, each of which is clear and approximately equal in importance, this pattern is most useful. It is not, however, a catch-all category for topics that do not seem to fit into any of the other patterns. Rather, this pattern should be regarded as one appropriate to the particular topic being considered. For example, the topical pattern is an obvious one for organizing a speech on the powers of the government. Here the divisions are clear:

The Powers of Government

  I. The legislative branch is controlled by Congress.

 II. The executive branch is controlled by the president.

III. The judicial branch is controlled by the courts.

Note that the topic itself, the powers of the government, divides itself into three parts: legislative, executive, and judicial. It remains for you to organize your various materials under these three logical headings.

A speech on the forms of communication would most likely be organized around a topical pattern. It would look something like this:

Forms of Communication

  I. Intrapersonal communication occurs within oneself.

 II. Interpersonal communication occurs between two people.

III. Public communication occurs between speaker and audience.

IV. Mass communication occurs through some audio or visual transmitter.

A speech on important cities of the world might be organized into a topical pattern, as might speeches on problems facing the college graduate, great works of literature, the world's major religions, and the like. Each of these topics would have several subtopics or divisions of approximately equal importance; consequently, a topical pattern seems most appropriate.

Problem-Solution Pattern

The problem-solution pattern is especially useful in persuasive speeches where you want to convince the audience that a problem exists and that your solution would solve or alleviate the problem.

Let's say you are attempting to persuade an audience that teachers should be given higher salaries and increased benefits. Here a problem-solution pattern might be appropriate. You might, for example, discuss in the first part of the speech the problems confronting contemporary education such as (1) industry lures away the most highly qualified graduates, (2) many excellent teachers leave the field after two or three years, and (3) teaching is currently a low-status occupation.

In the second part of your speech you might consider the possible solutions that you wish your audience to accept. These might include, for example: (1) salaries for teachers must be made competitive with salaries offered by private industry, and (2) the benefits teachers receive must be made as attractive as those offered by industry. Your speech, in outline form, might look like this:

I. Three major problems confront elementary education.

   A. Industry lures away the most qualified graduates.

   B. Numerous excellent teachers leave the field after two or three years.

   C. Teaching is currently a low-status occupation.

II. Two major solutions to these problems exist.

   A. Salaries for teachers should be increased.

   B. Benefits for teachers should be made more attractive.

Cause-Effect/Effect-Cause Pattern

Similar to the problem-solution pattern is the cause-effect or effect-cause pattern. This pattern is useful in persuasive speeches in which you want to convince your audience of the causal connection existing between two events or two elements. In the cause-effect pattern you divide the speech into two major sections, causes and effects.

For example, a speech on the reasons for highway accidents or birth defects might lend itself to a cause-effect pattern. Here you might first consider, say, the causes of highway accidents or birth defects and then some of the effects, for example, the number of deaths, the number of accidents, and so on.

A speech on hypertension, designed to spell out some of the causes and effects, might look like this:

I. There are three main causes of hypertension.

   A. High salt intake increases blood pressure.

B. Excess weight increases blood pressure.

C. Anxiety increases blood pressure.

II. There are three major effects of hypertension.

A. Nervousness increases.

B. Heart rate increases.

C. Shortness of breath increases.

The Motivated Sequence

Developed by Alan H. Monroe in the 1930s and widely used in all sorts of oral and written communications, the motivated sequence is a pattern of arranging your information so as to motivate your audience to respond positively to your purpose. In fact, it may be reasonably argued that all effective communications follow this basic pattern whether it is called the motivated sequence or given some other name.

As you will see, the motivated sequence is especially appropriate for speeches designed to move an audience to action (to persuade your listeners to do something). However, it is also useful for a wide variety of informative speeches.

The previous organizational patterns provided ways of organizing the main ideas in the body of the speech. The motivated sequence is a pattern for organizing the entire speech. Here the speech (introduction, body, and conclusion) is divided into five parts or steps: attention, need, satisfaction, visualization, and action.

Attention The attention step makes the audience give you their undivided attention. If you execute this step effectively, your audience should be anxious and ready to hear what you have to say. You can gain audience attention through a variety of means (more fully identified in Unit 11):

1. Ask a question (rhetorical or actual).
2. Make reference to audience members.
3. Make reference to recent happenings.
4. Use humor.
5. Use an illustration or dramatic story.
6. Stress the importance of the topic to this specific audience.
7. Use audiovisual aids, tell the audience to pay attention, use a quotation, refer to yourself, refer directly to your thesis or purpose, make reference to a little known fact or statistic.

Need In the second part of your speech, you would demonstrate that a need exists. The audience should feel that something has to be learned or something has to be done because of this demonstrated need. Monroe suggests that need be established in four parts:

1. State the need or problem as it exists or will exist.
2. Illustrate the need with specific examples.

What organizational pattern do most of the speeches you hear follow? What patterns do most of the college lectures follow? What advice would you give your instructors on organizing college lectures?

3. Further support the existence of the need with additional illustrations, statistics, testimony, and other forms of support (identified in Units 14, 16, and 17).

4. Show how this need affects your specific listeners, for example, how it affects their financial status, their career goals, their individual happiness.

Satisfaction Present the "answer" or the "solution" to satisfying the need that you demonstrated in Step 2. On the basis of this satisfaction step, the audience should now believe that what you are informing them about or persuading them to do will effectively satisfy the need. In this step you answer the question: How will the need be satisfied by what I am asking the audience to learn, to believe, to do? This satisfaction step usually involves:

1. a statement (with examples and illustrations if necessary) of what you want the audience to learn, believe, or do

2. a statement of how or why what you are asking them to learn, believe, or do will lead to satisfying the need identified in Step 2

Visualization Visualization intensifies the audience's feelings or beliefs. In this step you take the audience beyond the present time and place and enable them to imagine the situation as it would be if the need were satisfied as you suggested in Step 3. There are two basic ways of doing this:

1. Demonstrate the benefits that the audience will receive if your ideas are put into operation.

2. Demonstrate the negative effects that the audience will suffer if your plan is not put into operation.

Of course, you could combine these two methods and demonstrate both the benefits of your plan and the negative consequences of the existing plan or of some alternative plan.

Action   Tell the audience what they should do to ensure that the need (as demonstrated in Step 2) is satisfied (as stated in Step 3). That is, what should the audience do to satisfy the need? Here you want to move the audience in a particular direction, for example, to speak in favor of additional research funding for AIDS or against cigarette advertising, to attend the next student government meeting, to contribute free time to read for the blind. You can accomplish this step by stating exactly what the audience members should do, using an emotional appeal, or giving the audience guidelines for future action. These and other methods of concluding and motivating an audience are covered in depth in Units 11 and 18.

Here is a much abbreviated example of how these five steps would look in a speech designed to inform an audience about the workings of home computers.

[Attention]

By the time we graduate, there will be more home computers than automobiles. (You might then go on to explain the phenomenal growth of computers in education until you have the complete attention of your audience revolving around the importance and growth of computers.)

[Need]

Much as it is now impossible to get around without a car, it will be impossible to get around the enormous amount of information without a home computer. (You might then go on to explain how knowledge is expanding so rapidly that it will be extremely difficult to keep up with any field without computer technology.)

[Satisfaction]

Learning a few basic principles of home computers will enable us to process our work more efficiently, in less time, and more enjoyably. (You might then explain the various steps that your listeners could take to satisfy the needs you already identified.)

[Visualization]

With these basic principles firmly in mind (and a home computer), you'll be able to stay at home and do your library research for your next speech by just punching in the correct codes. (You might then go through in more or less detail the speech research process so that your listeners will be able to visualize exactly what the advantages of computer research will be.)

[Action]

These few principles should be supplemented by further study. Probably the best way to further your study is to enroll in a computer course. Another useful way is to read the brief paperback, The Home Computer for the College Student. *(You might then identify the several computer courses that are available and that would be appropriate for a beginning student. Further, you might identify a few other books or perhaps distribute a brief list of books that would be appropriate reading for the beginning student.)*

Notice that in an informative speech you could have stopped after the satisfaction step because you would have accomplished your goal of informing the audience about some principles of home computers. But, in some cases, you may feel it helpful to complete the steps to emphasize your point in detail.

In a persuasive speech, on the other hand, you must go at least as far as visualization (if your purpose is limited to strengthening or changing attitudes or beliefs) or to the action step (if you are attempting to motivate behavior).

Additional Organizational Patterns

The six patterns just considered are the most common and the most useful for organizing most public speeches. But, there are other patterns that might be appropriate for different topics. Here are several such patterns.

Structure-Function The structure-function pattern is useful in informative speeches in which you want to discuss how something is constructed (its structural aspects) and what it does (its functional aspects). This pattern might be useful, for example, in a speech to explain what an organization is and what it does, the parts of a university and how they operate, or the sensory systems of the body and their various functions. This pattern might also be useful in discussing the nature of a living organism: its anatomy (that is, its structures) and its physiology (that is, its functions).

Comparison and Contrast Arranging your material in a comparison-and-contrast pattern is useful in informative speeches in which you want to analyze two different theories, proposals, departments, or products in terms of their similarities and differences. In this type of speech you would not only be concerned with explaining each theory or proposal, but also would focus primarily on how they are similar and how they are different.

Pro and Con, Advantages and Disadvantages The pro-and-con pattern, sometimes called the advantages-disadvantages pattern, is useful in informative speeches in which you want to explain objectively the advantages (the pros) and the disadvantages (the cons) of each plan, method, or product.

Both the comparison-and-contrast and the pro-and-con patterns might be developed by focusing on the several qualities or aspects of each plan or product. For example, if you were comparing two health plans, your major propositions might center on such topics as costs to the worker, hospital benefits, and sick leave. Under each of these major propositions, you would show what Health Plan No. 1 provides and then what Health Plan No. 2 provides.

Both of these patterns are also useful in persuasive speeches where you wish to highlight the weaknesses in one plan or product and the strengths of another, much like advertisers do when they compare their product with Brand X.

Claim and Proof The claim-and-proof pattern is especially useful in a persuasive speech in which you want to prove the truth or usefulness of a particular proposition. It is the pattern that you see frequently in trials where the claim made by the prosecution is that the defendant is guilty and the proof is the varied evidence: the defendant had a motive; the defendant had the opportunity; the defendant had no alibi. In this pattern your speech would consist of two major parts. In the first part you would explain your claim (tuition must not be raised, library hours must be expanded, courses in AIDS education must be instituted). In the second part you would offer your evidence or proof as to why tuition must not be raised, for example.

Multiple Definition The multiple definition pattern is useful for informative speeches in which you want to explain the nature of a concept (What is a born-again Christian? What is a scholar? What is multiculturalism?). In this pattern each major heading would consist of a different type of definition or way of looking at the concept. A variety of definition types are discussed in Unit 13.

Who? What? Why? Where? When? This 5W pattern is the pattern of the journalist and is useful in informative speeches when you wish to report or explain an event, for example, a robbery, political coup, war, or trial. Here you would have five major parts to your speech, each dealing with the answers to one of these five questions.

Because your organizational pattern serves primarily to help your listeners follow your speech, you might want to tell your listeners (in your introduction or as a transition between the introduction and the body of your speech) what pattern you will be following. Here are just a few examples:

- *In touring southern Europe we'll travel from west to east.*
- *I'll first explain the problems with raising tuition and then propose a workable solution.*
- *First, we'll examine the causes of hypertension and then its effects.*

REMEMBER: **The most common organizational patterns:**
1. *Temporal:* main ideas are arranged in a chronological (or time) order
2. *Spatial:* main ideas are arranged in terms of dimensions of space, for example, left to right, top to bottom, east to west
3. *Topical:* main ideas (equal in value and importance) are itemized without any other order imposed on them
4. *Problem-solution:* main ideas are divided into problems and solutions
5. *Cause-effect:* main ideas are arranged into causes and effects
6. *Motivated sequence:* main parts of the speech are ordered in terms of attention, need, satisfaction, visualization, and action
7. Additional patterns: the *structure-function, comparison and contrast, pro and*

con, claim and proof, multiple definition, and *who? what? why? where? and when?* patterns

STRATEGIES OF INTERNAL ORGANIZATION

In addition to organizing your main ideas in terms of easy-to-follow patterns, consider the strategies of internal organization. For example, should you state your conclusion first and then give the audience your evidence or should you first present your evidence? Where do you put your strongest argument? Where do you put your weakest argument? These questions and at least some answers are considered in the following discussions of (1) climax and anticlimax orders and (2) primacy and recency.

Climax and Anticlimax

Climax and anticlimax orders refer to the use of inductive (beginning with specifics and working up to a generalization) or deductive approaches (beginning with a generalization and from it deriving a series of specifics).

In *climax order* you first present your evidence (your specifics) and then climax it with your conclusion or thesis. For example, you might say to a college class:

The athletic program will have to be cut because of inadequate funds; the student union, which operates at a loss each year will have to be closed; and class size will have to be increased 40 percent because a number of faculty will have to be fired since there is no money to pay them.

You would then climax these bits of information with the main issue: tuition must be raised.

In *anticlimax order* you would start out with the thesis that tuition must be raised (your general statement or conclusion) and then give your reasons (the specifics).

Whether you choose the climax or the anticlimax order depends a great deal on the attitudes and points of view of your audience. Here are some suggestions:

- Lead with the information the audience will object to least.
- If you anticipate great objection to your thesis, present your arguments and somehow soften the blow that is soon to come.
- If you anticipate little or no objection to your thesis or if your audience already supports it, lead with it and present the reasons or support for it later.

Primacy and Recency

The rule of *primacy* states that what you hear first will be remembered best and will have the greatest effect. The rule of *recency* states that what you hear last or most recently will be remembered best and will have the greatest effect.

Research findings on this controversy offer a few useful conclusions.

- What is in the middle is remembered least and has the least general effect. Thus, if you have a speech with three points, put the weakest one in the middle.

- If your listeners are relatively neutral and have no real conviction either way, lead with your best argument and in this way get the listeners on your side early.
- Lead with your best argument with an audience that is favorable to your point of view.
- If you are faced with a hostile audience or with an audience that holds very different views than you, put your most powerful argument last and work up to it gradually, assuming that you can count on the listeners staying with you until the end.

Research on memory tells us that the audience will remember very little of what you say in a speech. Interesting as your speech may be, listeners will forget most of what you say. Therefore, repeat your main assertions—whether you put them first or last in your speech—in your conclusion.

REMEMBER: Arrange your arguments and supporting materials in light of the research findings on:

1. Climax (ending with the major proposition or argument) and anticlimax (beginning with the major proposition or argument)
2. Primacy (giving greatest emphasis to what occurs first) and recency (giving greatest emphasis to what occurs last)

CRITICALLY SPEAKING

1. Select any unit in this book. What are the coordinate items in the unit? What items are immediately subordinate to the unit title? How are coordination and subordination illustrated visually in this text.
2. What organizational pattern would you use if you were giving a speech on the following topics?
   a. The fall of communism in the Soviet Union
   b. The layout of a football field
   c. How the game of baseball is played
   d. Why we need (don't need) national health insurance
   e. The process of electing the president of the United States
   f. The vice president of the United States should be elected separately
   g. Five guidelines in finding a job
   h. How to apply for graduate school admission
3. Bring what you feel is a particularly effective print ad to class. Does the ad contain all the elements considered in the motivated sequence?
4. In what ways do television commercials gain your attention? Might these techniques prove effective in public speaking.? How?
5. What strategies of internal organization would you use in each of the following situations? What reasons can you offer to support your choices?

a. Advocating expanding an abortion clinic to a group of right-to-lifers? Alternatively: advocating dismantling an abortion clinic to a group of pro-choice advocates?
b. Arguing in favor of increasing tuition to a group of first-year college students?
c. Supporting an increase in athletic scholarships to a group of physical education instructors?
d. Advocating the building of shelters for the homeless in a middle-class residential neighborhood?
e. Arguing against extending unemployment benefits beyond 26 weeks to a group of affluent business owners?

PRACTICALLY SPEAKING

10.1 GENERATING MAJOR PROPOSITIONS FROM THESIS STATEMENTS

One of the skills in organizing a speech is to ask a question of your thesis and from the answer generate your major propositions. Below we present 20 thesis statements suitable for a variety of informative or persuasive speechs. For each thesis statement, ask a question and generate two, three, or four major propositions that would be suitable for an informative or persuasive speech. Here is an example to get you started:

Thesis Statement: Mandatory retirement should (should not) be abolished.
Question: Why should mandatory retirement be abolished?

I.   Mandatory retirement leads us to lose many of the most productive workers.
II. Mandatory retirement contributes to psychological problems of those forced to retire.
III. Mandatory retirement costs corporations economic hardship because they have to train new people.

1. Buy (Do not buy) American.
2. Tax (Do not tax) property assets owned by religious organizations.
3. Require (Do not require) adoption agencies to reveal the names of birthparents to all children when they reach 18 years of age.
4. Permit (Do not permit) condom advertisements in all media.
5. Require (Do not require) sex education courses in elementary school.
6. Permit (Do not permit) gays and lesbians to adopt children.
7. Ban (Do not ban) all sales of wild-animal fur.
8. Make (Do not make) the death penalty mandatory for those convicted of selling drugs to minors.
9. Reinstate (Do not reinstate) the draft.
10. Eliminate (Expand) affirmative action programs.

11. Give (Do not give) political asylum to women who have been abused.

12. Elected political officials should (not) be allowed to serve as lobbyists at any time after their term of office has expired.

13. Courses on women's issues should (not) be required for all students at this college.

14. Expand (Reduce, Eliminate) ROTC Programs.

15. Abolish (Expand, Reduce) intercollegiate athletic competition.

16. Legalize (Do not legalize) soft drugs.

17. Build (Do not build) houses for the homeless.

18. Become (Do not become) computer literate.

19. Support (Do not support) mandatory instruction in AIDS prevention in all elementary and high schools.

20. Grant (Do not grant) full equality to gay men and lesbians in the military.

U N I T 11

Introductions, Conclusions, and Transitions

■ ■ ■ ■

UNIT OBJECTIVES

After completing this unit, you should be able to:

1. Explain the methods for gaining audience attention; establishing a connection among speaker, audience, and topic; and orienting the audience

2. Identify four common faults of introductions

3. Explain the methods for summarizing, motivating your audience, and closing the speech

4. Identify three common faults of conclusions

5. Explain the recommendations made for speaking "before the introduction" and "after the conclusion"

6. Explain the types and functions of transitions and internal summaries

*N*ow that you have the body of your speech organized, you need to devote attention to your introduction, your conclusion, and the transitions that will hold the pieces of your speech together.

■■■■ INTRODUCTIONS

Although you obviously will deliver the introduction to your speech first, you should construct it only after you have constructed the entire speech (body *and* conclusion). Begin collecting suitable material for your introduction as you prepare the entire speech, but wait until all the other parts are completed before you put the pieces together. In this way you will be better able to determine which elements should be included and which should be eliminated.

Your introduction should serve three functions: gain attention, establish a speaker-audience-topic connection, and orient the audience as to what is to follow. Let's look at each of these functions and at the ways you can serve these functions.

Gain Attention

In your introduction gain the attention of your audience and focus it on your speech topic. And, of course, maintain that attention throughout your speech. You can secure attention in a number of ways; here are just a few of them.

Ask a Question Questions are effective because they are a change from declarative statements and we automatically pay attention to change. *Rhetorical questions,* questions to which you don't expect an answer, are especially helpful in focusing the audience's attention on your subject: "Do you want to live a happy life?" "Do you want to succeed in college?" "Do you want to meet the love of your life?" Also useful are *polling-type questions,* questions which ask the audience for a show of hands: "How many of you have suffered through a boring lecture?" "How many of you intend to continue school after graduating from college?" "How many of you have suffered from loneliness?"

Richard Weaver (1991), in a speech on self-motivation delivered to fraternity members, uses a series of questions to gain attention and to focus such attention on his topic.*

> *Does it feel like you're being torn in all directions? Like you're getting stressed out? Like every teacher thinks his or her class is the only one you're taking? Like everything is coming down on you all at once, and you're not sure you can, or even want to, withstand the pressure? Do things feel like they are out of control? At least you know you're normal!*

Refer to Audience Members Reference to the audience makes them perk up and pay attention, because you are involving them directly in your talk. Harvey C. Jacobs (1985) gains attention by referring to members of the audience (and complimenting them) in his introduction:

*This excerpt is reprinted from a speech by Dr. Richard L. Weaver II entitled "Self Motivation: Ten Techniques for Activating or Freeing the Spirit," *Vital Speeches of the Day,* August 1, 1991, p. 520. It is used with his permission.

Winston Churchill once gave this advice to public speakers: "One, never walk up a wall that's leaning against you; two, never try to kiss a person who's leaning away from you; and, three, never speak to a group that knows more about the subject than you do." You work much closer to the readers than I do. You know readers very well, I'm sure. Editors are often referred to as the ivory tower crowd, while circulation people are out in the trenches trying to peddle the product we editors and reporters create.

Refer to Recent Happenings Referring to a previous speech, recent event, or prominent person currently making news helps gain attention because the audience is familiar with this and will pay attention to see how you are going to approach it. In a speech delivered by Lee Iacocca on the occasion of the minting of the $5 gold pieces commemorating the Statute of Liberty, Iacocca, whose Chrysler Corporation was hit by a strike, referred to this recent happening briefly and humorously:

This is my second ceremony involving a strike this week and the first one didn't turn out so well.

Use Humor A clever (and appropriate) joke or anecdote is always useful in holding attention. If you feel uncomfortable telling jokes in a public speaking situation, avoid this method. Similarly, avoid humor if you feel your joke or story will make any members of your audience uncomfortable or ill-at-ease. Further, make sure that your humor is integral to your speech topic. Use humor only if it relates directly to your specific speech topic. Unit 21 discusses suggestions for using humor.

Use an Illustration or Dramatic Story Much as people are drawn to soap operas, so are we drawn to illustrations and stories about people. Here is an example from a speech by Brenda Dempsey (Boaz and Brey, 1988), a student from Eastern Michigan University, in a speech on genetic counseling:

Mary Stewart was twenty-three, happily married, and pregnant. A prenatal test showed it was a boy. But, instead of the impending happiness which usually surrounds expectancy of a child, something was missing. You see, Mary's brother had been born with the crippling disease of Dishend's muscular dystrophy, a genetically inherited disease, which is passed on to boys from otherwise healthy mothers. Statistically, Mary stood a great chance of passing that disease to her unborn son.

Do be sure to make the connection between your opening illustration and the topic and purpose of your speech. Don't expect the audience to make the connections themselves. They may not do it and your great illustration will have no effect.

Stress Importance of Topic People pay attention to what they feel is important to them and ignore what seems unimportant and irrelevant. For example, in addition to telling them that budget cuts will hurt education in the state (again, too general to relate to), tell them what this means to them specifically. You might, for example, say:

Budget cuts in the abstract mean little. So, let me tell you what these cuts will mean to us. First, our class size is going to be increased from thirty to fifty. Just think what that will mean in a course like Public Speaking. Second, all our laboratory courses will be eliminated. Those of us majoring in Biology, Chemistry,

Why is it important for a lawyer to make the right impression in the introduction? What general purposes must a lawyer's introductory remarks serve (say, in defending someone accused of murder)?

Physics, Physiology, and similar sciences will receive no practical experience. All these courses will be conducted as pure lecture courses. Third, our tuition—already too high to suit me and I'm sure most of you as well—will be increased by thirty percent!

In short, tell the audience what your subject has to do with them, with their lives, with their money, with their jobs.

Additional Means of Gaining Attention   In addition to the means of gaining attention already illustrated, here are several more that you may find useful.

Use audiovisual aids. Audiovisual aids are valuable because they are something new and different. They engage our senses, and thus our attention. When used in the introduction they serve to quickly secure the attention of the audience and let the audience know that this speech is going to be something special. Unit 15 discusses audiovisual aids in depth.

Tell the audience to pay attention. A simple, "I want you to listen to this frightening statistic," or "I want you to pay particularly close attention to . . . ," used once or twice in a speech, will help gain audience attention.

Use a quotation. Quotations are useful because the audience is likely to pay attention to the brief and clever remarks of someone they have heard of or read about. Do make sure that the quotation is directly relevant to your topic. If you have to explain its relevance, it probably is not worth using.

Drawing by Brian Savage; © 1981 The New Yorker Magazine, Inc. Reprinted by permission.

Refer to yourself. Personal anecdotes gain attention because people enjoy hearing about other people's experiences or feelings. The popularity of tabloid journalism, television talk shows, and magazines like *People* and *Us* provide ample evidence of this universal interest in people.

Refer directly to your topic. If your topic focuses on the interests of the audience, you might begin by referring directly to it. If it is one whose relevance you have to prove, then this approach probably would not be appropriate.

Cite a little-known fact or statistic. Little-known facts or statistics will help perk an audience's attention. Headlines on unemployment statistics, crime in the schools, and political corruption sell newspapers because they gain attention.

Establish a Speaker-Audience-Topic Relationship

In addition to gaining attention, use your introduction to establish a connection among yourself as the speaker, the audience members, and your topic. Try to answer your listeners' inevitable question: Why should we listen to you speak on this topic? You can establish an effective speaker-audience-topic relationship in a number of ways.

Establish Your Credibility   The introduction is a particularly important time to establish your competence, character, and charisma (see Unit 20 for more detail). Here, for example, A. L. Jones (1972) establishes his credibility in his introduction in two ways. He establishes his good character by referring to his deep concern for the environment, and he establishes his competence by referring to his own studies in the field of ecology:

> *For several years I have been deeply concerned about reports of the destruction of our environment as a result of technological recklessness, overpopulation, and a religious and philosophical outlook that gives little consideration to the preservation of nature. My studies in this area of concern have turned up evidence that I feel compelled to share with you. I welcome this opportunity to do it.*

Refer to Others Present   Not only will this help you to gain attention, it will also help you to establish an effective speaker-audience-topic relationship. In this example Harvey Mackay (1991) refers not only to the audience but also to their present thoughts and feelings:

> *I'm flattered to be here today, but no so flattered that I'm going to let it go to my head. Yes, I was delighted to be asked to be your commencement speaker. But I also know the truth: by the time you're my age ninety-nine out of a hundred will have completely forgotten who spoke at your graduation.*
>
> *And, I can accept that. Because I can't remember the name of my commencement speaker either. What I do remember from graduation day is the way I felt: excited, scared and challenged. I was wondering what the world was like out there, and how I would manage to make an impact.*

Refer to the Occasion   Often your speech will be connected directly with the occasion. By referring to the reason the audience has gathered, you can establish a connection between yourself, the audience, and the topic. Here Joan David Ratteray (1987) refers to the occasion in her speech, "Escape to Freedom":

> *Thank you, Mr. Lustig. I am glad to be in Ohio today, for this is a State that has meant so much to Black Americans, a State that in the past has been a symbol of freedom. . . . I understand from your local newspapers that it was in this State also that a black man named John Brown, in the early 19th century, started some of the first independent schools for black children. And it was here that Harriet Tubman was buried with full military honors. Thus, the "underground railroad" and the State of Ohio are inextricably linked in the history of America's search for freedom.*
>
> *I have come to tell you today that I have found another "underground railroad" in America. This time it's helping inner-city youth all across this country escape the slavery imposed on them by traditional mass education in our inner cities.*

Express Your Pleasure in Speaking   Yukio Matsuyama (1992) effectively establishes a speaker-audience-topic relationship by humorously expressing his pleasure in addressing the audience:

> *I feel very happy to be invited here today. It is always a great pleasure for me to talk about Japan with those Americans who have a sincere interest in Japanese affairs and who don't find us inscrutable, but only intractable.*

Compliment the Audience Pay the audience an honest and sincere compliment, and they will not only give you their attention, they will feel a part of your speech. In this example Eric Rubenstein compliments the audience directly by noting the group's accomplishments:

Let me compliment your fine organization, Job Resources, on having counseled and job-trained more than 7,000 individuals, and having also obtained permanent employment for over 2,000 men and women since 1979.

Express Similarities with the Audience By stressing your own similarity with members of the audience, you create a bond with them and become an "insider" instead of an "outsider." Here Janice Payan (1990) uses this technique most effectively:

Thank you. I felt as if you were introducing someone else because my mind was racing back 10 years, when I was sitting out there in the audience at the Adelante Mujer conference. Anonymous. Comfortable. Trying hard to relate to our "successful" speaker, but mostly feeling like Janice Payan, working mother, glad for a chance to sit down.

I'll let you in on a little secret. I still am Janice Payan, working mother. The only difference is that I have a longer job title, and that I've made a few discoveries these past 10 years that I'm eager to share with you.

The first is that keynote speakers at conferences like this are not some sort of alien creatures. Nor were they born under a lucky star. They are ordinary Hispanic Women who have stumbled onto an extraordinary discovery.

Orient the Audience

The introduction should orient the audience in some way as to what is to follow in the body of the speech. Preview for the audience what you are going to say. The orientation may be covered in a variety of ways.

Give a General Idea of Your Subject

Tonight I'm going to discuss atomic waste.

My concern today is with pollution.

I want to talk with you about the problems our society has created for the aged.

Here Nannerl Keohane (1991) orients her audience by giving a general idea of the topic:

My topic is leadership—a sorely needed skill in our country and our world these days; and particularly women leaders—an even scarcer phenomenon; and how we might prepare more women to be leaders in the future.

Give a Detailed Preview S. J. Buchsbaum (1991) provides a detailed orientation that previews what he will cover in his speech:

Today, I want to review the problem of networked computer security, and establish some common perspectives on key aspects of this problem—along with some widely applicable security approaches. I will then discuss current forms of these securi-

*ty approaches in computer networks—ranging from very large computer net-
works, such as the AT&T telecommunications and information network to the
more limited computer networks that are pervading our corporate and national in-
frastructures. And I'll conclude with a look at emerging technological capabilities
for improving computer network security.*

Identify Your Goal   Here, Harold Carr (1987) identifies the thesis he hopes to establish:

*I'll argue today—and certainly will be happy to debate with you during the ques-
tion session—that communications during a "crisis"—however you define that
term—shouldn't be all that different from communications during routine times.*

Introduce the Topic and Its Importance   In this example, reprinted by permission,
C. Ray Penn (1990) introduces his speech on the importance of words by stressing the
topic's importance:

*"Sticks and stones may break my bones, but names will never hurt me"—this is the
most quoted axiom about the effect of words upon human life. Of course it is much
easier to say this to others than it is to have it said to us, even if the person intends
it to make us feel better. The cruel fact of life is that if you ask a person to recall his
or her most painful moment, it will most likely involve what someone said. Like a
never-ending echo, painful words reverberate within the cavernous psychic walls
of each one of us.*

*"Sticks and stones may break my bones, but names will never hurt me"—it is
my purpose today to replace these worn and dangerous words with another set of
words—"A choice of words is a choice of worlds."*

REMEMBER   Use your introduction to serve three essential purposes:

1. Gain attention by, for example, asking a question, referring to audience members, referring to recent happenings, using humor, using an illustration or dramatic story, stressing the importance of the topic.
2. Establish a connection among speaker, audience, and topic by, for example, establishing your credibility, referring to others present, referring to the occasion,
   expressing your pleasure in speaking with this audience, complimenting the audience, and expressing similarities with the audience.
3. Orient your audience by, for example, giving a general idea of your subject, giving a detailed preview of your main propositions, identifying the goals you hope
   to achieve, and introducing the topic and stressing its importance.

Some Common Faults of Introductions

The introduction is perhaps the most important single part of the speech so be especially careful to avoid the most common faults.

Don't Apologize   A common fault is to apologize for *something*. Don't do it. You
do not have to say, "I am not an expert on this topic" or "I didn't do as much reading
on it as I should have." And *never* start a speech with "I'm not very good at giving pub-

"How much would you pay for all the secrets of the universe? Wait, don't answer yet. You also get this six-quart covered combination spaghetti pot and clam steamer. Now how much would you pay?"

Drawing by Maslin; © 1981 The New Yorker Magazine, Inc. Reprinted by permission.

lic speeches." In your entire speech, but especially in your introduction, emphasize the positive; highlight your assets and your strengths.

Don't Pretend Do not pretend to be what you are not: an expert when you are not; an art critic when you are not. Be yourself at your best. Highlight your positive qualities.

Don't Make Hollow Promises A related fault, wisely captured in the accompanying cartoon, is to promise something that you will not in fact deliver. The speaker who promises to tell you how to solve your love life problems, how to make a fortune in the stock market, or how to be the most popular person on campus and fails to deliver such insight quickly loses credibility.

Don't Rely on Gimmicks Avoid gimmicks that gain attention but are irrelevant to the nature of the speech or inconsistent with your treatment of the topic. Thus, for example, slamming a book on the desk, yelling obscenities, or telling a joke that bears no relation to the rest of your speech may accomplish this very limited goal of gaining attention, but quickly the audience sees them for what they are—gimmicks and tricks that have fooled them into paying attention. Such actions are resented and will set up barriers between you and your listeners.

TIPS FROM PROFESSIONAL SPEAKERS

Never—but never—apologize. Follow the positive road all the way. "An apology," said Oliver Wendell Holmes, "is only egotism wrong side out." It starts the audience looking for the shortcomings in you and your message. All the things you may be tempted to apologize for should have been taken care of, and would have with a little planning, long before D-Day. If you failed to take the time needed to research, develop, and rehearse your talk, or if you did not know, or learn, enough about your subject, you won't improve matters by pointing this out. Instead, you will lessen the audience's interest and put them on the lookout for anything about you or your talk that may be deficient.

Dorothy Sarnoff, speech consultant and trainer and developer of the "Speech Dynamics and Cosmetics" course. *Speech Can Change Your Life* (New York: Dell, 1970), p. 214.

Don't Preface Your Introduction Do not preface your speech with such common but ineffective statements as:

> *I'm really nervous, but here goes.*

> *Before I begin my talk, I want to say . . .*

> *I hope I can remember everything I want to say.*

REMEMBER: **Avoid the major problems of introductions:**
1. **don't apologize**
2. **don't pretend**
3. **don't make hollow promises**
4. **don't rely on gimmicks**
5. **don't preface your introduction**

CONCLUSIONS

"A speech," noted Lord Mancroft, "is like a love affair. Any fool can start it, but to end it requires considerable skill." Although I would not agree that any fool can start a speech (or a love affair)—at least not effectively—it does take exceptional skill to end one.

Your conclusion is especially important because it is often the part of the speech that the audience remembers most clearly. It is your conclusion that in many cases determines what image of you is left in the minds of the audience. Devote special attention to this brief but crucial part of your speech. Let your conclusion serve three major functions: to summarize, motivate, and provide closure.

Summarize

The summary function is particularly important in an informative speech, less so in persuasive speeches or in speeches to entertain. You may summarize your speech in a variety of ways.

Restate Your Thesis In this type of brief summary, you restate the essential thrust of your speech, repeating your thesis or perhaps the goals you hoped to achieve. Here, in a speech on socially responsible investing, Clark Moeller (1984) uses this brief summary method:

> In summary, socially responsible investing is a viable strategy for making your investment behavior consistent with your principles and promoting social justice. And—you don't have to sacrifice a good return on your investment in the process.

Restate the Importance of the Topic Another method for concluding is to tell the audience again why your topic or thesis is so important. In a speech entitled "Corporate Fitness Programs Pay Off," Brenda W. Simonson (1986) restates her thesis:

> It is estimated that within the next five years, 25 percent of all major corporations in the United States will have established some sort of fitness programming. Indeed, corporate fitness programming has come of age. There's no doubt about it—healthy employees work more and cost less and that's why managers will embrace fitness, not as a fringe benefit, but as an integral part of their regular personnel and health care policies. The message is clear—fitness means profits.

Restate Your Major Propositions In this type of summary you restate your thesis and the major propositions you used to support it. Here, in a speech on compact disk technology, Barbara Seidl (Boaz and Brey, 1988), a student from the University of Wisconsin, demonstrates:

> Now having acquired a basic understanding of CDI technology, its applications in a number of areas, and some of the concerns over its future acceptance, you should now be able to draw your own conclusions about participating in this interesting evolution, because you'll soon be encountering the grandchild of this odd little disk, this miracle music technology. Compact Disk Interactive (CDI)—its the next electronic revolution.

Motivate

A second function of the conclusion—most appropriate in persuasive speeches—is to motivate your audience to do what you want them to do. In your conclusion you have the opportunity to give the audience one final push in the direction you wish them to take. Whether it is to buy stock, vote a particular way, or change an attitude, you can use the conclusion for a final motivation, a final appeal. Here are two excellent ways to motivate.

Ask for a Specific Response Specify what you want the audience to do after listening to your speech. Clarence Darrow (Peterson, 1965), in his summation speech in defense of Henry Sweet, a black man charged with murder, directed his conclusion at motivating the jury to vote not guilty in a case that drew national and worldwide attention because of the racial issues involved. A vote of not guilty was in fact quickly returned by a jury of twelve white men.

> *Gentlemen, what do you think of our duty in this case? I have watched day after day these black, tense faces that have crowded this court. These black faces that now are looking to you twelve whites, feeling that the hopes and fears of a race are in your keeping. This case is about to end, gentlemen. To them, it is life. Not one of their color sits on this jury. Their fate is in the hands of twelve whites. Their eyes are fixed on you, their hearts go out to you, and their hopes hang on your verdict. This is all. I ask you, on behalf of this defendant, on behalf of these helpless ones who turn to you, and more than that—on behalf of this great state, and this great city, which must face this problem and face it fairly—I ask you, in the name of progress and of the human race, to return a verdict of not guilty in this case!*

Provide Directions for Future Action Another type of motivational conclusion is to spell out, most often in general terms, the direction you wish the audience to take. Here is an example by David Archambault (1992), president of the American Indian College Fund, in a speech to the Rotary Club:

> *Let us make this anniversary a time of healing and a time of renewal, a time to wipe away the tears. Let us—both Indian and non-Indian—put our minds together and see what life we can make for our children. Let us leave behind more hope than we found.*

Provide Closure

The third function of your conclusion is to provide closure. Often your summary will accomplish this, but in some instances it will prove insufficient. End your speech with a conclusion that is crisp and definite. Make the audience know that you have definitely and clearly ended. Some kind of wrap-up, some sort of final statement, is helpful in providing this feeling of closure. You may achieve closure through a variety of methods.

Use a Quotation A quotation is often an effective means of providing closure. Note, for example, in the conclusion to the "I Have a Dream" speech by Martin Luther King, Jr. (1963), how effectively King used the words of an old spiritual to close his speech (see the Appendix).

Linda Reivitz (1985) uses a quotation in a humorous but pointed way to conclude her speech on women's equality:

> *I would like to close today with a salute to former President Grover Cleveland, who in 1905 said, "Sensible and responsible women do not want to vote." May all those who display equal enlightenment as that attain an equal place in history.*

Refer to Subsequent Events You may also achieve closure by referring to future events to take place either that day or soon afterwards. Notice how effectively John R. Silber (1985) uses this method in a speech on higher education:

Each of these three issues has relevance not only for Americans but for any country seriously concerned about higher education and its relation to democracy. They are not the only issues of importance I have raised today, but they form a basis for further discussion. I am looking forward to a fruitful exchange of ideas in the panels that will follow.

Pose a Challenge or Question   You may close your speech by leaving the audience with a provocative question to ponder or a challenge to consider. David T. Kearns (1987), Chief Executive Officer of Xerox, provides crisp closure with his briefly stated request:

Ladies and gentlemen, let me leave you with this thought. Today's kindergartners will be the first high school graduates of the 21st century. Let's give them a head start on their future. Let's start now.

Another method is to pose a question and answer it by recapping your thesis and perhaps some of your major arguments or propositions. Here Jeff Sculley (Reynolds and Schnoor, 1991), a student from Bradley University, in an after-dinner speech on homophobia, asks a question as a way of summing up his speech and then answers it:

How can we avoid this horrible fate? By simply giving up on hatred and fear, and remembering that the greatest guarantor of our civil liberties is mutual toleration.

REMEMBER: **Use your conclusion to accomplish three purposes:**

1. Summarize by, for example, restating your thesis or goals you hoped to achieve, the importance of the topic or thesis, or your major propositions.
2. Motivate your audience by, for example, asking for a specific response or providing the audience with general directions for future action.
3. Provide crisp closure by, for example, using a quotation and referring it to your thesis, referring to subsequent events, or posing a challenge or question to the audience.

Some Common Faults of Conclusions

Because the conclusion is such an important part of your speech, be careful to avoid the common problems.

Don't Apologize   Avoid apologizing for any inadequacies, real or imagined. Actually, apologies are not always ineffective. In the hands of the right person they may help to interject a needed note of modesty. In most cases, however, it is best not to apologize.

Don't Introduce New Material   You may, of course, give new expression to ideas covered in the body of the speech, but do not introduce new material in your conclusion. Instead, use your conclusion to reinforce what you have already said in your discussion and to summarize your essential points.

Don't Dilute Your Position   Here are some expressions you will want to avoid:

I know this is not that important, but . . .

We really don't know enough about inflation to offer any real advice, but anyway . . .

This information is probably dated, but it was all I could find.

Statements such as these are ineffective and only detract from the credibility you have already established.

Ethically, of course, you do have the obligation to qualify your assertions as warranted by the evidence, but do this in the body of your speech, not in the conclusion.

Don't Drag Out Your Conclusion   End your speech crisply. Avoid dragging out your conclusion. Beginning speakers often preface each statement of their conclusion with terms that lead the audience to think that this is the last statement. Expressions such as "in summary," "in conclusion," or "therefore" will often lead the audience to expect an ending. When you are ready to end, end. Do not linger at the podium.

REMEMBER: **Avoid the common problems with conclusions:**
1. **don't apologize**
2. **don't introduce new material**

"Your Honor, I believe that the court has heard quite enough."

3. don't dilute the strength of your position
4. don't drag out the conclusion

BEFORE THE INTRODUCTION AND AFTER THE CONCLUSION

Although it is convenient to consider your speech as beginning with your introduction, it actually begins as soon as the audience focuses on you as speaker. Similarly, your speech does not end after you have spoken the last sentence. It ends only after the audience directs its focus away from you to another speaker or another project. Here are a few suggestions for dealing with the speech before the introduction and after the conclusion.

Before the Introduction

Display enthusiasm when you get up from your seat and walk to your speaking position. Display no signs of discomfort or displeasure. Your listeners will respond more favorably if they feel you are enjoying the experience. Stand in front of the audience with a sense of control.

Do not start your speech as soon as you get up from your seat or even as soon as you get to the front of the room. Survey your audience; engage their attention. Pause briefly, then begin your speech.

After the Conclusion

If there is a question period following your speech and you are in charge of it, pause after you have completed your conclusion and ask the audience if they have any questions. If there is a chairperson who will recognize audience members, pause after your conclusion, and then nonverbally indicate to the chairperson that you are ready to entertain questions.

If there is no question period, pause after the last statement of your conclusion. Continue to maintain eye contact with the audience for a second or two and then walk (do not run) to your seat. Once you sit down, show no signs of relief, do not sigh, or in any other way indicate that you are relieved or pleased that the experience is over. Focus your attention on the chairperson or the next speaker or on whatever activity is taking place.

TRANSITIONS AND INTERNAL SUMMARIES

Remember that your audience will hear your speech just once. They must understand it as you speak it or lose it. Transitions and internal summaries help listeners understand your speech more effectively and efficiently.

Transitions

Transitions are words, phrases, or sentences that connect the various parts of your speech. They provide the audience with guideposts that help them follow the development of your thoughts and arguments. Use transitions in at least the following places:

- between the introduction and the body of the speech
- between the body and the conclusion
- between the main points in the body of the speech

Here are the major transitional functions and some stylistic devices that you might use to serve these functions.

To announce the start of a major proposition or piece of evidence:

- First, . . .
- A second argument . . .
- A closely related problem . . .
- If you want further evidence, look at . . .
- Next, consider . . .
- My next point . . .
- An even more compelling argument . . .

To signal that you are drawing a conclusion from previously given evidence and argument:

- Thus, . . .
- Therefore, . . .
- So, as you can see . . .
- It follows, then, that . . .

To alert the audience to your introducing a qualification or exception:

- But, . . .
- However, also consider . . .

To remind listeners of what has just been said and that it is connected with another issue that will now be considered:

- In contrast to . . . , consider also . . .
- Not only . . . , but also . . .
- In addition to . . . , we also need to look at . . .
- Not only should we . . . , but we should also . . .

To signal the part of your speech that you are approaching:

- By way of introduction . . .
- In conclusion . . .
- Now, let's discuss why we are here today . . .
- So, what's the solution? What should we do?

You can enhance your transitions by pausing between your transition and the next part of your speech. This will help the audience see that a new part of your speech is coming. You might also take a step forward or to the side after saying your transition. This will also help to reinforce the movement from one part of your speech to another.

The Internal Summaries

Closely related to the transition (and in some cases a special type of transition) is the internal summary. An *internal summary* is a statement that summarizes what you have already discussed. It is a statement that usually summarizes some major subdivision of your speech. The "REMEMBER" summaries throughout this book are examples of internal summaries. Their function is to summarize some major subdivision of a unit. Incorporate a number of internal summaries into your speech—perhaps working them into the transitions connecting, say, the major arguments or issues.

An internal summary that is also a transition might look something like this:

The three arguments advanced here were (1) . . . , (2) . . . , (3) . . . . Now, what can we do about them? I think we can do two things. First, . . .

Another example:

Inadequate recreational facilities, poor schooling, and a lack of adequate role models seem to be the major problems facing our youngsters. Each of these, however, can be remedied and even eliminated. Here is what we can do.

Note that these brief passages remind the listeners of what they have just heard and preview for them what they will hear next. The clear connection in their minds will fill in any gaps that may have been created through inattention, noise, and the like.

REMEMBER: **Transitions connect the parts of your speech and give your listeners guides to help them follow your speech. Use them:**
1. **between the introduction and the body**
2. **between the major propositions**
3. **between the body and the conclusion**

CRITICALLY SPEAKING

1. How do you gain attention interpersonally? Does this have any counterparts in the public speaking situation?
2. What other ways might you gain the attention of your classmates in your speech introduction?
3. What other faults do you see in speech introductions? What general recommendations would you offer speakers?
4. What types of emotional appeals would be most effective in motivating you to accept the position of a persuasive speaker?
5. What other faults do you see in speech conclusions? What general recommendations would you offer speakers?

6. What makes you really want to listen to a speaker? How might you incorporate this into a speech introduction?

7. What makes you remember a speech? How might you incorporate this into a speech?

8. How important are transitions in the lectures you hear in college? Would you like to see lecturers use more transitions or less? Are internal summaries used?

PRACTICALLY SPEAKING

11.1   ANALYZING INTRODUCTIONS

Read over each of these introductions to various kinds of speeches and identify the functions each of them serves and the means used to achieve these functions.

1. Let us ask ourselves, what is education? About all things, what is our ideal of a thoroughly liberal education?—of that education which, if we could begin life again, we would give ourselves—of that education which, if we could mould the fates to our own will, we would give our children. Well, I know not what may be your conceptions upon this matter, but I will tell you mine, and I hope I shall find that our views are not very discrepant.

—Thomas Henry Huxley, "A Liberal Education"

2. Mr. President: When the mariner has been tossed for many days in thick weather, and on an unknown sea, he naturally avails himself of the first pause in the storm, the earliest glance of the sun, to take his latitude, and ascertain how far the elements have driven him from his true course. Let us imitate this prudence, and, before we float farther on the waves of this debate, refer to the point from which we departed, that we may at least be able to conjecture where we now are. I ask for the reading of the resolution before the senate.

—Daniel Webster, "Second Speech on Foote's Resolution—Reply to Hayne"

3. I doubt if any young woman in this University ever approached a tough assignment with more trepidation than this not-so-young woman is experiencing over this assignment. For a commencement address is a tough assignment for the most experienced of speakers. But when the speaker is not experienced, when she is not even a speaker, you can, if you'll put yourselves in her quaking shoes, imagine her state of mind. I find myself explaining the familiar panic of that recurrent nightmare peculiar to actors in which a ghoulish bevy of directors and fellow players are bustling one onto a strange stage shouting "Hurry! Hurry! You're late!" And one has no idea of what one's part is, or for that matter what the play is. And one arrives before the audience completely speechless and, often as not, completely naked. Things are not quite that crucial for I do seem able to speak and I do appear to be clad.

—Cornelia Otis Skinner, "To Maximize One's Life"

4. I have come here today to speak to you about the San Min *Principles. What are the* San Min *Principles? They are, by the simplest definition, the principles for our nation's salvation. What is a principle? It is an idea, a faith, and a power. When men begin to study into the heart of a problem, an idea generally develops first; as the idea becomes clearer, a faith arises; and out of the faith a power is born. So a principle must begin with an idea, the idea must produce a faith, and the faith in turn must give birth to power, before the principle can be perfectly established. Why do we say that the* San Min *Principles will save our nation? Because they will elevate China to an equal position among the nations, in international affairs, in government, and in economic life, so that she can permanently exist in the world. The* San Min *Principles are the principles for our nation's salvation; is not our China today, I ask you, in need of salvation? If so, then let us have faith in the* San Min *Principles and our faith will engender a mighty force that will save China.*

—Sun Yat-Sen, *"The Three Principles of the People,"* 1924

11.2   CONSTRUCTING INTRODUCTIONS

Prepare an introduction to one of the topics listed, making sure that you (1) secure audience's attention and interest, (2) establish a connection among speaker, audience, and topic, and (3) orient the audience as to what is to follow. Be prepared to explain the methods you used to accomplish each of these aims.

1. College is not for everyone.
2. It is better never to love than to love and lose.
3. Tenure should be abolished.
4. Maximum sentences should be imposed even for first offenders of the drug laws.
5. All alcoholic beverages should be banned from campus.
6. Abortion should be declared illegal.
7. Psychotherapy is a waste of time and money.
8. Television should be censored for violence and sex.
9. Euthanasia should be legalized by the federal government.
10. Religion is the hope (opium) of the people.
11. Contribute to the Olympics.
12. Donate your organs to medicine after your death.
13. Switch to the new spreadsheet program.
14. Earn an M.B.A. Degree.
15. Laws restricting Sunday shopping should be abolished.

11.3   ANALYZING CONCLUSIONS

Read each of these conclusions to various kinds of speeches and identify the functions each serves and the means used to achieve these functions.

1. I am endeavoring to show to my countrymen that violent noncooperation only multiplies evil and that as evil can only be sustained by violence, withdrawal of support of evil requires complete abstention from violence. Nonviolence implies voluntary submission to the penalty for noncooperation with evil. I am here, therefore, to invite and submit cheerfully to the highest penalty that can be inflicted upon me for what in law is a deliberate crime and what appears to me to be the highest duty of a citizen. The only course open to you, the judge, is either to resign your post, and thus dissociate yourself from evil if you feel that the law you are called upon to administer is an evil and that in reality I am innocent, or to inflict on me the severest penalty if you believe that the system and the law you are assigning to administer are good for the people of this country and that my activity is therefore injurious to the public weal.

—Mohandas Gandhi, "Nonviolence"

2. I can conceive of nothing worse than a man-governed world except a woman-governed world—but I can see the combination of the two going forward and making civilization more worthy of the name of civilization based on Christianity, not force. A civilization based on justice and mercy. I feel men have a greater sense of justice and we of mercy. They must borrow our mercy and we must use their justice. We are new brooms; let us see that we sweep the right rooms.

—Lady Astor, "Women and Politics"

3. I am against our participation in this war not only because I hate war, but because I hate fascism and all totalitarianism, and love democracy. I speak not only for myself, but for my Party in summoning my fellow countrymen to demand that our country be kept out of war, not as an end in itself, but as a condition to the fulfillment of all our hopes and dreams for a better life for ourselves and our children, yes, and all the children of this great land. The extraordinary shifts and changes in European alliances should but confirm our resolution to stay out of Europe's war, and, ourselves at peace, to seek as occasion permits, the peace of the world.

—Norman Thomas, "America and the War"

4. And so, my fellow Americans, ask not what your country can do for you; ask what you can do for your country.

My fellow citizens of the world, ask not what America will do for you, but what together we can do for the freedom of man.

Finally, whether you are citizens of America or citizens of the world, ask of us here the same high standards of strength and sacrifice which we ask of you. With a good conscience our only sure reward, with history the final judge of our deeds, let us go forth to lead the land we love, asking His blessing and His help, but knowing that here on earth God's work must truly be our own.

—John Kennedy, "Inaugural Address"

11.4 CONSTRUCTING CONCLUSIONS

Prepare a conclusion to a hypothetical speech on one of the topics listed, making sure that you (1) summarize the speech's main points, (2) motivate the audience, and (3) provide closure. Be prepared to explain the methods you used to accomplish each of these functions.

1. Undergraduate degree programs should be five-year programs.
2. Proficiency in a foreign language should be required of all college graduates.
3. Children should be raised and educated by the state.
4. All wild-animal killing should be declared illegal.
5. Properties owned by churches and charitable institutions should be taxed in the same way that any other properties are taxed.
6. History is bunk.
7. Suicide and its assistance by others should be legalized.
8. Teachers—at all levels—should be prevented from going on strike.
9. Gambling should be legalized in all states.
10. College athletics should be abolished.
11. All crimes should have a statute of limitations.
12. Same-sex marriages should be legalized.
13. Divorce should be granted immediately when there is mutual agreement.
14. Courses in multiculturalism should be required for all students.
15. Privatization of elementary and high schools should be encouraged.

Outlining the Speech

■ ■ ■ ■

UNIT OBJECTIVES

After completing this unit, you should be able to:

1. Identify two functions that outlines serve

2. Identify two major types of outlines

3. Explain four suggestions concerning the mechanics of outlining

4. Describe the characteristics of an effective delivery outline

---

*T*he outline is a blueprint for your speech; it lays out the elements of the speech and their relationship to each other. With this blueprint in front of you, you can see at a glance all the elements of organization considered in the previous units—coordination and subordination, the functions of the introduction and conclusion, the transitions, the major propositions and their relationship to the thesis and purpose, and the adequacy of the supporting materials. And, like a blueprint for a building, the outline enables you to spot weaknesses that might otherwise go undetected.

Begin outlining at the time you begin constructing your speech. Do not wait until you have collected all your material, but begin outlining as you are collecting material, organizing it, and styling it. In this way you will take the best advantage of one of the major functions of an outline—to tell you where change is needed. The outline should be changed and altered as necessary at every stage of the speech construction process.

FUNCTIONS AND TYPES OF OUTLINES

An outline will help you to organize your speech. As you outline the speech, you clarify the major points of your speech, the major supporting materials, and the transitions. Once these can be easily examined visually, you may see, for example, if your assertions are properly coordinated, if your supporting materials do in fact support your assertions, and so on. If you are using a temporal or a spatial organizational pattern, for example, you can quickly see from the outline if, in fact, the temporal or spatial progression is clear or in need of further development.

Speech outlines provide an efficient way to assess the strengths and weaknesses of the speech as it is being constructed. Let's say you are preparing a speech on censorship and your major points concern sex and violence. Your outline will tell you at a glance if your supporting materials are adequately and evenly distributed between the two points. The outline may tell you that more material has to be collected on the sex issue, or that your speech is almost totally devoted to statistical information and you need some human interest material, and so on. In short, the outline can guide your collection of information.

TIPS FROM PROFESSIONAL SPEAKERS

Your presentation structure, to be of any use whatsoever, must be simple enough to be remembered. It must be simple enough so that *you'll* remember what you want to say, and *your audience* will have no difficulty remembering what you told them.

Ron Hoff, leading speaker and advertising and marketing director. *"I Can See You Naked": A Fearless Guide to Making Great Presentations* (Kansas City, MO: Andrews and McMeel, 1988), p. 144.

What is the value of a speech outline in addressing an audience that differs greatly in age, as pictured here, or on any other important variable? Is an outline less or more important as the audience becomes more homogeneous? Why?

The outline, when it is constructed from the beginning of the speech preparation process, helps you check the speech as a whole (or at least as much as you have constructed so far). When you work for a long time on a speech and when each part is constructed over a long period of time, it becomes difficult to "see the forest for the trees." The outline enables you to stand back and examine the entire forest.

Outlines may be extremely detailed or extremely general. Since you are now in a learning environment where the objective is to make you a more proficient public speaker, your instructor may wish to suggest one type of outline over another. And, of course, just as the type of outline will depend on the specific speaker, the type of outline that proves best for instructional purposes will vary with the instructor. I, for example, prefer that students construct rather detailed outlines, but I recognize that this is for instructional purposes and that once students have learned the art of public speaking, they will adjust the outlining procedures to what fits them best.

The more detail you put into the outline, the easier it will be to examine the parts of the speech for all the qualities and characteristics that were discussed in the previous units. Consequently, I suggest that, at least in the beginning, you outline your speeches in detail and in complete sentences. The usefulness of an instructor's criticism will often depend on the completeness of the outline.

With these factors in mind, then, I suggest that you do the following, especially in your beginning speeches. Begin constructing the outline as soon as you get the topic clearly in mind. Revise it constantly. Every new idea, every new bit of information will result in some alteration of basic structure. At this point keep the outline brief and perhaps in key words or phrases. Once you feel pretty confident that you are near completion, construct an outline in detail—using complete sentences—and follow the procedures and principles discussed in the next sections of this unit. Use this outline to test your organizational structure, following the questions provided in the Performance Checklist at the end of Part Three.

■■■■ CONSTRUCTING THE OUTLINE

After you have completed your research and have an organizational plan for your speech mapped out, put this plan (this blueprint) on paper. That is, construct what is called a "preparation outline" of your speech using the following guidelines.

Preface the Outline with Identifying Data

Before you begin the outline proper, identify the general and specific purposes as well as your thesis. This prefatory material (see Units 9, 13, and 15 for details) should look something like this:

General purpose: to inform
Specific purpose: to inform my audience of four major functions of the mass media
Thesis: the mass media serve four major functions

These identifying notes are not part of your speech proper. They are not, for example, mentioned in your oral presentation. Rather, they are guides to the preparation of the speech and the outline. They are like road signs to keep you going in the right direction and to signal when you have gone off course.

One additional bit of identifying data should preface the preface: the title of your speech.

Outline the Introduction, Body, and Conclusion as Separate Units

Each of these three parts of the speech, although intimately connected, should be labeled separately and should be kept distinct in your outline. Like the identifying data above, these labels are not spoken to the audience but are further guides to your preparation.

By keeping the introduction, body, and conclusion separate, you will be able to see at a glance if they do, in fact, serve the functions you want them to serve. You will be able to see where further amplification and support are needed. In short, you will be able to see where there are problems and where repair is necessary.

At the same time, do make sure that you examine and see the speech as a whole—where the introduction leads to the body and the conclusion summarizes your propositions and brings your speech to a close.

Insert Transitions and Internal Summaries

Insert [using square brackets] transitions between the introduction and the body, the body and the conclusion, the major propositions of the body, and wherever else you think they might be useful.

Insert your internal summaries (if these are not integrated with your transitions) wherever you feel they will help your audience to understand and remember your ideas.

Append a List of References

Some instructors require that you append a list of references to your speeches. If this is requested, then do so at the end of the outline or on a separate page. Some instructors require that only sources cited in the speech be included in the list of references, whereas others require that the full list of sources consulted be provided (those mentioned in the speech as well as those not mentioned).

Whatever the specific requirements, remember that these sources will prove most effective with your audience if you carefully integrate them into the speech. It will count for little if you consulted the latest works by the greatest authorities but never mention this to your audience. So, when appropriate, weave into your speech the source material you have consulted. In your outline, refer to the source material by author's name, date, and page in parentheses and then provide the complete citation in your list of references.

In your actual speech it might prove more effective to include the source with your statement. It might be phrased something like this:

> *According to John Naisbitt, author of the nationwide bestseller,* Megatrends, *the bellwether states are California, Florida, Washington, Colorado, and Connecticut.*

Regardless of what specific system is required (find out before you prepare your outline), make certain to include all sources of information, not just written materials. Personal interviews, information derived from course lectures, and data learned from television should all be included in your list of references.

REMEMBER: Outlines (which vary from key word to phrase to complete sentence):

1. help you organize your thoughts into a coherent pattern
2. help you assess the strengths and weaknesses of your speech, and for checking the speech as a whole

And in constructing outlines be sure to:

3. preface the outline with identifying data
4. outline the introduction, body, and conclusion as separate units
5. insert transitions and internal summaries
6. append a list of references (if required)

■■■■ SOME MECHANICS OF OUTLINING

Assuming that the outline you construct for your early speeches will be relatively complete, here are a few guidelines concerning the mechanics of outlining.

Use a Consistent Set of Symbols

The following is the standard, accepted sequence of symbols for outlining:

I.

  A.

    1.

      a.

        (1)
          (a)

Begin the introduction, the body, and the conclusion with Roman numeral I. That is, each of the three major parts should be treated as a complete unit.

Not This:	*This:*
Introduction	*Introduction*
I.	I.
II.	II.
Body	**Body**
III.	I.
IV.	II.
V.	III.
Conclusion	**Conclusion**
VI.	I.
VII.	II.

Use Visual Aspects to Reflect the Organizational Pattern

Use proper and clear indentation. This will help to set off visually coordinate and subordinate relationships.

Not This:

  I. Television caters to the lowest possible intelligence.

  II. Situation comedies

III. "Full House"

This:

I. Television caters to the lowest possible intelligence.

    A. Situation comedies illustrate this.

        1. "Full House"

        2. "Coach"

        3. "Wings"

    B. Soap operas illustrate this.

        1. "As the World Turns"

        2. "General Hospital"

        3. "Young and the Restless"

Use One Discrete Idea Per Symbol

If your outline is to reflect the organizational pattern among the various items of information, use just one discrete idea per symbol. Compound sentences are sure giveaways that you have not limited each item to a single idea. Also, be sure that each item is discrete, that is, that it does not overlap with any other item.

Not This:

I. Education might be improved if teachers were better trained and if students were better motivated.

This:

I. Education would be improved if teachers were better trained.

II. Education would be improved if students were better motivated.

    Note that in *This* items I and II are single ideas but in *Not This* they are combined.

Not This:

I. Teachers are not adequately prepared to teach.

    A. Teacher education programs are inadequate.

    B. Course syllabi are dated.

This:

I. Teachers are not adequately prepared to teach.

    A. Teacher education programs are inadequate

        1. Support for A

        2. Support for A

    B. In-service programs are inadequate.

        1. Support for B

        2. Support for B

    Note that A and B are discrete in *This* but overlap in *Not This*. In *Not This* B is actually a part of A (one of the inadequacies of teacher education programs is that course syllabi are dated).

Use Complete Declarative Sentences

Phrase your ideas in the outline in complete declarative sentences rather than as questions or as phrases. This will further assist you in examining the essential relationships. It is much easier, for example, to see if one item of information supports another if both are phrased in the declarative mode. If one is a question and one is a statement, this will be more difficult.

    Not This:

I. Who should raise children?

II. Should the state raise children?

    A. Equality for children

    B. Parents will be released for work.

    This:

I. Children should be raised by the state.

    A. All children will be treated equally.

    B. Parents will be released to work.

    Note that in *This* all items are phrased as complete declarative sentences and their relationship is therefore brought out clearly. In *Not This*, on the other hand, a mixture of question, sentence, and phrase obscures the important relationships among the items in the outline.

REMEMBER: **Follow these mechanics of outlining:**
1. **Use a consistent set of symbols.**
2. **Use visual aspects to reflect and reinforce the organizational pattern.**
3. **Use one discrete idea per symbol.**
4. **Use complete declarative sentences.**

A SAMPLE OUTLINE WITH ANNOTATIONS

The following outline, with side notes explaining its structures and functions, will help clarify the various facets of organization and outlining.

Revealing Yourself to Others

INTRODUCTION

I. If you want to get to know yourself better, reveal yourself: Self-disclose.
    A. This may sound peculiar, but it is supported by a great deal of scientific research.
    B. Self-disclosure can lead us to feel better about ourselves but can also lead to lots of problems.
    C. Understanding self-disclosure can lead us to make the most effective use of this most important form of communication.

II. I've immersed myself in self-disclosure for the last five years—as researcher and writer—and want to share some insights with you.
    A. As a researcher I conducted over two dozen studies.
    B. As a writer, I spent the last two years analyzing and synthesizing just about everything known about self-disclosure.

III. In order to understand self-disclosure we need to focus on two aspects.
    A. Self-disclosure is a form of communication in which you reveal information about yourself that is normally kept hidden.
    B. Self-disclosure involves both rewards and problems.

[Let me consider first the definition of self-disclosure.]

BODY

I. Self-disclosure is a form of communication in which you reveal information about yourself.
    A. Self-disclosure is a type of communication.
        1. Self-disclosure includes overt statements
            a. An overt confession of infidelity to your lover is self-disclosure.
            b. A letter explaining why you committed a crime is self-disclosure.

Here I try to gain attention by stating what appears to be a contradiction. I could have used a specific instance, a humorous story, an interesting quotation, and various other methods discussed in Unit 11. The introductory statement used here has the added advantage that it introduces the topic immediately. In these two brief statements I emphasize the importance of the topic to the audience to ensure their continued attention and interest.

Note that each statement in the outline is a complete sentence. You can easily convert this full sentence outline into a phrase or word outline.

Here I establish my connection with the topic and answer the inevitable question of the audience: why I am discussing this particular topic? I also establish my credibility. In this outline I overdo this aspect to emphasize some of the ways in which we may seek to establish credibility. In an actual speech I would have cut this considerably.

Notice also the parallel structure (the similarity in phrasing) used in these three examples: As a researcher . . . , As a writer. This structural similarity helps to unify these statements and helps the audience see this unity easily and quickly. In this section I explain exactly what I will cover in the speech. For the sake of clarity I state here the two main points that I cover in the body of the speech in the same language. Note also that these points are repeated in the summary in the conclusion. Different language may and often is used. Note, however, that although this repetition is obvious to you reading the speech, it will not necessarily be obvious to the audience. Listeners will not remember the exact wording used, and yet such repetition will help them remember your speech.

I also state here the specific purpose of the speech— "to understand self-disclosure."

The transitions (indicated here in brackets) are stated in rather obvious terms to emphasize their basic structure and function. As explained earlier, with practice you will develop transitional statements with more grace and subtlety.

This is the first major point of the speech, and here I focus on definitional aspects of self-disclosure. The entire definition is presented in I, and in A and B, each element in the definition is explained in more detail.

 2. Self-disclosure includes slips of the tongue and other unintentional communications.
   a. A slip of the tongue in which you reveal that you are really in love with your best friend's spouse is self-disclosure.
   b. An uncontrollable rage in which you tell your boss all the horrible things you've kept inside is self-disclosure.
B. Self-disclosure involves information about the self not previously known by the listeners.
   1. Telling people something about someone else is not self-disclosure.
     a. Self-disclosure involves the self.
     b. Self-disclosing statements begin with "I."
   2. Telling people what they already know is not self-disclosure.

[This, then, is what self-disclosure is; now let us focus on what self-disclosure may involve.]

II. Self-disclosure involves both rewards and problems.
   A. There are two main rewards of self-disclosure
      1. First, we get to know ourselves better.
        a. Talking about my fear of snakes led me to understand the reasons for such fears.
        b. Results from studies show that persons who disclose have greater self-awareness than do those who do not self-disclose.
      2. Second, we can deal with our problems better.
        a. Dealing with guilt is a prime example.
        b. Studies conducted by Civikly, Hecht, and me show that personal problems are more easily managed after self-disclosure.
   B. There are two major dangers of self-disclosure.
      1. First, self-disclosure may involve personal problems.
        a. The fear of rejection may be more damaging than retaining the secrets.
        b. Self-disclosure may bring to the surface problems that you are not psychologically ready to deal with.
      2. Second, self-disclosure may involve professional problems.
        a. A number of ex-convicts who disclosed their criminal records have been fired.
        b. Persons who are treated by psychiatrists

Observe how this transition connects what has been discussed with what is to follow.

Notice how this statement clues the listener to expect a two-part division: rewards and problems. Each of these divisions is further broken down to explain the specific rewards and problems that may be derived from self-disclosure.

Note that here, as in 2, I provide listeners with guide words ("first," "second,") to enable them to keep track of where I am. In the actual speech I might even make this clearer by stating something like "The first reward is that we get to know ourselves better" to emphasize that I am here talking about the first reward. This may seem like oversimplifying, but for an audience hearing the speech only once, it will prove helpful.

Note again the parallel structure throughout the speech outline. Focus, for example, on Body II A and B, on Body II B 1 and 2, and elsewhere throughout the speech. This parallel structure helps clarify significant relationships for both the speaker and the listener.

and who revealed this have had their political careers ruined.

[Let me now summarize in brief some of what we now know about self-disclosure.]

CONCLUSION

I. Self-disclosure is a unique form of communication.
  A. Self-disclosure is a form of communication in which you reveal information about yourself.
  B. Rewards and problems await self-disclosure.

II. Self-disclosure is probably our most significant form of communication.
  A. We all engage in it.
  B. It can lead to great advantages and great disadvantages.

III. So, if you want to get to know yourself better, self-disclose.

This transition tells the audience that the conclusion (containing a summary) is next.

Here I provide a summary of the main points in the speech. Notice that these points correspond to the orientation in the Introduction (III, A and B) and to the main points in the Body (I and II). Again, the same wording is used to add clarity.

This section serves two purposes. First, I provide a relatively clear-cut ending to the speech. The last sentence, especially, should make it clear that the speech is finished. Second, I recall the significance of the topic and of the speech. Notice that II C restates the significance of the topic originally provided in the Introduction I.

Here I provide closure by referring back to the opening lines of the speech.

A SKELETAL OUTLINE

Here is a skeletal outline that you might find useful in visualizing how your speech should be organized. Naturally, you would have to modify this for your specific purposes; if you had fewer or more than three main points, you would adjust the body of the speech outline accordingly.

Introduction

I. _____

II. _____

III. _____

  A. _____

  B. _____

  C. _____

[_____]

Body

I. _____

  A. _____

B. _____

[——]

II. _____

   A. _____

   B. _____

[——]

III. _____

   A. _____

   B. _____

[——]

Conclusion

I. _____

   A. _____

   B. _____

   C. _____

II. _____

III. _____

▪■■■■ THE DELIVERY OUTLINE

Now that you have constructed a preparation outline, you need to construct a *delivery outline,* an outline that will assist you in delivering the speech. Resist the temptation to use your preparation outline to deliver the speech. If you use your preparation outline, you will tend to read from the outline, which is not a very effective way to give a speech.

Instead, construct a brief delivery outline, one that will assist rather than hinder your delivery of the speech. Here are some guidelines in preparing this delivery outline.

Be Brief

Do not use full sentences. Instead, use key words that will trigger in your mind the ideas you wish to discuss with your audience. Follow, too, the principles for constructing the preparation outline: (1) use a consistent set of symbols (the same ones you used in your preparation outline) and (2) use the visual aspects to reflect and reinforce the organizational pattern. Try to limit yourself to one side of one sheet of paper.

Be Clear

Be sure that you can see the outline while you are speaking. Do not write so small that you will have to squint to read it; on the other hand, do not write so big that you will need reams of paper to deliver a 5-minute speech. Use different color ink, underline, and use any symbols or guidance system that will help you communicate your ideas to your audience most effectively.

Be Delivery Minded

This is your outline. You want it to help you deliver your speech most effectively. Therefore, include any guides to delivery that will help while you are speaking. For example, you might note in the outline when you will use your visual aid and when you will remove it. A simple "Show VA" or "Remove VA" should suffice. You might also wish to note some speaking cues such as "slow down" when reading a poetry excerpt, or perhaps a place where an extended pause might help.

Rehearse with the Delivery Outline

In your rehearsals, use the delivery outline only. Do not rehearse with your full-sentence outline. This is simply a specific application of the general rule: Make rehearsals as close to the real thing as possible.

A Sample Delivery Outline

Here is a sample outline suitable for delivery. Note the following features of this delivery outline:

1. it follows closely the preparation outline. [Compare this outline with the "Revealing Yourself to Others" annotated outline presented earlier in the unit.]
2. it is brief enough so that you can effectively deliver your speech without losing eye contact with the audience, it uses abbreviations (*SD* for self-disclosure; *C* for communication) and phrases rather than complete sentences
3. it is detailed enough to include all the essential parts of your speech, including transitions
4. it contains delivery notes specifically tailored to your own needs, for example, pause suggestions, terms to be emphasized, and guides to using visual aids
5. it is clearly divided into introduction, body, and conclusion (though to save space, the labels are omitted and lines are used instead) and uses the same numbering system as the preparation outline

Delivery Outline

PAUSE!

LOOK OVER AUDIENCE!

   I. Get to know self: SD

      A. Research supports: feel better

      B. *BUT*, problems too

      C. Understanding SD: effectiveness

PAUSE—SCAN AUDIENCE

   II. Immerse self in SD

      A. As researcher (SHOW BOOKS ON SD)

      B. As writer

 III. Understanding SD

WRITE 2 TOPICS ON BOARD

      A. SD: form of C

      B. SD: rewards and problems

[Let's examine SD as a form of C]

   I. SD: form of C

      A. Type of C

      B. *NEW* (not *OLD*) information

[Now that we know what SD is, let's look at some rewards and problems]

   II. SD: rewards *AND* problems

TAPE REWARDS/PROBLEMS VISUAL AND CHART TO BOARD

      A. Rewards: know self better and deal with problems

[*BUT*, there are problems too]

      B. Problems: personal and professional

PAUSE

STEP FORWARD

[Let's review what we now know about SD]

   I. SD: unique form of C

II. SD: most significant form of C

III. Get to know self: SD

PAUSE!

ASK FOR QUESTIONS

CRITICALLY SPEAKING

1. Many students who are required to write outlines actually write them after they have written the corresponding English composition or speech. Why is this ineffective?
2. What identifying data does your instructor want prefaced to the outline?
3. The skeletal outline provided in this unit used a topical, temporal, or spatial organizational pattern. How would you construct a skeletal outline for a speech using a problem-solution pattern? A cause-effect pattern? A motivated sequence pattern?
4. What suggestions might you offer for writing the delivery outline? That is, what devices have you incorporated into your delivery outline that might be useful to others?
5. What do you suppose the delivery outline for the typical college lecture looks like?
6. What outline guides would you suggest that your college lecturers make greater use of? Why would these be useful?

PRACTICALLY SPEAKING

12.1 ORGANIZING A SCRAMBLED OUTLINE

This exercise provides an opportunity to work actively with the principles of organization and outlining discussed in the previous units. Your task is to unscramble the following 19 statements from an outline on "Friendship," and fit them into a coherent and logical outline consisting of an introduction, a body, and a conclusion.

Friendship

1. We develop an acquaintanceship.
2. Friendship is an interpersonal relationship between two persons that is mutually productive, established and maintained through mutual free choice, and characterized by mutual positive regard.
3. We meet.

4. Without friendships we would not be able to function effectively in our daily lives.

5. In order to understand friendships we need to see what a friendship is and its stages of development.

6. Friendship is established and maintained through mutual free choice.

7. Friendship is one of the most important of our interpersonal relationships.

8. Friendship is characterized by mutual positive regard.

9. Friendship is mutually productive.

10. Without friendships our pleasures would not be expanded.

11. We develop an intimate friendship.

12. Friendship is an interpersonal relationship.

13. Without friendships our pain would not be lessened.

14. Friendships develop through various stages.

15. Friendships do not develop full-blown but rather go through various stages—from the initial meeting, through acquaintance, close friendship, to intimate friendship.

16. We develop a casual friendship.

17. By underestanding friendship we will be in a better position to develop and maintain productive and enjoyable friendship relationships.

18. Friendship—an interpersonal communication relationship which is mutually productive, established, and maintained through mutual free choice and characterized by mutual positive regard—is one of our most important interpersonal relationships.

19. We develop a close relationship.

■ PART THREE CHECKLISTS

Performance Checklist: Evaluating Your Organization

YES   **NO**   Have you:

☐   ☐   1. Derived your propositions from your thesis?

☐   ☐   2. Arranged the propositions in a logical order that the audience will find easy to follow?

☐   ☐   3. Considered the advantages of climax versus anticlimax and primacy versus recency orders

☐   ☐   4. Composed an introduction that gains attention, establishes a speaker-audience-topic relationship, and orients the audience?

☐   ☐   5. Avoided the common faults of introductions: apologizing, pretending, making hollow promises, using gimmicks, and prefacing your introduction?

☐   ☐   6. Composed a conclusion that summarizes, motivates, and provides closure?

☐   ☐   7. Avoided the common faults of conclusions: apologizing, introducing new material, diluting your position, and dragging out the ending?

☐   ☐   8. Inserted transitions and internal summaries at appropriate places?

☐   ☐   9. Composed a preparation outline that uses a consistent set of symbols, uses visual aspects to reinforce the organization, contains one discrete idea per symbol, and is phrased in complete sentences?

☐   ☐   10. Composed a delivery outline that is brief, clear, and delivery oriented?

Critical Thinking Checklist: Thinking Critically About Organization

YES   **NO**   Do you:

☐   ☐   1. Analyze propositions in terms of how effectively they support a specific thesis (Unit 10)?

☐   ☐   2. Organize propositions into a logical pattern that listeners will be
          able to follow easily (Unit 10)?

☐   ☐   3. Arrange your major arguments so that they will have the greatest
          impact on your intended audience (Unit 10)?

☐   ☐   4. Discover and use a wide variety of techniques to gain attention
          (Unit 11)?

☐   ☐   5. Organize and outline complex ideas and supporting materials into
          a coherent whole (Unit 12)?

PART FOUR

Elements
of Public Speeches

Part Four focuses in detail on the types of speeches as well as the types of materials that you will use in developing these speeches. The emphasis is on informative (Units 13, 14, and 15) and persuasive speeches (Units 16, 17, 18, and 19) since these are the ones you'll be called on to deliver most often.

In addition to explaining the types of informative and persuasive speeches and how these might be constructed, you will see how to use supporting materials (for esample, illustrations and definitions) and audiovisual aids, and how to develop and critically evaluate arguments and evidence, motivational appeals, and credibility appeals. Finally, Unit 20 covers a variety of speeches that are given on special occasions.

In **thinking critically** about the types of speeches, try to:

- analyze (as user, listener, and critic) appeals based on logic, emotion, and credibility as they occur in all types of public speeches as well as in interpersonal and small group encounters, and in writing; it can mean the difference between logical and illogical conclusions
- avoid polarization in preparing or in responding to persuasive speeches; you do not have to be totally for or against an issue; you can agree with parts and disagree with others
- recognize that the cultural norms of audiences vary greatly; the expected and accepted mixture of logical, emotional, or credibility appeals will vary greatly from one culture to another

The Informative Speech

UNIT OUTLINE

Principles of Informative Speaking
The Speech of Description
The Speech of Definition
The Speech of Demonstration
A Sample Speech with Annotations

Critically Speaking
Practically Speaking

■ ■ ■ ■

UNIT OBJECTIVES

After completing this unit, you should be able to:

1. Explain at least five principles for informative speaking

2. Explain *description, definition,* and *demonstration* as ways of communicating information

3. Identify the major strategies to use in describing, defining, and demonstrating

---

Your first speeches will probably be informative ones. You may describe a process, define a term, or perhaps demonstrate how something works. In this and the next two units, the focus is on the informative speech. Let's start with some general principles of informative speaking.

PRINCIPLES OF INFORMATIVE SPEAKING

When you communicate "information" you tell your listeners something they do not know, something new. You may tell them of a new way of looking at old things or an old way of looking at new things. You may discuss a theory not previously heard of or a familiar one not fully understood. You may talk about events that the audience may be unaware of or may have misconceptions about. Regardless of what type of informative speech you intend to give, the following principles should help.

Limit the Amount of Information

There is a limit to the amount of information that a listener can take in at one time. Resist the temptation to overload your listeners with information. Limit the amount of information that you communicate and instead, expand its presentation. It is better to present two new items of information and explain these with examples, illustrations, and descriptions than to present five items without this needed amplification.

Here, for example, is the type of thing you should avoid:

In this speech I want to discuss the differences between women and men. I'm going to focus on the physiological, psychological, social, and linguistic differences.

Clearly the speaker is trying to cover too much. The speaker is going to be forced to cover these four areas only superficially with the result that little new information will be communicated. Instead, select one area and develop it in depth:

In this speech I want to discuss some of the linguistic differences between women and men. I'm going to focus on two linguistic differences: differences in language development and differences in language problems. Let's look first at the way in which girls and boys develop language.

In this speech, the speaker now has the opportunity to cover an area in depth. As a result the listeners are more likely to learn something that they did not know.

Stress Relevance and Usefulness

Listeners will remember your information best when they see it as relevant and useful to their own needs or goals. Notice that as a listener you follow this principle all the time. For example, in a communication class you might attend to and remember the stages in the development of language in children simply because you will be tested on the information and you want to earn a high grade.

If you want the audience to listen to your speech, relate your information to their needs, wants, or goals. *Throughout your speech,* make sure the audience knows that the information is relevant and useful to them. For example, you might say something like:

> *We all want financial security. We all want to be able to buy those luxuries we read so much about in magazines and see every evening on television. Wouldn't it be nice to be able to buy a car without worrying about where you're going to get the down payment or how you'll be able to make the monthly payments? Actually, that is not an unrealistic goal as I'll demonstrate in this speech. In fact, I will show you several methods for investing your money that will enable you to increase your income by at least 20 percent.*

Relate New Information to Old

Listeners will learn information more easily and retain it longer when you relate it to what they already know. Here, for example, Betsy Heffernan, a student from the University of Wisconsin (Reynolds and Schnoor 1991), relates the problem of sewage to a familiar historical event:

> *During our nation's struggle for independence, the citizens of Boston were hailed as heroes for dumping tea into Boston Harbor. But not to be outdone, many modern day Bostonians are also dumping things into the harbor. Five-thousand gallons of human waste every second. The New England Aquarium of Boston states that since 1900, Bostonians have dumped enough human sewage into the harbor to cover the entire state of Massachusetts chest deep in sludge. Unfortunately, Boston isn't alone. All over the country, bays, rivers and lakes are literally becoming cesspools. Improper sewage disposal is having widespread effects on our environment, our health, and our quality of life. In order to understand how serious these effects are, we'll first look at the damage improper sewage disposal causes to our environment and to us, why this damage is occurring, and finally, ways that we can improve the efficiency of our sewage treatment facilities. Examination of these areas will reveal the extent of this problem and the urgent need that it be solved.*

TIPS FROM PROFESSIONAL SPEAKERS

Chronology and logic are built into the human brain. They are definite, predictable ways we gather, organize, and interpret information.

To introduce new material to an audience, you must allow their brains to hook into old, well-known, comfortable information-processing systems. To absorb new material or make sense of *any* material, your audience needs for you to follow a *logical* progression. In real life "A" does truly come before "B" and "C." So it must in your presentation. Start at the beginning.

Sonya Hamlin, communication consultant. *How to Talk So People Listen: The Real Key to Job Success* (New York: Harper & Row, 1988), p. 99.

What principle of information do you see violated most often in classroom speeches? What advice would you give to correct these difficulties?

For example, let's say you wanted to explain the *jicama*. You might relate it to things that the audience already knows by saying something like this:

> The jicama *is a Mexican potato. It looks like a brown-skinned turnip. It has a white inside and tastes something like crispy water chestnuts.*

Relate the new to the old, the unfamiliar to the familiar, the unseen to the seen, the untasted to the tasted. In this way you will help your listeners to perceive more clearly what they have never experienced before.

Vary the Levels of Abstraction

You can talk about freedom of the press in the abstract by talking about the importance of getting information to the public, by referring to the Bill of Rights, and by relating a free press to the preservation of democracy. That is, you can talk about the topic on a relatively high level of abstraction. But, you can also talk about freedom of the press by citing specific examples: how a local newspaper was prevented from running a story critical of the town council or about how Lucy Rinaldo was fired from the *Accord Sentinel* after she wrote a story critical of the mayor. You can talk about the topic on a relatively low level of abstraction, a level that is specific and concrete.

Combining the high abstraction and the specific seems to work best. Too many high abstractions without the specifics or too many specifics without the high abstractions will generally prove less effective than the combination of abstract and specific.

Here, for example, is an excerpt from a speech on the homeless. Note that in the first paragraph we have a relatively abstract description of homelessness. In the second paragraph, we get into specifics. In the last paragraph the abstract and the concrete are connected.

Homelessness is a serious problem for all metropolitan areas throughout the country. It is currently estimated that there are now over 200,000 homeless in New York City alone. But, what is this really about? Let me tell you what it's about.

It's about a young man. He must be about 25 or 30, although he looks a lot older. He lives in a cardboard box on the side of my apartment house. We call him Tom, although we really don't know his name. All his possessions are stored in this huge box. I think it was a box from a refrigerator. Actually, he doesn't have very much and what he has easily fits in this box. There's a blanket my neighbor threw out, some plastic bottles he puts water in, and some styrofoam containers he picked up from the garbage from Burger King. He uses these to store whatever food he finds.

What is homelessness about? It's about Tom and 200,000 other "Tom's" in New York and thousands of others throughout the rest of the country. And not all of them even have boxes to live in.

REMEMBER: these principles of informative speaking:
1. limit the amount of information you communicate
2. stress the relevance and the usefulness of the information
3. relate new information to old
4. vary the levels of abstraction

THE SPEECH OF DESCRIPTION

When you describe, you are concerned with explaining an object or person, or with explaining an event or process. Here are a few examples:

Describing an Object or Person
- the structure of the brain
- the contributions of Thomas Edison
- the parts of a telephone
- the layout of the Alamo
- the hierarchy of a corporation
- the human body
- the components of a computer system

Describing an Event or Process
- Andrew: the hurricane of the '90s
- the events leading to World War II

- organizing a body building contest
- Castro's takeover of Cuba
- how a newspaper is printed
- the process of buying a house
- purchasing stock
- how a child acquires language
- how to read a textbook

Strategies for Describing

Here are some suggestions for describing objects and people, events and processes.

Select an Appropriate Organizational Pattern Consider using a spatial or a topical organization when describing objects and people. Consider using a temporal pattern when describing events and processes. For example, if you were to describe the layout of Philadelphia you might start from the north and work down to the south (using a spatial pattern). If you were to describe the contributions of Thomas Edison, you might select the three or four major contributions and discuss each of these equally (using a topical pattern).

If you were describing the events leading up to World War II, you might use a temporal pattern and start with the earliest and work up to the latest. A temporal pattern would also be appropriate for describing how a hurricane develops or how a parade is put together.

Use a Variety of Descriptive Categories Describe the object or event with lots of descriptive categories. Use physical categories and ask yourself such questions as these:

- What color is it?
- How big is it?
- What is it shaped like?
- How high is it?
- How much does it weigh?
- How long or short is it?
- What is its volume?
- How attractive-unattractive is it?

Also, consider its social, psychological, and economic categories. In describing a person, for example, consider such categories as friendly-unfriendly, warm-cold, rich-poor, aggressive-meek, and pleasant-unpleasant.

Consider Using Audiovisual Aids Audiovisual aids will help you describe almost anything. Use them if you possibly can. In describing an object or person, show your listeners a picture. Show them pictures of the brain, the inside of a telephone, the skeleton of the body. In describing an event or process, create a diagram or flowchart to illustrate the various stages or steps. Show your listeners a flowchart representing the stages in buying stock, in publishing a newspaper, in putting a parade together.

Consider Who? What? Where? When? and Why? These categories are especially useful when you want to describe an event or process. For example, if you are going to describe how to purchase a house, you might want to consider the people involved (who?), the steps you have to go through (what?), the places you will have to go (where?), the time or sequence in which each of the steps have to take place (when?), and the advantages and disadvantages of buying the house (why?).

Developing the Speech of Description

Here are two examples of how you might go about constructing a speech of description. In this first example, the speaker describes the four steps in reading a textbook. Each main point covers one of the major steps. The organizational pattern is a temporal one. The speaker discusses the main points in the order in which they would normally occur. Here is how the body of such a speech might appear in outline form:

Specific purpose: to describe the four steps in reading a textbook
Thesis: you can increase your textbook reading effectiveness. (*How can we increase our textbook reading effectiveness?*)

I. Preview the text.

II. Read for understanding.

III. Read for retention.

IV. Review the text.

In delivering such a speech a speaker might begin by saying:

There are four major steps we should follow in reading a textbook. We should preview the text, read for understanding, read for retention, and review what we have read. Let's look at each of these steps in more detail.

The first step is to preview the text. Begin at the beginning and look at the table of contents. How is the book organized? What are the major parts of the text? In The Elements of Public Speaking *there are five major parts: preliminaries, subjects and audiences, organization, types of speeches, and style and delivery. Each part consists of several units. Let's look at how a unit is organized.*

Each unit begins with a series of objectives. These objectives are the goals of the unit. These objectives. . . .

In this second example, the speaker identifies four suggestions for increasing assertiveness (again, following a temporal sequence).

Specific purpose: to describe how we can become more assertive
Thesis: assertiveness can be increased (*How can assertiveness be increased?*)

I. Analyze assertive behaviors.

II. Record your own assertive behaviors.

III. Rehearse assertive behaviors.

IV. Act assertively.

▪▪▪▪ THE SPEECH OF DEFINITION

What is leadership? What is a born-again Christian? What is the difference between sociology and psychology? What is a cultural anthropologist? What is safe sex? These are all topics for informative speeches of definition.

A *definition* is a statement of the meaning or significance of a concept or term. Use definitions when you wish to explain difficult or unfamiliar concepts or when you wish to make a concept more vivid or forceful.

In defining a term or in giving an entire speech of definition, you may focus on defining a term, a system or theory, or the similarities and/or differences among terms or systems. It may be a subject new to the audience or one familiar to them but presented in a new and different way. Here are some examples:

Defining a Term
- What is multiculturalism?
- What is drug addiction?
- What is censorship?
- What is political correctness?

Defining a System or Theory
- What is the classical theory of public speaking?
- What are the parts of a generative grammar?
- Confucianism: its major beliefs
- The "play theory" of mass communication

Defining Similar and Dissimilar Terms or Systems
- Communism and socialism: some similarities and differences
- What do Christians and Muslims have in common?
- Oedipus and Electra: How do they differ?
- Love and infatuation: their similarities
- Freshwater and saltwater fishing

Strategies for Defining

There are several approaches to defining your topic. Here are some suggestions.

Use a Variety of Definitions When explaining a concept, it is helpful to define it in a number of different ways. Here are some of the most important ways to define a term.

Define by Etymology. In defining the word *communication*, you might note that it comes from the Latin *communis,* meaning "common"; in "communicating" you seek to establish a commonness, a sameness, a similarity with another individual.

And *woman* comes from the Anglo-Saxon *wifman*, which meant literally a "wife man," where the word *man* was applied to both sexes. Through phonetic change *wifman* became *woman*. Most larger dictionaries and, of course, etymological dictionaries will help you determine etymological definitions.

Define by Authority. You might, for example, define *lateral thinking* by authority and say that Edward deBono, who developed lateral thinking in 1966, has noted that "lateral thinking involves moving sideways to look at things in a different way. Instead of fixing on one particular approach and then working forward from that, the lateral thinker tries to find other approaches."

Or you might use the authority of cynic and satirist Ambrose Bierce and define *love* as nothing but "a temporary insanity curable by marriage," and *friendship* as "a ship big enough to carry two in fair weather, but only one in foul."

Define by Negation. You might also define a term by noting what the term is not, that is, defining by negation. "A wife," you might say, "is not a cook, a cleaning person, a baby sitter, a seamstress, a sex partner. A wife is . . . " or "A teacher is not someone who tells you what you should know but rather one who . . . ." Here Michael Marien (1992) defines *futurists* first negatively and then positively:

> *Futurists do not use crystal balls. Indeed, they are generally loathe to make firm predictions of what will happen. Rather, they make forecasts of what is probable, sketch scenarios of what is possible, and/or point to desirable futures—what is preferable and what strategies we should pursue to get there.*

Define by Direct Symbolization. You might also define a term by direct symbolization, by showing the actual thing or a picture or model of it.

Use Definitions to Add Clarity   If the purpose of the definition is to clarify, then it must do just that. This would be too obvious to mention except for the fact that so many speakers, perhaps for want of something to say, define terms that do not need extended definitions, something Lucy, in the cartoon, seems to be doing with enjoyment. Some speakers use definitions that do not clarify, and that, in fact, complicate an already complex concept. Make sure your definitions define only what needs defining.

Use Credible Sources   When you use an authority to define a term, make sure the person is in fact an authority. Tell the audience who the authority is and the basis for the individual's expertise.

In the following excerpt, note how Russell Peterson (1985) uses the expertise of Robert McNamara in his definition:

Peanuts by Charles Schultz. Copyright © 1992 United Features Syndicate. Reprinted by permission of UFS, Inc.

When Robert McNamara was president of the World Bank, he coined the term "absolute poverty" to characterize a condition of life so degraded by malnutrition, illiteracy, violence, disease and squalor, to be beneath any reasonable definition of human decency. In 1980, the World Bank estimated that 780 million persons in the developing countries lived in absolute poverty. That's about three times as many people as live in the entire United States.

Proceed from the Known to the Unknown   Start with what your audience knows and work up to what is new or unfamiliar. Let's say you wish to explain the concept of *phonemics* (with which your audience is totally unfamiliar). The specific idea you wish to get across is that each phoneme stands for a unique sound. You might proceed from the known to the unknown and begin your definition with something like this:

We all know that in the written language each letter of the alphabet stands for a unit of the written language. Each letter is different from every other letter. A "t" is different from a "g" and a "g" is different from a "b" and so on. Each letter is called a "grapheme." In English we know we have 26 such letters.

We can look at the spoken language in much the same way. Each sound is different from every other sound. A "t" sound is different from a "d" sound and a "d" sound is different from a "k" sound, and so on. Each individual sound is called a "phoneme." In English we have approximately 42 such sounds or phonemes.

Now, let me explain in a little more detail what I mean by a "phoneme."

In this way, you will build on what the audience already knows, a procedure that is useful in all learning.

Developing the Speech of Definition

Here are two examples of how you might go about constructing a speech of definition. In this first example, the speaker selects three major types of lying for discussion and arranges these in a simple topical pattern.

Specific purpose: to define lying by explaining the major types of lying misdirection
Thesis: there are three major kinds of lying (*What are the three major kinds of lying?*)

  I. Concealment is the process of hiding the truth.

 II. Falsification is the process of presenting false information as if it were true.

III. Misdirection is the process of acknowledging a feeling but misidentifying its cause.

In delivering such a speech, a speaker might begin the speech by saying:

A lie is a lie is a lie. True? Well, not exactly. Actually, there are a number of different ways we can lie. We can lie by concealing the truth. We can lie by falsification, by presenting false information as if it were true. And, we can lie by misdirection, by acknowledging a feeling but misidentifying its cause. Let's look at the first type of lie—the lie of concealment.

Most lies are lies of concealment. Most of the time when we lie we simply conceal the truth. We don't actually make any false statements. Rather we simply don't reveal the truth. Let me give you some examples I overheard recently.

In this next example, the speaker explains the parts of a résumé and follows a spatial order, going from the top to the bottom of the page.

Specific purpose: to define the essential parts of a résumé
Thesis: there are four major parts to a résumé. *(What are the four major parts of a résumé?)*

 I. Identify your career goals.

 II. Identify your educational background.

 III. Identify your work experience.

 IV. Identify your special competencies.

THE SPEECH OF DEMONSTRATION

In using demonstration (or in a speech devoted entirely to demonstration), you would explain how to do something or how something operates. Here are some examples:

Demonstrating How to Do Something
- giving mouth-to-mouth resuscitation
- how to balance a checkbook
- piloting a plane
- how to drive defensively
- how to mix colors
- how to develop your body

Demonstrating How Something Operates
- how the body maintains homeostasis
- the workings of a thermostat
- how a heart bypass operation is performed

Strategies for Demonstrating

In demonstrating how to do something or how something operates, consider the following guidelines.

Use Temporal Organization In most cases, a temporal pattern will work best in speeches of demonstration. Demonstrate each step in the sequence in which it is to be performed. In this way, you will avoid one of the major difficulties in demonstrating a process, backtracking. Do not skip steps even if you think they are familiar to the audience. They may not be.

Connect each step to the other with appropriate transitions. For example, in explaining the Heimlich maneuver you might say:

Now that you have your arms around the choking victim's chest, your next step is to. . . ."

Assist your listeners by labeling the steps clearly, for example, "the first step," "the second step," and so on.

Begin with an Overview It is often helpful when demonstrating to give a broad general picture and then present each step in turn. For example, let's say you were talking about how to prepare a wall for painting. You might begin with a general overview and say this:

> *In preparing the wall for painting, you want to make sure that the wall is smoothly sanded, free of dust, and dry. Sanding a wall is not like sanding a block of wood. So, let's look at the proper way to sand a wall.*

In this way, your listeners will have a general idea of how you will go about demonstrating the process.

Consider Using Visual Aids Visual aids are often helpful in showing the steps of a process in sequence. A good example of this is the signs in all restaurants demonstrating the Heimlich maneuver. These signs demonstrate each of the steps with pictures as well as words. The combination makes it easy for us to understand this important process.

Developing the Speech of Demonstration

Here are two examples of the speech of demonstration. In the first example, the speaker identifies and demonstrates how to listen actively.

Specific purpose: to demonstrate three techniques of active listening
Thesis: we can learn active listening (*How can we learn active listening?*)

  I. Paraphrase the speaker's meaning.

 II. Express understanding of the speaker's feelings.

III. Ask questions.

In delivering the speech, the speaker might begin by saying:

> *Active listening is a special kind of listening. It is listening with total involvement, with a concern for the speaker. It's probably the most important type of listening you can engage in. Active listening consists of three steps: paraphrasing the speaker's meaning, expressing understanding of the speaker's feelings, and asking questions.*
>
> *Your first step in active listening is to paraphrase the speaker's meaning. What is a paraphrase? A paraphrase is a restatement in your own words of the speaker's meaning. That is, you express in your own words what you think the speaker meant. For example, let's say that the speaker said . . . .*

In this next example, the speaker explains the proper way to argue by identifying the ways we should *not* argue. As you can see, these unproductive fight strategies are all about equal in value and are arranged in a topical order.

Specific purpose: to demonstrate how to fight fairly by identifying and demonstrating four unfair conflict strategies.

Thesis: conflict can be made more productive *(How can conflict be made more productive?)*

   I. Blame the other person.

  II. Unload all your previous grievances.

 III. Make light of the other person's displeasure.

 IV. Hit the other person with issues he or she cannot handle effectively.

REMEMBER: **the three major ways to communication information:**

1. **description: describing a process or procedure, an event, an object, or a person**
2. **definition: defining a term, system or theory, or similarities and/or differences among terms**
3. **demonstration: demonstrating how to do something or how something operates**

A SAMPLE SPEECH WITH ANNOTATIONS   ■■■■

The following speech is presented as a summary of some of the principles of informative speaking presented in this and earlier units. The annotations should help to illustrate further these principles of public speaking.

Where Has the Time Gone?

LIVING A PRODUCTIVE LIFE

Vincent Ryan Ruggiero

"Where has the time gone?" The question forces itself upon us even on special occasions like this one, flooding our thoughts with memories. The experience of soaring upward on that swing in the park, shouting excitedly, "Look, Mom and Dad, look! I can almost touch the sky." That precarious moment when we found the courage to try our bicycle without training wheels and were rudely introduced to the sidewalk. Our first taste of cotton candy. The delicious sinking sensation we got from the rides at the carnival. The joy of wondering what Santa Claus would bring us for Christmas.

So many memories from so long ago. Then suddenly the understanding we manage to shield ourselves from on lesser days flashes upon us—those times have fled and

Vincent Ryan Ruggiero is professor of humanities at the State University of New York at Delhi. He has written widely on critical thinking and so comes to this speech with considerable credibility references. In fact, it is likely that many of the graduating students in his audience used one or more of his textbooks in their college career. Note below how he further establishes his credibility and relates to the topic of the speech.

The speaker introduces his topic of managing time by involving his audience, by asking them to recall some memories from their past. The incidents he cites are common ones and he moves quickly through these to further illustrate how quickly time does pass.

He relates his topic to his listeners by reminding them that they have frequently asked the same question ("Where has the time gone?"), for example, after summer vacation.

The topic is surely a worthwhile one. It is a subject that we are all interested in because we all want to get the most out of time as possible. And the topic is particularly well suited to this audience since they will be starting their professional lives (or going on to postgraduate school) where effective time management will be important.

Observe that throughout these introductory examples, Ruggiero combines the abstract with the specific. The abstract concepts of time, its importance, and its rapid passing are combined with specifics of weddings, concerts and proms, and even Uncle George falling into the lake.

Notice how *time* is defined by authority. Observe the images created (thus appealing to a variety of senses): time as an enemy stealing little pieces of our lives and time as a prison from which we cannot escape.

Here the speaker recalls the paradoxes and ironies his audience has been confronted with and then offers a solution: use time wisely. This is his thesis. Notice that everything in the speech relates directly to this single idea.

will never return. And so in the midst of our celebration, our joy is tinged with sadness, our laughter intermingled with tears.

"Where has the time gone?" This is not the first time you've wondered. The question has followed summer vacations, athletic contests, trips to far away places, concerts and proms. You would eagerly await the occasion, anticipating the excitement and enjoyment, looking forward to savoring it . . . and then, no more than the moment had arrived, it was past.

Nor will this be the last time you will wonder. As you grow older, you will ask again and again, with increasing frequency, "Where did the time go?" The question will hover over every important gathering. Every wedding. Every birth. Every high school and college reunion. Every funeral. Sometimes it will be asked directly; at other times it will be cloaked in nostalgia. "Remember the family picnic when Uncle George fell into the lake?" "I'll never forget the trick we played on Sally in the dormitory."

As the months become years and the years decades, you will appreciate more deeply, as your parents and relatives do today, the meaning of the poet's words, "O time too swift. O swiftness never ceasing." You will also come to hear a voice from within asking more and more insistently, "What have you done—what are you doing—with your life?"

Because we humans exist in time and have no control over it, it is perhaps understandable that some philosophers have regarded time cynically, as an enemy that relentlessly steals little pieces of our lives until nothing remains, or as a prison to which we are consigned even before birth without hope of liberation, or as a cosmic curse on our existence. But that perspective only worsens the human condition, shrivelling our spirits, narrowing our expectations, diminishing hope. Hating time is little different from hating life, for as Benjamin Franklin sagely observed, time is really "the stuff life is made of."

We may not have any more control over the passing of time than our ancestors did, but we have more time available to us than any people in history. Not only is our lifespan longer, but our workday is shorter. Our grandparents and great-grandparents labored fourteen hours a day, six and sometimes seven days a week. The hours they had at their disposal to bring their special hopes and dreams to fruition were meager, yet they treated them as a precious gift and used them prudently.

One of the great sins of our age is taking the gift of time for granted. We mass-produce watches, clocks, and calendars, yet we ignore their constant reminder of our mortality. We squander our lives in trivial pursuits and rush to imitate the very lifestyles that have driven the rich and famous to psychiatrists' couches and then wonder why chronic depression, drug abuse, and apathy in the school and workplace are so prevalent.

This is truly an age of ironies. Our society is threatened by chronic laziness, yet it warns people against becoming workaholics. Business and professional groups call for excellence, and then subsidize the worship of the glamour, glitter, and superficiality that is destroying excellence. The communications and publishing industries lament America's intellectual decline, yet continue to give dieting and bodybuilding prominence over *mind*-building.

My message to you today is not a panacea for life's problems, nor a magic formula for fame and fortune. It is a prescription for avoiding the essential confusion and misdirection of our age and living a productive life, a life that will be an abiding source of pride and satisfaction. This message can be summed up in three words: USE TIME WISELY.

People often ask me how I have managed to stay abreast of the research in several disciplines, write articles and books, and maintain an active speaking and consulting schedule, usually while teaching a full course load. I explain that before I became a college professor, I spent four years as an industrial engineer. My duties in that position included conducting time and motion studies of innumerable employees in the large company I worked for. Those studies taught me a priceless lesson—that most people are filled with wasted time and motion.

I decided that by being thrifty with time and investing it with the same care wealthy people exercise in investing their money, I could, in effect, *lengthen my life*. So I set about developing some rules that would help me live more efficiently. I'd like to share with you the six I have found most helpful.

1. PLAN YOUR DAYS CAREFULLY. Don't make the mistake of planning only months and years ahead and letting your days organize themselves. You will achieve

This speech is probably best thought of as one of description, but it really is a combination of information and persuasion. It is informative in that Ruggiero describes the steps to successfully manage time, but he hopes to also change his listeners' attitudes toward time and consequently their behaviors.

Here is an especially good example of the speaker establishing his credibility because he identifies the specific characteristics that qualify him for speaking on the topic of time management.

Note here how effectively the speaker connects a concept new to his audience ("being thrifty with time and investing it") with an old and familiar concept (being thrifty with money and investing it wisely).

Observe the effective transition from his discussion of time passing quickly to his suggestions for managing time effectively: "So I set about developing some rules . . . I'd like to share with you the six I have found most helpful."

One way to view the organization of the speech is to say that it is organized in a topical pattern with each of the six suggestions for effective time management considered as a major proposition. However, we might also view the speech as being organized in a problem-solution pattern where the problem is considered first—that time passes quickly—and the solution is considered next—how to use the six principles of effective time management.

Here the speaker uses six major propositions and covers each one briefly. Although it is generally advisable to use four or less major propositions, each of these is still given approximately equal weight.

Note that for each of the propositions, he combines the abstract or general principle with specific, concrete suggestions. In No. 4, the general principle is "whenever possible, do two activities at once." This is then followed with specific, concrete suggestions; for example, "catch up on your professional reading while waiting in your doctor's office."

The language throughout the speech is clear and easily understood.

Notice that the conclusion relates back to the introduction and to the thesis of his talk. We know that the conclusion is coming because the speaker introduces it with the title of his speech, "Where has the time gone?" and then relates it back to the thesis when he says "My wish for you is that you will then be able to

much more if you define each day's tasks in advance, decide how much time each deserves, and honor that decision.

2. ESTABLISH FAVORABLE WORKING CONDITIONS. Find out whether you do your best work in the morning, afternoon, or evening; in silence or with music or other sounds surrounding you. Don't assume that familiar conditions are necessarily the best for you. Experiment. And when you learn what conditions are best, try to arrange your work accordingly.

3. SET ASIDE A SPECIAL TIME EACH DAY FOR REFLECTION. This time needn't be longer than fifteen minutes or a half hour, but it should be devoted exclusively to standing back from your daily activities and pondering these questions: What have I learned in the past twenty-four hours that can help me live my life better? How can I best apply that knowledge?

4. WHENEVER POSSIBLE, DO TWO ACTIVITIES AT ONCE. There are many occasions when two activities can be done at once without affecting performance. For example, you can balance your checkbook, iron your clothes, or plan your week's menu while watching television. Similarly, you can catch up on your professional reading while waiting in your doctor's office. The more such combinations you can think of, the more time you will save.

5. BUILD SOME SOLITUDE INTO YOUR ROUTINE. At least once or twice a week, get away from the crowd and spend your lunch and coffee breaks alone, taking a walk, reading a book, or sitting in the park. Not only will you be able to do a few things you haven't found time for, but you will return to work more refreshed.

6. ESCAPE FROM PROFITLESS DISCUSSIONS. Monitor your conversations to be sure they are worth the time they require. When you realize you have been going from person to person reporting the same news or expressing the same opinion, stop talking and turn to a more worthwhile activity. And when you find yourself involved in an extended gripe session, remind yourself that problems can often be *solved* in less time than people devote to complaining about them, and accept that thought as a personal challenge.

"Where has the time gone?" When you have grown old and are looking back over your life, you will ask this question once more. My wish for you is that you will then be able to respond, "Though it passed all too quickly, I used it well." Congratulations and good luck.

Copyright 1987 by Vincent Ryan Ruggiero. Delivered as the Commencement Address at Ohio University, Zanesville, Ohio, June 14, 1987. Reprinted by permission of the author.

respond, 'Though it passed all too quickly, I used it well.'"

CRITICALLY SPEAKING

1. Select an advertisement (television or print) and examine how closely it follows the principles of informative speaking identified speaking identified here. Which principle is most important to the success of an advertisement? Why?

2. How might you use the principle of relating new information to old if you wanted to describe a compact disc to someone who has never heard of one? Electricity to someone from the fifteenth century? Computers to someone from the nineteenth century?

3. How might you go about describing the registration process at your school? What would be your major propositions?

4. What categories might you use in describing a football? Forest? House? Infant? Movie? Book?

5. How would you organize a speech to define "the ideal professor"?

6. How many different types of definitions could you use to define wealth? Happiness? Entertainment? Economic hardship? Love? Anarchy?

7. How would you organize a speech in which you demonstrated the process of driving a car?

PRACTICALLY SPEAKING

13.1   ANALYZING AN INFORMATIVE SPEECH

This exercise is designed to help you identify the major parts of a speech and the way they fit together. Carefully read the speech by Joey Callow in the Appendix and respond to the questions appearing in the margins.

Amplifying Materials in Informative Speeches

UNIT OUTLINE

Examples and Illustrations

Testimony

Statistics

Critically Speaking

Practically Speaking

■ ■ ■ ■

UNIT OBJECTIVES

After completing this unit, you should be able to:

1. Explain the nature of examples and illustrations in the speech

2. Explain the suggestions for critically evaluating and using examples and illustrations

3. Explain the nature of testimony in the speech

4. Explain the suggestions for critically evaluating and using testimony

5. Explain the role of statistics in the speech

6. Explain the suggestions for critically evaluating and using statistics

*O*nce you have identified your specific purpose and your main assertions, devote your attention to supporting or amplifying these assertions. Develop these assertions so that the audience will understand each one easily and more fully. Three ways to amplify your assertions are explained in this unit: examples and illustrations, testimony, and statistics. Two other forms of amplifying materials are discussed elsewhere: definitions were discussed in Unit 13 and audiovisual aids are considered in Unit 15.

■■■■ EXAMPLES AND ILLUSTRATIONS

Examples and illustrations are specific instances that are explained in varying degrees of detail. A relatively brief specific instance is referred to as an *example.* a longer and more detailed example told in narrative or storylike form is referred to as an *illustration.*

Examples and illustrations are useful when you wish to make an abstract concept or idea concrete. For example, it is difficult for the audience to see exactly what you mean by such abstract concepts as "persecution," "denial of freedom," "friendship," and "love" unless you provide specific examples and illustrations of what you mean. Your examples and illustrations also encourage listeners to see your mental pictures of these concepts rather than seeing their own definitions of *love* or *friendship,* for example.

In a speech on lead poisoning, Brenda Dempsey (Boaz and Brey, 1988), a student from Eastern Michigan University, uses a specific example to stress the importance of her topic:

> When Denise Waddle and her family moved to a nice, middle-class section of Jersey City, New Jersey, they had dreams of healthy living, block parties, even a big backyard so their kid could make mud pies. In less than one year in their new home, their two-year old son had been poisoned, and their newborn showed high levels of poisoning in his bloodstream. Unknowingly, the Waddle's had been poisoned by their own backyard, for high levels of lead contaminated their water, and their lives.

Examples and illustrations may be real and factual on the one hand or hypothetical and imagined on the other. Thus, in explaining friendship, you might tell the story of the behavior of an actual friend. Here you would be using a real or factual example or illustration. Or you might formulate a composite of an ideal friend and describe how this person would act in such-and-such a situation. Here you would have a hypothetical or imagined example or illustration. Both types are useful. Both types are effective.

David Rockefeller (1985) uses a particularly effective real example to illustrate how people can make charitable contributions in creative ways:

> One of the most fascinating ventures along these lines has been the actor Paul Newman's venture into salad oil. Some three years ago—as a lark—he and a friend started a company to market his home-made salad oil and other products such as

Newman's Own Industrial Strength Venetian Spaghetti Sauce, and then donate any profits to charity. Last year the company netted some $1.19 million which it gave to support 80 different nonprofit groups!

Critically Evaluating Examples and Illustrations

Ask yourself (as speaker, listener, and critic) the following questions about your examples and illustrations.

1. Is the example or illustration typical or representative? Generally, use an example that is representative of the class of objects about which you are speaking. Training schools that advertise on television frequently show a particularly successful graduate. The advertiser assumes, of course, that the audience will see this example as representative. Perhaps this person is representative; more often than not, however, representativeness is not achieved or perhaps even desired by the advertiser.

At times you may want to draw an example or illustration that is purposefully far-fetched. Perhaps you wish to poke fun at a particular proposal or show the inadequacies of an alternative point of view. The important point is that both you and the audience see the example and the illustration in the same way. If you assume that the example is typical and logical and the audience assumes that it is a caricature, it will prove ineffective and backfire.

2. Is the example relevant? Use examples that relate directly to the proposition you wish to explain. Leave out irrelevant examples, however interesting or entertaining. Be certain too that the audience sees the relevance. Notice how Marvin Alisky (1985) uses his example to make his point:

In his play Pygmalion, *George Bernard Shaw observes, "If you treat a girl like a flower girl, that's all she will ever be. If you treat her like a princess she may become one."*
If we treat those around us like extensions of our modern technology, that is all they will be. If we treat them like important assets with individual and changing needs, then they will become assets to our organizations and communities.

Using Examples and Illustrations

In using the example and illustration, keep in mind that their function is to make your ideas vivid and easily understood. They are useful for explaining a concept; they are not ends in themselves. Make them only as long as necessary to ensure that your purpose is achieved. Details for the sake of details are useless. Similarly, use enough examples to make your point. Make sure that the examples are sufficient to re-create your meaning in the minds of your listeners, but be careful not to use too many. If you use too many examples the audience may become bored and may lose the very point you wish to make.

Make the relationship between your assertion and your example explicit. Remember that this relationship is clear to you because you have constructed the speech. The audience is going to hear your speech only once. Show the audience exactly how your example relates to the assertion or concept you are explaining. Consider the following excerpt in which Stella Guerra (1986) uses a series of examples to illustrate the progress made by women in government and the military. Notice how much more effective these examples are than if she had simply said, "Women have made great progress in government and in the military."

> *In short, we are continuing to help America forge an environment that says "opportunities are abundant."*
>
> *In this environment of prosperity we've seen many firsts:*
> *The first female brigadier general*
> *The first female astronaut*
> *The first female sky marshall*
> *The first female ambassador to the United Nations*
> *The first female justice of the Supreme Court*
> *The first female director of Civil Service*
> *The first female U.S. Customs rep in a foreign country*
> *The first female to graduate at the very top of the class in a service academy—*
> *Navy '84; Air Force '86*
> *The list goes on and on—and this same progress can be seen in all sectors of our society.*

Make clear the distinction between real and hypothetical illustrations. Do not try to foist a hypothetical illustration on the audience as a real one. If they recognize it, they will resent your attempt to fool them. Use statements such as the following to let the audience know when you are using a hypothetical example.

> *We could imagine a situation such as . . .*
>
> *I think an ideal friend would be someone who . . .*
>
> *A hypothetical illustration of this type of friendship would be like this.*

If the example or illustration is real, let the audience know this as well. Such statements as "A situation such as this occurred recently; it involved . . . ," or "I have a friend who . . . ," or simply "An actual example of this was reported . . . " will help the audience see what you want them to see.

REMEMBER: Examples and illustrations are specific instances explained in varying degrees of detail and are especially useful in making ideas vivid.

Examples and illustrations may be:

1. real or hypothetical

    and should be:

2. representative and relevant

    and are most effective when:

3. used to explain a concept rather than as ends in themselves

4. the relationship between the concept and the example or illustration is made explicit

5. the distinction between a real and a hypothetical example or illustration is made clear

TESTIMONY

Testimony refers to the opinions of experts or to the accounts of witnesses. Testimony helps to amplify your speech by adding a note of authority to your arguments. Testimony may, therefore, be used in either of two ways. First, you might be concerned with the opinions, beliefs, predictions, or values of some authority or expert. You might, for example, want to state an economist's predictions concerning inflation and depression, or you might want to support your analysis by citing an art critic's evaluation of a painting or art movement.

As you can see, testimony is also of value when you wish to persuade an audience. Thus, you may use the testimony of a noted economist to support your predictions about inflation, or you may wish to cite an education professor's opinion about the problems confronting education in an effort to persuade your listeners that certain changes must be made in our schools.

In the following excerpt, for instance, U.S. Congresswoman Shirley Chisholm addresses the Independent Black Women's Caucus of New York City and uses the testimony of noted psychologist Rollo May to bolster her argument that black women must assume political power rather than wait for it to be given to them.

> As Rollo May has put it: "Power cannot, strictly speaking, be given to another, for then the recipient still owes it to the giver. It must in some sense be assumed, taken, asserted, for unless it can be held against opposition, it is not power and will never be experienced as real on the part of the recipient." And those of us in this room know all too well that whatever is given to us is almost always a trap.

Second, you might want to use the testimony of an eyewitness to some event or situation. You might, for example, cite the testimony of someone who saw an accident, the person who spent two years in a maximum-security prison, or the person who had a particular operation.

One way for you to present testimony is to use direct quotations. Quotations are often useful, but at times they become cumbersome. Too often they are not related directly to the point you are trying to make and their relevance gets lost. If the quotation is in technical language that members of the audience will not understand, it then becomes necessary to interject definitions as you go along. Therefore, unless the quotation is short, comprehensible to the audience, and related directly to the point you are trying to make, use your own words; paraphrase in your own words the essence of the testimony. Do note, of course, when the ideas are borrowed from your authority or source.

Critically Evaluating Testimony

Test the adequacy of your testimony by asking yourself the following questions. You might find it interesting to apply these questions to the beaver in the cartoon.

1. *Is the testimony presented fairly?* In using the testimony of others, present it fairly. Include, for example, any qualifications made by the expert. When presenting the ideas of an authority, present them as that authority would want. The accompany-

"*I ask that the record show that the witness does not presume to speak for the animal kingdom but is testifying here strictly in his capacity as a beaver.*"

Drawing by Maslin; © 1992 The New Yorker Magazine, Inc. Reprinted by permission.

ing "TIP" from Claude C. Cox, in his talk on speech writing, offers sound advice concerning accuracy in general and of testimony in particular.

2. Is the person an authority on this subject? Authorities, especially today, reign over very small territories. Doctors, professors, and lawyers—to name just a few authorities—are experts on very small bodies of knowledge. A doctor may be an expert on the thyroid gland but may know little about skin, muscles, or blood. A professor of history might know a great deal about the Renaissance but little about American history. When an authority is used, be certain that the person is in fact an authority *on your specific subject.*

3. Is the person unbiased? This question should be asked of both expert and witness accounts. Try to discover if there are any biases in the sources being cited. The real estate salesperson who tells you to "Buy! Buy! Buy!" and the diamond seller who tells you "Diamonds are your best investment" obviously have something to gain and are biased. Be suspicious of the conclusions of any biased source. This does not mean that normally biased sources cannot provide unbiased testimony. Surely they can. This does mean that once a bias has been detected, you should be on the lookout for how this bias *might* figure into the testimony.

■-■-■-■

TIPS FROM PROFESSIONAL SPEAKERS

One of the first and most important commandments for any writer is: "Thou shalt check and recheck your facts." A parallel commandment is: "Never assume anything."

A writer should never place himself in the position of having his credibility questioned. Actually, the writer's credibility represents the credibility of the TV or radio station, a sponsor, the talent reading the script, or a cable channel.

If a quotation is used, it must be exact, and left in context as much as possible when time allows. If time is not available to use a complete quote, the script should place the quotation into its proper perspective.

Dates and numbers must be accurate. References to sources need to be given whenever possible. It is far better to omit a fact or figure than to use it if there is any question about its accuracy.

Claude C. Cox, director of marketing, Southern Baptist Radio-TV Commission. "Everyone Is a Writer," *Vital Speeches of the Day* 51 (June 1, 1985): 507.

Using Testimony

When you cite testimony, first, stress the competence of the person whether that person is an expert or a witness. To cite the predictions of a world-famous economist of whom your audience has never heard will mean little unless you first explain the person's competence. You might say, for example:

> *This prediction comes from the world's leading economist, who has successfully predicted all major financial trends over the past 20 years.*

Now the audience will be prepared to lend credence to what this person says.

Similarly, establish the competence of a witness. Consider the following two excerpts.

> *My friend told me that in prison drugs are so easy to get that all you have to do is pay the guard and you'll get whatever you want.*

> *My friend, who was a guard in three different prisons over the past 15 years, told me that in prisons drugs are so easy to get that all you have to do is pay the guard and you'll get whatever you want.*

Notice that in the second statement, you establish the credibility of your source. Your audience is much more likely to believe this second testimony.

Second, stress the unbiased nature of the testimony. If the audience perceives the testimony to be biased—whether or not it really is—it will have little effect. You want to check out the biases of a witness so that you may present accurate information. But, you also want to make the audience see that the testimony is in fact unbiased.

Third, stress the recency of the statement to the audience. Notice that in the first excerpt that follows, we have no way of knowing when the statement was made and

If you could interview anyone you wished for your next speech, whom would you choose? What questions would you ask?

therefore no way of knowing how true this statement would be today. In the second excerpt, however, the recency of the statement is stressed. As demonstrated by this example, recency is often a crucial factor in determining whether or not we will believe a statement.

> *General Bailey has noted that the United States has over twice the military power of any other world power.*

> *General Bailey, who was interviewed last week in the* Washington Post, *noted that the United States has twice the military power of any other world power.*

REMEMBER: Testimony is used when the opinions of experts or the accounts of witnesses are needed to lend authority or otherwise amplify your propositions.
  Testimony should be:

1. presented fairly
2. authoritative on the specific subject
3. unbiased

   and is most effective when:

4. the competence of the authority is stressed
5. the unbiased nature of the testimony is stressed
6. the recency of the observation or opinion is stressed

STATISTICS

Statistics are summary numbers. Statistics help us to see at a glance the important characteristics of an otherwise complex set of numbers. For a teacher to read off 50 grades on the last examination would not help you to grasp where your score fell in relation to the others in your class. In such cases, statistical information is much more helpful.

Measures of Central Tendency Measures of *central tendency* tell you the general pattern of a group of numbers. The *mean* is the arithmetic average of a set of numbers; for example, the mean grade on the mid-term was 89, the mean expenditure on personal grooming items is $40 per year, the mean income for scientists is $64,000.

The *median* is the middle score; 50 percent of the cases fall above the median and 50 percent fall below it. For example, if the median score on the mid-term was 78, it means that half the class scored higher than 78 and half scored lower.

The *mode* is the most frequently occurring score. It is the single score that most people received. If the mode of the mid-term was 85, it means that more students received 85 than any other single score.

Measures of Correlation Measures of *correlation* tell you how closely two or more things are related. You might say, for example, that there is a high correlation between smoking and lung cancer or between poverty and crime. Recognize that high correlations do not mean causation. The fact that two things vary together (that is, are highly correlated) does not mean that one causes the other. They may each be caused by some third factor.

Measures of Difference Measures of *difference* tell you the extent to which scores differ from the average or from each other. For example, the *range* tells us how far the lowest score is from the highest score. The range is computed by subtracting the lowest from the highest score. If the lowest score on the mid-term was 76 and the highest was 99, the range was 23 points. Generally, a high range indicates great diversity, whereas a low range indicates great similarity.

Percentiles Percentiles are useful for specifying the percentage of scores that fall below a particular score. For example, if you scored 700 on the College Entrance Examination Board test, you were approximately in the ninety-seventh percentile. This means that 97 percent of those taking the test scored lower than 700. Generally, the twenty-fifth, fiftieth, and seventy-fifth percentiles (also called, respectively, the first, second, and third quartiles) are distinguished. The second quartile, or fiftieth percentile, is also the median since exactly half the scores are above and half are below.

In the following excerpts the speakers use statistical figures to make their assertions more vivid and more meaningful. Ernest L. Boyer, U.S. Commissioner of Education, uses the arithmetic mean to demonstrate that children are avid television viewers.

Young children—2 to 5 years old—now watch television over 4 hours every day, nearly 30 hours a week. That's more than 1500 hours every year. And by the time a youngster enters first grade he or she has had 6000 hours of television viewing.

Critically Evaluating Statistics

In critically evaluating statistics, ask the following questions.

1. Are the statistics based on a large enough sample? The size of the sample is always important. This is one reason why few advertisers ever report the size of their sample. Advertisers may tell you, for example:

> *Buy Blotto milk for the health of your baby. Four out of five nutritionists surveyed chose Blotto milk.*

But, you are not told how large the entire sample was. If they merely tested groups of five until they found one group where four would endorse Blotto, you would not put much confidence in those statistics. (Note too that the statement does not say what they chose Blotto milk over. We assume it was other brands of milk but nowhere does the advertiser make this explicit.) The sample must be large enough to expect that if another group were selected, the results would be the same as those reported in the statistics. Enough nutritionists should have been surveyed so that if you went out and selected 100 at random, 80 would endorse Blotto.

2. Is the sample a fair representation of the entire population? If you wish to make inferences about an entire class of people, sample the group fairly and include representatives of all subgroups. Thus, it would be unfair to make inferences about the attitudes of college professors if you surveyed only communication professors. Nor, however, would it be fair if you surveyed only biology or only history professors.

3. Is the statistic based on recent sampling? Recency is particularly important since things change so rapidly. To report mean income, church attendance, or smoking statistics without ensuring recency would be meaningless. Here, for example, Martha Lamkin (1986), in a speech delivered October 24, 1986, uses the September 1986 issue of *American Demographics* for her statistics. Note too that she cites not only the current status of women in these professions but also what these figures mean in terms of growth:

> *Despite the persistence of occupational segregation, women's representation in several areas is growing rapidly. The September issue of* American Demographics *reports that, since 1970:*
>
> *. . . women now make up over 20 percent of all lawyers—an increase of 400 percent; . . . we now comprise 18 percent of all doctors—up 80 percent; and . . . women now constitute 28 percent of all computer scientists—a 100 percent increase.*

4. Are the statistics collected and analyzed by an unbiased source? Remember our advertisers! They are intent on selling a product; they make their living that way. When they say "four out of five," ask who collected the data and who analyzed it?

Using Statistics

Keep in mind that the audience will ask essentially the same questions that a good researcher would ask in analyzing statistics. Answer these questions for your audience. For example, answer their questions about whether the source is biased. Stress the unbiased nature of the source who collected and analyzed the statistics, the representativeness of the sample, and the recency of the statistical collections and computations.

Further, make the statistics clear to an audience that will hear the figures only once. Round off figures so they are easy to comprehend and retain. Don't say that the median income of workers in this city is $12,347. This may be accurate, but it will be difficult to remember. Instead, say that it is "around $12,300" or even "a bit more than $12,000."

Make numbers meaningful to the audience. To say, for example, that the Sears Tower in Chicago is 1559 feet tall does not visualize its height. So, consider saying something like:

> *The Sears Tower is 1559 feet tall. Just how tall is 1559 feet? Well, it's as tall as the length of more than four football fields. That's how tall. It's as tall as 260 6-foot people standing on each other's heads.*

Make explicit the connection between the statistics and what they show. To say, for example, that college professors make an average of $42,000 per year needs to be related specifically and to the proposition that teachers' salaries should be raised or lowered, depending on your point of view.

Here Geneva Johnson (1991) uses statistics to dramatize the rapid population growth of the elderly:

> *Today's population is growing at a steady rate of 1 percent per year and now includes 6 million elderly. By 2030, we will have 17 million and by 2050, 26 million. Implication, today, is that 1 in 40 people are 80 or older. By 2050, 1 in 12 will be 80 or older.*

REMEMBER: Statistics are an organized summary of figures that clarify trends or other important characteristics of an otherwise complex set of numbers.

Statistics should be:

1. based on a large enough sample
2. based on a representative sample
3. based on recent sampling
4. collected and analyzed by unbiased sources

   and are most effective when:

5. the unbiased nature of the statistics is stressed
6. the statistics are clearly understandable to an audience hearing them just once
7. the statistics are made meaningful to the audience
8. the connection between the statistics and what they support or amplify is stressed

CRITICALLY SPEAKING

1. What kind of an example might you use to explain the feeling of love? Loneliness? Joy? Sadness? Poverty? Excellence of mind? Physical strength?

2. How effectively do your instructors use examples and illustrations? What suggestions for improvement might you offer?

3. What specific person or type of person would prove an effective spokesperson for:
   a. the best way to bake a cake
   b. how to lead a happy life
   c. what the government has to do to solve economic problems
   d. why religion is (not) important in everyday life

4. For what propositions would you be an effective spokesperson? Why?

5. How effectively do advertisements use statistics? What principles for using statistics do you think advertisers generally follow? Why?

6. What kinds of statistics would help you support the following propositions?
   a. robotics engineering pays well
   b. Golden Gate Bridge is long
   c. adventure films are the most financially successful
   d. college graduates are significantly happier than nongraduates
   e. WhiterWhite fights tooth decay better than any other toothpaste
   f. excessive television viewing distorts the viewer's perceptions of reality

PRACTICALLY SPEAKING

14.1   AMPLIFYING STATEMENTS

Here are some rather bland, uninteresting statements. Select one of them and amplify it using at least three different methods of amplification. Identify each method used. Since the purpose of this exercise is to provide greater insight into forms and methods of amplification, you may, for this exercise, manufacture, fabricate, or otherwise invent facts, figures, illustrations, examples, and the like. In fact, it may prove even more beneficial if you go to extremes in constructing these forms of support.

1. Significant social and political contributions have been made by college students.
2. The Sears Tower in Chicago is the world's tallest building.
3. Dr. Kirk is a model professor.
4. My grandparents left me a fortune in their will.
5. The college I just visited seems ideal.
6. The writer of this article is a real authority.
7. I knew I was marrying into money as soon as I walked into the house.
8. Considering what they did, punishment to the fullest extent of the law would be mild.
9. The fortune teller told us good news.
10. The athlete lived an interesting life.

14.2 EVALUATING TESTIMONY

The exercise explores some of the standards for evaluating testimony. At the same time, it will suggest ways in which you can select and present testimony to an audience more effectively. Therefore, consider two questions together: (1) What would the person's (ideal) qualifications be, before you would accept his or her testimony on the following issues and purposes, or, alternatively, (2) if you were presenting testimony on the following issues, how would you establish the person's qualifications so that your class members would accept what he or she says?

1. a report of an accident
2. the importance of a proper diet
3. lose weight now
4. improve your communication skills
5. follow the advice given by astrology
6. buy real estate now
7. ways to prevent the spread of AIDS
8. the real Oprah Winfrey
9. how to read the stock market page
10. tips on buying a computer
11. the near-death experience
12. schizophrenia
13. rising in the corporation
14. how to feed your pet
15. why a particular food is good for you
16. writing a book
17. overcoming test anxiety
18. how to lose your fear of public speaking
19. improve your memory
20. life on Mars

Audiovisual Aids

UNIT OUTLINE

The Functions of Audiovisual Aids
Types of Audiovisual Aids
Critically Evaluating Audiovisual Aids
Using Audiovisual Aids

Critically Speaking
Practically Speaking

■ ■ ■ ■

UNIT OBJECTIVES

After completing this unit, you should be able to:

1. Explain the functions of audiovisual aids

2. Identify at least ten types of audiovisual aids

3. Explain the four tests to use in critically evaluating the effectiveness of audiovisual aids

4. Explain the guidelines for using audiovisual aids

When you are planning to give a speech, consider using some kind of audio-visual aid—a visual or auditory means of clarifying or amplifying your speech. At the start, ask yourself if you should you use an AV aid. How would the aid make your speech more effective? What type of aid should you use? Charts? Slides? Models? There are many types to choose from. How should you go about creating the AV aid? What principles should you follow to make sure that your aid helps you achieve your public speaking purpose? How should you use the aid during your speech?

■■■■■ THE FUNCTIONS OF AUDIOVISUAL AIDS

AV aids are not an added frill. They are integral parts of your speech and serve important functions. Let's look at some of the more important functions.

Audiovisuals Gain Attention and Maintain Interest

We are a generation that grew up on audiovisual entertainment. We are used to it and we enjoy it. It's not surprising then that we, as members of the audience, appreciate it when a speaker makes use of such aids. We perk up when the speaker says, "I want you to look at this chart showing the employment picture for the next five years" or "Listen to the way Springsteen uses vocal variety."

Audiovisual aids also help maintain attention and interest because they break up the speech and provide some variety in what we see and what we hear. Audiences will appreciate this and will respond more favorably to you when you provide them with this variety, with this differently packaged message.

Audiovisuals Add Clarity

Let's say you want to illustrate the growth of the cable television industry in the United States over the last 30 years. You could say, for example, "In 1952 there were 14,000 subscribers, in 1955 there were 150,000 subscribers, in 1960 there were 650,000 subscribers, in 1965 there were 1,275,000 subscribers, . . . " This gets pretty boring and you still haven't covered the '70s and the '80s. Note how much easier this same information is communicated in the bar graph in Figure 15.1. At a glance we can see the rapid growth from practically nothing to over 41,000,000 subscribers.

Audiovisuals Reinforce Your Message

Audiovisuals help to add the redundancy that is so necessary in making sure the audience understands and remembers what you have said. With a visual aid you present the same information in two different ways—verbally as they hear you explain the aid and visually as they see the chart, map, or model. The same is true with audio aids. The audience hears you speak of vocal variety but they also hear examples of it from

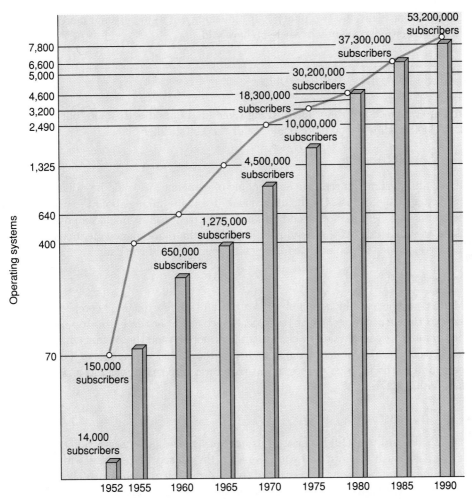

FIGURE 15.1 Growth of the cable TV industry in the United States as of January of each year. (*Sources:* Figures for 1952 to 1974: *Television Factbook,* services vol. no. 44 [1974–1975 ed.]. Figures for 1975: National Cable Television Association. Figures for 1978: *Television Factbook,* services vol. no. 47 [1977–1978 ed.]. Figures for 1980: *Television Digest, Inc.* Figures for 1983, 1985, and 1987: *Broadcasting/Cablecasting Yearbook.* Warren K. Agee, Phillip H. Ault, and Edwin Emery, *Introduction to Mass Communication,* 10th ed., New York: HarperCollins, 1991, p. 268.)

the recording. This one-two punch helps the audience to understand more clearly and to remember more accurately what you have said.

■■■■ TYPES OF AUDIOVISUAL AIDS

You are convinced of the value of using some kind of audiovisual aid, but what kind? Let's look at some of the more popular aids used by speakers.

The Actual Object

If you are speaking on the care and feeding of elephants, it would be difficult to bring the actual thing to class. On the other hand, if you are talking about the workings of a computer or a lie detector or certain kinds of tropical fish, it might be possible to use these as visual aids. As a general rule (to which there are many exceptions), the best audiovisual aid is the object itself; bring it to your speech if you can.

Models

Models—replicas of the actual object—are useful when explaining complex structures such as the hearing mechanism, the vocal mechanism, or the brain. You may remember from biology or physiology class that these models (and the pictures of them in the textbooks) made a lot more sense than just the verbal explanations. These models helped to clarify the size of the various structures, their position, and how they interface with each other.

The Chalkboard

The chalkboard is useful because of its ease of use and general availability. All classrooms have such a board and you have seen them used by teachers with greater or lesser effect; in some way, you have had some "experience" with them. The chalkboard may be used effectively to record key terms or important definitions or even to outline the general structure of your speech. The chalkboard does, however, have disadvantages. Don't use it when you can present the same information with a preplanned chart or model. The reason is that it is difficult for the novice speaker to use the chalkboard without losing the attention of the audience. Often, for example, speakers will turn their backs to the audience while they write on the board. In this brief time, they can easily lose the attention of the audience.

Transparent and Opaque Projections

Serving a purpose similar to the chalkboard are transparent and opaque projections. Most communication departments have such projectors readily available. A *transparency* is a clear, acetate page onto which any carbon imprint (pencil, photocopy, or laser printing, for example) can be transferred and then projected onto the wall or a screen, making a relatively small image large enough to be seen from all parts of the room. This is useful for terms or outlines that are complex and that you want your listeners to see as well as hear.

Another advantage is that you can write on the transparencies while you are

THE
BASES OF
POWER

REFERENT POWER

LEGITIMATE POWER

REWARD POWER

COERCIVE POWER

EXPERT POWER

INFORMATION POWER

FIGURE 15.2   Transparency master.

speaking. You can circle important items, underline key terms, and draw lines connecting different terms. Here, for example, is a transparency I use in teaching a large interpersonal communication class (Figure 15.2).

Opaque projections serve a similar function as transparencies but use the actual page or photograph rather than a specially made transparency. Both can be presented on an opaque projector. Perhaps the greatest advantage of such projections is that they can be presented to the audience and then removed from sight just by flicking the "off" switch.

In using transparencies or opaque projections, do not clutter them up with too much material. Use the transparency to highlight a few essential points. Depending on your specific purpose, you may find it helpful to disclose what is contained on the transparency gradually rather than all at once. A piece of lightweight cardboard works well to cover the page. You can then disclose each point when you wish the audience to attend to it. You can add color by using transparencies of different colors and also by using grease pencils or marking pencils in a variety of colors.

Some projectors generate a great deal of noise, so you may have to adjust your speech volume to combat this extra noise.

Handouts

Handouts (printed material) are helpful in explaining complex material and also in providing listeners with a permanent record of some aspect of your speech. Handouts are also useful for presenting complex information that you want your audience to refer to throughout your speech.

Handouts can cause problems if they contain information not yet covered in your speech. Audience members may peruse them when you would rather they devote their attention to what you are saying. You don't want to have to remind your listeners to ignore the handout and concentrate on what you're saying.

Charts

Charts are useful in communicating lots of different types of information. Simple *word charts* will help you to highlight the major points you wish to cover in your speech. For example, in a speech on "How to read a book," the word chart presented in Figure 15.3 clearly identifies the major steps the speaker is discussing. This chart may be used with the orientation in the introduction, with the major points in the body, or with the conclusion's summary. Or, it may be set up and referred to throughout the speech. Note that its simplicity is especially helpful because it identifies the major concepts but will not distract the listeners as your speak.

A chart of a somewhat different type is the *flip chart*. This is actually a pad of paper, usually very large paper of about 24 × 24 inches. The pad is mounted on a stand and as you deliver your speech, you flip the pages of the pad to reveal the visuals you want your audience to see. For example, if you were to discuss the various departments in an organization, you might have the key points relating to each department on a separate page of your flip chart. As you discuss the advertising department, you would show the chart relevant to the advertising department. When you move on to discuss the personnel department, you would flip to the chart dealing with personnel.

Graphs

Graphs are useful for showing differences over time, for showing how a whole is divided into parts, and for showing different amounts or sizes.

The *bar graph* illustrating the growth of the cable television industry presented in Figure 15.1 is a good example of a graph designed to show differences over time.

HOW TO READ A BOOK

1. PREVIEW

2. READ FOR UNDERSTANDING

3. READ FOR RETENTION

4. REVIEW

FIGURE 15.3   A word chart.

Another bar graph, presented in Figure 15.4, illustrates the changes taking place in college majors. Figure 15.5 presents a very simple bar chart to illustrate the differences in the volume of selected sounds.

Use a *pie graph* (*pie chart*) if you want to show how some whole is divided into its parts. Pie charts clearly depict how a whole is divided into several parts and the relative sizes of these parts.

FIGURE 15.4   A bar graph. (*Source:* "1985 Facts & Figures for New York State Public Schools," NYS School Boards Association.)

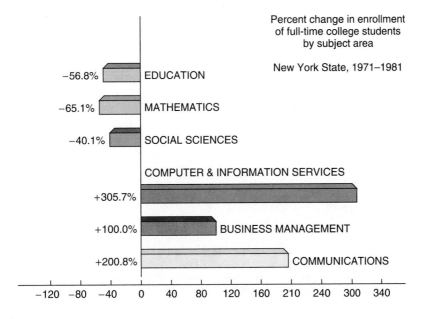

Percent change in enrollment
of full-time college students
by subject area

New York State, 1971–1981

−56.8% EDUCATION

−65.1% MATHEMATICS

−40.1% SOCIAL SCIENCES

COMPUTER & INFORMATION SERVICES

+305.7%

+100.0% BUSINESS MANAGEMENT

+200.8% COMMUNICATIONS

−120 −80 −40 0 40 80 120 160 210 240 300 340

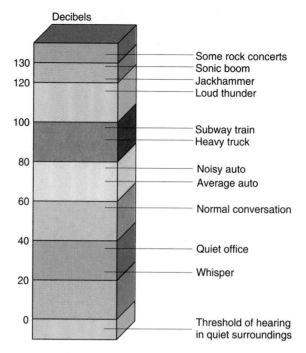

FIGURE 15.5   A scale of decibels showing values of familiar sounds for comparison. (From *Psychology in Perspective* by James Hassett and Kathleen M. White. Copyright © 1989 by Harper & Row, Publishers, Inc. Reprinted by permission of HarperCollins Publishers, Inc.)

FIGURE 15.6   A line chart.

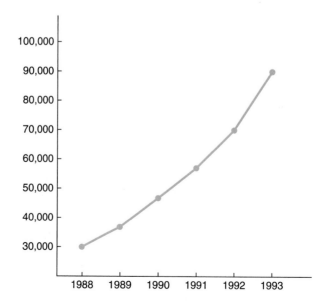

Line charts are useful when you want to show changes or trends over a particular time period. Look at the line chart in Figure 15.6. This illustrates the sales for a small grocery store over a six-year period and clearly communicates how rapidly the business has grown.

Maps

Maps are useful for showing geographic elements as well as changes throughout history: population density, immigration patterns, economic conditions, the location of various resources, and hundreds of other issues you may wish to develop in your speeches. The map in Figure 15.7 shows the area of the country covered by the Sunbelt.

People

Oddly enough, *people* can function effectively as "audiovisual aids." For example, if you wanted to demonstrate the muscles of the body, you might use a bodybuilder. If you wanted to demonstrate different voice patterns, skin complexions, or hairstyles, you might use people as your aids. Aside from the obvious assistance they provide in

FIGURE 15.7   A map as a visual aid. (From *Understanding Society*, 2nd ed., by Caroline Hodges Persell. Copyright © 1987 by Harper & Row, Publishers, Inc. Reprinted by permission of HarperCollins Publishers, Inc.)

The Sunbelt

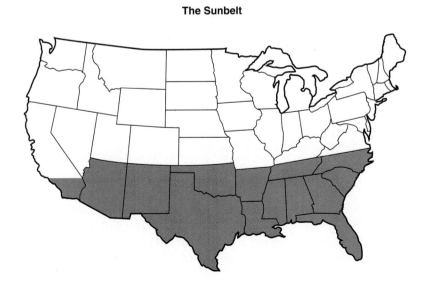

demonstrating their muscles or voice qualities, people help to secure and maintain the attention and interest of the audience.

Slides

Slides are useful for showing various scenes or graphics that you cannot describe in words. The great advantages of slides are their visual appeal (and hence their attention-getting value) and their ease of preparation and use. Again, most departments of communication have slide projectors, so you should have no trouble getting the equipment. When planning to use slides, be sure you allow yourself sufficient time to shoot, develop, and organize them.

Films, Filmstrips, and Videotapes

I use a variety of *films* to illustrate some of the breakdowns in interpersonal communication, the techniques for and the progress made in teaching animals to communicate, and various other topics. *Filmstrips* are also useful because they enable you to regulate timing more closely. If there are a number of questions during a lecture, you can easily stop a filmstrip to address them; stopping a film it is a bit more cumbersome. Although it is a great deal to undertake, you might consider making your own *videotape* to illustrate your talk. But remember, a bad film is a bad audiovisual aid and detracts rather than adds to the effectiveness of your speech.

Pictures and Illustrations

Assuming that you do not have films or slides, the next best visual aid is a *picture*. There, however, many hazards involved in using this type of aid, so I recommend its use only with reservations. If the picture is large enough for all members of the audience to see clearly (say, poster size), if it clearly illustrates what you want to illustrate, and if it is mounted on cardboard, then use it; otherwise, do not.

Do not pass pictures around the room. This only draws attention away from what you are saying. Listeners will look for the pictures to circulate to them, will wonder what the pictures contain, and will miss a great deal of your speech in the interim.

Illustrations may at times be more useful than pictures. For example, Figure 15.8 presents an illustration of the human ear to show the structures of the ears, their shape, and how they are related to each other.

Records and Tapes

To deliver a speech about music and not provide the audience with samples would seem strange. Very likely the audience's attention will be drawn away from your speech to wonder why you have not provided the actual music. Records and tapes, of course, can be useful for many other types of speeches as well. A speech on advertising would be greatly helped, for example, by having actual samples of advertisements as played on radio or television. A tape of such examples would go a long way to help clarify your point. It would also provide for variety by breaking up the oral presentation most effectively.

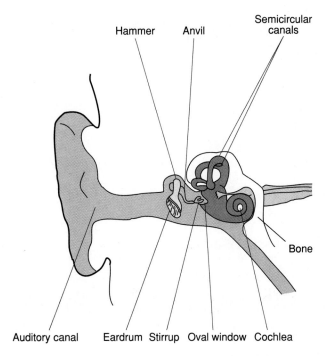

FIGURE 15.8   The structure of the human ear. (From *Psychology in Perspective* by James Hassett and Kathleen M. White. Copyright © 1989 by Harper & Row, Publishers, Inc. Reprinted by permission of HarperCollins Publishers, Inc.)

REMEMBER: **Audiovisual aids serve a number of important functions by helping you to:**

1. **gain attention and maintain the interest of your listeners**
2. **clarify concepts**
3. **reinforce your message**

and come in many forms, for example: the actual object, models, the chalkboard, transparent and opaque projections, handouts, charts (word, organization, and flip), graphs (bar, pie, and line), maps, people, slides, films, filmstrips, and videotapes, pictures and illustrations, and records and tapes.

CRITICALLY EVALUATING AUDIOVISUAL AIDS

In using audiovisual aids, ask yourself the following questions.

Is the Aid Clear?

This is the most important test of all. If the aid is not clearly visible, it will not serve its purpose. Therefore, make the aid large enough so that everyone can see it. Poster-board paper is readily available and relatively inexpensive. The 24×36-inch size seems

Maps are an often neglected form of visual aid. How might you incorporate a map into your next speeches?

large enough for most purposes. It contains enough space for most charts or graphs and it can be seen from any point in most classrooms. Black print on a white background is probably the clearest combination you can use. Also, make the aid simple so that its meaning is clear. Too many words or pictures will obscure your meaning.

Is the Aid Relevant?

It may be attractive, well-designed, easy to read, and possess all the features one could hope for in an audiovisual aid, but if it is not relevant to the topic, leave it at home.

Is the Aid Appealing?

Audiovisual aids work best when they are appealing. Sloppy, poorly designed, and dirty visual aids will detract from the purpose they are intended to serve. Visual aids should be attractive enough to engage the attention of the audience, but not so attractive that they are distracting. The almost nude body draped across a car may be effective in selling underwear, but would probably detract if your object is to explain the profit-and-loss statement of the Chrysler Corporation.

USING AUDIOVISUAL AIDS

Keep the following guidelines for using audiovisual aids clearly in mind.

Use the Aid When It Is Relevant

Use the aid only when it is relevant. Show it when you want the audience to concentrate on it and then remove it. If you are using the chalkboard, write the terms or draw the diagrams when you want the audience to see them and then erase them. If you do not remove the visual, the audience's attention may remain focused on the board when you want to go on to something else.

Know Your Aids Intimately

When planning to use an audiovisual aid, know it intimately. This is especially true when you are planning to use several audiovisual aids. Be sure you know in what order they are to be presented and how you plan to introduce them. Know exactly what goes where and when.

Test the Aids Before Using Them

Test the audiovisual aids prior to your speech. Be certain that they can be easily seen from all parts of the room. An inability to see a visual aid clearly is probably the greatest error speakers make. They assume that listeners in all parts of the room will be able to see the aid without actually testing it out. Always test your aids and make sure they can be seen without difficulty.

Rehearse your speech with the audiovisual aids incorporated into the presentation. Practice your actual movements with the aids you will use. If you are going to use a chart, how will you use it? Will it stand by itself? Will you tape it to the board (and do you have tape with you)? Will you ask another student to hold it for you? Will you hold it yourself?

Do Not Talk to Your Audiovisual Aid

Avoid the common mistake that many speakers make when using audiovisuals—they talk to the aid instead of the audience. Both you and the aid should be focused on the audience. Talk to your audience at all times. Know your aids so well that you can point to what you want without breaking eye contact with your audience.

REMEMBER: **Audiovisual aids should be:**

1. **clear**
2. **relevant to the topic and issue at hand**
3. **attractive and appealing**

and are most effective when:

4. **used only at the time they are relevant**
5. **you are especially familiar with them**
6. **you have previously tested them for clarity and workability**
7. **they do not hinder speaker-audience contact**

CRITICALLY SPEAKING

1. What other functions do audiovisual aids serve?
2. What persuasive functions do audiovisual aids serve?
3. What might be appropriate audiovisual aids for such topics as these:
highway safety
the need for prison reform
expanding health care programs
eliminating core requirements in colleges
the history of the mystery novel
children's television commercials
economic problems and the American family
4. Recall the last college lecture you heard. Did the instructor use any audiovisual aids? What particular aids might have helped improve the class?
5. What's the worst possible scenario you can imagine concerning the misuse of audiovisual aids?

PRACTICALLY SPEAKING

15.1   ANALYZING VISUAL AIDS

Select a print advertisement and analyze the visuals. For purposes of this exercise, consider the text of the ad as the spoken speech and the visual in the ad as the visual aid for the speech.

1. What types of aids were used?
2. What functions did the visual aids serve?
3. Were the aids clear?
4. Were they relevant?
5. Are the aids appealing?

15.2   CREATING VISUAL AIDS

Create an appropriate visual aid for one of the speeches contained in this book. Explain how your visual aid gains attention, clarifies concepts, helps the audience to remember the speech, and reinforces the message.

The Persuasive Speech

■ ■ ■ ■

UNIT OBJECTIVES

After completing this unit, you should be able to:

1. Define *attitude, belief,* and *behavior* as used in persuasion

2. Explain the following principles of persuasion: the credibility principle, the attractiveness principle, the audience participation principle, the inoculation principle, and the magnitude of change principle

3. Explain the foot-in-the-door and the door-in-the-face techniques

4. Explain the two types of persuasive speeches and at least three strategies for achieving each persuasive goal

---

*M*ost of the speeches you hear are persuasive speeches. The speeches of politicians, advertisers, and religious leaders are perhaps the clearest examples. In most of your own speeches, you too will aim at persuasion. You will try to change your listeners' attitudes and beliefs or perhaps change their behaviors. In school you might try to persuade others to (or not to) expand the core curriculum, use a plus-minus or a pass-fail grading system, disband the basketball team, allocate increased student funds for the school newspaper, establish competitive majors, or eliminate fraternity hazing. On your job you may be called upon to speak in favor of (or against) having a union, a wage increase proposal, a health benefit package, or Tim Doolan for shop steward.

Persuasive speaking is and will continue to be an important part of your academic and professional life. Your persuasive abilities will enable you to achieve your goals more effectively and will help to distinguish you as a leader.

This and the next two units focus on the important skills of persuasion and explain what persuasion is and how you can become a more successful persuasive speaker.

ATTITUDES, BELIEFS, AND BEHAVIORS

In your persuasive speeches you might want to strengthen or change the attitudes or beliefs of your listeners. Or, you might want to get them to do something; that is, you might want to influence their behaviors. Let's define more specifically what is meant by attitudes, beliefs, and behaviors.

Think of an **attitude** as a tendency to behave in a certain way. For example, if you have a favorable attitude toward chemistry, you will be more apt to elect chemistry courses, to read about chemistry, to talk about chemistry, and to conduct chemistry experiments. If you have an unfavorable attitude toward chemistry, you will avoid chemistry courses, not read about chemistry, and so on. If you have a negative attitude toward horror films, you will resist going to see them and might try to discourage your friends or family from seeing them as well.

A **belief** is a conviction in the existence or reality of something or in the truth of some assertion. You may believe that there is justice in the world or that there is life after death. You may believe that democracy (or socialism or communism) is the preferred system of government or that children should be seen and not heard. You may believe that censorship is wrong, that power corrupts, or that television contributes to teenage violence.

Behavior in persuasion refers to overt, observable actions: voting for Tania for class president, buying a Ford, reading to a sightless student, studying for an economics final, and saying "Yes, I will marry you" are all examples of behaviors. They are all actions and you can observe each of them.

Keep these definitions in mind as the major types of persuasive speeches are identified: (1) speeches to strengthen or change attitudes or beliefs, and (2) speeches designed to actuate or to stimulate action.

PRINCIPLES OF PERSUASION

Your success in strengthening or changing attitudes or beliefs and in moving your listeners to action will depend on your use of the principles of persuasion. These six major principles will be useful to you in all your attempts at persuasion.

The Credibility Principle

You will be more persuasive if your listeners see you as credible, a principle apparently not realigned by the television announcer and newscaster in the accompanying cartoon. If your listeners see you as competent, knowledgeable, of good character, and charismatic or dynamic, they will think you credible. As a result you will be more effective in changing their attitudes or in moving them to do something.

Here, for example, Willard C. Butcher (1987) establishes his credibility by referring to his commitment to and association with high ethical standards:

> *For example, my own company, like most others, has a Corporate Code of Conduct—a blueprint that spells out the value standards we expect our employees to live up to. But having a written document is no guarantee that decisions will be made in an ethical way.*

"And now here's Andy to horse around with the news."

Drawing by Mort Gerberg; © 1977 The New Yorker Magazine, Inc. Reprinted by permission.

We must constantly work at making our Code of Conduct a "living document" and the practice of corporate ethics, a "living spirit" throughout the Chase organization.

Stated another way, "Church on Sunday, Sin on Monday" ethics will not cut it. We must practice what we preach and incorporate ethics into every decision we make.

You may wish to review Unit 19 ("Credibility and Ethics") for more specifics on how you can enhance your more credibility.

The Selective Exposure Principle

Your listeners (in fact, all audiences) follow the "law of selective exposure." It has at least two parts:

1. Listeners will actively seek out information that supports their opinions, beliefs, values, decisions, and behaviors.
2. Listeners will actively avoid information that contradicts their existing opinions, beliefs, attitudes, values, and behaviors.

Of course, if you are very sure that your opinions and attitudes are logical and valid, then you might not bother to seek out supporting information. And, you may not actively avoid nonsupportive messages. People exercise selective exposure most often when their confidence in their opinions and beliefs is weak.

Some Implications This principle of selective exposure suggests a number of implications. For example, if you want to persuade an audience that holds very different attitudes from your own, anticipate selective exposure operating and proceed inductively; that is, hold back on your thesis until you have given them your evidence and argument. Only then relate this evidence and argument to your initially contrary thesis.

If you were to present them with your thesis first, they might tune you out without giving your position a fair hearing. So, become thoroughly familiar with the attitudes of your audience if you want to succeed in making these necessary adjustments and adaptations.

Let's say you are giving a speech on the need to reduce spending on college athletic programs. If your audience was composed of listeners who agreed with you and wanted to cut athletic spending, you might lead with your thesis. Your introduction might go something like this:

Our college athletic program is absorbing money that we can more profitably use for the library, science labs, and language labs. Let me explain how the money now going to unnecessary athletic programs could be better spent in these other areas.

On the other hand, let's say that you were addressing alumni who strongly favored the existing athletic programs. In this case, you might want to lead with your evidence and hold off stating your thesis until the end of your speech.

Why are the principles of persuasion more difficult to apply to large audiences than they are to small audiences?

The Audience Participation Principle

Persuasion is greatest when the audience participates actively in your presentation. In experimental tests the same speech is delivered to different audiences. The attitudes of each audience are measured before and after the speech. The difference between their attitudes before and after the speech is taken as a measure of the speech's effectiveness. For one audience the sequence consists of (1) pretest of attitudes, (2) presentation of the persuasive speech, and (3) posttest of attitudes. For another audience the sequence consists of (1) pretest of attitudes, (2) presentation of the persuasive speech, (3) audience paraphrases or summarizes the speech, and (4) posttest of attitudes. Researchers consistently find that those listeners who participated actively (as in paraphrasing or summarizing) are more persuaded than those who received the message passively. Demagogues and propagandists who succeed in arousing huge crowds often have the crowds chant slogans, repeat catch phrases, and otherwise participate actively in the persuasive experience.

The implication here is simple: persuasion is a transactional process. It involves both speaker and listeners. You will be more effective if you can get the audience to participate actively in the process.

The Inoculation Principle

The principle of inoculation can be explained with the biological analogy on which it is based. Suppose that you lived in a germ-free environment. Upon leaving this germ-free environment and upon exposure to germs, you would be particularly susceptible to infection because your body has not built up an immunity—it has no resistance. Resistance, the ability to fight off germs, might be achieved by the body, if not naturally, then through some form of inoculation. You could, for example, be injected with a weakened dose of the germ so that your body begins to fight the germ by building up antibodies that create an "immunity" to this type of infection. Your body, because of the antibodies it produced, is able to fight off even powerful doses of this germ.

The situation in persuasion is similar to this biological process. Some of your attitudes and beliefs have existed in a "germ-free" environment, they have never been attacked or challenged. For example, many of us have lived in an environment in which the values of a democratic form of government, the importance of education, and the traditional family structure have not been challenged. Consequently, we have not been "immunized" against attacks on these values and beliefs. We have no counterarguments (antibodies) prepared to fight off these attacks on our beliefs, so if someone were to come along with strong arguments against these beliefs, we might be easily persuaded.

Contrast these "germ-free" beliefs with issues that have been attacked and for which we have a ready arsenal of counterarguments. Our attitudes on the draft, nuclear weapons, college athletics, and thousands of other issues have been challenged in the press, on television, and in our interpersonal interactions. As a result of this exposure, we have counterarguments ready for any attacks on our beliefs concerning these issues. We have been inoculated and immunized against attacks should someone attempt to change our attitudes or beliefs.

Some Implications If you are addressing an inoculated audience, take into consideration the fact that they have a ready arsenal of counterarguments to fight your persuasive assault. For example, if you are addressing heavy smokers on the need to stop smoking or alcoholics on the need to stop drinking, you might assume that these people have already heard your arguments and that they have already inoculated themselves against the major arguments. In such situations, be prepared, therefore, to achieve only small gains. Don't try to reverse totally the beliefs of a well-inoculated audience. For example, it would be asking too much to get the smokers or the alcoholics to quit their present behaviors as a result of one speech. But, it might not be too much to ask to get them—at least some of them—to attend a meeting of a smoking clinic or Alcoholics Anonymous.

If you are trying to persuade an uninoculated audience, your task is often much simpler since you do not have to penetrate a fully developed immunization shield. For example, it might be relatively easy to persuade a group of high school seniors about the values of a college core curriculum since they probably have not thought much about the issue and probably do not have arguments against the core curriculum at their ready disposal.

Do recognize, however, that even when an audience has not immunized itself, they often take certain beliefs to be self-evident. As a result they may well tune out any attacks on such cherished beliefs or values. This might be the case, for example, if you try to persuade an audience of communists to support capitalist policies. Although they may not have counterarguments ready, they may accept their communist beliefs as so fundamental that they simply will not listen to attacks on such beliefs. Again, proceed slowly and be content with small gains. Further, an inductive approach would suit your purposes better here. Attacking cherished beliefs directly creates impenetrable resistance. Instead, build your case by first presenting your arguments and evidence and gradually work up to your conclusion.

If you try to strengthen an audience's belief, give them the antibodies they will need if ever under attack. Consider raising counterarguments to this belief and then demolishing them. Much as the injection of a small amount of a germ will enable the body to build an immunization response, presenting counterarguments and then refuting them will enable the listeners to immunize themselves against future attacks on these values and beliefs. This procedure has been found to confer greater and longer-lasting resistance to strong attacks than merely providing the audience with an arsenal of supporting arguments.

The Magnitude of Change Principle

The greater and more important the change you want to produce in your audience, the more difficult your task will be—a lesson apparently not learned by Santa's visitor in the cartoon. The reason is simple: we normally demand a greater number of reasons

"I want an immediate end to wordwide inflation, a drop in Arabian oil prices, and a crack at Ernie Filkin's job."

Courtesy H. Martin.

and lots more evidence before we make important decisions—career changes, moving our families to another state, or investing our life savings in certain stocks.

On the other hand, we may be more easily persuaded (and demand less evidence) on relatively minor issues—whether to take "Small Group Communication" rather than "Persuasion," or to give to the United Heart Fund instead of the American Heart Fund.

People change gradually, in small degrees over a long period of time. And although there are cases of sudden conversions, this general principle holds true more often than not. Persuasion, therefore, is most effective when it strives for small changes and works over a considerable period of time. For example, a persuasive speech stands a better chance when it tries to get the alcoholic to attend just one AA meeting rather than to give up alcohol for life. If you try to convince your audience to change their attitudes radically or to engage in behaviors to which they are initially opposed, your attempts may backfire. In this type of situation, the audience may tune you out, closing its ears to even the best and most logical arguments.

When you have the opportunity to try to persuade your audience on several occasions (rather than simply delivering one speech), two strategies will prove relevant: the foot-in-the-door and the door-in-the-face techniques.

Foot-in-the-Door Technique   As its name implies, this technique involves getting your foot in the door first. That is, you first request something small, something that your audience will easily comply with. Once this compliance has been achieved, you then make your real request (Freedman and Fraser, 1966; DeJong, 1979; Cialdini, 1984; Pratkanis and Aronson, 1991). Research shows that people are more apt to comply with a large request after they have complied with a similar but much smaller request. For example, in one study the objective was to get people to put a "Drive Carefully" sign on their lawn. When this (large) request was made first, only about 17 percent of the people were willing to comply. However, when this request was preceded by a much smaller request, in this case to sign a petition, between 50 and 76 percent granted permission to install the sign.

In using this strategy, be sure that your first request is small enough to gain compliance. If it isn't, then you miss the chance ever to gain compliance with your desired and larger request.

Door-in-the-Face Technique   This technique is the opposite of foot-in-the-door (Cialdini and Ascani, 1976; Cialdini, 1984). In this strategy you first make a large request that you know will be refused (for example, "We're asking most people to donate $100 for new school computers). Later, you make a more moderate request, the one you really want your listeners to comply with (for example, "Might you be willing to contribute $10?"). In changing from the large to the more moderate request, you demonstrate your willingness to compromise and your sensitivity to your listeners. The general idea here is that your listeners will feel that since you have made concessions, they will also make concessions and at least contribute something. Listeners will probably also feel that $10 is actually quite little, considering the initial request and, research shows, are more likely to comply and will donate the $10.

In using this technique, be sure that your first request is significantly larger than your desired request but not so large as to seem absurd and be rejected out of hand.

REMEMBER: these principles of persuasion:

1. *credibility principle:* demonstrate competence, character, and charisma
2. *selective exposure principle:* (a) proceed inductively if you anticipate initial resistance; (b) analyze your audience's attitudes and beliefs thoroughly; and (c) deal with potential counterarguments to your thesis
3. *audience participation principle:* actively involve the audience.
4. *inoculation principle:* (a) try for small gains with an inoculated audience; (b) proceed inductively when attacking an uninoculated audience's long-held beliefs; and (c) when strengthening an audience's beliefs, refute potential counterarguments
5. *magnitude of change principle:* strive for small changes in short speeches or when advocating particularly important changes. The *foot-in-the-door* (request something small and follow it with your desired request) and the *door-in-the-face* (request something large and follow it with your desired request) techniques are especially useful when making several attempts at persuasion.

THE SPEECH TO STRENGTHEN OR CHANGE ATTITUDES OR BELIEFS

Many speeches seek to strengthen existing attitudes or beliefs. Much religious and political speaking, for example, tries to strengthen attitudes and beliefs. People who listen to religious speeches usually are already believers, so these speeches strive to

TIPS FROM PROFESSIONAL SPEAKERS

Know exactly what response you hope to evoke. This should be thought through and determined in advance. Are you in the spotlight to motivate your audience, to rouse them, to produce or sell more, to educate, share information, raise their morale, or challenge them? You should know specifically what you want to accomplish and organize your thoughts, material, and delivery to that end. . . . In preparing your speech, isolate the most important points and make sure you present them in the most dynamic and positive way possible. Don't bury them among a hodge-podge of thought or sandwich them between your laughs. Give them the kind of attention you'd expect from an advertising agency—that is, make sure that the most important points are distinguishable and as memorable as possible.

Buck Rogers, former vice president of marketing at IBM and, according to *USA Today*, one of the most requested speakers in America. *Getting the Best Out of Yourself and Others* (New York: HarperCollins, 1987), pp. 203–204.

strengthen the attitudes and beliefs the people already hold. Here the audience is already favorable to the speaker's purpose and is willing to listen.

Speeches designed to change attitudes or beliefs are much more difficult to construct. Most people resist change. When you attempt to get people to change their beliefs or attitudes you are fighting an uphill (but not impossible) battle.

Speeches designed to strengthen or change attitudes or beliefs come in many forms. Depending on the initial position of the audience, you can view the following examples as topics for speeches to strengthen or change attitudes or beliefs.

- Marijuana should be legalized.
- General education requirements should be abolished.
- Expand college athletic programs.
- History is a useless study.
- Television shows are mindless.
- Records should be rated for excessive sex and violence.
- Puerto Rico should become the fifty-first state.

Strategies for Strengthening or Changing Attitudes and Beliefs

When you attempt to strengthen or change your listeners' attitudes and beliefs, consider the following principles.

Estimate Listeners' Attitudes and Beliefs Carefully estimate—as best you can—the current state of your listeners' attitudes and beliefs. If your goal is to strengthen these attitudes and beliefs, then you can state your thesis and your objectives as early in your speech as you wish. Since your listeners are in basic agreement with you, your statement of your thesis will enable you to create a bond of agreement between you.

You might say, for example:

Like you, I am deeply committed to the fight against abortion. Tonight, I'd like to explain some new evidence that has recently come to light that we must know if we are to be effective in our fight against legalized abortion.

If, however, you are in basic disagreement and you wish to change their attitudes, then reserve your statement of your thesis until you have provided them with your evidence and argument. Get them on your side first by stressing as many similarities between you and your audience as you can. Only after this should you try to change their attitudes and beliefs. Continuing with the abortion example (but this time with an audience that is opposed to your antiabortion stance), you might say:

We are all concerned with protecting the rights of the individual. No one wants to infringe on the rights of anyone. And it is from this point of view—from the point of view of the inalienable rights of the individual—that I want to examine the abortion issue.

In this way, you stress your similarity with the audience before you state your antiabortion position to this pro-abortion audience.

Seek Small Changes When addressing an audience that is opposed to your position and your goal is to change their attitudes and beliefs, seek change in small increments. Let's say, for example, that your ultimate goal is to get an antiabortion group to favor abortion on demand. Obviously, this goal is too great to achieve in one speech. Therefore, strive for small changes. Here, for example, is an excerpt in which the speaker attempts to get an antiabortion audience to agree that some abortions should be legalized. The speaker begins as follows:

> *One of the great lessons I learned in college was that most extreme positions are wrong. Most of the important truths lie somewhere between the extreme opposites. And today I want to talk with you about one of these truths. I want to talk with you about rape and the problems faced by the mother carrying a child conceived in this most violent of all the violent crimes we can imagine.*

Notice that the speaker does not state a totally pro-abortion position but instead focuses on one area of abortion and attempts to get the audience to agree that in some cases abortion should be legalized.

Demonstrate Your Credibility Show the audience that you are knowledgeable about the topic, have their own best interests at heart, and that you are willing and ready to speak out in favor of these important concerns.

Give Listeners Good Reasons Give your audience good reasons for believing what you want them to believe. Give them hard evidence and arguments. Show them how such attitudes and beliefs relate directly to their goals, their motives. (Evidence and argument are covered in Unit 17 and motivational appeals in Unit 18.)

Developing the Speech to Strengthen or Change Attitudes and Beliefs

Here are some examples to clarify the nature of this type of persuasive speech. These examples present the specific purpose, the thesis, and the question asked of the thesis to help identify the major propositions of the speech. In this first example, the speaker uses a problem-solution organizational pattern, first presenting the problems created by cigarette smoking, and then the solution.

Specific purpose: to persuade my audience that cigarette advertising should be banned from all media
Thesis: cigarette advertising should be abolished (*Why should it be abolished?*)

    I. Cigarette smoking is a national problem.

        A. Cigarette smoking causes lung cancer.

        B. Cigarette smoking pollutes the air.

        C. Cigarette smoking raises the cost of health care.

   II. Cigarette smoking will be lessened if advertisements are prohibited.

  III. Fewer people would start to smoke.

  IV. Smokers would smoke less.

In delivering such a speech a speaker might begin like this:

I think we all realize that cigarette smoking is a national problem that affects each and every one of us. No one escapes the problems caused by cigarette smoking— not the smoker and not the nonsmoker. Cigarette smoking causes lung cancer. Cigarette smoking pollutes the air. And cigarette smoking raises the cost of health care for everyone.

Let's look first at the most publicized of all smoking problems: lung cancer. There can be no doubt—the scientific evidence is overwhelming—that cigarette smoking is a direct cause of lung cancer. Research conducted by the American Cancer Institute and by research institutes throughout the world all come to the same conclusion: cigarette smoking causes lung cancer. Consider some of the specific evidence. A recent study—reported in the November 1989 issue of the . . . .

Here is an example dealing with birth control. A topical organizational pattern is used here.

Specific purpose: to persuade my audience that advertisements for birth control devices should be allowed in all media

Thesis: media advertising of birth control devices is desirable (*Why is media advertising desirable?*)

I. Birth control information is needed.

A. Birth control information is needed to prevent disease.

B. Birth control information is needed to prevent unwanted pregnancies.

II. Birth control information is not available to the very people who need it most.

III. Birth control information can best be disseminated through the media.

REMEMBER: **Consider the following strategies in the speech to strengthen or change attitudes and beliefs:**

1. **estimate the current status of your listeners' attitudes and beliefs**
2. **seek change in small increments**
3. **demonstrate your own credibility**
4. **give your listeners both logical and motivational reasons**

THE SPEECH TO STIMULATE ACTION

Speeches designed to stimulate the audience to action or to engage in some specific behavior are referred to as speeches to actuate. The persuasive speech addressed to motivating a specific behavior may focus on just about any behavior imaginable. Here are some possible topics:

▪ Vote in the next election.
▪ Vote for Smith.

- Do not vote for Smith.
- Give money to the American Cancer Society.
- Buy a ticket to the football game.
- Listen to "20/20."
- Major in economics.
- Take a course in computer science.
- Buy a Pontiac.

Strategies for Stimulating Listeners to Action

When designing a speech to get listeners to do something, keep the following principles in mind.

Be Realistic Be realistic in what you want the audience to do. Remember you have only 10 or 15 minutes and in that time you cannot move the proverbial mountain. So, ask for small, easily performed behaviors—to sign a petition, to vote in the next election, to donate a small amount of money.

Demonstrate Your Own Compliance As a general rule, never ask the audience to do what you have not done yourself, a rule the cartoon's encyclopedia sales representative obviously didn't learn. So, demonstrate your own willingness to do what you want the audience to do. If you don't, the audience will rightfully ask, "Why haven't you done it?" In addition to your having done what you want them to do, show them that you are pleased to have done so. Tell them of the satisfaction you derived from donating blood or from reading to blind students.

Reprinted by permission of Rex May.

Stress Specific Advantages Stress the specific advantages of these behaviors to your specific audience. Don't ask your audience to engage in behaviors solely for abstract reasons. Give them concrete, specific reasons why they will benefit from the actions you want them to engage in. Instead of telling your listeners that they should devote time to reading to blind students because it is the right thing to do, show them how much they will enjoy the experience and how much they will personally benefit from it.

Developing the Speech to Stimulate Action

Here are a few examples of the speech to actuate. In this first example the speaker tries to persuade the audience to buy a personal computer.

Specific purpose: to persuade my audience to buy a personal computer
Thesis: personal computers are useful (*Why are personal computers useful?* or *In what ways are personal computers useful?*)

  I. Personal computers are useful for word processing.

    A. You can type faster with a word processor.

    B. You can revise documents easily with a word processor.

  II. Personal computers are useful for bookkeeping.

  III. Personal computers are useful for research.

In delivering such a speech a speaker might say:

Have you ever added up all the hours you have spent typing your college papers? Have you ever tried to keep your finances in order only to lose the little pieces of paper you wrote your figures on? And then you had to start all over again. Have you ever gone to our college library and not found what you were looking for? Or, maybe I should say, have you ever gone to our library and found exactly what you were looking for?

Typing, bookkeeping, and research are a computer's three greatest strengths and I'd like to tell you in more detail about how a computer can simplify your life. I'm sure that by the end of this brief talk you will want to run, not walk, to your nearest computer dealer and buy your own personal computer.

I think typing is probably the most boring of all college chores.

Here is a speech on devoting time to helping the handicapped. Here the speaker asks for a change in the way most people spend their leisure time. It utilizes a topical organizational pattern; each of the subtopics is treated about equally.

Specific purpose: to persuade my audience to devote some of their leisure time to helping the handicapped
Thesis: leisure time can be well used in helping the handicapped (*How can leisure time be spent helping the handicapped?* or *What can we do to help the handicapped?*)

I. Read for the blind.

   A. Read to a blind student.

   B. Make a recording of a textbook for blind students.

II. Run errands for students confined to wheelchairs.

III. Type for students who can't use their hands.

REMEMBER: **In the speech to stimulate action, consider the following strategies:**

1. be realistic in what you ask your listeners to do; ask for small, easily performed behaviors

2. demonstrate your own willingness to do as you want your listeners to do

3. stress the specific (rather than the general or abstract) advantages of this behavior

A SAMPLE PERSUASIVE SPEECH WITH ANNOTATIONS

The following speech is presented as a summary of some of the basic principles of persuasion covered in this unit. The speech was given by Jan Moreland, a student at Illinois State University, and was judged the best persuasive speech in the 1987 National Championship Tournament.

Recently, I saw a commercial on television for a major pest control company. The commercial depicted a young couple frantic that their home would be consumed by termites. So, like many Americans they called the Terminix man who came to their house, killed the termites, and saved the day. As I watched the commerical, though, I thought about Beatrice Nelson. Beatrice Nelson, a middle-aged Colorado housewife, found herself lost and disoriented one evening two years ago. Her husband rushed her to a nearby emergency room where she was examined by toxicologist, Dr. Daniel Tautlebaum.

Tautlebaum found that Beatrice was so confused that she could not remember days of the week or the names of any U.S. Presidents. He was bewildered until he was told that a month earlier Beatrice had an exterminator at her house to spray for termites, as she puts it, just to be safe. Ironically, the result of that action made Beatrice anything but safe. The exterminator used a nerve-damaging pesticide called chlordane, which was not only effective

Moreland gains attention through the retelling of an incident depicted on a television advertisement and continues to maintain attention by the sharp contrast between the commercial and the real-life consequences of the pesticide.

The speaker establishes the importance of the topic through the dramatic example of Beatrice Nelson's mental problems and the statistic of over 7,500 phone calls concerning chlordane.

in ridding the home of termites, but in robbing Beatrice of part of her mind. Even now, Bea cannot pass simple neurological tests, or remember simple details of her life.

Unfortunately, Bea is not alone. In fact, the Environmental Protection Agency Hotline, which is an 800-number set up for reporting complaints, problems, and illnesses associated with pesticides, received over 7,500 phone calls concerning chlordane last year alone. And, according to the National Coalition Against the Misuse of Pesticides, or N-CAMP, there are currently eighty-four cases in litigation against the manufacturers of chlordane and the pest control companies who use it.

Obviously, the problem of chlordane poisoning is not a small one. But what is more frightening is that there is nothing being done to prevent exterminators from using the chemical around our homes. Now, the impact of chlordane poisoning cannot be fully understood until we first look at the problem surrounding the chemical, then, examine why it's still on the market, and, finally, discuss some solutions that prevent any further harm.

Perhaps the director of the citizens group People Against Chlordane, Pat Manichino, said it best when he said, "The problem is not the use or application of the chemical. The problem is chlordane, and until we face that fact, the problem will never be solved. You see, chlordane is a termiticide that attacks the central nervous systems in termites. Unfortunately, it can have the same effect on human beings as well."

The chemical is so dangerous, in fact, that in 1982 the National Academy of Sciences conducted a study for the United States Air Force to determine the level of chlordane contamination in their on base homes. The study's finding, there is no level below which no adverse biological effects will occur. And the study went on to say that at a level of only five micrograms per cubic meter of air, a home should be evacuated. Now the frightening fact here is that according to a January 1987 report on National Public Radio, over three-hundred thousand homes will be treated with chlordane this year alone. Three-hundred thousand homes treated with a chemical that is unsafe at any level.

Now, the EPA disputes this evidence, and believes that proper training of exterminators and proper application of the chemical would prevent contaminations. But the EPA should have done their homework. Four years

Moreland provides a clear orientation, identifying the major points of her speech:" . . . the impact of chlordane poisoning . . . we *first look at the problem surrounding the chemical,* then, *examine why it's still on the market,* and finally discuss some *solutions that prevent any further harm.* The organizational pattern is basically problem-solution.

Moreland introduces her first point through the testimony of the director of People Against Chlordane. We also learn here that there is an organization devoted to fighting this problem which helps the speaker establish credibility. After all, others are also concerned with the issue.

In establishing that chlordane is dangerous the speaker effectively combines the results of a scientific study on its dangers and the statistics on the number of homes that will be exposed to this toxic substance.

Although the Enviromental Protection Agency was mentioned earlier, note that it might have been help-

ago, health officials in New York and Massachusetts were so concerned about chlordane poisoning that they placed several restrictions on the chemical's use and application. But, according to Nancy Ridley of the Massachusetts Health Department, none of the restrictions were effective. She said. "We had just as many cases reported and our restrictions were much tighter than the ones the EPA is proposing."

In addition, the Belsicoff Corportion, the manufacturers of chlordane, stated in a June 1984 issue of *Pest Control Technology* that, "It is impossible to eliminate risks, spills, or accidents on any given job using chlordane." And there's a catch. Even when the chemical is applied properly, contaminations occur.

According to a study conducted by Ross Lighty, chemist at North Carolina State University, air samples were taken in homes where the application of chlordane was strictly supervised and label instructions were followed to the letter. The air samples revealed levels approaching five micrograms per cubic meter, the same level at which the NAS recommends evacuation. Pat Manichino states that any regulation that allows for the use and application of the chemical cannot prevent spills or accidents and, therefore, they are all inadequate.

Manichino's point is well taken. The continued use of chlordane has prompted thousands of phone calls yearly to organizations such as the EPA hotline and N-CAMP complaining of adverse symptoms from chlordane. For example, Kelly Purdell of Houston, Texas began to feel so confused and, well, "crazy" as she puts it, that she was ready to admit herself to a psychiatric ward before officials found high levels of chlordane in her home and condemned it. The home of the Delaney family was so contaminated that Charleston officials condemned it as well. But perhaps the worst example is that of Charles Hanson. When his home became contaminated two years ago, he and his family were forced to evacuate, forced to live in rented houses and motels. They're still making mortgage payments on their contaminated home.

You see, what we need to understand is that when a family evacuates their home, they are likely never to return. According to a 1983 publication entitled "EPA Facts," published by the EPA, once a home is contaminated with chlordane, it cannot be decontaminated until the chemical dissipates which can take twenty to twenty-five years.

ful to indicate that the acronym EPA would be used when the agency was first introduced or identify the agency in full the first time the acronym is used. Moreland did this for National Coalition Against the Misuse of Pesticides (N-CAMP).

The research cited seemed appropriate to this speech. She made use of *Pest Control Technology*, the testimony of scientists in the field, Department of Health officials, and citizens groups. The sources from which the evidence and argument were drawn, however, were not clearly identified, except for the individuals named, "EPA Facts," and *Pest Control Technology*. But, for the most part, we don't know if Moreland talked with them directly, read their statements in newspapers, or heard them on radio or television.

In establishing the dangers of chlordane, Moreland uses the technique of attacking one of the opposing arguments that listeners might raise, namely, that the chemical is not dangerous if precautions are taken.

The specific examples of people affected by chlordane are most effective in making the point that chlordane is dangerous.

Note the effective transition connecting the first point with the second point: "Well, now that we know that we are dealing with such a dangerous chemical you might be asking yourself, 'Why is it still on the market?' This single sentence reminds us that the speaker has covered the dangers of the chemical and will now discuss why it is still on the market.

In explaining why chlordane is still on the market, Moreland directly involves the audience by asking rhetorical questions (questions whose answers are obvious but which are used to involve the audience and make them come up with the answer you want to suggest).

This paragraph provides a needed internal summary of the main points the speaker has already made.

The speaker introduces her third point, the solution: "Now, at this point it should be obvious that some kind of a solution needs to be found."

Well, now that we know that we are dealing with such a dangerous chemical you might be asking yourself, "Why is it still on the market?" Good question. And the EPA believes they have an answer. EPA official Doug Camp states that there is not enough evidence to suggest that enough people have been harmed. Good answer, Doug. But, in defense of the agency, it is important to understand that evidence is not always readily available, because the public is generally uninformed. For example, when was the last time you asked your Orkin representative what he uses to kill termites? Or better yet, when was the last time you suffered a headache, sore throat, sinus problems, or any number of other minor ailments and attributed them to your exterminator? It never comes to mind, does it? And, according to Diane Baxter of N-CAMP, that's part of the problem. She states that some of the symptoms can begin so subtly, that we don't even consider the idea that we may have been poisoned.

Now, at this point it is important for me to tell you that no deaths have been linked to chlordane so far. And, according to Leah Wise of the Massachusetts Health Department, that's another reason the chemical hasn't been removed from the market. She says, "In this country we tend to be more concerned with mortality than morbidity, so if people are just getting sick we don't pay too much attention."

The scope of the chlordane problem has become too broad for any of us to ignore any longer. Especially when we consider that homes have been contaminated to the point of condemnation and people have suffered permanent neurological damage while the EPA sits by and watches. Well, they say there is not enough evidence to suggest that enough people have been harmed. Until and if that evidence is found, the EPA will not ban chlordane. Not enough evidence? How many people have to suffer permanent neurological damage before we have enough evidence?

Now, at this point it should be obvious that some kind of a solution needs to be found. Perhaps a solution like the one implemented by New York, Massachusetts and the Federal Government of Japan: ban chlordane. But we have already heard the EPA's answer to that request. So, it appears then that we are faced with two choices. Either run the risk of termites eating us out of house and home so to speak, or endangering our health in an effort to stop them. Well, lucky those are not our only two choices. Since their banning of chlordane in 1984, New York and Massachusetts have been using a new chemical called Dursban. Now Dursban is as effective as chlordane, but doesn't produce the same devastating effects.

Well, it seems these two states are on the right track, but the EPA is standing firm. As consumers, though, we don't have to remain passive victims of chlordane poisoning. There are solutions we can actively pursue now without waiting for the EPA.

Of course, each one of us has already taken a step toward one solution: we are informed. It is now our responsibility to inform others. Make your family and friends aware that their health may be in danger every time an exterminator comes to their home.

The second solution. As responsible consumers we need to be aware of the steps that we can take to protect ourselves against poisoning. The first is to call an exterminator before he comes to your home and ask him if he uses chlordane or if we have a choice as to which chemical he will use around our home. If the exterminator tells you he uses chlordane, tell him you will not patronize his services for that reason. If pest control companies become aware that they are losing business because of chlordane, they may stop using it.

Also, we need to make agencies such as the EPA aware when we do experience problems with a chemical. They want evidence, let's give it to them. We can do this by notifying the Environmental Protection Agency Hotline. Now, if you would like that phone number I will be available after this speech to give you that number and the numbers of N-CAMP and People Against Chlordane. These can get you in touch with someone who can help you if you feel that you or someone you know has been poisoned. Also, if you have any questions about the chemical. The final step that we as individuals can take is to ask our local health departments to check any home that we are considering to buy or rent for high levels of chlordane.

The use of chlordane must be stopped. And the responsibility lies with us. A combination of the individual steps that we can take and the national level steps the EPA should take, can prevent our families, our friends, and ourselves from ever suffering the painful conse-

---

The steps to a solution to the problem are carefully and clearly identified. The solution concerns both attitudes and behaviors. The attitude change Moreland calls for is to recognize the importance of the problem, to become more informed, and to be determined not to allow chlordane to be used. The behavioral change Moreland calls for is questioning pest control companies, checking out any future homes for chlordane poisoning, and making our attitudes known to the EPA, N-CAMP, and People Against Chlordane. The speaker makes this especially easy for the audience by having the relevant phone numbers available.

The supporting materials consisted basically of testimony and specific instances or examples. These were most effective though the speech would have profited from including a greater variety of supporting materials, for example, definitions, analogies, illustrations, and especially statistics.

Moreland effectively establishes her credibility through the use of governmental agencies and scientists as source material (demonstrating competence in research), a readiness to answer further questions (demonstrating commitment, concern, and knowledge), and having the phone numbers of relevant organizations (demonstrating her own commitment and belief in what she is saying).

Moreland concludes her speech with a motivation to assume the responsibility for dealing with this problem. She achieves closure by referring back to her introduction and at the same time effectively repeats her main point, namely, that this business is dangerous—"we should be afraid of the exterminator as well."

The language used was clear, appropriate, and personal.

quences from chlordane poisoning. Yes, as that commercial depicted we may be frantic over the fear of termites, but perhaps we should be afraid of the exterminator as well.

Speeches by Jan Moreland in *1987 Championship Debates and Speeches*. Copyright © 1987 by the American Forensic Association. Reprinted by permission.

CRITICALLY SPEAKING

1. On what topics would you be a credible spokesperson? Why?
2. How might you use the audience participation principle in your classroom persuasive speeches?
3. Can you give a personal example of how the inoculation principle operated in your own life?
4. Formulate another principle of persuasion. How might this principle be used by the persuasive speaker?
5. What persuasion principles would be of most value to you if you were trying to persuade your class that government must do more for the homeless? That class members should give blood during the upcoming blood drive?
6. Why is it generally easier to strengthen attitudes and beliefs than to change them? Are there situations where the reverse would be true?

PRACTICALLY SPEAKING

16.1   ANALYZING A PERSUASIVE SPEECH

This exercise is designed to help you identify the major parts of a speech and the ways in which they fit together. Carefully read one of the speeches in the Appendix by Shelley Schnathorst, Martin Luther King, Jr., or William Banach. Respond to the questions presented in the margins.

16.2   APPLYING THE PRINCIPLES OF PERSUASION

For each of the following persuasive purposes (and intended audience), indicate how you might apply at least one principle of persuasion discussed in this unit. Note that in some of these examples the audience is extremely heterogeneous.

1. I and my entire administration have been scrupulously honest (audience: political leaders whose endorsement this candidate wants and who fear that rumors of dishonesty may be found to be true).

2. Try a sample of this new cologne and take advantage of our sale price (audience: the department store browser as well as people who have come specifically to buy cologne).

3. Women should be allowed full participation in the religious community (audience: conservative religious leaders and women actively involved in feminist issues).

4. Vote for unknown candidate A, not for unknown candidate B (audience: the general voter).

5. Get out of pre-law (audience: first year pre-law students).

6. Contribute $25 to the college's voluntary landscaping fund (audience: this public speaking class).

7. Don't drink while driving (audience: first-time teen offenders).

8. Condoms should be distributed to all students beginning in the third grade (audience: parents of third and fourth grade children, teachers, and school administrators).

9. Invest in our new play that is sure to be next year's Broadway sensation (audience: conservative business executives who are considering a first investment in the theatre and long-time theatre investors).

10. Exercise at least three times a week (audience: professors in their 50s and 60s who are being treated for high blood pressure and their relationship partners).

11. Follow a proper diet (audience: teenagers with diabetes).

12. Consider a career in medicine (audience: high school students from poor rural areas).

13. Avoiding sexual harassment (audience: teachers from all educational levels).

14. Privatize highways (audience: moderate wage-earning commuters and business developers).

15. Give drug addicts free needles to reduce the spread of AIDS (audience: doctors, nurses, and other health-care workers).

Developing Arguments for Persuasive Speeches

■ ■ ■ ■

UNIT OBJECTIVES

After completing this unit, you should be able to:

1. Define *argument* and *evidence*

2. Identify the three general tests for reasoning

3. Explain the nature of reasoning from specific instances to a generalization and from a generalization to specific instances, the major tests, and the guidelines to follow in using these forms of reasoning effectively

4. Explain the nature of reasoning by analogy, the major tests, and the guidelines to follow in using reasoning from analogy effectively

5. Explain the nature of cause-effect reasoning, the major tests, and the guidelines to follow in using cause-effect reasoning effectively

6. Explain the nature of reasoning by sign, the major tests, and the guidelines to follow in using reasoning by sign effectively

323

*T*his unit continues the study of supporting materials, this time focusing on materials that prove or attempt to prove the validity of a proposition or conclusion.

ARGUMENT AND EVIDENCE

An *argument* consists of evidence (for example, facts) and a conclusion. *Evidence* plus the *conclusion* that the evidence supports equal an argument. *Reasoning* is the process you go through in forming conclusions on the basis of evidence. For example, you might reason that since college graduates earn more money than nongraduates (*evidence*), Jack and Jill should go to college if they wish to earn more money (*conclusion*).

When you present an argument in a public speech, you attempt to prove something to your listeners. You want to prove that what you say is true or practical or worth pursuing. In the vast majority of cases, you cannot prove in any objective sense that marijuana should or should not be legalized or that the death penalty would benefit or harm society. Rather, you seek, as a speaker, to establish the probability of your conclusions in the minds of the listeners. Thus, the process is in part a *logical* one of demonstrating that what you say is probably true. The process is, however, also a *psychological* one of persuading your listeners to accept the conclusions as you have drawn them.

The information presented here applies to the speaker in constructing the speech, to the listener in receiving and responding to the speech, and to the speech critic or analyst in analyzing and evaluating the speech. A poorly reasoned argument, inadequate evidence, and stereotypical thinking, for example, need to be avoided by the speaker, recognized and responded to by the listener, and negatively evaluated by the critic.

Before getting to the specific forms of argument or reasoning, let's review some general tests of support applicable to all forms of argument. These general tests (and, in fact, all the tests of adequacy) are presented as questions so that you may use them to evaluate your evidence and test the adequacy of your argument.

Is the Support Recent?

We live in a world of rapid change. What was true 10 years ago is not necessarily true today. Economic strategies that worked for your parents will not work for you. As the world changes, so must our strategies for coping with it. And what is true of economics is also true of other areas; no area, in fact, is immune to change. Therefore, it is important that your supporting materials be as recent as possible. Recency alone, obviously, does not make an effective argument. Yet, other things being equal, the more recent the evidence and support, the better.

Is There Corroborative Support?

Very few conditions in this world are simple. Most issues worthy of discussion are complex. Consequently, in reasoning about any issue, support the proposition from differ-

Drawing by Stevenson; © 1991 The New Yorker Magazine, Inc. Reprinted by permission.

ent sources and perspectives. Let's say, for example, that you are considering majoring in accounting. Before you make that decision, you should look at the issue from different perspectives. Your evidence should come not only from educational authorities attesting to, say, the value of your particular college program, but also from government statistics on the need for accountants, from economic forecasts concerning probable earnings, and so on. That is, in drawing a conclusion (or in supporting a thesis) gather evidence and argument from numerous and diverse sources. When all or most of the evidence points in the same direction, you are on pretty firm ground. If some evidence points to "yes" and some evidence points to "no," then perhaps you should reevaluate your conclusion. Just as you would be convinced by evidence all pointing in the same direction, so will your listeners. Note that the corroboration must itself stand the tests of evidence to be discussed—a condition our hapless hero in the cartoon seems not to have learned.

Are the Sources Unbiased?

We each see the world through our own individual filters. We see the world not objectively, but through our prejudices, our biases, our preconceptions, our stereotypes; others see the world through their own filters. No one is totally objective.

Consequently, in evaluating evidence, establish how biased the sources are and in what direction they are biased. Do not treat a tobacco company report on the connection between smoking and lung cancer with the same credibility as a report by some impartial medical research institute. Question research conducted and disseminated by any special interest group. As a speaker and as a listener, be careful to recognize biases in your sources. It is always legitimate to ask: To what extent might this source be biased? Might this source have a special interest that leads her or him to offer this evidence or this conclusion?

REMEMBER: **Materials supporting argument and reasoning should be:**

1. **recent**
2. **corroborated by other evidence**
3. **unbiased**

REASONING FROM SPECIFIC INSTANCES AND GENERALIZATIONS

In reasoning from specific instances (or examples), you examine several specific instances and then conclude something about the whole. This form of reasoning is useful when you want to develop a general principle or conclusion but cannot examine the whole. For example, you sample a few communication courses and conclude something about communication courses in general; you visit several Scandinavian cities and conclude something about the whole of Scandinavia.

You probably follow this same general process in dealing with another person. For example, you see Samantha in several situations and conclude something about Samantha's behavior in general; you date Pat a few times, or maybe even for a period of several months, and on that basis draw a general conclusion about Pat's suitability as a spouse.

Carol Howard (1984), in a speech delivered at the 75th Anniversary Conference of Women in Communication, effectively uses numerous specific instances (only some of which are included here) to support her thesis:

> *Join me, if you would, on a random walk through the pages of the business press over the last few months:*
>
> The New York Times *on July 5 published an article that said putting a woman on your board is no longer in vogue, so progress has gotten slower. Today women fill only about 3 percent of the 14,000 directorships covered by the Fortune 1000 companies.*
>
> The Wall Street Journal *on July 16 carried an article on research about men's views on women as bosses. The fact that there are enough women bosses to warrant a study* is *good news. The fact that it's news at all says we've a way to go.*
>
> Fortune *magazine published a cover story in the August 20 issue on corporate spouses. The good news is that they kissed the so-called traditional corporate wife goodbye and used the word* spouse. *The bad news is that the only examples of women executives were in a sidebar, literally and figuratively set apart from the main story describing male CEOs and their wives.*

Technically, you may also argue in the other direction—namely, from a general principle to some specific instance. That is, you begin with some general statement or axiom that is accepted as true by the audience and argue that since something is true of the entire class, it must also be true of the specific instance, which is a member of that class.

Reasoning from general principles—actually, more a way of presenting your argument than a type of reasoning—is useful when you wish to argue that some unexamined instance has certain characteristics. You would, for example, note the general principle and show that an unexamined item is a member of that general principle. You would then draw the conclusion that, therefore, the item also possesses the qualities possessed by the whole (or covered by the general principle).

For example, listeners may all accept the notion that Martians are lazy, uncooperative, and dull-witted. This is the general principle or axiom that is accepted. The argument from generalization would then apply this general principle to a specific instance, for example, "Obviously we should not hire Delta X since we do not want a lazy, uncooperative, stupid colleague."

Note in this excerpt from Ken Lonnquist's speech, "Ghosts," how he argues against abortion from the general principle that one does not have control over the body of another.

> We say that it is our right to control our bodies, and this is true. But there is a distinction that needs to be made, and that distinction is this: Preventing a pregnancy is controlling a body—controlling your body. But preventing the continuance of a human life that is not your own is murder. If you attempt to control the body of another in that fashion, you become as a slave master was—controlling the lives and the bodies of his slaves—chopping off their feet when they ran away, or murdering them if it pleased him. This was not his right; it is not our right.

Critically Evaluating Reasoning from Specific Instances to a Generalization

Apply these tests in reasoning from specific instances.

1. Were enough specific instances examined? Obviously there will be a limit to the number of specific instances you can examine. After all, your time, energy, and resources are limited. Yet it is important that you examine enough instances to justify your conclusion. Exactly how much is enough will vary from one situation to another. You cannot spend three days in a foreign country and conclude something about the entire country. You cannot interact with three Ethniquians and conclude something about all Ethniquians. Two general guidelines might prove helpful in determining how much is enough.

First, the larger the group you wish covered by your conclusion, the greater the number of specific instances you should examine. If you wish to draw conclusions about a class of 75 million Martians, you will have to examine a considerable number of Martians before drawing any valid conclusions. On the other hand, if you are attempting to draw a conclusion about a bushel of 100 apples, sampling a few is probably sufficient.

Second, the greater the diversity of items in the class, the more specific instances you will have to examine. Some classes or groups of items are relatively homogeneous, whereas others are more heterogeneous; this will influence how many specific instances constitute a sufficient number. Spaghetti in boiling water are all about the same, thus, sampling one usually tells you something about all the others. On the other hand, communication courses are probably very different from each other, so valid conclusions about the entire group of communication courses will require a much larger sample.

2. Were the specific instances examined representative? Specific instances must be representative. If you wish to draw conclusions about the entire class, examine specific instances coming from all areas or subclasses within the major class. If you wanted to draw conclusions about the student body of your school, you could not simply examine communication majors or physics majors or art majors. Rather, you would have to examine a representative sample. If you wish to draw conclusions about the whole, be sure you examine all significant parts of that whole.

3. Are there significant exceptions? When you examine specific instances and attempt to draw a conclusion about the whole, take into consideration the exceptions. Thus, if you examine a number of Venusians and discover that 70 percent have I.Q.s of less than 80, you might be tempted to draw the conclusion that Venusians are stupid. But what about the 30 percent who have I.Q.s of over 140? This is a significant exception that must be taken into account when drawing your conclusion and would necessitate qualifying your conclusion in significant ways. Exactly how many exceptions will constitute "significant exceptions" is not easy to determine and will certainly vary from one situation to another.

As a speaker, you should disclose significant exceptions to your listeners. To hide these would be dishonest and also usually ineffective from a persuasive point of view because, more often than not, the audience either has heard or will hear of these exceptions. If you have not mentioned them, they will become suspicious of your overall honesty and your credibility will quickly decline.

Critically Evaluating Reasoning from a Generalization to Specific Instances

In testing reasoning from general principles to specific instances, apply these two tests.

1. Is the general principle true or at least probably true? Obviously, if the general principle is not true, it would be useless to apply it to any specific instance. In most instances you cannot know if a general principle is true simply because you cannot examine all instances of the class. If you did examine all instances of the class, there would be no reason to use this form of reasoning since you would have already examined the instance to which you wish to apply the general principle. For example, if you examine all the apples in the bushel, there is no reason to formulate the general conclusion that all the apples are rotten and to say that, therefore, one particular apple is rotten. In examining all the apples you will have examined that specific apple. Consequently, what we are really dealing with is a general principle that seems to be "usually" and "probably" true. Thus, our conclusions about any specific instance will also only be "usually" or "probably" true.

2. Is the unknown or unexamined item clearly a specific member of the class? If you want to draw a conclusion about a particular Atlantan and want to reason that this person is assertive because all Atlantans are assertive, you have to be certain that this person is in fact a member of the class of Atlantans.

Using Specific Instances and Generalizations

In reasoning from specific instances to general principles, stress that your specific instances are sufficient in number to warrant the conclusion you are drawing, that the specific instances are in fact representative of the whole, that your sample was not drawn disproportionately from one subgroup, and that there was an absence of significant exceptions. That is, you will be more convincing if you answer the questions that an intelligent and critical listener will ask of your evidence.

In using reasoning from general principles to specific instances, make certain that the audience accepts your general principle. If it is not accepted, any attempt to use it as evidence concerning a specific instance will be doomed to failure. To say, "We all know that . . ." or "You and I believe that . . ." does not mean that the audience "knows that . . ." or "believes that. . . ." Conduct a thorough audience analysis before using this type of argument. The general principle must be accepted *before* you use it as a basis for a conclusion about an unexamined specific instance.

REMEMBER: **When reasoning from specific instances to generalizations:**
1. a valid number of specific instances must be examined
2. the specific instances examined must be representative of the whole
3. the significant exceptions must be accounted for

and is most effective when you:
4. stress the sufficiency and representativeness of the sample
5. account for exceptions

When reasoning from a generalization to a specific instance:
1. the general principle should be true or at least probably true
2. the unknown or unexamined instance is clearly a specific instance that falls under the generalization

and is most effective when:
3. the general principle is accepted by the audience

REASONING FROM ANALOGY

In reasoning from analogy, you compare like things and conclude that since they are alike in so many respects, they are also alike in some as-yet unknown or unexamined respect. For example, you reason that since the meat at Grand Union is fresh, the fish will be also. In this simple bit of reasoning, you compared two like things (the two foods, meat and fish) and concluded that what was known to be true about one item (that the meat was fresh), would also be true of the unknown item (the fish).

Analogies may be literal or figurative. In a *literal analogy* the items being compared are from the same class—foods, cars, people, countries, cities, or whatever. For example, in a literal analogy one might argue that (1) word processing, database, and desktop publishing software are all similar to tax preparation software—they are all popular, have been around for about the same number of years, and have been revised repeatedly; (2) these software packages have all been easy to learn and use; (3) therefore, tax preparation software will be easy to learn and use. Here, then, we have taken a number of like items belonging to the same class (types of computer software), and then reasoned that the similarity would also apply to the unexamined item (tax preparation software).

In a *figurative analogy,* the items compared are from different classes. These analogies are useful for amplification but do not constitute logical proof. Here, for example, Tom Doyle (Boaz and Brey, 1987) uses a figurative analogy to argue against the usefulness of tariffs affecting Japanese products:

> *The Reagan administration responded to recent trade problems with the Japanese by announcing a policy of limited protectionism, where tariffs are slapped upon Japanese electronic chips, the equivalent of bonking your friend over the head with a pool cue when he beats you at the game.*

As this example illustrates, the figurative anology only creates an image. It does not prove anything. Its main purpose is to clarify, and it is particularly useful when you wish to make a complex process or relationship clearly understandable to the audience.

In the accompanying "TIP," Sonya Hamlin explains the power of the analogy.

Critically Evaluating Reasoning from Analogy

In testing the adequacy of an analogy—here of literal analogies—ask yourself two general questions:

1. Are the two cases being compared alike in essential respects? In the example of the tax preparation software, one significant difference was not noted: to use that software effectively, you really have to know the rules and regulations governing taxes. You can learn to use word-processing software without going beyond the information contained in the manual; but to learn to use tax-preparation software you have to know what is in the manual as well as the tax code.

2. Do the differences make a difference? In any analogy, regardless of how literal it is, the items being compared will be different: no two things are exactly the same. But in reasoning with analogies, ask yourself if the differences make a difference. Obviously, not all differences make a fundamental difference. The difference in the knowledge you need for the various software programs, however, is a substantial difference that needs to be considered.

Using Reasoning from Analogy

Stress the numerous and significant similarities between the items being compared and minimize the difference between them. Mention differences that do exist and that the

TIPS FROM PROFESSIONAL SPEAKERS

[Analogies] are one of the best devices for clarifying a complex or abstract concept. Since they're usually a story or an example drawn from life, they have instant appeal for any audience.

By turning away from a hard-nosed pragmatic approach to your message and finding a basic story, fable, folk legend, quote from classical literature, or example from current events that suits the basic principle involved, you cause people to be persuaded on much more familiar territory. It's reinforcing as well as amusing to listen to. Your audience doesn't have to work too hard to tune right into your wavelength, unlike the unfamiliar material you're asking them to stretch and reach for.

Analogies provide a change of pace and build in a sense of suspense. The audience looks forward to the end when the point of your story comes clear and they can see the connection with what you've been saying. Analogies can underline a basic truth with a seemingly light-hearted moment.

Using an example from daily life puts every member of the audience directly into the story, as well as humanizing you, the teller.

A word of caution: Think through your analogy to see how apt it is for making an instant connection between your point and the point of the story. Will everyone get the punch line? Does it really fit?

Sonya Hamlin, communication consultant and Emmy award-winning television host, producer, and writer. *How to Talk So People Will Listen: The Real Key to Job Success* (New York: Harper & Row, 1988), p. 183. Reprinted by permission

audience will think of, but show that these do not destroy the validity of your argument. If the audience knows that there are differences, but you do not confront these differences squarely, your argument is going to prove ineffective. The listeners will be wondering, "But what about the difference in . . . ?"

For example, let us say you are giving a speech in favor of instituting the honor system at your college. You might argue from the analogy of West Point and say something like:

> *The honor system has worked at other colleges. West Point is perhaps the most famous example. At West Point students take their examinations without any proctors. They are totally on their own honor.*

But, your audience may well reject this analogy and say to themselves (and perhaps in the question period) that West Point is a very different type of college. Therefore, you need to confront the difference between West Point and your school. You might begin by saying:

> *I know that many of you are thinking that West Point is a very different type of school from ours. But, in matters that relate to the honor system, it is not different. Let me show why these two colleges are actually alike in all essential respects. First, both our schools enroll students of approximately the same academic abili-*

ties. SAT scores, for example, are almost identical as are high school grades. Second, both schools. . . .

REMEMBER: **When using analogies:**
1. use cases that are alike in essential respects
2. use cases in which the differences do not make a significant difference

and are most effective when:
3. similarities are stressed
4. the importance of differences is minimized
5. differences are confronted squarely

REASONING FROM CAUSES AND EFFECTS

In reasoning from causes and effects, you may go in either of two directions. You may reason from cause to effect (from observed cause to unobserved effect) or from effect to cause (from observed effect to unobserved cause).

In causal reasoning you would argue, for example, that X results from Y; and since X is undesirable, Y should be eliminated. In an actual speech, the reasoning might be presented like this:

The Surgeon General and all the available evidence show unmistakably that Cancer [X] results from smoking [Y]. Smoking is personally destructive [X]; we have no choice but to do everything we can to eliminate smoking entirely [Y].

Alternatively, of course, you might argue that X results from Y; and since X is desirable, Y should be encouraged. In a speech, you might say something like this:

We know that general self-confidence [X] results from positively reinforcing experiences [Y]. Therefore, if you wish to encourage the development of self-confidence in your children [X], give them positively reinforcing experiences [Y].

Critically Evaluating Reasoning from Causes and Effects

In testing reasoning from cause to effect or from effect to cause, ask yourself the following questions.

1. Might other causes be producing the observed effect? If you observe a particular effect (say, high crime or student apathy), you need to ask if causes other than the one you are postulating might be producing these effects. Thus, you might postulate that poverty leads to high crime, but there might be other factors actually causing the high crime rate. Or poverty might be one cause, but it might not be the most important cause. Therefore, explore the possibility of other causes producing the observed effects.

2. Is the causation in the direction postulated? If two things occur together, it is often difficult to determine which is the cause and which is the effect. For example, a lack of interpersonal intimacy and a lack of self-confidence are often seen in the same person. The person who lacks self-confidence seldom has intimate relationships with others. But which is the cause and which is the effect? It might be that the lack of intimacy creates or "causes" low self-confidence; it might also be, however, that low self-confidence leads to or "causes" a lack of intimacy. Of course, it might also be that some other previously unexamined cause (a history of negative criticism, for example) might be producing both the lack of intimacy and the low self-confidence.

3. Is there evidence for a causal rather than merely a time-sequence relationship? Two things might vary together, but they may not be related in a cause-effect relationship. Divorce frequently results after repeated instances of infidelity, but infidelity itself may not be the cause of the divorce rate. Rather, some other factor may be leading to both infidelity and divorce. Thus, even though infidelity may precede divorce, it may not be the cause of it. When you assume that a temporal relationship implies a causal relationship, you are committing a fallacy of reasoning called *post hoc ergo propter hoc* ("after this, because of this").

Here Richard Snyder (1984) uses reasoning from cause to effect but without offering any real evidence of the connection linking the assumed cause and assumed effect:

> *We have been through two tumultuous decades: the '60s and the '70s, in which the liberals dominated the media and the trends. What happened—*Education lagged badly. *Look at the SAT scores. Look at illiteracy, absenteeism, crime in city schools. How do you study with the TV turned on? Higher education is currently under fire for mushy curricula and poor scholarship. Compare us to foreigners. We suffer.*
>
> Family life *came apart in many ways. Employed wives are part of the explanation, but it is difficult not to associate the trends with TV viewing. TV cannot tell us that its commercials have big appeal to consumers and at the same time disavow any connection between violent programs and the wife abuse, child abuse, shootings, stabbings, batteries, and the overall upsurge in crime.*

Using Cause-Effect Reasoning

Stress the causal connection by pointing out that:

1. other causes are not significant and may for all practical purposes be ruled out,
2. the causal connection is in the direction postulated, that is, that the cause is indeed the cause and the effect is the effect, and
3. the evidence points to a causal connection—that the relationship is not merely related in time.

Furthermore, depending on the specific purpose of your speech, make the audience realize that this causal connection can be altered to their advantage. Tell them that the effect may be strengthened (if the effect is desirable) or broken (if the effect is undesirable).

REMEMBER: When reasoning from causes and effects, make certain that:
1. other causes are not producing the observed effect
2. the causation is in the direction postulated
3. there is evidence for a causal rather than simply a temporal relationship

and is most effective when:

4. other possible causes may be ruled out
5. the causation is indeed in the postulated direction
6. the relationship is indeed a causal one

■■■■ REASONING FROM SIGN

Some years ago I went to my doctor because of a minor skin irritation. Instead of looking at my skin, the doctor focused on my throat, noticed that it was enlarged, felt around a bit, and began asking me a number of questions. Did I tire easily? Yes. Did I drink lots of liquid? Yes. Did I always feel thirsty? Yes. Did I eat a great deal without gaining any weight? Yes. She then had me stretch out my hand and try to hold it steady. I couldn't do it. Lastly, she took a close look at my eyes and asked if I had noticed that they had expanded. I hadn't been aware of it, but when it was pointed out I could see that my eyes had expanded a great deal. These indicators were signs of a particular illness. Based on these signs, she made the preliminary diagnosis that I had a hyperthyroid condition. The results of blood and other tests confirmed the preliminary diagnosis. I was promptly treated, and the thyroid condition was corrected.

Medical diagnosis is a good example of reasoning by sign. The general procedure is simple. If a sign and an object, event, or condition are frequently paired, the presence of the sign is taken as proof of the presence of the object, event, or condition. Thus, the tiredness, extreme thirst, and overeating were taken as signs of hyperthyroidism since they frequently accompany the condition. When these signs (or symptoms) disappeared after treatment, it was taken as a sign that the thyroid disease had been arrested. Further tests confirmed this as well.

The same general kind of reasoning is used in legal matters to determine guilt or innocence. Recall any of a hundred television or film dramas: someone is killed, the detective looks for signs of guilt. A motive, a history of violence, an inability to account for the time during which the murder took place are signs that together support the conclusion that "Higgins" did it.

In a disco, bar, or party, if someone asks you to dance, buys you a drink, engages you in conversation, and stares longingly into your eyes, you would normally take these as signs that this individual is interested in you and would like to pursue the relationship beyond this initial point. We reason from sign all the time.

Critically Evaluating Reasoning from Sign

In reasoning from sign, ask yourself these questions.

1. Do the signs necessitate the conclusion drawn? Given the extreme thirst, overeating, and the like, how certain may I be of the "hyperthyroid" conclusion? With most medical and legal matters we can never be *absolutely* certain, but we can be certain beyond a reasonable doubt.

2. Are there other signs that point to the same conclusion? In the thyroid example, the extreme thirst could have been brought on by any number of factors.

Similarly, the swollen throat and the overeating could have been attributed to other causes. Yet, taken together they seemed to point to only one reasonable diagnosis. This was later confirmed with additional and more sophisticated signs in the form of blood tests and thyroid scans. Generally, the more signs that point toward the conclusion, the more confidence we can have that it is valid.

3. Are there contradictory signs? Are there signs pointing toward contradictory conclusions? If, for example, "Higgins" had a motive and a history of violence (signs supporting the conclusion that Higgins was the murderer), but also had an alibi for the time of the murder (a sign pointing to the conclusion of innocence), the conclusion of guilt would have to be reconsidered or discarded.

Using Reasoning from Sign

Stress the certainty of the connection between the sign and the conclusion. Make the audience see that because these signs are present, no other conclusion is likely. Let them see that for all practical purposes, all other conclusions are ruled out.

This is the procedure followed in law. The guilt of an individual must be established not conclusively but beyond all *reasonable* doubt. The audience should be made to see that your conclusion drawn from sign is the best—the most reasonable—conclusion possible.

Student government debates, such as the one in which this speaker is engaged, rely heavily on logical arguments. What types of logical arguments (specific instances, analogy, causes-effects, and sign) would prove most effective in convincing an audience of your peers that (1) gays and lesbians should (not) be permitted in the U.S. military; (2) abortion should be made legal (illegal) in all states; or (3) this college should (not) be declared smoke-free?

Make the connection between the signs and the conclusions clear to the audience. If you, as a speaker, know of the connection between, say, enlarged eyes and hyperthyroidism, this does not mean that the audience knows it. State explicitly that enlarged eyes can only be produced by hyperthyroidism and that, therefore, the sign (enlarged eyes) can lead to only one reasonable conclusion (hyperthyroidism).

As with other forms of reasoning, try to anticipate and answer the objections of your audience to your line of reasoning. For example, let us say that you are trying to argue that women are discriminated against in jobs in higher education. You might use reasoning by sign and say something like this:

> *What evidence is there for the claim that women are discriminated against in higher education? Let's look. First, there are few women at the higher ranks of associate and full professor. Second, few women are chairpersons of departments. Third, there are extremely few women at the level of dean or president. Fourth, few women serve on really important committees that determine college policy, tenure, and promotion.*

One frequently raised objection to this line of reasoning is that few women go into higher education. Hence, this counterargument goes, there would naturally be fewer women in these higher positions. Anticipate a rebuttal such as this and confront it in your speech. You might continue your reasoning by sign and confront this anticipated objection by saying:

> *One frequently raised objection to these facts is that fewer women go into higher education. Let's look at the validity—I should say invalidity—of that argument. First, the figures for women are disproportionately lower. That is, the percentage of women in the higher ranks of associate or full professor is significantly lower than it is for men. Further, the percentage of women at the lower ranks of instructor and assistant professor is higher than it is for men. So, the difference has nothing to do with the number of men or women entering higher education. The difference is due to the fact that the percentage of men promoted to higher ranks is higher than the percentage of women.*

REMEMBER: **When reasoning from sign:**
1. the signs should support the conclusion you have drawn
2. other signs should point in the same direction
3. contradictory signs should be accounted for

and is most effective when:
4. the certainty of the connection between the sign and the conclusion is stressed and is made clear
5. the major counterarguments that the audience is likely to raise are answered

CRITICALLY SPEAKING

1. Why is it important to ask each of these three questions of any argument and its evidence: Is the support recent? Is there corroborative support? Are the

sources unbiased? Answer these questions for each of the following propositions:

    a.   Broccoli helps prevent cancer.
    b.   Happiness results from doing good for others.
    c.   The economic situation will improve significantly.
    d.   Crime in the cities will decline for the next three years.

2. Select two or three advertisements from a newspaper or magazine. What is their main argument? What form of reasoning did the advertiser use to support the argument?

3. In what cases would the recency of support be irrelevant to the validity of your argument?

4. What form of reasoning would be most appropriate to proving the following propositions?

    a.   Foreign language mastery should be required of all college graduates.
    b.   Women are better judges of people than are men.
    c.   As a group, college professors are happier than lawyers or medical doctors.
    d.   Brand A is better than Brand B.
    e.   Unemployment will increase over the next five years.

5. What form of reasoning would a good detective use most often? Can you give a hypothetical example of such reasoning?

PRACTICALLY SPEAKING

17.1   EVALUATING THE ADEQUACY OF REASONING

Here are, in brief, a few arguments. Read each of them carefully and (1) identify the type of reasoning used, (2) apply the tests of adequacy discussed this unit, and (3) indicate what could be done to make the reasoning more logical *and* more persuasive.

1. Last year, the three campus theater productions averaged 250 paid admissions. In a college of 12,000 students and with a theater that seats 1,000, the record is not particularly good. It seems clear that students are apathetic and simply don't care about theater or about campus activities in general. Something should be done about this—to encourage an appreciation for the arts and support for college-sponsored activities in general.

2. Students are apathetic. This is true of high school as well as college students, at urban as well as campus schools. We see it all around us. So, why bother to build a new theater; the students are not going to attend the productions. Let's direct that money to something that will be used, something that will be useful to the students and to the community as a whole.

3. Dr. Manchester should be denied tenure for being an ineffective teacher. Two of my friends are in Manchester's statistics course and they hate it; they haven't learned a thing. Manchester's student evaluation ratings are way below the

department and college average, and the readings Manchester assigns are dull, difficult, and of little relevance to students.

4. The lack of success among the Martians who have settled on Earth is not difficult to explain. They simply have no ambition, no drive, no desire to excel. They're content to live on welfare, drink cheap wine, and smoke as much grass as they can get their hands on.

5. I went out with three people I met at clubs—they were all duds. In the club they were fine but once we got outside I couldn't even talk with them. All they knew how to do was wear freaky clothes and dance. So when Pat asked me out I said, "No." I decided it would be a waste of time.

6. College professors are simply not aware of the real world. They teach their courses in an atmosphere that is free of all the problems and complexities of real life. How could they possibly advise me as to how to go about preparing for and finding a job?

7. I took Smith's course in rhetorical theory and it was just great—and easy. In fact, only one test was given and it was simple. Everybody got an A or B+. We didn't even have a term paper, and the lectures were all really interesting and relevant. This semester I have room for an elective so I'm taking Smith's psycholinguistics course.

8. One recent sociological report indicates some interesting facts about Theta Three. In Theta Three there are, as most of us know, few restrictions on premarital sexual relations. Unlike in our country, the permissive person is not looked down on. Social taboos in regard to sex are few. Theta Three also has the highest suicide rate per 100 inhabitants. Suicide is not infrequent among teenagers and young adults. This condition must be changed. But, before it is changed, life must be accorded greater meaning and significance. Social, and perhaps legal, restrictions on premarital sexual relations must be instituted if the individual is to have self-respect. Only in this way will the suicide rate— Theta Three's principal problem today—be significantly reduced.

9. In 1936 the *Literary Digest* took a poll to predict whether Landon or Roosevelt would win the presidential election. The *Digest* sent pre-election ballots to 10 million people, chosen at random from telephone directories and from lists of registered owners of automobiles. Two million ballots were returned and the *Digest* concluded that Landon would win the election.

10. Pat and Chris are unhappy and should probably separate. The last time I visited, Pat told me that they just had a big fight and mentioned that they now fight regularly. Chris spends more time with the kids than with Pat and frequently goes out after work with people from the office. Often, Chris has told me, they sit for hours without saying a word to each other.

17.2   ANALYZING ARGUMENTS: THE TOULMIN MODEL

An excellent way to analyze arguments is with the model developed by Stephen Toulmin, a British philosopher and logician. In Toulmin's model there are three essential parts and an additional three parts that may be used depending on the argument and the audience. The three essential parts are **claim, data,** and **warrant.**

The *claim* is the conclusion you wish the audience to accept; it is the proposition you want the audience to believe is true or justified or right. For example: *Tuition must be increased.*

The *data* are the facts and opinions—the evidence—used to support your claim. For example: *The college has recently incurred vast additional expenses.*

The *warrant* is the connection leading from the data to the claim. The warrant is the principle or the reason why the data justify (or warrant) the claim. For example: *Tuition has been in the past and is likely to continue to be the principal means by which the college pays its expenses.*

In addition to these three elements (which are essential to all arguments), there are three other optional elements that may or may not be present depending on the type of argument advanced and the nature of the audience to be persuaded.

The *backing* is the support for the warrant—the supporting material that backs up the principle or reason expressed in the warrant. Backing is especially important if the warrant is not accepted or believed by the audience. For example: *Over the last 40 years, each time the college incurred large expenses, it raised tuition.*

The *qualifier* is the degree to which the claim is asserted; it is an attempt to modify the strength or certainty of the claim. The qualifier is used only when the claim is presented with less than total certainty. For example: *probably.*

The *reservation* (or rebuttal) specifies those situations under which the claim might not be true. For example: . . . *unless the college manages to secure private donations from friends and alumni.*

Usually these six parts of an argument are laid out in diagrammatic form to further illustrate the important relationships.

The main value of Toulmin's system is that it provides an excellent method for analyzing arguments, which is especially appropriate to the public speaking situation. The following questions may also help you to analyze the validity and possible effectiveness of your arguments:

1. Are the data sufficient to justify the claim? What additional data are needed?
2. Is the claim properly (logically) qualified? Is the claim presented with too much certainty?
3. Is the warrant adequate to justify the claim on the basis of the data? Does the audience accept the warrant or will it need backing? What other warrants might be utilized?
4. Is the backing sufficient for accepting the warrant? Will the audience accept the backing? What further support for the warrant might be used?
5. Are the essential reservations stated? What other reservations might the audience think of that should be included here?

Test your understanding of these six elements of the Toulmin model by identifying which element each of the following statements represents. They are presented here in random order.

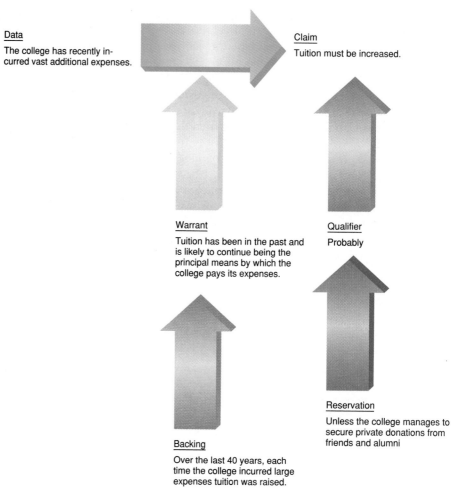

Data

The college has recently incurred vast additional expenses.

Claim

Tuition must be increased.

Warrant

Tuition has been in the past and is likely to continue being the principal means by which the college pays its expenses.

Qualifier

Probably

Reservation

Unless the college manages to secure private donations from friends and alumni

Backing

Over the last 40 years, each time the college incurred large expenses tuition was raised.

FIGURE 17.1

A diagram of the parts of an argument in a Toulmin analysis.

_____ 1. Cicero College must adopt a policy of training all its students in computer literacy.

_____ 2. Employers are demanding computer literacy for all positions.

_____ 3. This new emphasis must take place as soon as possible.

_____ 4. Colleges are obligated to prepare students for the job market.

_____ 5. Colleges that have failed to prepare students for the job market have found themselves without students.

_____ 6. unless the job market changes drastically

_____ 7. unless Cicero becomes a college devoted solely to the fine arts

_____ 8. Tawny Bay, Middlecenter, and Mt. Hill Colleges all neglected computer literacy and have declined 30% in enrollment.

_____ 9. All students should be trained in computer science with the possible exception of those in the fine arts.

Answers: 1 = claim; 2 = data; 3 = qualifier; 4 = warrant; 5 = backing; 6 = reservation; 7 = reservation; 8 = backing; 9 = qualifier.

Now that the mechanics of this model are clear, select one of the "claims" that follow and construct and diagram an argument using Toulmin's system. Include all six parts of the argument: claim, data, warrant, backing, qualifier, and reservation. After each person has constructed and diagrammed one argument, the papers should be collected, randomized, and redistributed so that each student has a diagrammed argument developed by someone else. In groups of five or six (or with the class as a whole), each student should analyze the argument, evaluating its validity and its potential rhetorical effectiveness for an audience composed of students from your class. The five questions presented previously might provide a useful starting place.

Claims

1. Senator Smiley should be reelected.
2. College football should be abolished.
3. Everyone has ESP.
4. Take a course in critical thinking.
5. Exercise daily.
6. Support the college athletic fund.
7. Keep a daily journal.
8. Express your opinions to your local representative.
9. Trace your family origins.
10. Visit India.

U N I T **18**

Motivating Behavior in Persuasive Speeches

■ ■ ■ ■

UNIT OBJECTIVES

After completing this unit, you should be able to:

1. Explain the role of psychological appeals in motivating behavior

2. Explain Maslow's hierarchy of needs

3. Identify at least three principles of motivation and explain their relevance to the public speaking transaction

4. Explain the operation of at least eight motivational appeals

---

*P*sychological appeals—appeals to needs, desires, and wants—are the most powerful means of persuasion you possess. Because of their importance, this entire unit is devoted to explaining what psychological appeals are and how you can use them effectively.

When you use psychological appeals you direct your appeals to your listeners' needs and desires. Although psychological appeals are never totally separate from rational appeals—appeals to reasoning and logic—they are considered separately here. The concern here is with *motives*, with those forces that energize or move or motivate a person to develop, change, or strengthen particular attitudes or ways of behaving. For example, one motive might be the desire for status. This motive might lead you to develop certain attitudes about what occupation to enter, the importance of saving and investing money, and so on. It may move you to behave in certain ways—to buy Gucci shoes, a Rolex watch, or a Tiffany diamond. As these examples illustrate, appeals to status (or to any motive) may motivate different persons in different ways. Thus, the status motive may lead one person to enter the poorly paid but respected occupation of nursing; it may influence another to enter the well-paid but often disparaged real estate or diamond business.

One of the most useful analyses of motives is Abraham Maslow's fivefold classification, reproduced in Figure 18.1. One of the assumptions contained in it is that you would seek to fulfill the need at the lowest level first and only then the need at the next higher level. Thus, for example, you would not concern yourself with the need for security or freedom from fear if you were starving (that is, if your need for food had not been fulfilled). Similarly, you would not be concerned with friendship or affectional relationships if your need for protection and security had not been fulfilled. I have used the insights of Maslow—as well as of various other theorists and researchers—in developing the principles of motivation that follow.

▪▪▪▪ PRINCIPLES OF MOTIVATION

Let's consider some principles of motivation so that you will be able to use motivational appeals more effectively in your own speeches.

Motives Differ

Motives are not static, nor do they operate in the same way with different people. Motives differ from one time to another and from one person to another.

Motives change with time. Think of the motives that are crucial to you at this time in your life and that motivate your current thinking and behavior. These motives, however, may not be significant in 10 or even 2 years. They may fade and others may take their place. Now, for example, attractiveness may be one of the more dominant motives in your life. You have a strong need to be thought attractive by your peers. Later in life this motive may be replaced by, for example, the desire for security, for financial independence, for power, or for fame.

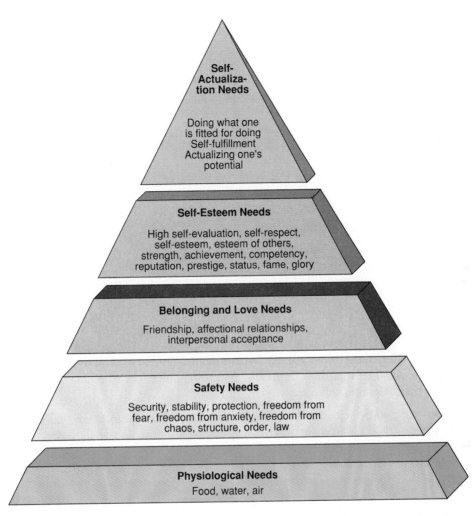

FIGURE 18.1   Maslow's "hierarchy of needs." (*Source:* Based on Abraham Maslow, *Motivation and Personality.* New York: HarperCollins, 1970.)

Motives function differently with different people. This is simply a specific application of the general principle: people are different. Consequently, different people will respond differently to the very same motive. Further, different motives in different people may lead to the same behavior. Thus, three persons may choose to become college professors—one because of its security, one because of its relative freedom, and one because of its status. The resulting behavior in all three cases is essentially the same, but the motivational histories are very different.

Motives Are Ordered

Not all motives are equal in intensity. Some are powerful and exert a strong influence on behavior; others are less powerful and may influence behavior only slightly. Further, motives may be ordered in terms of their degree of generality or specificity. Let's look at each of these characteristics of motives.

Strong and Weak Motives Motives exist in varying degrees of intensity. Some motives are strong, some are weak, and the vast majority are somewhere in between. To complicate matters a bit more, the intensity of the various motives will vary from one time to another and from one communication situation to another.

Since motives vary in intensity and strength, they vary in the influence they have on the individual. It is obvious that people will be influenced more by motives that are strong and less by motives that are weak. Determining which motives your audience holds strongly and which weakly may be one of your most difficult tasks; but if you can identify those motives that will strongly influence the audience, you need not waste time on motives that are ineffective in influencing behavior.

Maslow's Hierarchy Revisited The notion of an ordered hierarchy of motives comes from the work of Abraham Maslow. Recall that in this system certain needs have to be satisfied before other needs can motivate behavior (Figure 18.1). Thus, you need to determine what needs of the audience have been satisfied and, therefore, what needs you might use to motivate them. In most college classrooms, for example, you may assume that the two lowest levels—physiological needs and safety needs—have been reasonably fulfilled. In many students, however, the third level (love needs) is not fulfilled, and propositions may be linked to these with great effectiveness. Thus, to assure the audience that what you are saying will enable them to achieve more productive interpersonal relationships or greater peer acceptance will go a long way toward securing their attention and receptiveness.

General and Specific Motives Motives are general classes of needs and desires. For example, the achievement motive may include a host of specifics that, taken together, make up and define achievement for a specific person. People are not motivated by appeals to abstract and general motives but rather to specific aspects of these motives. Thus, to appeal to status—defined in abstract and general terms—does nothing (or at best very little) to motivate specific attitudes and behaviors. Rather, you need to appeal to, for example, the desire to be recognized by others on the street, having a job that is respected by family and friends, or having a home in an exclusive part of town.

The more specific your appeal, the more effective your appeal will be in persuading your audience. Consider, for example, the difference between the teacher's appeal to read this book because it will help to make you an educated person versus the appeal to read this book because it will help you to pass this course or the next test.

Motives Interact

Motives rarely operate in isolation; usually a collection of motives operate together. Sometimes these motives operate in the same direction, all influencing behavior in the same way. At other times, motives conflict with one another, each stimulating behavior in somewhat different directions.

In cases where a number of motives influence behavior in the same direction, your appeal should be directed to a number of motives rather than limited to just one. For example, if you want an audience to contribute money to AIDS research, appeal to a variety of influential motives—safety for oneself and one's family and friends, altruism, control over the environment, and so on.

In cases where motives conflict with one another, your task is a more difficult one. Let us say that humanitarian motives would lead your audience to give money to AIDS research, but their desire for self-gain or for using their money to do other things would lead them not to donate funds. In this case you might propose that the humanitarian motives are more noble or perhaps that the amount of money involved is not so great that they would impoverish themselves.

REMEMBER: **The following principles of motivation:**

1. motives differ from one time to another and from one person to another
2. motives are ordered, varying in intensity and generality
3. motives interact, sometimes in concert and sometimes in conflict

MOTIVATIONAL APPEALS

In employing motivational appeals, you can address many specific motives. Naturally each audience will be a bit different, and motives that are appropriately appealed to in one situation might be inappropriate or ineffective in another. You will always have to exercise judgment and taste. Before examining the list of specific motives to which you may direct your appeals, consider the general advice offered by Sonya Hamlin in the accompanying "TIP."

TIPS FROM PROFESSIONAL SPEAKERS

Making the listener want to hear you is primary.

Right. But now that you think about it, why would someone else spontaneously get interested in your vested stuff? You'd need a propellant—something that could make a difference, something that could *actively* turn your audience to your pursuit and away from theirs. What?

When what you have to say clearly intersects with what the other person wants or needs or cares about.

If your message obviously relates to one or more of the listener's "hot buttons," you have given a primary, compelling reason for listening. You're not actually demanding that he/she give up self-involvement. You're just piggy-backing on some part of the listener's own momentum; his/her self-involvement. You're defining your message as another facet of his or her ongoing life concerns.

Sonya Hamlin, president, Sonya Hamlin Communications, a communications consulting firm. *How to Talk So People Listen: The Real Key to Job Success* (New York: Harper-Collins, 1988), pp. 22–23. Reprinted by permission.

Altruism

Altruism, some argue, does not exist. It is said that all of our motives are selfish, and perhaps this is right. Any action, any belief, any attitude can usually be traced to a motive that might be regarded as selfish—to greed, to sensory pleasure, to personal power. But it is equally true that most of us want to believe that our motives are altruistic, at least sometimes. We want to do what we consider the right thing; we want to help others; we want to contribute to worthy causes. We want to help the weak, feed the hungry, cure the sick. The fact that we derive some kind of selfish pleasure from these actions does not militate against our viewing them as being motivated by altruism. Appeals to altruism are most effective when done with moderation. If they are not moderate, they will seem unrealistic and out of touch with the way real people think in a world that is practical and difficult to survive in.

Here is an especially good example of the use of the appeal to altruism. In this speech Charlotte Lunsford (1988) appeals to altruism but also to a wide variety of other motives. She effectively uses the principle that appeals to a wide variety of motives:

> Volunteerism still combines the best and the most powerful values in our society—pride in the dignity of work, the opportunity to get involved in things that affect us, the freedom of choice and expression, the chance to put into practice an ethic of caring, and the realization that one person can make a difference.
>
> To these altruistic reasons for volunteering, we can add some very specific rewards for giving of one's time in the service of others:
>
> —a chance to do the things that one does best
> —working with a respected community organization
> —seeing the results of one's own work
> —the opportunity to make business and professional contacts—"networking"
> —the opportunity to develop social skills
> —and the chance to move to paid employment

Fear

We are motivated in great part by a desire to avoid fear. We fear the loss of those things we desire. We fear the loss of money, family, friends, love, attractiveness, health, job, and just about everything we now have and value. We also fear punishment, rejection, failure. We fear the unknown, the uncertain, the unpredictable.

The use of fear in persuasion has been studied extensively, and the results show that strong amounts of fear work best (Boster and Mongeau, 1984; Allen and Preiss, 1990). With low or even moderate levels of fear, the audience is not motivated sufficiently to act; with high levels of fear they perk up and begin to listen.

A good example of the use of fear in persuasion can be seen in the American Express Traveler's Checks commercial, where you are led to believe that if you lose traveler's checks other than American Express', they will not be refunded; in fact, you will find yourself stranded in a foreign country with no money and no one willing to help you.

Here an audience of soldiers hears about protecting themselves from nerve gas attacks. If you were giving such a speech, what motives would you appeal to in order to secure their interest and attention? To convince them to follow your advice and warnings?

The other side of fear is safety. We all have a need for safety. Maslow put safety at the second level, just above the satisfaction of the physiological need for food and drink. We want to feel protected, to be free of fear. Sometimes the safety motive is seen in the individual's desire for order, structure, and organization. We fear what is unknown, and order and structure make things predictable and, hence, safe.

In this excerpt Michael Marien (1984) appeals to fear in his speech on the need to control our modern technologies:

> *And the bad news is awesome. There are some 50,000 to 60,000 nuclear warheads in the world today, with a total explosive yield of 1.6 million times that of the 1945 Hiroshima bomb that we use as a benchmark. A single 20 megaton bomb, which could be dropped on New York City, has 1600 times the yield of the Hiroshima bomb. Our modern arsenal amounts to 5000 times the destructive power of all munitions used in World War II. So we do indeed have the potential to end all life on our planet, as a group of scientists recently warned in sketching a scenario of a possible nuclear winter.*

Individuality and Conformity

These two conflicting motives are discussed together because they are opposite sides of the same coin and often operate at the same time. Each pulls us in a different direction and each lessens the effects of the other. Clearly, we have a need for uniqueness, for individuality. We want to stand out from the crowd. Many people fear being lost in the crowd, being indistinguishable from everyone else.

Yet we also want to conform, to be one of the crowd, to be "in." We want to be like those we admire and respect. Consider, for example, the way we dress, the way we talk, even the way we think and act. In large part we do what we do because we desire to conform to some standard, or, perhaps, we wish to imitate some person we admire.

Successful motivation depends on your making your listeners see themselves as standing out from the crowd but never as "outsiders." Make your listeners see themselves as individuals who have a unique identification but who are nevertheless closely identified with the positively evaluated groups.

Power, Control, and Influence

We want power, control, and influence. First, we want power over ourselves—we want to be in control of our own destinies, we want to be responsible for our own successes. As Emerson put it, "Can anything be so elegant as to have few wants, and to serve them one's self?"

We also want control over other persons. We want to be influential—we want to be opinion leaders, we want others to come to us for advice, for guidance, for instruction. Similarly, we want control over events and things in the world. We want to control our environment. Practically every communication book designed for the popular market (that is, a non-textbook) emphasizes how the knowledge of communication will enable you to achieve power, control, and influence—in sales, in work, and in love. You will motivate your listeners when you enable them to believe that they can increase their power, control, and influence as a result of their learning what you have to say or doing as you suggest.

In a commencement address at Ohio University, Vincent Ryan Ruggiero (1987) appealed to his listeners' desire to control their lives more efficiently; this speech is reprinted in its entirety at the end of Unit 13 ("Where Has the Time Gone?," see paragraphs 10–12).

Self-Esteem and Approval

"In his private heart," wrote Mark Twain, "no man much respects himself." And perhaps because of this, we have a need for a positive self-image, to see ourselves in the best possible light. We want to see ourselves as self-confident, as worthy and contributing human beings. Inspirational speeches, speeches of the "you are the greatest" type, never seem to lack receptive and suggestive audiences.

Self-esteem is, at least in part, attained by gaining the approval of others. College students are especially concerned with peer approval, but also want approval from family, teachers, elders, and even children. Somehow the approval of others makes us feel positive about ourselves. If others approve of us, we assume that we must deserve such approval. Approval from others also ensures the attainment of a number of related goals. For example, if we have peer approval, we probably also have influence. If we have approval, we will likely have status. In relating your propositions to your audience's desire for approval, avoid being too obvious. Few people want to be told that they need or desire approval.

Love and Affiliation

We are motivated to love and be loved. We want to be assured that someone loves us (preferably lots of people). At the same time we want to be assured that we are capable of loving in return. For most persons, love and its pursuit occupy a considerable amount of time and energy. If you can teach your audience how to be loved and how to love, you will have not only an attentive but also a grateful audience.

We also want affiliation—friendship and companionship. We desire to be a part of a group despite our equally potent desire for independence and individuality. Notice how advertisements for discos, singles bars, and dating services emphasize this need for affiliation. On this basis alone they successfully gain the attention, interest, and participation of thousands. Again, such affiliation seems to assure us that we are in fact worthy creatures. If we have friends and companions, surely we are people of some merit.

In this excerpt Leo Buscaglia (1988), noted author and lecturer, appeals to our desire for love and affiliation:

> It is not uncommon these days to form relationships based on nothing more than mutual physical attraction. On this shaky foundation we set high standards and impossible expectations. We insist that the "magic" continue, that the honeymoon last forever. We resist the reality that love can also mean carrying out the trash, meeting car payments, standing in line at the grocery store and doing the laundry. Relationships that are based on little more than a steamy attraction more often than not end by leaving us bewildered, wondering what went wrong when we find that we are no longer "happily-ever-aftering." We usually discover that it was the small conflicts, the petty peeves, the infantile rigidity and stubbornness, the disillusionment and the refusal to forgive.
>
> There is no simple formula for making us better lovers. At best we can base our love on certain tried-and-true rules that can make a positive beginning.

Achievement

We want to achieve in whatever we do. As students you want to be successful students. As a teacher and writer I, too, want to be successful. We want to achieve as friends, as parents, as lovers. This is why we read books and listen to speeches that purport to tell us how to be better achievers. We also want others to recognize our achievements as real and valuable. "Being successful in my work" was noted as "extremely important" by 63 percent of entering college students.

In using the achievement motive, be explicit in stating how your speech, ideas, and recommendations will contribute to the listeners' achievements. If you tell the listeners how they can learn to increase their potential, earn better grades, secure more prestigious jobs, and become more popular with friends, you will have a highly motivated audience.

In a speech on the values of networking, Peter B. Stark (1985) appeals to the achievement motive of his audience and in the process effectively establishes his credibility:

> *Networking is the most powerful success tool to get you where you want to go. To be honest, networking is one of the greatest assets I have ever owned.*
>
> *At the age of 21, I was the Executive Assistant to the President of a 25-million dollar company. An unadvertised position I had gained through a management consultant I had met in Toastmasters International.*
>
> *At the age of 23, I was the Director of Marketing for the local Caterpillar Tractor Dealer, a 100-million dollar company. Another unadvertised position I received through a community contact. And, at the age of 25, I had enough contacts to open Photomation West, a printing and advertising firm.*[*]

Financial Gain

"Money," said George Bernard Shaw, "is the most important thing in the world. It represents health, strength, honor, generosity, and beauty as conspicuously as the want of it represents illness, weakness, disgrace, meanness, and ugliness. Not the least of its virtues is that it destroys base people as certainly as it fortifies and dignifies noble people."

Most people are motivated to some extent by the desire for financial gain—for what it can buy, for what it can do. We may be concerned with buying necessities, luxuries, or even time—time to do the things we all want to do and not be tied to the pedestrian and the mundane, like ironing, washing, typing, painting, and so on.

Concern for lower taxes, for higher salaries, for fringe benefits are all related to the money motive. Show the audience that what you are saying or advocating will make them money and they will listen with considerable interest, much as they read the current get-rich-quick books that are flooding the bookstores.

In a speech designed to motivate the audience to take action against certain proposed budget cuts, Cyril F. Brickfield (1985) appeals to the financial motive of his senior citizen audience:

> *Congress is now considering freezing Social Security COLA's [cost-of-living adjustments]. Congress is willing to force more than a half million of us into poverty. But the defense budget is exempt from any freeze.*
>
> *Ladies and gentlemen, let me ask you, is it fair that older Americans must lose their inflation protection while the Pentagon doesn't?*

Status

One motive that accounts for a great deal of our behavior is our desire for status, a principle the car dealer in the cartoon hopes will work. In our society our status is measured by our occupation and wealth; often job and money are positively related.

But there are other kinds of status: the status that comes from competence on the athletic field, from excelling in the classroom, or from superiority on the dance floor.

[*]Reprinted from *Networking* by permission of the author.

BUMPER SNICKERS — BY BUNNY HOEST

"It's recommended by nine out of 10 doctors."

Bumper Snickers by Bunny Hoest. Copyright © 1992 by Bunny Hoest. Reprinted courtesy of Bunny Hoest and The National Enquirer.

To be most effective, link your propositions with your specific audience's desire for status.

Beginning college students give considerable attention to their future jobs but rank interest and the utilization of skills and abilities as more important than other qualities we normally think of as being part of status. For example, in a recent survey, 17,000 students were asked what would make for future job satisfaction. Of those qualities listed as "very important," 93 percent noted "interesting to do" and 74 percent noted "uses skills and abilities." On the issues normally considered characteristic of status, a "chance to earn a good deal of money" was noted by 47 percent, "a job most people look up to, respect" by 37 percent, and "high status, prestige" by 36 percent. I suspect that these percentages change considerably with age, giving greater importance to status in the form of financial gain and societal approval.

In this excerpt Kelly Zmak (Boaz and Brey, 1987), a student from San Jose State University, appeals to the audiences' desire for status and success:

> You know, as college people we all have something in common. We want to be successful. The levels of our success vary, but to be successful is something that we all strive for. Having an advantage in today's world is something none of us would mind. But having a disadvantage is something that none of us can afford. I would say that there are many of you here today that are not capitalizing on your potential, because you do not own a personal computer. And for those of you who do, listen up. Your computer may not have the power, the capabilities, and the features needed to give the home user, the student, and the businessperson an advantage in today's world.

Self-Actualization

According to Abraham Maslow, the self-actualization motive only influences our attitudes and behaviors after all other needs are satisfied. And since these other needs are very rarely all satisfied, the time spent appealing to self-actualization might better be spent on other motives. And yet I suspect that regardless of how satisfied or unsatisfied our other desires are, we all have in some part a desire to self-actualize, to become what we feel we are fit for. If we see ourselves as poets, we must write poetry. If we see ourselves as singers, we must sing. If we see ourselves as teachers, we must teach. Even if we do not pursue these as occupations, we nevertheless have a desire to write poetry, to sing, or to teach—even if only in our imaginations. Appeals to self-actualization encourage listeners to strive for their highest ideals and are always welcomed.

Here, for example, William Jackson (1985) appeals to self- actualization in his speech on happiness in life:

> One of the greatest wastes of our national resources is the number of young people who never achieve their potential. If you think you can't, you won't. If you think you can, there is an excellent chance you will. The cost of excellence is discipline. The cost of mediocrity is disappointment. Only a mediocre person is always at his best. There should be two goals in your life; one is to get what you want in life, and the other is to enjoy your successes. Only the wisest people achieve the latter.

REMEMBER: the usefulness of the following motives:
1. altruism
2. fear
3. individuality and conformity
4. power, control, and influence
5. self-esteem and approval
6. love and affiliation
7. achievement
8. financial gain
9. status
10. self-actualization

▪■▪■ A SAMPLE SPEECH WITH ANNOTATIONS

Claude Pepper, U.S. Representative from Florida, delivered this speech to the National Council of Senior Citizens in Washington, D.C., on June 6, 1977. The rights of the elderly have been so neglected in this youth-oriented society that it is appropriate to give specific consideration to the elderly. We will all be "the elderly" of tomorrow, and people close to us are the elderly of today, so raising our consciousness seems particularly worthwhile. Like the Billups speech ("Black History"), this speech also effectively blends the specific instances with the broad generalizations so important in public speaking effectiveness. The text of the speech is reprinted by permission of The Pepper Foundation, Tallahassee, Florida.

Mandatory Retirement

Claude Pepper

In 1776, the Colonists, rebelling against the tyrannies of George the Third, issued a Declaration of Independence and Bill of Rights. In 1848, a group of women, disenfranchised in the country they helped to found, met in Seneca Falls, New York, and issued a declaration of sentiments patterned on the Declaration of Independence. In 1948, in the wake of the horrors of Nazi Germany, the U.N. issued a declaration of human rights. Today I call for a declaration of independence for the elderly from mandatory retirement, forced institutionalization, hazardous nursing homes, and criminal victimization. I call for a bill of rights guaranteeing the elderly the right to work as long as they are willing and able, the right to home health alternatives to institutionalization, the right to safe nursing homes and security in their homes and in the streets.

Mandatory retirement is a cruel euphemism camouflaging age discrimination and forced unemployment. With the surety of a guillotine, it severs productive persons from their livelihood, shears their sense of self-worth and squanders their talents. The elderly of this country who want to work and are able to work deserve the opportunity to work. They are tired of aphorisms. They demand action.

Each day of the year more than 4,000 Americans reach the age of 65. There is no evidence that on that day their ability to function productively in the economy vanishes. There is, in fact, ample evidence to support Shaw's observation that "some are younger at 70 than most at 17." Who would tell Margaret Mead, who is 75, that her contributions to the study of sociology ended at age 65? Who would tell Arthur Fiedler, who is 83, or Leopold Stokowski, who is 94, that those over 65 cannot contribute meaningfully to our appreciation of music? To waste the talents of the older worker is as shameful as it is to waste natural resources.

Why then does mandatory retirement exist? In part, because Social Security arbitrarily set a certain age for receipt of benefits. In part because Congress refused to protect workers over 65 in the Age Discrimination in

The late Claude Pepper spoke widely on the rights of senior citizens and on the obligations of others toward the elderly. In addressing the National Council of Senior Citizens, Pepper came to the speech with considerable credibility; he was viewed as a competent spokesperson and as one who had his audience's interest foremost in mind. Because of his previous record in support of the elderly, the audience was already familiar with his position on the issues he raises and, we can assume, will be in basic agreement with him. The speaker is concerned, then, not with changing attitudes but with strengthening them and ultimately motivating the audience to specific actions.

In this introduction Pepper accomplishes a great deal. (1) He secures audience favor early in the speech by expressing a position with which they agree. Recall that the audience is composed of senior citizens and that the speaker (also a senior citizen) is committing himself to fight for their rights. (2) Pepper orients the audience by identifying his major points: mandatory retirement, forced institutionalization, hazardous nursing homes, and criminal victimization. The organizational pattern is thus a topical one. (3) Pepper places the issues in historical perspective with a few provocative examples. (4) He gives these issues greater significance by comparing them to, for example, the Declaration of Independence and the United Nations Declaration of Human Rights.

Here, Pepper introduces his first major topic: mandatory retirement. Immediately he states his position: "Mandatory retirement is a cruel euphemism. . . ." In the next few paragraphs Pepper gives his arguments against mandatory retirement.

With just a few specific instances, Pepper makes a good case against mandatory retirement. Who would argue that people like Mead, Fiedler, and Stokowski should be forced to retire? At the same time, he is telling this audience that they are in good company with Mead, Fiedler, and Stokowski, and thus stimulates an agreement response from the audience.

Pepper makes the reasons for mandatory retirement seem feeble, at best. They seem, from his analysis, to be based on accident and misperception. He fails to mention, for example, that one of the major reasons for mandatory retirement is unemployment. Without mandatory retirement, unemployment might be more serious than it is now. But Pepper's purpose is not to offer an argumentative brief against mandatory retirement, but to strengthen the existing beliefs of the audience.

Here, Pepper offers an internal summary of his position and provides a brief transition ("But that is not the only cruel act. . . .") connecting what has been said to what will be said. Pepper thus glides neatly from his first major point (mandatory retirement) to his second point (institutionalization).

Again, Pepper immediately states his position with regard to his second topic: "Every year, thousands of older Americans are unnecessarily institutionalized."

Pepper offers his first major fear appeal—the fear of being institutionalized with inadequate service. He also cites numerous statistics to further impress upon the audience the pervasiveness of the inequities.

Notice here the clear statement of one of Pepper's major arguments: "Criteria for nursing homes are even hazier." This statement serves to connect the previous argument with the one to follow and clearly signals to the audience that he will now illustrate and document the "haziness" of the criteria. Note, too, that the statistics cited give us the impression that Pepper is in full command of his subject matter and is therefore a credible spokesperson.

Employment Act. And in part because we have not rid ourselves of the stereotype of the enfeebled older worker. In fact, older workers perform as well and often better than younger workers in jobs requiring experience.

Mandatory retirement creates a host of additional problems. There is evidence that forced retirement accelerates the aging process, brings on physical and emotional problems, causes economic deprivation, and strains an already overburdened Social Security system.

Age-based mandatory retirement is discriminatory, unjust, unnecessary and a waste of human talent.

Depriving the person who is able and willing to continue to work of the right to work because by some arbitrary standard that person is old is a cruel act. But that is not the only cruel act perpetrated against the elderly.

Every year, thousands of older Americans are unnecessarily institutionalized. More than one million older people live in nursing homes, mental hospitals, general hospitals, old age and retirement homes and other institutional settings which, in general, suffer from misdirection and inadequate service. Criteria for admission to these facilities are usually vague and variable. For example, one-third of the aged residents of state mental hospitals have no serious mental impairment at all, but simply have no place else to go.

Criteria for nursing homes are even hazier. State hospitals discharge many of their elderly, including those who are mentally disturbed and require psychiatric care, to nursing homes. One study of nursing home patients in Massachusetts concluded that as many as 40 percent of its residents could be treated at home for a lower cost if the law allowed. Testimony provided by HEW revealed that between 14 to 25 percent of the one million institutionalized elderly may be unnecessarily maintained in an institutional setting. Tragically, the federal government perpetuates needless institutionalization of the elderly. Of Medicaid's $3.2 billion budget for the elderly—almost 70 percent goes to nursing homes and only 1 percent for home health alternatives. The vast majority of elderly must rely largely on Medicare and Medicaid support, neither of which will pay for home health care services, and the government compounds the problem. Although preventive health care is far cheaper for both the patients and the government—Medicare and Medicaid do not provide coverage for annual checkups, professional and nutrition counseling, and diagnostic services. And while those over 75 suffer visual and hearing losses at rates two to three times that of those less their age, Medicare and Medicaid do not cover the elderly's eyeglasses, hearing aids, and dentures and other necessary medical appliances.

While many nursing homes are properly labelled homes because they offer compassionate care, others are more properly labelled nursing houses or nursing facilities—places where those whom society has abandoned are sent to die—uprooted, isolated, treated with condescension rather than compassion. It is not surprising to discover that death often occurs soon after institutionalization.

Here, Pepper provides the needed transition to connect his second topic (institutionalization) with his third topic, the closely related hazardous nursing home conditions.

The 23 million elderly people in this country want and deserve an alternative to institutionalization. Congress is beginning to view home health care as that alternative. Just last month, the House Committee on Aging was able to defeat a proposal to cut back funding for home health services.

Although "23 million" is a huge number, Pepper might have made it more meaningful by relating it to other examples: 23 million represents about one out of every nine people in the country; or, it is the approximate population of California.

Institutionalization of the elderly should cease to be society's place of first resort. Rather, it should be the place of last resort—for only those who choose and need such services. Home health care offers the elderly the flexibility of choice and the option to remain independent—an ideal which must be preserved in our democratic society.

Another brief internal summary and a restatement of one of Pepper's major propositions.

Those elderly who require institutionalization deserve federal standards which guarantee that nursing homes are not tinderboxes. After 32 elderly persons died needlessly in a nursing home fire last year, I introduced legislation mandating sprinkler systems in nursing homes funded by Medicare and Medicaid. The legislation authorizes low interest government loans to underwrite the cost of the sprinkler systems. After an investigation, initiated at my request, the General Accounting Office concluded that there has never been a multiple death fire in a nursing home protected by an automatic sprinkler system. The Comptroller General of the United States concluded that "Federal fire safety requirements do not insure life safety in nursing homes" and supported the sprinkler recommendation. Nursing home safety is the special concern of all persons who will grow old and whose loved ones will grow old and will face the possibility of care in such a facility. These persons are not com-

Notice how effectively Pepper builds his credibility by noting, for example, that he introduced legislation mandating sprinkler systems in nursing homes and that an investigation was conducted at his initiation. The speaker's record of fighting for the elderly does much to make him a more credible spokesperson.

Note how effectively Pepper connects the previously discussed mandatory retirement and forced institutionalization with his next point, victimization. It is an effective transition and helps us to see the speech as a cohesive whole.

More fear appeal. Notice that Pepper does not draw detailed scenes or portraits of such violent acts. Often overly strong fear appeals may not work as well and cause the audience to withdraw and stop listening. Note, too, that the incidents that Pepper mentions are probably too familiar to the audience; such acts have probably happened to them or to persons they know, so detailed descriptions are unnecessary.

Note here the use of "guide phrases": "two antithetic stereotypes. One claims that. . . ." And, in the next

forted by a New York State subcommittee report which found that because of fire hazards, nursing homes rank first on a list of unsafe places to live.

The elderly person forced out of a job or forced into an institution is in a very real sense a victim—a victim of societal stereotypes and misdirected legislation. But victimization of the elderly does not stop in the labor force or in health care. Crime against the elderly exacts a financial, physical and psychological cost which is immeasurable. The committee heard elderly victims tell of being raped, beaten, mugged, and assaulted, their savings depleted by medical costs, spending days in hunger waiting for the next Social Security check. Ironically the elderly victim is the least likely to report crime either because he or she fears retaliation or is unable to afford the pursuit of justice.

Every year, nearly 20,000 senior citizens are robbed of their Social Security checks, usually by direct looting of their mailboxes. During these first days of the month, when Social Security, pensions, public assistances, and other checks arrive, robberies, burglaries and assaults escalate. The tragedy of crime is compounded for those elderly to whom Social Security checks mean food and shelter. The physical and financial scars of crime are deepened by the psychological scars. One elderly couple in New York City committed suicide rather than live out their lives in fear of being beaten again. Others imprison themselves behind bolted doors and barred windows dreading their next trip to the grocery store, afraid to attend civic and religious functions.

Hearings held by Mr. Roybal have revealed that the elderly are frequently the victims of property crimes—burglary, robbery, and larceny. Older victims, who are most frequently on fixed incomes with little or no savings, are unable to recoup monetary losses. They also lack the resources to replace stolen items or repair damaged property. Even the loss of $20, an amount of money considered too insignificant to register on the FBI crime index, can represent a loss of food, heat or needed medicine to the older person on a small, fixed income. Recognizing this the Committee on Aging has recommended passage of a victim compensation bill, with special provisions to provide coverage for property loss and damage to needy elderly victims.

At the base of governmental response to the elderly are two antithetic stereotypes. One claims that to be old is to be feeble-minded and worthless; the other claims that to be old is to be just like everybody else. The misguided belief that an arbitrary age signals senility is perpetuated in the Age Discrimination in Employment Act which fails to protect the worker over 65 from age discrimination. That stereotype also fosters the custodial mentality which drives the elderly into costly and often needless institutionalization. By demanding an end to mandatory retirement and by demanding home health alternatives we fracture the hold that stereotype currently has on legislative philosophy.

The second stereotype claims that the elderly do not differ in any significant respect from any other segment of the population. This stereotype spawns legislation which resembles the trickle down theory of economics: design social programs for the population at large and the elderly will presumably benefit. This legislative philosophy ignores the special needs of the elderly. Protection from age discrimination, safety in nursing homes, and protection from fraudulent marketing of hearing aids and dentures are among those special concerns.

We cannot banish these pernicious stereotypes by Congressional mandate. We can guarantee that they are not embodied in legislation.

It is time to declare that the elderly persons in this country will no longer be victimized by mandatory retirement, forced institutionalization, hazardous nursing homes, and criminal assault. I ask you to join in rebellion against the indignities imposed on the elderly.

While you are here for your legislative convention I urge you to talk to and write your congressman, pressing enactment of H.R. 1115, ending mandatory retirement and age discrimination for federal employees, so that the federal government can take the initiative and provide an example for all public and private employers to follow.

Talk to and write your congressman and let him know that you support the upcoming Labor-HEW appropriations bill. This legislation, at the Aging Committee's urging, contains an additional $92 million for programs for the elderly. For example, it doubles the funds for senior citizen centers (from $20 million to $40 million), increases nutrition programs (from $225 to $250 million) and increases home health demonstrations (by $5 million), The National Institution on Aging (also by $5 million), and Senior Companions (a $½ million increase) as well as other programs.

paragraph: "The second stereotype. . . ." Phrases such as these help the audience to follow the speaker more closely.

Note the effectiveness of this restatement of Pepper's main points.

Here, Pepper asks for specific action and, in general terms at least, identifies the benefits that such actions could generate. Usually, such statistics are more effective when they are individualized for the members of the audience. For example, the increase from $20 million to $40 million for senior citizens' centers is most impressive but more specific figures might help; for example, how many additional seniors these centers might service, what services the centers might provide that they are now unable to provide, and, specifically, what this money will mean to the senior citizens sitting in *this* audience.

Again, Pepper asks for specific actions and thereby involves the audience directly. He, in effect, asks the audience to join him in this fight for the rights of the elderly and thus establishes a most effective bond—a working relationship—between himself and the members of his audience.

Although the entire speech was addressed to an audience of senior citizens, Pepper here gives the speech wider appeal and stresses the relevance of this topic and these issues to all people and not just the elderly.

In this conclusion Pepper summarizes his four main points and, in the last paragraph, ends crisply by again identifying himself closely with the audience and by complimenting and praising the audience: "the generation that survived the great depression and two world wars."

Last week, during consideration of this bill in the Appropriations Committee, an amendment was offered to cut many of these increases, together with other labor and health programs. This amendment lost by only one vote and will be offered on the House floor about June 15. I hope you will urge your congressman to support the Labor-HEW bill and oppose the Michel Amendment's cuts and I hope you will write President Carter and urge him to sign the bill.

France supported the colonists in their rebellion against Britain. Men joined women in their battle for suffrage and equal rights. I call on persons of all ages to defend the rights of the elderly because every person in this nation has a stake in the well-being of the elderly. Many are themselves elderly; others have elderly loved ones. All will themselves age. And if they do not now join in this rebellion, they will find when they become senior citizens that the injustices they have suffered and the problems they have encountered are compounded by age-based mandatory retirement, by a governmental philosophy which favors costly and often needless institutionalization, by nursing homes which are too often tinderboxes, by the spectre of criminal attack, and by pernicious stereotypes.

Let us declare that those who sow promises, reap votes, and then spurn the elderly until the next election will harvest indignation. Contrary to the stereotype, the elderly do not forget the promises of vote-seeking politicians. Thus, I am particularly pleased that the Carter administration is moving to keep the promises made to the elderly in the 1976 campaign.

As leaders in the cause of the elderly, I ask you to join me in affirming the tenacity of the generation that survived the great depression and two world wars. We have declared our independence. We demand our rights. Thank you.

CRITICALLY SPEAKING

1. How would you describe your own motives in terms of Maslow's hierarchy of needs?

2. Do you know people you would describe as "self-actualizers"? How do they differ from most people?

3. Have your motives changed since starting college? How?

4. What motives influence you the most in regard to:
   a. attending college
   b. your interpersonal relationships
   c. the choice of your occupational goal
   d. your activities over the last weekend
5. Do you have conflicting motives pulling you in different directions? If so, how do you think you will eventually resolve the conflict?
6. How do you respond to the fear appeals that are currently used in popular advertisements?
7. Are you motivated by both the desire to be different and the desire to be one of a group? Does this create difficulties?
8. Can you identify three ways in which you are influenced by the motives discussed here?
9. Which single motive is the most influential in your life right now? Which is the least influential? How do you feel about this?
10. What motives would you appeal to in persuading your class to:
    a. support Channel 1?
    b. vote against affirmative action proposals?
    c. support a multiculturalism requirement?
    d. exercise at least 30 minutes a day?
    e. support the building of a homeless shelter in their neighborhood?
11. What motives are used in popular television advertisements to sell:
    a. soft drinks?
    b. cosmetics?
    c. automobiles?
    d. diet products?
    e. fast-food restaurants?
    f. breakfast cereals?

PRACTICALLY SPEAKING

18.1 CONSTRUCTING MOTIVATIONAL APPEALS

Select one of the specific "Purposes" and "Audiences" that follow and develop a motivational appeal based on one or more of the motivational appeals discussed in this unit. After constructing these appeals, share the results of your labors with others, either in small groups or in the class as a whole. In your discussion you may wish to consider some or all of the following questions.

1. Why did you select the specific motivational appeal(s) you did?
2. Why did you assume that this (these) appeal(s) would prove effective with the topic and the audience selected?

3. How effective do you think such an appeal would be if actually presented to such an audience?

4. Might some of the appeals backfire and stimulate resentment in the audience? Why might such resentment develop? What precautions might be taken by the speaker to prevent such resentment from developing?

5. What are the ethical implications of using these motivational appeals?

6. Where in the speech do you think you would place this (these) appeal(s)? In the beginning? Middle? End? Why?

Purposes

1. Marijuana should (not) be made legal for all those over 18 years of age.

2. Cigarette smoking should (not) be banned in all public places.

3. Capital punishment should (not) be law in all states.

4. Social Security benefits should be increased (decreased) by at least one-third.

5. Retirement should (not) be mandatory at age 65 for all government employees.

6. Police personnel should (not) be permitted to strike.

7. National health insurance should (not) be instituted.

8. Athletic scholarships should (not) be abolished.

9. Domestic partnerships should (not) be accorded the same rights and privileges as marriages

10. Required courses in college should (not) be abolished.

11. Teachers should (not) be paid according to performance rather than (but according to) seniority, degrees earned, or publications.

12. Divorce should (not) be granted immediately when the parties request it.

Audiences

1. Senior citizens of Metropolis

2. Senior Club of DeWitt Clinton High School

3. Small Business Operators Club of Accord

4. American Society of Young Dentists

5. Council for Better Housing

6. Veterans of Vietnam

7. Los Angeles Society of Interior Designers

8. Catholic Women's Council

9. National Council of Black Artists

10. Parent–Teachers Association of New Orleans Elementary Schools

11. Midwestern Council of Physical Education Instructors
12. Society for the Rehabilitation of Ex-Offenders

18.2 PERSUADING WITH COMPLIANCE-GAINING STRATEGIES

Here are a few strategies for getting others to do as you wish (Marwell and Schmitt, 1967; Miller and Parks, 1982). Review the strategies and identify at least two ways in which you might use these in your next persuasive speech.

Promise. Pat promises to reward Chris if Chris complies with Pat's request.
Pat: *I'll give you anything you want if you will just give me a divorce. You can have the house, the car, the stocks, the three kids; just give me my freedom.*

Threat. Pat threatens to punish Chris for noncompliance.
Pat: *If you don't give me a divorce, you'll never see the kids again.*

Expertise. Pat promises that Chris will be rewarded for compliance (or punished for noncompliance) because of "the nature of things."
Pat: *It will be a lot easier for everyone involved if you don't contest the divorce.*

Self-feelings. Pat promises that Chris will feel better if Chris complies with Pat's request and worse if Chris does not.
Pat: *You'll see. You'll feel a lot better if you donate blood during the blood drive.*

Altercasting. Pat casts Chris in the role of the "good" person (or "bad" person) and argues that Chris should comply because a person with "good" qualities would comply while a person with "bad" qualities would not.
Pat: *Any intelligent person would vote for additional funding for the homeless. Or Only a cruel and selfish tightwad would deny the homeless additional funding.*

Esteem. Pat tells Chris that people will think more highly of Chris (relying on the need for the approval of others) if Chris complies with Pat's request, or people will think less if Chris does not comply.
Pat: *Everyone will respond your decision to volunteer at the homeless shelter. Or Everyone will think you're lazy and selfish if you don't volunteer your free time.*

How would you use any one of these strategies to persuade others and accomplish each of the following five goals?

1. to persuade a friend to cut classes and go to the movies
2. to persuade a group to vote in favor of building a senior citizen center
3. to persuade an audience to reaffirm their faith in the government
4. to persuade an audience to manage their time more efficiently
5. to persuade an audience to change their telephone company to Expand-a-Phone

Credibility
and Ethics

■ ■ ■ ■

UNIT OBJECTIVES

After completing this unit, you should be able to:

1. Define *speaker credibility*

2. Explain the ways in which credibility impressions may be formed

3. Explain the three components of credibility

4. Identify at least ten suggestions for increasing your credibility

5. Describe the ethical speaker and the ethical listener

---

*H*ow believable are you as a speaker? How believable are you apart from any evidence or argument you might advance? What is there about you as a person that makes us believe or not believe you? These are questions of *credibility*, the focus of the first part of this unit.

A related question also concerned with the character of the speaker is, What is an ethical speaker? How does an ethical speaker differ from an unethical one? These are questions of *ethics*, questions concerning the morality or immorality, the honesty or dishonesty of a person. Because public speaking influences other people's thoughts and behaviors, questions of ethics are crucial. Ethics is covered in the second half of this unit.

■■■■ SPEAKER CREDIBILITY

You have probably made judgments about speakers apart from any arguments, evidence, or motivational appeals they offered. Often you believe or disbelieve a speaker because of who the speaker is, not because of anything the speaker said. You may, for example, believe certain information or take certain action solely by virtue of Lee Iacocca's or Shirley MacLaine's reputation, personality, or character. Alexander Pope put it more poetically in his "Essay on Criticism":

> *Some judge of author's names, not works, and then*
> *Nor praise nor blame the writings, but the men.*

We call this quality of believability *speaker credibility*. Credibility is not something the speaker has or does not have in any objective sense. In reality the speaker may be a stupid, immoral person. If the audience perceives the speaker as intelligent and moral, then that speaker has high credibility. Further, research tells us, the audience will believe this speaker.

Much contemporary research focuses on what makes a person believable. Advertisers are interested because it relates directly to the effectiveness or ineffectiveness of their ad campaigns. Is Michael Jackson an effective spokesperson for Pepsi-Cola? Is Bill Cosby an effective spokesperson for Jell-O?

Credibility is important to the politician because it determines in great part how people vote. It influences education—the students' perception of teacher credibility will determine the degree of influence the teacher has on a class. There seems no communication situation that credibility does not influence.

We form a *credibility impression* of a speaker on the basis of two sources of information (Figure 19.1). First, we assess the reputation of the speaker as we know it; this is *initial* or what theorists call *extrinsic credibility*. Second, we evaluate how that reputation is confirmed or refuted by what the speaker says and does during the speech. This is *derived* or *intrinsic credibility*. In other words, we combine what we know about the speaker's reputation with the more immediate information we get from present interactions. Information from these two sources—reputation and present encounters—interact and the audience forms some collective final assessment of credibility.

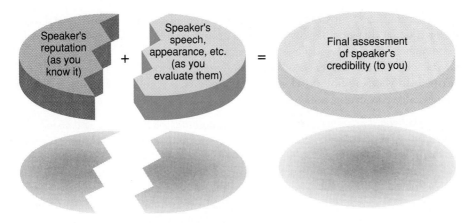

FIGURE 19.1   How we form credibility impressions.

We can identify three major qualities of credibility. *Competence* refers to the knowledge and expertise the audience thinks the speaker possesses. *Character* refers to the intentions and concern of the speaker for the audience. *Charisma* refers to the personality and dynamism of the speaker. We consider each of these three characteristics and the ways in which you may effectively demonstrate them as a speaker.

As a public speaker, part of your task is to make your audience see you as a believable spokesperson. Here are some ways in which you may convey a favorable impression of your competence, your character, and your charisma.

Competence

Competence refers to the knowledge and expertise a speaker is thought to have. The more knowledge and expertise the audience perceives the speaker as having, the more likely the audience will be to believe the speaker. For example, we believe a teacher to the extent that we think he or she is knowledgeable on the subject.

Competence is logically subject-specific. Usually, competence is limited to one specific field. A person may be competent in one subject and totally incompetent in another. Your political science instructor, for example, may be quite competent in politics but quite incompetent in mathematics or economics. Often, however, we do not make the distinction between areas of competence and incompetence; thus, we may perceive a person we think is competent in politics as competent in general. We will, therefore, perceive this person as credible in many fields. We refer to this as the *halo effect*—when listeners generalize their perception of competence to all areas. Listeners see the speaker's competence as a general trait of the individual.

This halo effect also has a counterpart—the *reverse halo*. Here the person, seen as incompetent in, say, mathematics, is perceived to be similarly incompetent in most other areas as well. As a critic of public speaking, be particularly sensitive to competence being subject-specific. Be sensitive to both the halo and reverse halo effects.

Demonstrate your competence to your audience. You want your audience to see you as knowledgeable and expert. Here are some methods you can use.

Tell Listeners of Your Competence Let the audience know of your special experience or training that qualifies you to speak on this specific topic. If you are speaking on communal living and you have lived on a commune yourself, then include this in your speech. Tell the audience of your unique and personal experiences when these contribute to your credibility. Here, for example, G. J. Tankersley (1984) establishes his knowledge concerning educational issues:

> *I've probably had more occasions than many other businessmen to consider these subjects over the years. This is largely because I've spent a good part of my own "extracurricular" time on education.*
>
> *Currently, I'm co-chairman of a drive to raise funds for Auburn University, which is my alma mater. I'm a member of the Business-Higher Education Forum, a group of about 80 business leaders and college presidents who concern themselves with some of the issues I'm going to discuss today. And I've been working at the University of Pittsburgh, where I'm a Vice Chairman of the Board of Trustees and Chairman of the Board of Visitors at the Business School.*
>
> *Also, I used to teach. Just after World War II and before I started my career in the gas business, I taught thermodynamics for four years at Auburn's Engineering School.*

Cite a Variety of Research Sources Make it clear to your audience that you have thoroughly researched your topic. Do this by mentioning some of the books you have read, the persons you have interviewed, the articles you have consulted. Weave these throughout your speech. Don't bunch them together at one time.

Look again at Jay Lane's speech on dust (Unit 2). Note that he cites several books, articles, and interviews. Because of these citations—neatly woven into the speech—we get the impression that Lane is knowledgeable about the topic and has thoroughly researched it.

Stress the Competencies of Your Sources If your audience is not aware of them, then emphasize the particular competencies of your sources. For example, saying simply, "Senator Smith thinks . . . " does nothing to establish the senator's credibility. Instead, consider saying something like:

> *Senator Smith, who headed the finance committee for three years and was formerly Professor of Economics at MIT, thinks. . . .*
>
> *Senator Smith, who has fought in the last two wars and who knows what war is firsthand, has argued that. . . .*

In this way it becomes clear to the audience that you have chosen your sources carefully and with a view toward providing the most authoritative sources possible.

Demonstrate Confidence If you followed the nine steps for preparing a public speech, you probably have considerable confidence in your speech. Communicate that confidence to the audience. Let them know that you are comfortable and at ease speaking to them. If, for example, you are using visual aids, become so familiar with them that you know exactly what order they are in and exactly at what point you will use each.

Avoid Apologizing Do not needlessly call attention to your inadequacies as a spokesperson or to any gaps in your knowledge. No one can know everything. Your audience does not expect you to be the exception. It is not necessary, however, to remind them of any possible shortcoming. Stress your competencies, not your inadequacies. Avoid such statements as:

I know I'm no expert in toxic waste but. . . .

I really should have looked into this more carefully but time was short. But, I did read. . . .

I didn't read the opposing arguments because I don't believe they can possibly be right.

Here is an excerpt from former Vice-President Dan Quayle's (1988) speech of acceptance of the Republican Nomination for Vice-President of the United States. How effectively does Quayle establish his competence?

Many this week have asked, who is Dan Quayle? The people of Indiana know me and now the nation will.

 Since 1980, I have been a United States Senator from Indiana—and proud of it.

 Before that, I was a member of the United States House of Representatives—and proud of it.

 And, as a young man, I served six years in the National Guard. And, like the millions of Americans who have served in the Guard and who serve today—I am proud of it. In Indiana they call us "Hoosiers" and if you saw the movie Hoosiers *you have a feeling for what life is like in the small towns of our state.*

 My hometown of Huntington is a little bigger than the town in the movie, and the high school I graduated from was a little bigger than the one that fielded the basketball team in the film. Still, I identify with that movie, Hoosiers, *because it reflects the values I grew up with in our small town. We believe very strongly in hard work, in getting an education, and in offering an opportunity to our families. We love basketball, we love underdogs, but most important, we love our country.*

Character

We perceive a speaker as credible if we perceive that speaker as having high moral *character*. Here our concern is with the individual's honesty and basic nature—we want to know if we can trust that person. We believe a speaker we can trust. An individual's motives or intentions are particularly important in judging character.

 When the audience perceives your intentions as good for them (rather than for your personal gain), they will think you credible and they will believe you.

 As a speaker, demonstrate those qualities of character that will increase your credibility. Here are some suggestions for demonstrating character.

Stress Fairness If delivering a persuasive speech, stress that you have examined both sides of the issue (if, indeed, you have). If you are presenting both sides, then make it clear that your presentation is an accurate and fair one. Be particularly careful not to omit any argument the audience may already have thought of—this is a sure sign that your presentation is not a fair and balanced one. Tell the audience that you would not advocate a position if you did not base it on a fair evaluation of the issues.

Stress Concern for Enduring Values We view speakers who are concerned with small and insignificant issues as less credible than speakers who demonstrate a concern for lasting truths and general principles. Thus, make it clear to the audience that your position—your thesis—is related to higher-order values; show them exactly how this is true.

Notice how former President George Bush (1988) stresses his concern for such enduring values as family, religion, tradition, and individual power in his speech accepting the Republican nomination:

> At the bright center is the individual. And radiating out from him or her is the family, the essential unit of closeness and of love. For it is the family that communicates to our children—to the 21st century—our culture, our religious faith, our traditions and history.
>
> From the individual to the family to the community, and so out to the town, to the church and school and, still echoing out, to the country, the state, the nation—each doing only what it does well, and no more. And I believe that power must always be kept close to the individual, close to the hands that raise the family and run the home.

Stress Similarities Emphasize the ways in which you are similar to your audience, particularly in beliefs, attitudes, values, and goals. We perceive as believable people who are like ourselves, especially in basic values. The more similar people are to our own attitudes, beliefs, and goals, the more likely we will perceive them as credible.

Consider this excerpt from former President Bush's (1988) acceptance speech. Note how he attempts to achieve similarity with his widely diverse audience:

> But that's not what community means, not to me. For we are a nation of communities, of thousands and tens of thousands of ethnic, religious, social, business, labor union, neighborhood, regional and other organizations, all of them varied, voluntary and unique.
>
> This is America: the Knights of Columbus, the Grange, Hadassah, the Disabled American Veterans, the Order of Ahepa, the Business and Professional Women of America, the union hall, the Bible study group, LULAC, Holy Name—a brilliant diversity spread like stars, like a thousand points of light in a broad and peaceful sky.

Demonstrate Long-term Consistency We feel more comfortable putting our trust in someone who has been consistent over time. We become leery of persons who flit from one issue to another or from one team to another. If you have been in favor of XYZ for the last three years, then tell the audience. For example:

> I began working as a volunteer for the Drug Hotline when I first entered college, four years ago. Now that I'm ready to graduate I want to tell you about the work

the Hotline is doing and why you should get involved in one of the most important projects I have ever worked on.

Stress Concern for Audience Make it clear to the audience that you are interested in their welfare rather than seeking self-gain. If the audience feels that you are "out for yourself," they will justifiably downgrade your credibility. Make it clear that the audience's interests are foremost in your mind.

Here is an excerpt from Richard Nixon's "Checkers Speech." How effectively does Nixon establish his character?

Then, in 1942, I went into the service. Let me say that my service record was not a particularly unusual one. I went to the South Pacific. I guess I'm entitled to a couple of battle stars. I got a couple of letters of commendation.

But I was just there when the bombs were falling. And then I returned to the United States, and in 1946 I ran for Congress.

When we came out of the war, Pat and I—Pat during the war had worked as a stenographer, and in a bank, and as an economist for a government agency, and when we came out, the total of our savings, from both my law practice, her teaching, and all the time I was in the war, the total for that entire period was just a little less than $10,000—every cent of that, incidentally, was in government bonds— well, that's where we start, when I got into politics.

Charisma

Charisma is a combination of the speaker's personality and dynamism as seen by the audience. We perceive as credible or believable speakers we like rather than speakers we do not like. We perceive as credible speakers who are friendly and pleasant rather than aloof and reserved. Similarly, we favor the dynamic over the hesitant, nonassertive speaker. We perceive as less credible the shy, introverted, soft-spoken individual than the extroverted and forceful individual. The great leaders in history have been dynamic people. Perhaps we feel that the dynamic speaker is open and honest in presenting herself or himself. The shy, introverted individual may be seen as hiding something. As speakers there is much that we can do to increase our charisma and hence our perceived credibility.

Demonstrate a Positive Outlook Show the audience that you have a positive orientation to the public speaking situation and to the entire speaker-audience encounter. We see positive and forward-looking people as more credible than negative and backward-looking people. Stress your pleasure at addressing the audience. Stress hope rather than despair; stress happiness rather than sadness. Note how Donald Ed Engen (1985) demonstrates a positive orientation in the following excerpt:

This annual fly-in is truly one of the greatest events in aviation. It is a true reflection of the energy, excitement, sense of adventure, and triumph of technology in our society. As many of you know, I was an active member of EAA until I became FAA administrator.

I wouldn't miss the opportunity to return to Oshkosh each summer. Paul Poberezny, his wife, Audrey, and his son, Tom, make all of us feel at home here.

"*Your lecture agent just called. Your whole schedule has been revised. It seems you've lost your charisma since the FBI destroyed their dossier on you.*"

Courtesy Scotty.

EAA is truly a strong membership organization, with its many members sustaining aviation through both their activities, and the ideas that they promote with aviation. As FAA administrator, I am grateful that I can count on EAA members who want to keep the fun and adventure in flying.

Act Assertively Show the audience that you are a person who will stand up for your rights. Show them that you will not back off simply because the odds may be against you or because you are outnumbered.

Demonstrate Enthusiasm The lethargic speaker, the speaker who somehow plods through the speech, is the very opposite of the charismatic speaker. Try viewing a film of Martin Luther King, Jr., or Billy Graham speaking—they are totally absorbed with the speech and with the audience. They are excellent examples of the enthusiasm that makes speakers charismatic. Lilyan Wilder, in the accompanying "TIP," provides some useful suggestions for developing this needed enthusiasm.

Be Emphatic Use language that is emphatic rather than colorless and indecisive. Use gestures that are clear and decisive rather than random and hesitant. Demonstrate a firm commitment to the position you are advocating; the audience will be much more likely to agree with a speaker who believes firmly in the thesis of the speech.

Although it is difficult to evaluate charisma without hearing the speaker's voice and seeing the speaker gesture, focus on those aspects that you can identify from just the written word in examining the following excerpt from Martin Luther King Jr.'s "I Have a Dream" speech. (The entire speech appears in the Appendix.) How effectively does King establish his charisma?

> *I say to you today, my friends, so even though we face the difficulties of today and tomorrow, I still have a dream. It is a dream deeply rooted in the American dream.*
>
> *I have a dream that one day this nation will rise up and live out the true meaning of its creed: "We hold these truths to be self-evident; that all men are created equal."*
>
> *I have a dream that one day on the red hills of Georgia the sons of former slaves and the sons of former slaveowners will be able to sit down together at the table of brotherhood; I have a dream—*
>
> *That one day even the state of Mississippi, a state sweltering with the heat of injustice, sweltering with the heat of oppression, will be transformed into an oasis of freedom and justice; I have a dream—*
>
> *That my four little children will one day live in a nation where they will not be judged by the color of their skin but by the content of their character; I have a dream today.*

General Guidelines

In addition to these specific suggestions for projecting competence, character, and charisma, here are four general guidelines. These should further assist you in establishing your credibility.

Develop Credibility Characteristics Develop or strengthen these characteristics of competence, character, and charisma as a person as well as as a speaker. This is easy

---

TIPS FROM PROFESSIONAL SPEAKERS

Sometimes . . . you have to work at uncovering why the material is important to you. Here are two helpful rules:

1. Learn everything you can about your subject. The more you know about it, the more excited and passionate you'll become.

2. As you learn, ask yourself: "How does this relate to me?" "Do I care?" "What does this mean to me?" For example: "The disease of muscular dystrophy, which I am discussing with this group, could it strike my little girl?" Or, "The beautiful car I am presenting to this customer, would it make my own family happy?"

Lilyan Wilder, communication consultant and coach. *Talk Your Way to Success* (New York: Simon & Schuster (Fireside Book), 1986).

The Anita Hill–Clarence Thomas hearings revolved largely around credibility. Whom did you believe? What specific credibility factors can you point to in explaining why you believed one person more than the other?

to say but may be extremely difficult to put into practice; nevertheless, it is important to have these goals. The actual development of these qualities is the best insurance to make you credible in public speaking situations.

Demonstrate Credibility Whether you introduce yourself or whether someone else does it, it is helpful to legitimize yourself to the audience, especially in the introduction—a principle the candidate in the cartoon so clearly violates. If you have a broad knowledge of the topic or firsthand experience, tell the audience as early as possible. For example, a speaker might say something like this:

> *I've just returned to the states after spending two years in the Peace Corps. I worked in Guatemala for 10 months and in Chile for 14 months. I taught the people about farming, irrigation, and crop rotation. In just the short time that I was in these places, we managed to increase the vegetable crops by over 300 percent. I want to apply some of that same information we used in Guatemala and Chile to the problems you are now facing on your own farms.*

If there is a formal introduction to your speech, you may have references integrated into this introduction to help establish your credibility. When teachers introduce themselves to their classes, they often establish their credibility. They might, for example, refer to their degrees, where they studied, or some research project on which they are working. At first glance this may seem immodest, but as long as the references are true, such credibility-establishing references allow the audience to appreciate better the information the teacher will communicate.

"My heartfelt thanks to Kitty Lundell for writing my speeches, and to Keith Donegan for delivering them."

Drawing by Weber; © 1992 The New Yorker Magazine, Inc. Reprinted by permission.

Use Varied Methods to Establish Credibility Do not rely on the same few methods to build your credibility. Use a number of different methods. Be sure to consider all three components of credibility: competence, character, and charisma.

An excerpt from Senator Edward Kennedy's "Chappaquiddick" speech follows. How effectively does Kennedy establish his general credibility?

The people of this state, the state which sent John Quincy Adams and Daniel Webster and Charles Sumner and Henry Cabot Lodge and John Kennedy to the United State Senate, are entitled to representation in that body by men who inspire their utmost confidence.

For this reason, I would understand full well why some might think it right for me to resign. For me this will be a difficult decision to make.

It has been seven years since my first election to the Senate. You and I share many memories—some of them have been glorious, some have been very sad. The opportunity to work with you and serve Massachusetts has made my life worthwhile.

And so I ask you tonight, People of Massachusetts, to think this through with me. In facing this decision, I seek your advice and opinion. In making it, I seek your prayers. For this is a decision that I will have finally to make on my own.

Figure 19.2 presents a sample rating scale for evaluating a speaker's credibility—it's a visual summary of some of the more essential qualities of credibility.

REMEMBER: the components of credibility:

1. *competence:* the knowledge and expertise the speaker is thought to possess
2. *character:* the honesty and integrity the speaker is perceived to possess
3. *charisma:* the speaker's personality and dynamism as perceived by the audience

SPEAKER ETHICS

Ethics concern the rightness or wrongness of both the public speaker's *and* the listener's behaviors. What standards should the speaker and the listener follow? What principles should speakers and listeners follow if their public speaking behaviors are to be ethical?

FIGURE 19.2   **Rating Scale for Evaluating a Speaker's Credibility**

Speaker

Knowledgeable	7	6	5	4	3	2	1	Unknowledgeable
Experienced	7	6	5	4	3	2	1	Inexperienced
Confident	7	6	5	4	3	2	1	Not confident
Informed	7	6	5	4	3	2	1	Uninformed
Fair	7	6	5	4	3	2	1	Unfair
Concerned	7	6	5	4	3	2	1	Unconcerned
Consistent	7	6	5	4	3	2	1	Inconsistent
Similar	7	6	5	4	3	2	1	Dissimilar
Positive	7	6	5	4	3	2	1	Negative
Assertive	7	6	5	4	3	2	1	Unassertive
Enthusiastic	7	6	5	4	3	2	1	Unenthusiastic
Active	7	6	5	4	3	2	1	Passive

The first four qualities refer to *competence;* the second four to *character;* the last four to *charisma.*

The standards applied here grow out of the belief that each person has a right to make his or her own choices. Each person has a right to the information and the knowledge necessary to make informed choices. Of course, we assume that the individual is intellectually and emotionally capable of making reasoned and reasonable choices. We further assume that these choices will not restrict or prevent other persons from making their choices. Thus, we cannot always grant freedom of choice to young persons, mentally ill persons, and those who would prevent others from exercising their right of choice. Mothers and fathers, doctors and psychiatrists, and judges and law enforcement officers may have to prevent the exercise of some individual choices.

The aim of this unit is not to prime you to accept the ethical position set forth here; rather, it is to provide you with one point of view. This should serve as a starting point for you to examine your own system of ethics. You will eventually formulate a system of ethical public speaking that you find workable and consistent with your own beliefs and values.

Five guidelines prove useful in evaluating the ethics of the public speaker. These guidelines are, at the same time, the *ethical responsibilities* of a public speaker. As you review these guidelines, think about your own ethical standards and behaviors—these should provide an initial framework for structuring your own system of ethics.

Truth

Present the truth as you understand it. Your audience does not expect universal Truths (with a capital *T*). It does, however, have a right to expect that you speak the truth as you see it. Obviously, you should not lie. You should also avoid misrepresenting the truth because it better fits your purpose, as we might assume happened in the Motley's Crew cartoon. Avoid distorting some bit of information because in undistorted form it would not be as useful.

Further, be truthful about the sources of your materials. If you are going to use a quotation, then cite it exactly as it was written or spoken and credit the source. For example, you might say simply: "Bob Hope put it this way: 'Middle age is when your age

Motley's Crew. Copyright © Tribune Media Services, Inc. Reprinted by permission.

starts to show around your middle.'" If you are using the ideas of another person but are not quoting directly, you still have to acknowledge your source. For example, you might say, "Rupert Murdoch once claimed that newspapers reflect our tastes, they don't change them. And that is what I want to talk about—the role of newspapers in reflecting our culture." In this way it is clear to your audience that the words and/or the ideas are legitimately taken from others.

Follow the same rules for crediting sources as you would in writing a paper for history or anthropology. And just as you would be guilty of plagiarism if you didn't cite the sources in your history paper, you would be guilty of plagiarism if you don't credit your sources in your speech. Whenever you use the materials of others, acknowledge this in your speech. Much as readers of an essay have the right to know where your arguments or data came from, so do listeners. Therefore, weave into your speech the sources of your materials. Do this with subtlety and without disturbing the natural flow and rhythm of your speech. Here are a few examples.

A recent article in Time *magazine noted that. . . .*

Professor Fox, in her lecture last week on Western Civilization, argued that. . . .

This week Nielsen reported that the number of homes with color televisions. . . .

It is also unethical—and illegal—to defame another person. We defame (or commit defamation against) another person when we falsely attack the person's reputation, causing damage to that person's reputation. We call such defamation *libel* when it is done in print or in pictures and *slander* when it is spoken. So, be careful of your facts, especially when talking against another person.

Knowledge

If you speak on a specific subject—as a teacher lecturing or as a political candidate debating—prepare yourself thoroughly. Be so informed that the audience will be able to get the information they need to make reasoned and reasonable choices.

Audience Centered

Have the audience's interests foremost in mind. This is not to say that you should not speak out of personal interest; it is to say that speakers should never exploit their audiences. If a speaker asks an audience to listen to a speech and to do certain things, it should be for their ultimate benefit. It would be unethical, for example, to persuade an audience to take up arms in a self-destructive war or to buy homes in a flood zone. It would be unethical to ask an audience to donate money to an embezzling organization.

It is also unethical (and illegal) to create what is legally termed a *clear and present danger* (Verderber, 1991). This ruling, which derives from a Supreme Court decision (Oliver Wendell Holmes presiding in *Schenck* v. *U.S.,* 1919), prohibits speech that is potentially dangerous to the welfare of the people and the country: causing people to riot or to commit illegal acts may actually prove illegal if it can be determined that the speech posed a clear and present danger.

Preparation

The audience has a right to expect that you have done your best at all stages of the public speaking process. As a student, you know how horrible it is to listen to boring lecturers. You probably tune out the lecturer who fails to make the lecture relevant or does not deliver it in a dynamic and interesting manner. Such teaching (speaking) is unethical because inept delivery, organization, and the like leave you uninformed and less able to make reasoned choices about computers, politics, or economics.

Understandable

Closely related to preparedness is understandability (Jensen, 1970). As a speaker you have an obligation to make your speech understandable to your audience. In talking above the level of the audience, for example, you prevent the audience from clearly understanding what you are arguing or explaining. In talking in oversimplified terms, you can fool your audience into thinking they understand what they really do not. Both approaches are unethical because they prevent the audience from learning what it needs to learn to make its choices.

You can see clear examples of this practice every day. The doctor or lawyer who speaks in "medicalese" or "legalese" to prevent you from understanding what she or he means is unethical. The salesperson who makes insurance contracts seem so simple that you think you understand them (until you file a claim) is unethical.

This does not mean that it is unethical for you to phrase ideas in complex language or to simplify abstract concepts. As with the other principles noted here, it is your intention that counts. If you intend to present information necessary for the audience to make their own choices, then you would be ethical. If, on the other hand, you intend to prevent the audience from securing such information, you would be unethical.

ETHICAL LISTENING

Most discussions of ethics focus exclusively on the speaker. Public speaking, however, is a two-way process. Both speaker *and* listener share in the success or failure of the interaction, and both share in the moral implications of the public speaking exchange. Two major principles should govern your behavior as a listener.

An Honest Hearing

First, as a listener, give the speaker an honest hearing. Listen fully and openly. Try to put aside prejudices and preconceptions so you can evaluate the speaker's message fairly. Then, accept or reject the speaker's ideas on the basis of the information offered, and not on the basis of some bias. Of course, you will see any given topic from your own point of view. As a listener, however, try to see the topic, and particularly the specific purpose, from the speaker's point of view as well.

Empathize with the speaker. You don't have to agree with the speaker. Try, however, to understand emotionally as well as intellectually what the speaker means. Only after you have achieved empathic understanding should you evaluate the speaker, the speech, or the purpose.

Honest Responses

Second, as the speaker should be honest with the listener, the listener should be honest with the speaker. This means giving open and honest feedback to the speaker. It means reflecting honestly on the questions that the speaker raises; it means providing an appropriate evaluation and critique. Much as the listener has a right to expect an active speaker, the speaker has the right to expect an active listener. The speaker has a right to expect a listener who will actively deal with, rather than just passively hear, the message.

REMEMBER: **The ethical public speaker is:**

1. **truthful in presenting what is known to be true and in crediting others**
2. **informed as thoroughly as possible**
3. **concerned with the audience's ultimate welfare**
4. **prepared in content and form**
5. **understandable to the audience**

and the ethical listener:

6. **gives the speaker a fair hearing**
7. **gives the speaker honest feedback**

CRITICALLY SPEAKING

1. What aspects of your competence would you stress if you were giving a speech on how to succeed in college to a group of high school seniors? A speech on managing your time more effectively? A speech on how to make friends?
2. What aspects of your character would you stress to an audience of senior citizens in a speech on the need for increased health care for pregnant teenagers?
3. How would you stress your charisma to an audience of sports fans in a speech on supporting the Olympics?
4. What other ethical guidelines would you suggest be added to those given here?
5. What additional ethical responsibilities does the listener have?
6. In what ways are the ethical responsibilities of the public speaker different from those of the interpersonal communicator? The newscaster or journalist?
7. Should elected officials (or teachers, doctors, or therapists) be held to a higher standard of ethics than, say, the post office worker or the owner of a small hardware store? Why?

PRACTICALLY SPEAKING

19.1 EVALUATING THE CREDIBILITY OF THE FAMOUS

Listed here are 28 famous personalities. For each person, identify the subject matter area(s) in which he or she would be perceived as credible and give at least one reason why you think so. Use your public speaking class as the target audience.

Ted Koppel	Edward Kennedy	Cher	Al Gore
Michael Jackson	Francis Ford Coppola	Bill Clinton	Abigail Van Buren
Elizabeth Taylor	Coretta King	Alice Walker	Ross Perot
Boris Yeltsin	Calvin Klein	Henry Kissinger	Hillary Clinton
Woody Allen	Leo Buscaglia	Michael Jordan	Oprah Winfrey
Billy Graham	Spike Lee	Helen Gurley Brown	Bill Cosby
Phil Donahue	David Brinkley	Perry Ellis	Pete Rose

After completing this exercise, discuss your responses with others, either in small groups or in the class as a whole. From an analysis of these responses, the following should be clear and may also serve as springboards for further discussion:

1. Each individuals will be perceived in a somewhat different way by each other individual.
2. Each person—regardless of "expertise" or "sophistication"—will be perceived as credible on some topics by some audiences.
3. Credibility exists in the perception of the audience rather than in the person-speaker.

19.2 COMPOSING A 60-SECOND CREDIBILITY BUILDER

Write a brief introduction (approximately 1 minute in length or about 130–150 words) about yourself for someone else to use in introducing you and your next speech. In this introduction mention at least three specific details that would help establish your credibility—competence, moral character, charisma, or, ideally, all three.

19.3 COMPARATIVE CREDIBILITY JUDGMENTS

Credibility judgments are made both absolutely and comparatively. Thus, for example, you may judge the credibility of a witness at a trial or a newspaper reviewer or a local religious leader on the basis of some absolute standards you may have. But, even in making this absolute judgment, you are probably also comparing this person with similar others and are probably positioning this person somewhere on a scale along with these others. Similarly, you may make a comparison credibility judgment of the three candidates running for Mayor and vote for the one to whom you attribute the highest credibility. So, your judgment for Senator Smith is made not just absolutely but also in comparison with the others in the race.

This exercise emphasizes this concept of comparative credibility judgments and asks you to rank order the following people, roles, and institutions; use 3 for the highest credibility and 1 for the lowest.

After completing these ratings, consider, for example:

■ What reasons did you use in constructing your rankings? That is, what qualities of credibility did you consider in your ranking? Why did you single out these particular qualities?

■ Do any of your rankings illustrate the notion that credibility depends on the subject matter?

■ Are there certain qualities that make you believe someone regardless of the subject matter?

■ Which of the three major characteristics of credibility (competence, character, charisma) would you consider the most and the least important for: (a) a family physician, (b) a college professor, (c) a divorce lawyer, (d) a romantic-life partner, (e) a best friend?

■ Are any of your credibility judgments gender-related? That is, do you attribute higher credibility to women on some issues and to men on others?

■ Are any of your credibility judgments culture-related? That is, might you attribute high or low credibility ratings to people or products or institutions because of their culture?

1. talk show hosts on the causes of divorce
   _____ Oprah Winfrey
   _____ Joan Rivers
   _____ Sally Jesse Raphael

2. talk show hosts on the male reluctance to express himself
   _____ Jerry Springer
   _____ Phil Donahue
   _____ Geraldo Rivera

3. actors on the art of acting
   _____ Robert DeNiro
   _____ Meryl Streep
   _____ Elizabeth Taylor

4. Newspapers on international business
   _____ *The New York Times*
   _____ *The Wall Street Journal*
   _____ *The Washington Post*

5. Middle-East leaders on the Middle East in 2000
   _____ Chairman Yasir Arafat (P.L.O.)
   _____ Prime Minister Yitzhak Rabin (Israel)
   _____ King Hussein (Jordan)

6. United States politicians on the role of the politician in today's world
   _____ Bill Clinton
   _____ Ross Perot
   _____ Al Gore

7. Speaker on leading a happy life
   _____ professor
   _____ physician
   _____ lawyer

8. Institutions on community service
   _____ bank
   _____ Insurance company
   _____ hospital corporation

9. Writers on the craft of mystery writing

_____ P.D. James
_____ Stephen King
_____ Michael Crichton

10. Speakers on minority rights

_____ military speaker
_____ religious speaker
_____ political speaker

11. Authors of exercise books on the proper way to exercise

_____ Richard Simmons
_____ Jane Fonda
_____ Arnold Schwartzennegger

12. Company representatives on car safety

_____ Representative from Toyota
_____ Representative from Ford
_____ Representative from Mercedes-Benz

13. Sources of accurate and up-to-date information on film and television stars

_____ "Entertainment Tonight"
_____ *The National Enquirer*
_____ *People Magazine*

14. Scholar on the meaning of life

_____ philosopher
_____ minister/priest/rabbi
_____ scientist

15. Speaker on truth in advertising

_____ Speaker representing cable television
_____ Speaker representing network television
_____ Speaker representing the Associated Press

19.4 MAKING ETHICAL JUDGMENTS

This exercise raises some of the significant issues concerning the ethics of public speaking and should stimulate you to consider the way in which you think you should act in each of the following situations.

Read over the following situations and respond to each of the questions posed.

1. You are pressed to deliver a speech in your public speaking class. You find a *Reader's Digest* article that, it seems, could be used without anyone being aware that it was not your work. Should you use this article for your speech? Should you use it if there were no chance of anyone finding out? Explain.

2. You have been put in charge of an advertising campaign to sell a new deodorant hand soap. You are considering printing ads with sexual terms and symbols embedded in the soap bubbles below the level of conscious awareness. This technique, you understand, is used quite often by some of the leading advertisers. It sells liquor, cars, and perfume and should be effective in selling soap as well. Would this be ethical? Explain.

3. You are running for student body president and need to deliver speeches to the various clubs on campus. But you do not have the time or the abilities needed to construct these speeches. A few friends offer to write your speeches for a slight fee which you could easily afford. Would this be ethical? Explain.

U N I T 20

The Special Occasion Speech

■ ■ ■ ■

UNIT OBJECTIVES

After completing this unit, you should be able to:

1. Explain the speech of introduction, the principles to follow and the pitfalls to avoid

2. Explain the speech of presentation or acceptance, the principles to follow and the pitfalls to avoid

3. Explain the speech to secure goodwill, the principles to follow and the pitfalls to avoid

4. Explain the speech of tribute, the principles to follow and the pitfalls to avoid

When you give a "special occasion" or "ceremonial" speech, you are giving a speech that is part information and part persuasion. These special occasion speeches are reviewed separately because their purposes are a bit more limited in scope. We discuss four special occasion speeches: (1) the speech of introduction, (2) the speech of presentation or acceptance, (3) the speech designed to create goodwill, and (4) the speech of tribute.

THE SPEECH OF INTRODUCTION

The speech of introduction is usually designed to introduce another speaker or to introduce a general topic area and a series of speakers. Often, for example, before a speaker addresses an audience, another speaker sets the stage by introducing both the speaker and the topic. At conventions, where a series of speakers address an audience, a speech of introduction might introduce the general topic on which the speakers will focus and perhaps provide connecting links among the several presentations.

In giving a speech of introduction your main purpose is to gain the attention and arouse the interest of the audience. Your speech should pave the way for favorable and attentive listening. It should seek to create an atmosphere conducive to achieving the particular speech purpose. The speech of introduction is basically informative and follows the general patterns already laid down for the informative speech. The main difference is that instead of discussing a topic's issues, you would discuss who the speaker is and what the speaker will talk about.

Principles to Follow

In your speeches of introduction, follow these four general principles.

Establish the Significance of the Speech Your major concern in introducing another speaker is to establish the importance of the speech for this specific audience. In this way you focus the audience's attention and interest on the main speaker.

Establish Relevant Connection Establish a connection or relationship among the essential elements in the public speaking act. At a minimum draw connections among the speaker, the topic, and the audience. Answer the implicit questions of the audience: Why should we listen to this speaker on this topic? Why is this speaker appropriate to speak on this topic? What do we (the audience) have to do with this speaker and this speech topic?

If you can answer such questions satisfactorily, you will have done your job of establishing a ready and receptive audience for the speaker.

Stress the Speaker's Credibility Establish the speaker's credibility. The speech of introduction is the ideal opportunity to present those accomplishments of the speaker that the speaker could not mention with modesty. Review the ways of establishing credibility (Unit 19) for some useful suggestions. The most general guideline is to try to answer the audience's question: What is there about this speaker that has earned her or him the right to speak on this topic, to this audience? In answering this question, you will inevitably establish the speaker's credibility.

Be Consistent with the Main Speech Make your speech of introduction consistent in style and manner with the major speech. To introduce a speaker on terminal diseases in a humorous and flippant style would clearly be inappropriate. Conversely, to introduce a humorist in a somber and formal style would be equally inappropriate.

In judging style and manner, predict the tone that the main speech will take. As you answer an invitation with the same degree of formality with which it is extended, you would introduce a speaker with the same degree of formality that will prevail during the actual speech. Otherwise, the speaker will have to counteract an inappropriate atmosphere created by the speech of introduction.

Pitfalls to Avoid

Here are a few of the more common faults that speakers encounter when they introduce another speaker.

Don't Cover the Speaker's Topic Don't cover the substance of the topic or what the speaker will discuss. Clever stories, jokes, startling statistics, or historical analogies, which are often effective in speeches of introduction, will prove a liability if the guest speaker intended to use this same material. It is not uncommon to find a speaker without an introduction or a conclusion because the material was used in the speech of introduction. If you have any doubts, check with the speaker well in advance of the actual speech. In this way you will avoid duplication and embarrassing the speaker and yourself.

Don't Oversell the Speaker Speakers giving introductions have a tendency to oversell the guest speaker, the topic, or both. The speech of introduction should be complimentary but should not create an image impossible to live up to. To say, for example, that "Morso Osrom is not only the world's greatest living expert on baldness but a most fascinating, interesting, and humorous speaker as well" only adds difficulties to the speaker's task. It would be better to let the speaker demonstrate his or her own communicative abilities.

The same is true for the topic. To say that "this is the most important topic today" or "without the information given here we are sure to die paupers" will only encumber the speaker by setting unrealistic expectations for the audience.

Don't Take Too Long Be brief. Remember that the audience has come to hear the main speaker so be brief. In actual practice, speeches of introduction vary considerably in length—from "Ladies and Gentlemen, the President" to pages and pages. You will have to judge how long is long enough. If the main speech is to be brief—say, 10 or 20 minutes—your speech of introduction should be no longer than 1 or 2 minutes. If, on the other hand, the main speech is to be an hour long, then your introduction might last 5 or 10 minutes or even longer. In estimating length, visualize yourself as a member of the audience listening to your own speech of introduction. How much would you want to hear?

A Sample Speech of Introduction

Here, for example, is the introductory speech, transcribed from television, given by Hal Bruno at the Vice-Presidential Debates, October 13, 1992.

> *Good evening from Atlanta and welcome to the Vice-Presidential Debates sponsored by the Nonpartisan Commission on Presidential Debates. It's being held here in the Theatre for the Arts on the campus of Georgia Tech. I'm Hal Bruno from ABC News and I'm going to be moderating tonight's debate.*
>
> *The participants are Republican Vice-President Dan Quayle, Democratic Senator Al Gore, and Retired Vice-Admiral James Stockdale who is the Vice-Presidential nominee for independent candidate Ross Perot.*
>
> *Now, the ground rules for tonight's debate. Each candiidate will have two minutes for an opening statement. I will then present the issues to be discussed. For each topic the candidates will have a minute and fifteen seconds to respond. Then this will be followed by a five-minute discussion period in which they can ask questions of each other if they so choose.*
>
> *Now the order of response has been determined by a drawing and we'll rotate with each topic. At the end of the debate each candidate will have two minutes for a closing statement. Our radio and TV audience should know that the candidates were given an equal allocation of auditorium seats for their supporters, so I'd like to ask the audience here in the theater to please refrain from applause or any partisan demonstration once the debate is under way because it takes time away from the candidates.*
>
> *So, with that plea from your moderator, let's get started and we'll turn first to Senator Gore for his opening statement.*

REMEMBER: **The speech of introduction should:**

1. establish a connection or relationship among speaker, topic, and audience
2. establish the speaker's credibility
3. be consistent in style and manner with the major speech

and should avoid:

4. covering what the speaker intends to discuss
5. overselling the speaker
6. taking too much time

▮■■▮ THE SPEECH OF PRESENTATION OR ACCEPTANCE

We consider speeches of presentation and speeches of acceptance together because they frequently occur together and because the same general principles govern both types of speeches.

In a speech of presentation you would seek to (1) place the award or honor in some kind of context, and (2) give the award an extra air of dignity or status. A speech of presentation may focus on rewarding a colleague for an important accomplishment (Teacher of the Year) or recognizing a particularly impressive performance (Academy Award winner). It may honor an employee's service to a company or a student's outstanding grades or athletic abilities.

The speech of acceptance is the counterpart to this honoring ceremony. Here the recipient accepts the award and also attempts to place the award in some kind of context. At times the presentation and the acceptance speeches are rather informal and amount to a simple "You really deserve this" and an equally simple and direct "Thank you." At other times, as, for example, in the presentation and acceptance of a Nobel Prize, the speeches are formal and are prepared in great detail and with great care. Such speeches are frequently reprinted in newspapers throughout the world. Somewhere between these two extremes lies the average speech of presentation and acceptance.

Principles to Follow

In your speeches of presentation, follow these two principles.

State the Reason for the Presentation As the presenter, make clear why this particular award is being given to this particular person. If a scholarship is being awarded for the best athlete of the year, then say so. If a gold watch is being awarded for 30 years of faithful service, say this.

State the Importance of the Award The audience (as well as the group authorizing or sponsoring the award) will no doubt want to hear something of the importance of the award. You can state this in a number of different ways. For example, you might refer to the previous recipients (assuming they are well known to the audience), the status of the award (assuming that it is a prestigious award), or its influence on previous recipients.

A Sample Speech of Presentation

Here, for example, communication Professor Raymie McKerrow presents an award to a colleague.

> *On behalf of Darlyn Wolvin, immediate Past President of ECA, I am pleased to present the Everett Lee Hunt Scholarship Award.*
>
> *This year's award recognizes an essay close to Hunt's own scholarly inquiry—the role of rhetoric in moral education. Professor Takis Poulakos, from the University of Pittsburgh, receives the award for his essay, "Isocrates' Use of Narrative in the Evagoras: Epideictic Rhetoric and Moral Action." The essay clearly demonstrates Isocrates' pivotal role in the emergence of the epideictic genre as both a prose form of praise that carried on the earlier poetic tradition, and as a piece of moral instruction to political leaders. The Isocratean tradition in rhetoric is enjoying something of a renaissance in the form of new studies, and to this trend. Takis Poulakos has contributed an excellent essay, uncommonly clear in its argument, and convincing as a piece of rhetoric in its own right.*

> *Therefore, I ask Professor Poulakos to come forward to receive the ECA 1988 Everett Lee Hunt Award for Scholarship.*

This speech is reprinted from *ECA News* 16 (Fall 1988), p. 8. It is reprinted by permission of Raymie McKerrow.

In preparing and presenting your speech of acceptance, follow these three principles.

Express Thanks Thank the people responsible for sponsoring and awarding you the award—the academy members, the board of directors, the student body, your fellow teammates.

Acknowledge Others Who Helped Much as an author will thank those persons who helped her or him in the writing of a particular book (see, for example, the acknowledgments in the preface of this book), the award recipient should thank those instrumental in achieving the award. In thanking such people, be specific without boring the audience. It is not necessary to detail exactly what each person contributed, but it is interesting to the audience to learn, for example, that Pat Tarrington gave you your first role in a soap opera or that Chris Willis convinced you to play the role in the film that led to your first Academy Award.

Convey Your Feelings Put the award into personal perspective. Tell the audience what the award means to you right now and perhaps what it will mean to you in the future. Allow the audience a personal closeness to you that they might not experience otherwise.

A Sample Speech of Acceptance I

Here is an exceptionally moving and provocative acceptance speech that clearly illustrates how closely tied together are the speaker, audience, and occasion. The speech was given by Elizabeth Taylor in acceptance of the Jean Hersholt Humanitarian Award, given for her great humanitarian work on behalf of people with AIDS. It was presented by Angela Lansbury for the Academy of Motion Picture Arts and Science on March 29, 1993. The speech was transcribed from television.

> *I have been on this stage many times as a presenter. I have sat in the audience as a loser. And I've had the thrill and the honor of standing here as a winner. But, I never, ever thought I would come out here to receive this award.*
>
> *It is the highest possible accolade I could receive from my peers. And for doing something I just have to do, that my passion must do.*
>
> *I am filled with pride and humility. I accept this award in honor of all the men, women, and children with AIDS who are waging incredibly valiant battles for their lives—those to whom I have given my commitment, the real heroes of the pandemic of AIDS.*
>
> *I am so proud of the work that people in Hollywood have done to help so many others, like dearest, gentle Audrey.* And while she is, I know, in heaven, for-*

---

*Audrey Hepburn, who had been presented with a posthumous award for her humanitarian work, especially for UNICEF.

ever guarding her beloved children, I will remain here as rowdy an activist as I have to be and, God willing, for as long as I have to be. [Applause]

Tonight I am asking for your help. I call upon you to draw from the depths of your being, to prove that we are a human race, to prove that our love outweighs our need to hate, that our compassion is more compelling than our need to blame, that our sensitivity to those in need is stronger than our greed, that our ability to reason overcomes our fear, and that at the end of each of our lives we can look back and be proud that we have treated others with the kindness, dignity, and respect that every human being deserves.

Thank you and God bless.

Pitfalls to Avoid

Speeches of presentation and acceptance have similar pitfalls.

Don't Misjudge the Importance of the Award Neither underestimate nor overestimate the importance or significance of an award. Most speakers—rather like the presenter in the cartoon—err in the direction of exaggeration. When this is done the pre-

Drawing by M. Stevens; © 1992 The New Yorker Magazine, Inc. Reprinted by permission.

senter, the recipient, and the entire situation can appear ludicrous. Be realistic. A good guideline to follow is to ask yourself what this award will mean next year or 5 years from now to these very same people. Will they remember it? Will it have exerted a significant influence on their lives? Will the local or national newspapers report it? Is it a likely item for a television spot? Obviously, the more questions you answer "yes," the less likelihood of your exaggerating. The more "no" answers, the more reserved you need to be.

Don't Be Long-Winded Few people want to hear long speeches of presentation or acceptance. Normally, these awards are given at dinners or at some other festive function, and people are generally anxious to get on with other activities—eating, playing ball, or whatever. If there are many awards to be given on this same occasion, then you have added reason to be especially brief. We see this very commonsense principle violated yearly on the Academy Awards show.

The story told by news correspondent Charles Osgood in the accompanying "TIP" may be taken as a reminder (rather than as specific advice) against delivering a too-long speech of acceptance.

Generally, the length of the speech should be proportional to the importance of the award. Awards of lesser importance should be presented and accepted with short speeches. Awards of greater significance may be presented and accepted with longer speeches. When acknowledging those who helped you, be selective. Do not include everyone you have ever known; select the most significant few and identify these. Everyone knows that there were others who influenced you, so it is unnecessary to state the obvious: "And there are many others too numerous to mention who helped me achieve this wonderful award."

Don't Talk in Platitudes and Clichés Platitudes and clichés abound in speeches of presentation and acceptance. Be especially careful not to include expressions that will lead your audience to think that this is a canned presentation and that the entire ceremony is perfunctory. Obvious examples to avoid are these:

This award-winner is so well known that no introduction is necessary.

I really don't deserve this award.

There is no one more deserving of this award than this year's recipient.

TIPS FROM PROFESSIONAL SPEAKERS

When Marlene Dietrich sent Mikhail Baryshnikov to pick up her award from the Council of Fashion Designers in New York, the great dancer asked her what she wanted him to say. She said, "Take the thing, look at it, thank them, and go." Mikhail said, "That's it?" and she said, "That's it! They don't have time to listen anyway."

Charles Osgood, CBS news correspondent and anchor of the "CBS Sunday Night News." *Osgood on Speaking: How to Think on Your Feet Without Falling on Your Face* (New York: Morrow, 1988), p. 39.

Speeches at graduation are often of the "inspirational" type. What principles would you suggest the inspirational speaker follow? What pitfalls would you suggest this speaker avoid?

A Sample Speech of Acceptance II

Here is another example of a most effective acceptance speech. William Faulkner, one of the leading American writers of the twentieth century, is the speaker. He was awarded the Nobel Prize for Literature in 1949 and the Pulitzer Prize in 1955. Faulkner delivered the following Nobel Prize acceptance speech on December 10, 1950, in Stockholm, Sweden, reportedly in his first dress suit and before television cameras for the first time. The speech is one of the best acceptance speeches ever recorded. It is especially noteworthy for its clarity of style and purpose and for its universal theme.

> *I feel that this award was not made to me as a man, but to my work—a life's work in the agony and sweat of the human spirit, not for glory and least of all for profit, but to create out of the materials of the human spirit something which did not exist before. So this award is only mine in trust. It will not be difficult to find a dedication for the money part of it commensurate with the purpose and significance of its origin. But I would like to do the same with the acclaim too, by using this moment as a pinnacle from which I might be listened to by the young men and women already dedicated to the same anguish and travail, among whom is already that one who will someday stand here where I am standing.*
>
> *Our tragedy today is a general and universal physical fear so long sustained by now that we can even bear it. There are no longer problems of the spirit. There is only the question: when will I be blown up? Because of this, the young man or woman writing today has forgotten the problems of the human heart in conflict with itself which alone can make good writing because only that is worth writing about, worth the agony and the sweat.*

He must learn them again. He must teach himself that the basest of all things is to be afraid; and, teaching himself that, forget it forever, leaving no room in his workshop for anything but the old verities and truth of the heart, the old universal truths lacking which any story is ephemeral and doomed—love and honor and pity and pride and compassion and sacrifice. Until he does so, he labors under a curse. He writes not of love but of lust, of defeats in which nobody loses anything of value, of victories without hope, and, worst of all, without pity or compassion. His griefs grieve on no universal bones, leaving no scars. He writes not of the heart but of the glands.

Until he relearns these things, he will write as though he stood among and watched the end of man. I decline to accept the end of man. It is easy enough to say that man is immortal simply because he will endure; that when the last ding-dong of doom has clanged and fades from the last worthless rock hanging tideless in the last red and dying evening, that even then there will still be one more sound: that of his puny inexhaustible voice, still talking. I refuse to accept this. I believe that man will not merely endure: he will prevail. He is immortal, not because he alone among creatures has an inexhaustible voice, but because he has a soul, a spirit capable of compassion and sacrifice and endurance. The poet's, the writer's, duty is to write about these things. It is his privilege to help man endure by lifting his heart, by reminding him of the courage and honor and hope and pride and compassion and pity and sacrifice which have been the glory of his past. The poet's voice need not merely by the record of man; it can be one of the props, the pillars, to help him endure and prevail.

REMEMBER: Speeches of presentation should:
1. state the reason for the presentation
2. state the importance of the award being presented

and speechs of acceptance should:
3. express thanks to those who gave you the award
4. acknowledge others who helped you
5. indicate the meaning of the award to you

Both speeches of presentation and acceptance should avoid:
6. misjudging the importance of the award
7. giving too long a speech
8. talking in platitudes and clichés

■■■■ THE SPEECH TO SECURE GOODWILL

The speech to secure goodwill is a peculiar hybrid. It is part information and part persuasion, and it is difficult to determine where one ends and the other begins. In fact, the strength of the goodwill speech often depends on the extent to which the information and the persuasion are blurred in the minds of the audience.

On the surface, the speech to secure goodwill functions to inform the audience about a product, company, profession, institution, way of life, or person. (When this "person" is the speaker, we often refer to this as a speech of "self-justification.") Beneath this surface, however, lies a more persuasive purpose: to heighten the image of a person, product, or company—to create a more positive attitude toward this person or thing.

Many speeches of goodwill have a still further persuasive purpose: to get the audience ultimately to change their behavior toward the person or company. Such a speech functions to create goodwill but invariably also functions to alter behavior. The securing of goodwill and the changing of behavior are not, in reality, separable.

A variant of the speech to secure goodwill is the speech of self-justification, where the speaker seeks to justify his or her actions to the audience. Political figures do this frequently. Richard Nixon's "Checkers Speech," his Cambodia-bombing speeches, and, of course, his Watergate speeches are clear examples of self-justification. Edward Kennedy's Chapaquiddick speech, in which he attempted to justify what happened when Mary Jo Kopechne drowned, is another example. (Excerpts from these speeches are provided in Unit 19.)

Whenever there is a significant loss of credibility, the speaker will be called upon to offer a speech of self-justification. As any political leader's image goes down, the frequency of the self-justifying speeches goes up.

Principles to Follow

In securing goodwill, whether for another person or for yourself, the following principles should prove helpful.

Demonstrate the Contributions that Deserve Goodwill Demonstrate how the audience may benefit from this company, product, or person. Or at least (in the speech of self-justification), show how the audience has not been hurt or not been hurt willfully. Often this is accomplished obliquely. When IBM demonstrates that they have accomplished a great deal through research, they also stress implicitly and sometimes more directly that these developments make it easier to function in business or in the home. General Electric's "We bring good things to life" is designed to secure goodwill and to demonstrate that the company benefits the audience—with more free time, less hard labor, and more accessible and inexpensive entertainment.

Stress Uniqueness In a world dominated by competition, the speech to secure goodwill must stress the uniqueness of the specific company, person, profession, and so on. Distinguish it clearly from all others, otherwise, any goodwill you secure will be spread over the entire field. IBM clearly distinguishes itself from its competitors.

Establish Credibility Speeches to secure goodwill must also establish credibility, thereby securing goodwill for the individual or commodity. To do so, concentrate on those dimensions of credibility discussed earlier (see Unit 19). Demonstrate that the subject is competent, of good intention, and of high moral character. Examine how Lee Iacocca does this in his speech on the odometer that follows. Who could not have goodwill toward such an individual, product, or business?

Pitfalls to Avoid

The following are three faults found in many speeches designed to secure goodwill. Try to avoid them.

Don't Be Obvious An ineffective goodwill speech is an obvious advertisement; an effective one is not. The effective goodwill speech looks, on the surface, very much like an objective informative speech. It will not appear to ask for goodwill, except on close analysis.

Don't Plead for Goodwill This admonition is especially appropriate in the speech of self-justification. Criers may achieve some goals, but in the long run they seem to lose out. Few people want to go along with someone who appears weak. If you attempt to justify some action, justify it with logic and reason. Do not beg for goodwill— demonstrate that it is due you. Most audiences are composed of reasonable people who prefer to act out of logic, who recognize that not everyone is perfect, and who are ready to establish or reestablish goodwill toward an individual.

Don't Overdo It Overkill is ineffective. You will turn off your audience rather than secure their goodwill. Remember: your perspective and the perspective of your audience are very different. Your acquaintance with the product may fully convince you of its greatness, but your audience does not have that acquaintance. Consequently, they will not appreciate too many superlatives.

A Sample Speech to Secure Goodwill

A particularly good example of the speech to secure goodwill is the following speech by Lee Iacocca, reprinted by permission. Here Iacocca was presented with a particularly difficult problem. Chrysler was accused of disconnecting its odometers so that the cars would appear to be new, despite the 40 miles of road test. This was not a particularly horrible offense since most car buyers know that their cars are put through various tests, yet it presented Iacocca with a credibility problem. He met this head on with a series of print and television advertisements in which he admitted the error and spelled out what he would do to correct this error of judgment.

> *"Testing cars is a good idea. Disconnecting odometers is a lousy idea. That's a mistake we won't make again at Chrysler. Period."*
> —LEE IACOCCA

Let me set the record straight.

1. *For years, spot checking and road testing new cars and trucks that come off the assembly line with the odometers disengaged was standard industry practice. In our case, the average test mileage was 40 miles.*

2. *Even though the practice wasn't illegal, some companies began connecting their odometers. We didn't. In retrospect, that was dumb. Since October 1986, however, the odometer of every car and truck we've built has been connected, including those in the test program.*

3. *A few cars—and I mean a few—were damaged in testing badly enough that*

they should not have been fixed and sold as new. That was a mistake in an otherwise valid quality assurance program. And now we have to make it right.

What we're doing to make things right.

1. *In all instances where our records show a vehicle was damaged in the test program and repaired and sold,* we will offer to replace that vehicle *with a brand new 1987 Chrysler Corporation model of comparable value. No ifs ands or buts.*
2. *We are sending letters to everyone our records show bought a vehicle that was in the test program and offering a free inspection. If anything is wrong because of a product deficiency, we will make it right.*
3. *Along with free inspection, we are extending their present 5 year or 50,000 mile protection plan on engine and powertrain to 7 years or 70,000 miles.*
4. *And to put their minds completely at ease, we are extending the 7 year or 70,000 mile protection to* all major systems: *brakes, suspension, air conditioning, electrical, and steering.*

 The quality testing program is a good program. But there were mistakes and we were too slow in stopping them. Now they're stopped. Done. Finished. Over.
 Personally, I'm proud of our products. Proud of the quality improvements we've made. So we're going to keep right on testing. Because without it we couldn't have given America 5 year 50,000 mile protection five years ahead of everyone else. Or maintained our warranty leadership with 7 years 70,000 mile protection. I'm proud, too, of our leadership in safety-related recalls.
 But I'm not proud of this episode. Not at all.
 As Harry Truman once said, "The buck stops here." It just stopped. Period.

REMEMBER: **The speech to secure goodwill should:**
1. stress the benefits the audience members may derive from this product, person, or company
2. stress the uniqueness of this product, person, or company
3. establish your credibility and the credibility of the subject

and avoid:
4. being obvious in your attempts to secure goodwill
5. pleading for goodwill
6. overdoing the superlatives

THE SPEECH OF TRIBUTE

The speech of tribute encompasses a wide variety of speeches. All, however, are designed to pay some kind of tribute to a person or event. They include the eulogy, designed to praise the dead; the farewell; the dedication; the commendation, praising some living person; and the commemoration of some particular event or happening.

The general purpose of the speech of tribute is to inform the audience of some accomplishment or of the importance of some event. It should also heighten the audience's awareness of the occasion, accomplishment, or person; strengthen or create positive attitudes; and make the audience more appreciative. On the surface, then, the purpose is informative; below the surface, it is persuasive.

Principles to Follow

In the speech of tribute, these three principles should prove effective.

Involve the Audience   Involve the audience in some way. This is not always easy—some tributes seem only to involve the individual being praised and some abstraction such as history, posterity, or culture. Make any history, posterity, or culture relevant to this specific audience. For example, if you were giving a eulogy, you would relate the meaning and accomplishments of the individual being eulogized to the specific audience. You would, in other words, answer the listeners' question, "What did this person's life mean to me?"

State the Reason for the Tribute   It is frequently helpful to give the audience some idea of why you are making this tribute. Oftentimes it is obvious: the teacher praises the student; the president congratulates the employee; the student eulogizes the teacher, and so on. The connections in these cases are obvious, and when they are, do not belabor them. But when they are not obvious to the audience, then tell the audience why you are the person giving this tribute.

Be Consistent with the Occasion   Construct and present a speech that is consistent with the specific occasion. This does not mean that all eulogies must be somber or that all sports award presentations must be frivolous. It is to say only that the speech should not contradict the basic mood of the occasion.

Pitfalls to Avoid

Avoid the following major problems in your speeches of tribute.

Don't Go Overboard   The speech of tribute records the positive, and the speech should be positive. But don't go overboard and overplay the specific accomplishments of an individual. This is dishonest and usually ineffective. State the person's accomplishments realistically. With some eulogies it is difficult to recognize the real person for all of the unrealistic and undeserved (and dishonest) praise.

Don't Qualify Negatively   Do not qualify negatively; qualify positively. There are ways of qualifying what you want to say without appearing negative, and in speeches of tribute this is especially important. For example, the same information is communicated in each of the following two statements:

- Although our guest is not the world's greatest scientist, she is one of the top ten.
- Our guest is one of the top ten scientists in the world.

Both statements say essentially the same thing, but only the second is really positive. The first is positive with a negative tone. Be particularly careful of terms such as *but, however, although,* and *even though.* These terms may qualify the accomplishments of an individual in a negative rather than a positive manner.

A Sample Speech of Tribute

In the following speech former President Ronald Reagan pays tribute to the astronauts who died in the shuttle *Challenger* explosion in 1986. The occasion was an extremely sad one. Most of the nation watched the tragedy on television just hours before. The speech reflects this sadness and mourning.

Ladies and gentlemen, I planned to speak to you tonight to report on the State of the Union, but the events of earlier today have led me to change those plans. Today is a day for mourning and remembering. Nancy and I are pained to the core by the tragedy of the shuttle Challenger. We know we share this pain with all of the people of our country. This is truly a national loss.

Nineteen years ago, almost to the day, we lost three astronauts in a terrible accident on the ground, but we've never lost an astronaut in flight; we've never had a tragedy like this. And perhaps we've forgotten the courage it took for the crew of the shuttle but they, the Challenger seven, were aware of the dangers and overcame them and did their jobs brilliantly.

We mourn seven heroes: Michael Smith, Dick Scobee, Judith Resnik, Ronald McNair, Ellison Onizuka, Gregory Jarvis and Christa McAuliffe. We mourn their loss as a nation, together.

The families of the seven—we cannot bear, as you do, the full impact of this tragedy but we feel the loss and we're thinking about you so very much. Your loved ones were daring and brave and they had that special grace, that special spirit that says, "Give me a challenge and I'll meet it with joy." They had a hunger to explore the universe and discover its truths. They wished to serve and they did—they served all of us.

We've grown used to wonders in this century; it's hard to dazzle us. For 25 years the United States space program has been doing just that. We've grown used to the idea of space, and perhaps we forget that we've only just begun. We're still pioneers. They, the members of the Challenger crew, were pioneers.

And I want to say something to the schoolchildren of America who were watching the live coverage of the shuttle's takeoff. I know it's hard to understand that sometimes painful things like this happen. It's all part of the process of exploration and discovery; it's all part of taking a chance and expanding man's horizons. The future doesn't belong to the fainthearted. It belongs to the brave. The Challenger crew was pulling us into the future, and we'll continue to follow them.

I've always had great faith in and respect for our space program, and what happened today does nothing to diminish it. We don't hide our space program, we don't keep secrets and cover things up. We do it all up front and in public. That's the way freedom is and we wouldn't change it for a minute. We'll continue our quest in space. There will be more shuttle flights and more shuttle crews and, yes, more volunteers, more civilians, more teachers in space. Nothing ends here. Our hopes and our journeys continue.

I want to add that I wish I could talk to every man and woman who works for NASA, or who worked on this mission, and tell them: "Your dedication and professionalism have moved and impressed us for decades, and we know of your anguish. We share it."

There's a coincidence today. On this day 390 years ago, the great explorer Sir Francis Drake died aboard ship off the coast of Panama. In his lifetime the great frontiers were the oceans, and a historian later said. "He lived by the sea, died on it, and was buried in it." Well, today we can say of the Challenger crew, their dedication was, like Drake's, complete. The crew of the space shuttle Challenger honored us by the manner in which they lived their lives. We will never forget them nor the last time we saw them this morning as they prepared for their journey and waved goodbye and "slipped the surly bonds of earth to touch the face of God."

Thank you.

Source: Reprinted from *The New York Times* (January 29, 1986), p. A9.

REMEMBER: **The speech of tribute should:**

1. **involve the audience in some way**
2. **state the reason for the tribute**
3. **deliver a speech that is consistent with the occasion**

and avoid:

4. **praising the individual disproportionately**
5. **qualifying negatively**

CRITICALLY SPEAKING

1. What principles of the speech of introduction do talk show hosts use when they introduce their guests? What would you like to hear them include more of?

2. What would an ideal speech of introduction sound like if it were introducing you to the class for your next speech?

3. What would you say if you were presenting the Teacher of the Year Award?

4. What would you say if you were given the award for Outstanding United States College Student of the year?

5. How do corporations secure goodwill in their newspaper and magazine advertisements?

6. How would you build a speech designed to secure the goodwill of the community for your college?

7. What main propositions would you seek to include in a speech of tribute to "body builder of the year," "the world's happiest couple," or "the current Nobel Peace Prize winner"?

PRACTICALLY SPEAKING

20.1   DEVELOPING THE SPEECH OF INTRODUCTION

Prepare a speech of introduction approximately two minutes in length. For this experience you may assume that the speaker you introduce will speak on any topic you wish. Do, however, assume a topic appropriate to the speaker and to your audience—your class. You may wish to select your introduction from one of the following suggestions:

1. Introduce a historical figure to the class.
2. Introduce a favorite or famous teacher.
3. Introduce a contemporary religious, political, or social leader.
4. Prepare a speech of introduction that someone might give to introduce you to your class.
5. Introduce your favorite author—alive or dead.
6. Introduce a famous media (film, television, radio, recording) personality—alive or dead.
7. Introduce a famous sports figure.

20.2   DEVELOPING THE SPEECH OF PRESENTATION/ACCEPTANCE

Form pairs of students. One student should serve as the presenter and one as the recipient of a particular award or honor. The two students can select a situation from the list presented below or make one up themselves. The presenter should prepare and present a two-minute speech in which she or he presents one of the awards to the other student. The recipient should prepare and present a two-minute speech of acceptance.

The situations noted below are purposely stated in rather general terms. The two students should specify in greater detail how they will define the nature and purpose of the award.

1. full scholarship to college
2. Academy Award for best performance
3. gold watch for service to the company
4. Athlete of the Year
5. Ms. or Mr. America
6. medal for bravery
7. $5 million for the college library
8. award to the graduating senior with the highest grade-point average
9. award to the Mayor of Goatsville for greatest improvement in educational services

10. book award
11. Mother (Father) of the Year award
12. honorary Ph.D. in communication for outstanding contributions to the art and practice of effective communication
13. "Rocky" award for greatest improvement
14. award for outstanding achievement in architecture
15. best-dressed student at the college
16. congeniality award
17. award for raising a prize hog
18. award for a gold record
19. Man (Woman) of the Year award
20. award for outstanding contributions to the organization

20.3   DEVELOPING THE SPEECH TO SECURE GOODWILL

Prepare a speech approximately three to five minutes in length in which you attempt to secure the goodwill of your audience toward one of the following:

1. your college (visualize your audience as high school seniors)
2. a particular profession or way of life (teaching, religious life, nursing, law, medicine, bricklaying, truck driving, etc.)
3. this course (visualize your audience as college students who have not yet taken this course)
4. the policies of a particular foreign country now in the news
5. a specific multinational corporation

20.4   DEVELOPING THE SPEECH OF TRIBUTE

1. Prepare a speech approximately three to five minutes in length in which you *welcome* one of the following persons to your college:
   a. political official
   b. movie star
   c. scientist
   d. astronaut
   e. visitor from another planet
   f. famous athlete
   g. author
   h. criminal
   i. millionaire
   j. comedian

2. Prepare a *eulogy* approximately three to five minutes in length. Even if you select a person who has been dead for some time, the eulogy should be placed in the present. That is, focus on the contributions of this person to the present time and the present audience.

■ PART FOUR CHECKLISTS

Performance Checklist: Evaluating Your Purpose and Supporting Materials

YES   NO   Have you:

☐   ☐   1. Composed a speech purpose appropriate to the speech situation and sufficiently limited it?

☐   ☐   2. Followed the principles for informative speaking: limit the amount of information, stress relevance, present information at the appropriate level, relate new information to old, present information through several senses, and vary the levels of abstraction?

☐   ☐   3. Amplified your ideas with definitions, examples and illustrations, testimony, and statistics? Have you tested their usefulness to the speech?

☐   ☐   4. Considered the advantages of audiovisual aids? If you are including such an aid, is it clear and relevant? Does it reinforce the message? Is it appealing?

☐   ☐   5. Followed the principles for persuasive speaking: credibility, attractiveness, selective exposure, audience participation, inoculation, and magnitude of change?

☐   ☐   6. Supported your propositions with appropriate arguments and evidence? Tested your reasoning adequacy? Is it recent? Corroborated by additional support? Unbiased?

☐   ☐   7. Used such motivational appeals as: altruism; fear; individuality and conformity; power, control, and influence; self-esteem and approval; love and affiliation; achievement; financial gain; self-actualization; and status?

☐   ☐   8. Established your credibility by demonstrating competence, moral character, and charisma?

☐   ☐   9. Adhered to traditional ethical guidelines? Are you truthful? Informed? Audience centered? Well prepared? Easily understood?

☐   ☐   10. Followed the principles and avoided the pitfalls for special occasion speaking?

Critical Thinking Checklist:
Thinking Critically about the Elements of Public Speeches

YES	NO	Do you:
☐	☐	1. Apply the principles of information processing to construct informative messages (Unit 13)?
☐	☐	2. Describe, define, and demonstrate in a logical and clearly organized manner so that others can easily understand (Unit 13)?
☐	☐	3. Locate, evaluate, and use examples and illustrations, testimony, and statistics to support an assertion (Unit 14)?
☐	☐	4. Construct, evaluate, and use audiovisual aids to support assertions (Unit 15)?
☐	☐	5. Apply the principles of persuasion to constructing persuasive messages (Unit 16)?
☐	☐	6. Evaluate arguments and evidence in terms of recency, corroboration, and bias (Unit 17)?
☐	☐	7. Develop arguments (from specific instances and generalizations, analogy, causes and effects, and sign) to support an assertion (Unit 17)?
☐	☐	8. Evaluate arguments (your own and those of others) in terms of their validity and usefulness in persuasion (Unit 17)?
☐	☐	9. Analyze and use motivational appeals in persuasion (Unit 18)?
☐	☐	10. Develop and present assertions supported by evidence of credibility (competence, character, and charisma) (Unit 19)?
☐	☐	11. Evaluate the credibility appeals of others (Unit 19)?

PART FIVE

Elements of Style and Delivery

Once the basics of speech construction are firmly established, you can devote your attention to improving your style (Units 21 and 22) and delivery (Units 23 and 24). In Part Five you will see how to make language effective in public speaking, for example, how to select words and phrase sentences for greatest effect.

Units 23 and 24 focus on the methods of delivery (impromptu, manuscript, memorized, and extemporaneous), characteristics of effective delivery, and how to use your voice and body to help communicate your meaning. In addition Unit 24 offers practical advice on how to rehearse your speech so that it achieves the effect you want.

In **thinking critically** about style and delivery, try to:

- view style and delivery as a reflection of who you are and how you feel about your topic, audience, and purpose
- find a style and a delivery that you feel comfortable with and that will work for you; polish and fine-tune it
- apply the principles of style—clarity, vividness, appropriateness, personalness, and forcefulness—to other forms of oral and written communication; modify these general qualities on the basis of your topic, audience, and purpose.
- appreciate the great variation in the ways in which different cultures view what constitutes effective style and effective delivery

Characteristics of Style

UNIT OUTLINE

How Language Works
Oral Style
The Humorous Style
Critically Speaking
Practically Speaking

■ ■ ■ ■

UNIT OBJECTIVES

After completing this unit, you should be able to:

1. Define and explain directness, abstraction, objectivity, formality, and accuracy as they apply to style in public speaking

2. Define *denotation* and *connotation*

3. Explain the five thinking errors

4. Explain the major differences between oral and written style, as produced and as received

5. Identify the functions of humor in public speaking

6. Explain the guidelines for using humor in public speaking

Y ou are a successful public speaker when your listeners create in their minds the meanings you want them to create. You are successful when your listeners adopt the attitudes and behaviors you want them to adopt. The language choices you make—for example, the words you select and the sentences you form—will influence greatly the meanings your listeners receive and thus how successful you are.

HOW LANGUAGE WORKS

Directness, abstraction, objectivity, and formality are four aspects of language that relate directly to successful public speaking. Your ability to manipulate these four qualities of language will influence your ability to inform or persuade an audience.

Language Varies in Directness

Consider the following sentences:

1. We should all vote for Halliwell in the next election.
2. Vote for Halliwell in the next election.
3. It should be apparent that we should abandon the present system.
4. Abandon the present system.
5. Many people would like to go to Xanadu.
6. How many of you would like to go to Xanadu?

The odd-numbered sentences are clearly less direct than the even-numbered sentences. Note, for example, that sentences 2, 4, and 6 address the audience directly. Sentences 1, 3, and 5 are more distant, more indirect. Indirect sentences address only an abstract, unidentified mass of individuals. The sentences might as well address just anyone. When you use direct sentences, you address your specific and clearly defined audience.

If you want to achieve directness, use active rather than passive sentences. Say "The professor invented the serum" rather than "The serum was invented by the professor." Use personal pronouns and personal references. Refer to your audience as "you" rather than "the audience" or "my listeners."

Language Varies in Abstraction

Consider the following list of terms:

- entertainment
- film
- American film

"Any new tax legislation must be studied by the committee, the IRS, and the Treasury Department . . . To make sure NOBODY understands it!"

■ recent American film

■ *Jurassic Park*

At the top is the general or abstract *entertainment*. Note that *entertainment* includes all the other items on the list plus various other items—television, novels, drama, comics, and so on. *Film* is more specific and concrete. It includes all of the items below it as well as various other items such as Indian film or Russian film. It excludes, however, all entertainment that is not film. *American film* is again more specific than *film* and excludes all films that are not American. *Recent American film* further limits *American film* to a time period. *Batman Returns* specifies concretely the one item to which reference is made.

Choose words from a wide range of abstractions. At times a general term may suit your needs best; at other times a more specific term may serve better. Generally, the specific term is the better choice.

Notice that a more general term—*entertainment*—conjures up a number of different images. One person in the audience may focus on television, another on music, another on comic books, and still another on radio. To some, "film" may bring to mind the early silent films. To others, it brings to mind postwar Italian films. To still others, it recalls Disney's animated cartoons. As you get more specific—less abstract—you more effectively guide the images that come to your listeners' minds. Specific rather than abstract language will aid you in both your informative and persuasive goals.

Language Varies in Objectivity

The best way to explain how language varies in objectivity is to introduce two new terms: *denotation* and *connotation*.

Denotation The *denotative* meaning of a term is its objective meaning. This is the meaning that you would find in a dictionary. This meaning points to specific references. Thus, the denotation of the word *book* is, for example, the actual book, a collection of pages bound together between two covers. The denotative meaning of *dog* is a four-legged canine; the denotative meaning of *to kiss* is, according to the *Random House Dictionary*, "to touch or press with the lips slightly pursed in token of greeting, affection, reverence, etc."

Connotation *Connotative* meaning, however, is different. The connotative meaning is our affective, our emotional meaning for the term. The word *book* may signify boredom or excitement. It may recall the novel you have to read or perhaps this textbook that you are reading right now. Connotatively, *dog* may mean friendliness, warmth, and affection. *To kiss* may, connotatively, mean warmth, good feeling, and happiness.

Using Denotative-Connotative Meanings All words (other than *function* words such as prepositions, conjunctions, and articles) have both denotative and connotative meaning. The relevance of this to you, as a public speaker, is considerable. Seldom do listeners misunderstand the denotative meaning of a term. When you use a term with which the audience is not familiar, you define it and thus make sure that the term is understood. Similarly, arguments seldom center on denotation. Differences in denotative meaning are pretty easy to handle.

Differences in connotative meanings, however, pose difficulties. You may, for example, use the term *neighbor* and may wish to communicate security and friendliness. To some of your listeners, however, the term may connote unwanted intrusions, sneakiness, and nosiness. Notice that both you and your listeners would surely agree that denotatively *neighbor* means one who lives near another. What you and they disagree on—and what then leads to misunderstanding—is the connotation of the term.

Consider such terms as *politician, jock, lady, police, sex, religion, professor,* and *education.* I'm sure you can easily appreciate the varied connotative meanings that an audience may have for these terms. In public speaking remember that your connotative meaning for a term is not necessarily the same as that of your audience. Select words with your audience's meanings in mind.

As a speaker, consider the audience's evaluation of key terms before using them in your speech. When you are part of the audience, as in a public speaking class, you often already know (generally at least) the meanings members have for various terms. When you address an audience very different from yourself, however, this prior investigation becomes crucial. When there is any doubt, select another word or qualify the word to make clear exactly what you wish to communicate.

Language Varies in Formality

Language varies from formal to informal or colloquial. Linguist Mario Pei (1956), for example, identified five levels of formality. He illustrates these (from the most formal to the most informal) with the "same" sentence.

1. Those individuals do not possess any.
2. Those men haven't any.
3. Those men haven't got any.
4. Those guys haven't/ain't got any.
5. Dem guys ain't got none.

Formal style is the style of written prose and the style of strangers speaking in a formal context. As the above examples illustrate, formal style uses big words (*individuals* rather than *men*) and infrequently used words (*possess* rather than *have* or *got*).

In formal style, the sentences often contain written-language expressions such as "the former," "the latter," and "the aforementioned." When you are reading, you can easily locate what "the former" or what "the latter" refers to by simply looking back at the previous sentence. When listening to a speech, however, you can't go back and relisten to the previous sentence. You would have to pause to discover which item was the former and which the latter. In the process you would probably lose attention and miss much of what the speaker is saying.

No single guideline for selecting an appropriate level of formality-informality can be offered. Generally, however, it is wise to speak at a level a bit more formal than the conversational level of the audience. Therefore, use common words but avoid slang. Use informal constructions (for example, contractions and personal pronouns), but avoid forms that your audience would consider incorrect (for example, "ain't got none").

Language Varies in Accuracy

Language can reflect reality faithfully or unfaithfully. It can describe reality (as science tells us it exists) with great accuracy or distortion. For example, we can use language to describe the many degrees that exist in, say wealth, or we can describe it inaccurately in terms of two values, rich and poor. We can discuss these ways in which language may vary in terms of the **five thinking errors**, central to the area of language study known as "General Semantics" (Korsybski, 1933; DeVito, 1973; Hayakawa and Hayakawa, 1989), and now so much a part of critical thinking instruction (Johnson, 1991).

Polarization *Polarization* refers to the tendency to look at the world in terms of opposites and to describe it in terms of extremes—good or bad, positive or negative, healthy or sick, intelligent or stupid, rich or poor, and so on. It is often referred to as the "fallacy of either-or." So destructive is either-or thinking that the American Psychiatric Association (1980) identifies it as one of the major behaviors characteristic of "borderline personality disorder"—a psychological disorder that lies between neurosis and psychosis and is characterized by unstable interpersonal relationships and confusion with one's own identity.

Most people, events, and objects, of course, exist somewhere between the extremes of good and bad, health and sickness, intelligence and stupidity, wealth and poverty. Yet there is a strong tendency to view only the extremes and to categorize people, objects, and events in terms of these polar opposites.

Problems arise when polar opposites are used in inappropriate situations; for example, "The politician is either for us or against us." Note that these options do not include all possibilities. The politician may be for us in some things and against us in other things, or may be neutral. Beware of speakers implying and believing that two extreme classes include all possible classes—that an individual must be pro-rebel forces or antirebel forces, with no other alternatives.

Fact-Inference Confusion You can make statements about the world you observe, and you can make statements about what you have not observed. In form or structure these statements are similar and cannot be distinguished by any grammatical analysis. For example, you can say, "This proposal contains 17 pages" as well as "This proposal contains the seeds of self-destruction." Both sentences look similar in form, yet they are very different types of statements. You can observe the 17 pages, but how do you observe "the seeds of self-destruction"? Obviously, this is not a descriptive but an *inferential statement,* a statement you make on the basis not only of what you observe, but on what you conclude.

There is nothing wrong with making inferential statements. You must make them to talk about much that is meaningful. The problem arises in acting as if those inferential statements are factual statements. Distinguishing between these two types of statements does not imply that one type is better than the other—we need both types. Both are useful, both are important—you simply must not confuse the two.

When you hear inferential statements, treat them as inferential and not as factual. Recognize that such statements may prove to be wrong, and be aware of that possibility. Inferential statements should leave open the possibility of alternatives. If, for example, you treat the statement "The United States should enforce the blockade" as factual, you eliminate the possibility of any alternatives.

Allness Because the world is infinitely complex, we can never know all or say all about anything—at least we cannot logically say all about anything. Beware of speakers who present information as if it is all that there is or as if it is all you need to know to make up your mind.

Disraeli once said that "to be conscious that you are ignorant is a great step toward knowledge." That observation is an excellent example of a *nonallness* attitude. If, as a critical listener, you recognize that there is more to learn, more to see, and more to hear, you will treat what the speaker says as part of the total picture, not the whole, not the final word.

Static Evaluation Often when you form an abstraction of something or someone—when you formulate a verbal statement about an event or person—that statement remains static and unchanging. But, the object or person to whom it refers has changed. Everything is in a constant state of change.

As critical listeners, respond to the statements of speakers as if they contained a tag that identified the time frame to which they refer. Visualize each such statement as containing a date. Look at that date and ask yourself if the statement is still true today. Thus, when a speaker says that 10 percent of the population now lives at or below the poverty level, ask yourself about the date to which that statement applies. When was the statistic compiled? Does the poverty level determined at that time adequately reflect current conditions?

Indiscrimination Nature seems to abhor sameness at least as much as vacuums. Nowhere in the universe can we find two things that are identical. Everything is unique—everything is unlike anything else.

Our language, however, provides us with common nouns (such as *teacher, student, friend, enemy, war, politician,* and *liberal*) which lead us to focus on similarities. Such nouns lead you to group all teachers together, all students together, and all politicians together. These words divert attention away from the uniqueness of each individual, each object, and each event. The misevaluation of *indiscrimination,* then, is one in which the focus is on classes of individuals, objects, or events rather than on the unique individual, object, or event.

There is nothing wrong with classifying. No one would argue that classifying is unhealthy or immoral. It is, on the contrary, an extremely useful method of dealing with any complex matter. Classifying helps us to deal with complexity. It puts order into our thinking. The problem arises from applying some evaluative label to that class, and then using that label as an "adequate" map for each individual in the group. Put differently, indiscrimination is a denial of uniqueness.

Beware, therefore, of speakers who group large numbers of unique individuals under the same label. Beware of speakers who tell you that "Democrats are . . . ," that "Catholics believe . . . ," that "Mexicans are. . . ." Ask yourself, which Democrats, how many Catholics, which Mexicans, and so on.

REMEMBER: **Language varies in:**
1. directness-indirectness
2. abstraction-specificity
3. objectivity-subjectivity
4. formality-informality
5. accuracy-inaccuracy (**polarization, fact-inference confusion, allness, static evaluation,** and **indiscrimination**).

ORAL STYLE

Oral style is a quality of spoken language that clearly differentiates it from written language. You do not speak as you write—the words and sentences you use differ. The major reason for this difference is that you compose speech instantly. You select your words and construct your sentences as you think your thoughts. There is very little time in between the thought and the utterance. When you write, however, you compose your thoughts after considerable reflection. Even then you probably often rewrite and edit as you go along. Because of this, written language has a more formal tone. Spoken language is more informal, more colloquial.

Spoken and written language not only *do* differ, they *should* differ. The main reason why spoken and written language should differ is that the listener hears a speech only once; therefore, speech must be instantly intelligible. The reader can reread an essay or look up an unfamiliar word. The reader can spend as much time as he or she wishes with the written page. The listener, however, must move at the pace you set as the speaker. The reader may reread a sentence or paragraph if there is a temporal attention lapse. The listener doesn't have this option.

These two forms of communication differ in the way we produce and receive them. These differences lead speakers and writers to compose differently. At the same time, the differences between the way we read and the way we listen demand that speakers and writers employ different principles to guide them in composing messages.

The words you use to speak and to write differ from each other. Generally, spoken language consists of shorter, simpler, and more familiar words than does written language. There is a great deal more qualification in speech than in writing. For example, when speaking you probably make greater use of such expressions as *although, however, perhaps,* and the like. When writing, however, you probably edit out many such expressions.

Although each politician has his or her own unique speaking style, there are generalizations that some theorists claim characterize "political speaking" in general. What are some of these generalizations? Can you give examples to support or refute such generalizations?

Spoken language has a greater number of self-reference terms (terms that refer to the speaker herself): *I, me, our, us,* and *you.*

Spoken language also has a greater number of "allness" terms such as *all, none, every, always, never.* You are probably more careful when you write to edit out such allness terms when you realize that such terms are probably not very descriptive of reality.

Spoken language contains more specific and concrete terms; written language contains more general and abstract terms.

Spoken language has more pseudo-quantifying terms (for example, *many, much, very, lots*), and terms that include the speaker as part of the observation (for example, *it seems to me that . . .* or *as I see it . . .*). Further, spoken language contains more verbs and adverbs, whereas writing contains more nouns and adjectives.

For the most part, retain this "spoken" style in your public speeches. The public speech, however, is composed much like a written essay. There is considerable thought and deliberation and much editing and restyling. Because of this, you will need to devote special effort to retaining and polishing your oral style. In the following unit specific suggestions for achieving this goal are presented.

To further clarify the differences, examine the contrasting examples of "Oral and Written Style" on pages 418–419.

REMEMBER: **Compared to written style, oral style is characterized by:**
1. shorter words
2. simpler words
3. more familiar words
4. greater qualification
5. more self-reference terms
6. more "allness" terms
7. more concrete terms
8. more pseudo-quantifying terms
9. more terms that include the speaker
10. more verbs and adverbs

and can be achieved by incorporating the above characteristics and by using:
11. short sentences
12. guide phrases such as *next, first,* and *therefore*
13. informal and personal terms
14. sentences that involve the listener
15. repetition of key terms
16. parallel structure

THE HUMOROUS STYLE

It is important to understand the role of humor in public speaking as a speaker (to use it more effectively), as a listener (to better appreciate the speaker's strategies), and as a

Oral and Written Style: A Comparative Example

To distinguish more clearly the characteristics of oral and written style, two excerpts—one in written style and one in oral style—are presented below. Read each carefully and note as many differences as you can.

Written Style

There are three major ways of lying that have been identified. The omission of information that is true is referred to as concealment. An example of this type of lie would occur when an individual answers one's parents, who ask "What did you do last night?", with the phrase, "Listened to records," but without any reference to drinking. To present false information as if it were the truth would be considered an instance of falsification. An example of this latter type of lie would be if someone who owed money said, "The check is in the mail" when it really was not. Misidentifying the causes of an emotion, as in saying, "I'm not crying; I just got something in my eye," would be considered an example of misdirection.

Oral Style

We can identify three major ways of lying: concealment, falsification, and misidentification. First, concealment involves omitting true information. A good example of this occurs when your parents ask, "What did you do last night?" If you answer, "listened to records" but omit drinking, then you've lied by concealment. Second, falsification involves presenting false information as if it were true. A popular example of falsification is when your friend who borrowed money tells you, "The check is in the mail" when it isn't. Third, misdirection involves misidentifying the causes of an emotion. For example, let's say you don't want others to know you're crying. You might lie by misdirection and say, "No, I'm not crying; I just got something in my eye."

Note some of the differences between these two styles. The oral style version uses the active voice; the written style version relies on the more indirect passive voice. In the oral style version we included a preview of the three types of lies to help the audience follow the discussion. No such preview is presented in the written style version, largely because the reader can easily glance ahead or back for orientation. In the oral version the sentences are shorter, and there are guide phrases to help the listener follow the discussion (for example, *first, second, third*). The language in the oral version is more informal and more personal; it makes use of personal pronouns (*we, you*) and contractions (*you've, isn't, you're*). It also involves the listener in the examples (*your parents, your friend borrows money, you don't want others to know you're crying*). The written version depersonalizes the examples and makes use of "written style" expressions such as "the individual," "one," and "latter." Note, too, that in the oral version the key terms (*concealment, falsification,* and *misdirection*) are repeated to help the audience remember and follow the examples. Further, the oral version uses parallel structure. Consider these three sentences:

1. First, concealment involves omitting true information.
2. Second, falsification involves presenting false information as if it were true.
3. Third, misdirection involves misidentifying the causes of an emotion.

Notice, for example, that (1) guide phrases begin each sentence; (2) key terms are introduced next; (3) the verb "involves" is used in all three sentences; and (4) the gerund (the -*ing* form of the verb) is used to begin the defining phrase.

critic (to better evaluate and judge the entire speech). Although humor is an important element in some public speeches, it is not a necessary element, nor is it always desirable. It is effective in some situations, with some speakers, and with some audiences. Analyze each specific speaking situation, then make a judgment as to whether or not to try humor. It is extremely difficult to use humor effectively. At the same time, it may be extremely effective in the right situation. With this disclaimer, consider humor—its role in public speaking and some guidelines for its effective use.

You can use humor in your speeches to achieve a number of important purposes. In a speech that is long and somber, humor breaks up the mood and lightens the tone. At times, humor serves as a creative and useful transition. Humor is excellent support material. It can help you emphasize a point, crystallize an idea, or rebut an opposing argument.

Some of you are probably excellent humorists. You can look at a situation, find the humor in it, and convey this humor to an audience easily and clearly. Others are probably ineffective humorists. In between these extremes lie most of us. All of us, however, could probably improve the humor in our communications. Effective humor in public speaking is relevant, brief, spontaneous, tasteful, and appropriate.

Relevance

Like any other type of supporting material, the humorous anecdote or story must be germane to your topic and your purpose. If it is not, don't use it. If you must go to exceptional lengths to make the story fit, or if you have to distort seriously the proposition it should support, then reconsider your material.

Brevity

Humor works best in public speaking when it is brief. If it occupies too great a portion of your speech, the audience may question your sincerity or seriousness. Humor in

■-■-■-■

TIPS FROM PROFESSIONAL SPEAKERS

Fancy, sesquipedalian words—like the six-shooter I've just fired off—should be avoided by speakers on nine out of ten occasions. This is a member of the Buckley clan telling you to keep your vocabulary simple *when you are delivering a talk.*

Every speaker is inherently in the business of education, true, but the field is not semantics, nor philology, nor etymology. Leave that to literary types. You want to be down to earth. You want your audience to understand just exactly what it is you wish to put across. . . . If there are two words that will do the job, strike out the longer one. Had President Roosevelt on that solemn occasion told the American people that we had nothing to fear but phobophobia, would he have carried half the country?

Reid Buckley, prominent lecturer and director of the Buckley School of Public Speaking in Camden, South Carolina. *Speaking in Public* (New York: HarperCollins, 1988), pp. 144–145.

special occasion speeches, however, may logically occupy a greater part of the entire speech than in informative or persuasive speeches. Here David Awl (Boaz and Brey, 1988), a student from Bradley University, uses humor (very briefly) in an after-dinner speech to introduce his topic:

> *What is it about so many of the great technological breakthroughs of the Twentieth Century, like Eggzilla, that are leaving us with the feeling that time is running out. Well, there's a name for this problem. No, not Olivia DeHaviland. The good names are always taken. It's called time sickness, and it's sapping the enjoyment out of our lives.*

Spontaneity

Humor works best when it seems spontaneous, something Mr. Kendall in the cartoon doesn't seem to understand. If humor appears studied or too well practiced, it may lose its effectiveness. In telling a humorous anecdote, for example, always keep your eyes on the audience, not on your notes. Never, never read your punch line. At the same time that humor should appear spontaneous, recognize the difficulty of getting a laugh. So, test your humor on your friends or family first to gauge their reactions and improve your delivery.

Don't telegraph your humorous material by long prefaces or by telling the audience that you are going to tell a funny story—you'll be lost if it fails to get the expected laugh. Let the humor of the story speak for itself.

Try also to develop a spontaneous retort just in case your humorous story turns out to be a dud. Don't look surprised, hurt, or as though you've lost control of yourself and your material. Instead develop a clever response. Johnny Carson is a master of these rejoinders, which are often a great deal more humorous than even his best jokes.

"Mr. Kendall would like to see one of those flashes of oddball humor."

Drawing by Leo Cullum; © 1992 The New Yorker Magazine, Inc. Reprinted by permission.

Tastefulness

Humor should be tasteful. Reject vulgar and "off-color" expressions. Coarseness is never a substitute for wit. If there is even the smallest possibility that your humor might make your listeners uncomfortable, then eliminate it. Avoid poking fun at any group, race, religion, nationality, sex, sexual minority, occupation, or age group. Especially avoid ethnic jokes; they have no place in a public speech.

At the same time, be careful of telling jokes at your own expense, of poking too much fun at yourself. Although we are often our own best foils, in a public speaking situation poking fun at yourself can damage your credibility. The audience may see you as a clown rather than as a responsible advocate.

Avoid sarcasm and ridicule. It is rarely humorous and it is often difficult to predict how an audience will respond. Your listeners may well wonder when your sarcasm or ridicule will be directed at them.

Appropriateness

Like all forms of support, humor must be appropriate to you as the speaker. Tell jokes in your own style—not in the style of Roseanne Arnold or Jay Leno. Invest time in developing a style that is your own and with which you are comfortable.

Similarly, use humor that is appropriate to your audience and to the occasion. Jokes about babies or anecdotes about the singles' scene are not likely to prove effective with a group of retired teamsters. The topic of the joke and its implications must be relevant and appropriate to all elements of the public speaking act.

REMEMBER: Humor in a public speech is most effective when:
1. relevant to your topic and your purpose
2. brief
3. spontaneous or seemingly spontaneous
4. tasteful rather than vulgar, off-color, or sarcastic
5. appropriate to you as a speaker, to your audience, and to the occasion

CRITICALLY SPEAKING

1. How might indirect, abstract, subjective, formal, and inaccurate language actually help the speaker achieve her or his purpose?
2. How many of the thinking errors (polarization, fact-inference confusion, allness, static evaluation, and indiscrimination) can you identify in one evening of prime-time television (comedies and hour dramas usually contain numerous examples)?
3. Can you recall any of the thinking errors in the speeches you've heard this semester?
4. How do differences between the processes of reading and listening necessitate differences between effective writing and effective speaking?
5. What other differences can you identify between oral and written language?
6. How do you respond to humor, say, in a history or mathematics lecture?
7. What common mistakes do you observe when people use humor? Can you use these mistakes to help you formulate general principles for using humor effectively?
8. How would you characterize the humor of Jay Leno, Eddie Murphy, or Roseanne Arnold? Can you identify the principles that characterize these persons' styles of humor?

PRACTICALLY SPEAKING

21.1   MAKING CONCEPTS SPECIFIC

One of the major skills in public speaking is learning to make your ideas specific so that your listeners will understand exactly what you want them to understand. Here are ten sentences. Rewrite each of the sentences making the italicized terms more specific.

1. The *woman* walked up the *hill* with her *children.*
2. The *teacher* was discussing *economics.*
3. The *player scored.*
4. The *teenager* was listening to a *record.*
5. No one in the *city* thought the *mayor* was doing anything useful.
6. The *girl* and the *boy* each received lots of *presents.*
7. I read the *review* of the *movie.*
8. The *couple* rented a great *car.*
9. The *detective* wasn't much help in solving the *crime.*
10. The *children* were playing an old *game.*
11. The *dinosaur approached* the *baby.*
12. He *walked up* the *steep hill.*
13. They loved playing *games.*
14. The *cat climbed* the *fence.*
15. The *large house is* in the *valley.*

Effective Style in Public Speaking

■ ■ ■ ■

UNIT OBJECTIVES

After completing this unit, you should be able to:

1. Define the five qualities of effective style

2. Identify the suggestions for achieving clarity, vividness, appropriateness, a personal style, and forcefulness

3. Identify the specific suggestions for constructing effective sentences

4. Define and provide examples of parallel, antithetical, and periodic sentences

5. Explain the principles for making your speech easy to remember

---

Now that the general principles of language and style are understood, specific suggestions can be identified for improving your speech style.

■■■■ CHOOSING WORDS

Choose carefully the words you use in your public speeches. Choose words to achieve clarity, vividness, appropriateness, a personal style, and forcefulness.

Clarity

Clarity in speaking style should be your primary goal. Here are some guidelines to help you make your speech clear.

Be Economical Don't waste words. Two of the most important ways to achieve economy are to avoid redundancies and to avoid meaningless words. Notice the redundancies in the following expressions:

- at 9 A.M. *in the morning*
- we *first* began the discussion
- the full *and complete* report
- I *myself personally*
- blue *in color*
- *over*exaggerate
- you, *members of the audience*
- *clearly* unambiguous
- about *approximately* 10 inches *or so*
- cash *money*

By withholding the italicized terms you eliminate unnecessary words. You thus move closer to a more economical and clearer style.

Similarly, eliminate meaningless phrases such as:

- *the amount of* $10 was paid
- *conduct a* study *on* the increasing divorce rate
- *there are* three people *who* want to

Rework meaningless phrases into expressions that are more economical and more direct. Instead of saying "would seem to show," say "shows." Instead of saying "the function of this plug. . . ," say "this plug. . . ." Instead of saying "for the reason that," say "because."

Use Specific Terms and Numbers Picture these items:

- a bracelet
- a gold bracelet

- a gold bracelet with a diamond clasp
- a braided gold bracelet with a diamond clasp

Notice that as we get more and more specific, we get a clearer and more detailed picture. Be specific. Don't say *dog* when you want your listeners to picture a St. Bernard. Don't say *car* when you want them to picture a limousine. Don't say *movie* when you want them to think of *Lethal Weapon 3*.

The same is true of numbers. Don't say "earned a good salary" if you mean "earned $90,000 a year." Don't say "taxes will go up" when you mean "taxes will increase 22 percent." Don't say "the defense budget was enormous" when you mean "the defense budget was $17 billion."

Use Guide Phrases Listening to a public speech is difficult work. Assist your listeners by using *guide phrases* to help them see that you are moving from one idea to another. Use phrases such as "now that we have seen how. . . , let us consider how. . . ," and "my next argument. . . ." Terms such as *first, second, and also, although,* and *however* will help your audience follow your line of thinking.

Use Short, Familiar Terms Generally, favor the short word over the long one. Favor the familiar word over the unfamiliar word. Favor the more commonly used term over the rarely used term. Here are a few examples:

Poor choices	Better choices
innocuous	harmless
elucidate	clarify
utilize	use
ascertain	find out
erstwhile	former
eschew	avoid
expenditure	cost or expense

Use Repetition and Restatement Repetition, restatement, and internal summaries will all help to make your speech clearer. *Repetition* means repeating something in exactly the same way. *Restatement* means rephrasing an idea or statement in different words. *Internal summaries* are periodic summary statements or reviews of subsections of your speech. All will help listeners to follow what you are saying.

Distinguish Between Commonly Confused Words Many words, because they sound alike or are used in similar situations, are commonly confused. Learn these terms and avoid such confusions. Here are ten of the most frequently confused words:

- Use *accept* to mean *to receive* and *except* to mean *with the exclusion of* (She accepted the award and thanked everyone except the producer).
- Use *to affect* to mean *to have an effect* or *to influence,* and *to effect* to mean *to produce a result* (The teacher affected his students greatly and will now effect an entirely new curriculum).
- Use *between* when referring to two items (It is between this one and that one)

THE NEXT 10 MILES
FEATURE ARRID ARROYOS,
BEAUTIFUL BUTTES,
MESMERIC MESAS,
PONDEROUS PONDEROSAS,
AND CARVED CANYONS.
(FORGIVE THE ALLITERATION)

Courtesy Harbrough.

and *among* when referring to *more than two items* (I want to chose from among these five items).

- Use *can* to refer to *ability* and *may* to refer to *permission* (I can scale the mountain but I may not reveal its hidden path).
- Use *cheap* to refer to something that is *inferior* and *inexpensive* to something that *costs little* (Inexpensive items are usually but not always cheap).
- Use *discover* to refer to the act of *finding something out* or *to learn something previously unknown* and use *invent* to refer to the act of *originating something new* (We discover unknown lands but we invent time machines).
- Use *explicit* to mean *specific* and *implicit* to mean the act of *expressing something without actually stating it* (He was explicit in his denial of the crime but was implicit concerning his whereabouts).
- Use *to imply* to mean *to state indirectly* and *to infer* to mean *to draw a conclusion* (She implied that she would seek a divorce; we can only infer her reasons).
- Use *tasteful* to refer to one's *good taste* and use *tasty* to refer to something that tastes good (The wedding was tasteful and the food most tasty).
- Use *uninterested* to mean *a lack of interest* and use *disinterested* to mean *objective* or *unbiased* (The student seemed uninterested in the lecture. The teacher was disinterested in who received what grades).

▨■■▨ TIPS FROM PROFESSIONAL SPEAKERS

Avoid showy language. Speak the way you talk in everyday conversation. Your everyday speech is spontaneous, new, like freshly baked bread. Speech is alive. It has music to it. In one of his speeches, F. D. Roosevelt changed "We are endeavoring to construct a more inclusive society" to the way it would be spoken: "We're going to make a country where no one is left out." Say it the easy way, "trippingly on the tongue."

Elayne Snyder, corporate consultant and speech coach. *Persuasive Business Speaking* (New York: American Management Association, 1990), p. 145.

Vividness

Select words to make your ideas vivid and come alive in the minds of your listeners.

Use Active Verbs Favor verbs that communicate activity rather than passivity. The verb *to be*, in all its forms—*is, are, was, were, will be*—is relatively inactive. Try using verbs of action instead. Rather than saying "The teacher was in the middle of the crowd," say "The teacher *stood* in the middle of the crowd." Instead of saying "The report was on the President's desk for three days," try "The report *rested* (or *slept*) on the President's desk for three days." Instead of saying "Management will be here tomorrow," consider "Management will descend on us tomorrow" or "Management jets in tomorrow."

Use Strong Verbs The verb is the strongest part of your sentence. Choose verbs carefully, and choose them so they accomplish a lot. Instead of saying "He walked through the forest," consider such terms as *wandered, prowled, rambled,* or *roamed.* Consider whether one of these might not better suit your intended meaning. Consult a thesaurus for any verb you suspect might be weak.

A good guide to identifying weak verbs is to look at your use of adverbs. If you use lots of adverbs, you may be using them to strengthen weak verbs. Consider cutting out the adverbs and substituting stronger verbs.

Use Figures of Speech Use figures of speech to help you achieve vividness. Figures of speech are stylistic devices that have been a part of rhetoric since ancient times. Table 22.1 contains ten figures you might use in your speech, along with definitions and examples.

Use Imagery Appeal to the senses, especially our visual, auditory, and tactile senses. Make us see, hear, and feel what you are talking about.

Visual Imagery. In describing people or objects, create images your listeners can see. When appropriate, describe such visual qualities as height, weight, color, size, shape, length, contour. Let your audience see the sweat pouring down the faces of the coal miners; let them see the short, overweight executive in a pin-striped suit smoking a cigar. Here Stephanie Kaplan (Reynolds and Schnoor, 1991), a student from the University of Wisconsin, uses visual imagery to describe the AIDS Quilt:

TABLE 22-1   FIGURES OF SPEECH

TYPE	DEFINITION	EXAMPLE
Alliteration	repetition of the same initial sound in two or more words; initial sound in two or more words	fifty famous flavors; the cool calculating leader
Antithesis	presentation of contrary ideas in parallel form	my loves are many; my enemies are few; "It was the best of times, it was the worst of times" (Dickens)
Climax	the arrangement of individual phrases or sentences in ascending order of forcefulness	as a child he lied, as a youth he stole, as a man he killed
Hyperbole	the use of extreme exaggeration	your obedient and humble servant; I'm so hungry I could eat a cow; he cried like a faucet
Irony	the use of a word or sentence whose literal meaning is the opposite of that which is intended	a teacher handing back failing examinations might say, "So pleased to see how many of you studied so hard."
Metaphor	the comparison of two unlike things	She's a lion when she wakes up; all nature is science; he's a real bulldozer
Metonymy	the substitution of a name for a title with which it is closely associated	"City Hall issued the following news release" where *City Hall* is used instead of *the mayor* or *the city council*
Personification	the attribution of human characteristics to inanimate objects	this room cries for activity; my car is tired and wants a drink
Rhetorical question	the use of a question to make a statement or to produce some desired effect rather than to secure an answer	Do you want to be popular? Do you want to get well?
Simile	the comparison of two unlike objects by using *like* or *as*	He takes charge like a bull; the manager is as gentle as a lamb

The Names Project is quite simply a quilt. Larger than 10 football fields, and composed of over 9,000 unique 3-feet by 6-feet panels each bearing a name of an individual who has died of AIDS. The panels have been made in homes across the country by the friends, lovers, and families of AIDS victims.

Auditory Imagery.   Appeal to our sense of hearing by using terms that describe sounds. Let your listeners hear the car *screeching*, the wind *whistling*, the bells *chiming*, the angry professor *roaring*.

Tactile Imagery.   Use terms referring to temperature, texture, and touch to create tactile imagery. Let your listeners feel the cool water running over their bodies and the punch of the fighter; let them feel the smooth skin of the newborn baby.

Appropriateness

Use language that is appropriate to you as the speaker. Also, use language that is appropriate to your audience, the occasion, and the speech topic. Here are some general guidelines to help you achieve this quality.

Speak on the Appropriate Level of Formality The most effective public speaking style is less formal than the written essay. One way to achieve an informal style is to use contractions. Say *don't* instead of *do not*, *I'll* instead of *I shall*, and *wouldn't* instead of *would not*. Contractions give a public speech the sound and rhythm of conversation, a quality that most listeners react to favorably.

Use personal pronouns rather than impersonal expressions. Say "I found" instead of "it has been found," or "I will present three arguments" instead of "three arguments will be presented."

Avoid Unfamiliar Terms Avoid using terms the audience does not know. Avoid foreign and technical terms unless you are certain the audience is familiar with them. Similarly, avoid jargon (the technical vocabulary of a specialized field) unless you are sure the meanings are clear to your listeners. Some acronyms (NATO, UN, NOW, and CORE) are probably familiar to most audiences; most, however, are not. When you wish to use any of these types of expression, explain fully their meaning to the audience.

Avoid Slang Avoid offending your audience with language that embarrasses them or makes them think you have little respect for them. Although your listeners may themselves use such expressions, they often resent their use by public speakers.

Avoid Offensive Terms Avoid terms that your listeners might see as sexist or racist. Do not use the masculine pronoun to refer to the hypothetical person; that is, do not use *he* or *him* generically. Change your sentences around so you can use the plural *they* or *them*, or say *he and she* or *her and him*. Do not refer to professions or positions by masculine names: avoid such expressions as *chairman*, *policeman*, or *salesman* when applied to both sexes; substitute *chair* or *chairperson*, *police officer*, and *salesperson*. Similarly, avoid using *man* when referring to the human race. *Human* serves as well and is more descriptive.

Alternatively, avoid terms that were at one time used to refer to a woman specifically. These terms developed from the masculine forms and may prove offensive. Avoid, for example, *poetess*, *Negress*, *Jewess*, *heroine*, and the like. Don't imply that the hypothetical doctor or lawyer is male by using sex identifiers such as "woman doctor" or "female lawyer."

Show this same equality to members of different races, nationalities, religions, and affectional orientations. Avoid referring to such groups with terms that carry negative connotations or picturing them in stereotypical and negative ways. At the same time, avoid slighting members of minority groups. Include references to minority groups and minority members in your examples and illustrations.

Personal Style

Audiences favor speakers who speak in a personal rather than an impersonal style, who speak *with* them rather than *at* them.

Use Personal Pronouns Say *I* and *me* and *he* and *she* and *you*. Avoid such impersonal expressions as *one* (as in "One is lead to believe . . . ") or "this speaker," or "you, the listeners." These expressions distance the audience and create barriers rather than bridges.

Use Questions Ask the audience questions to involve them. In a small audience, you might even briefly entertain responses. In larger audiences, you might ask the question, pause to allow the audience time to consider their responses, and then move on. When you direct questions to your listeners, they feel a part of the public speaking transaction.

Create Immediacy Immediacy is a connectedness, a relatedness with one's listeners. Immediacy is the opposite of disconnected and separated. Create a sense of immediacy by using the "you approach." Say "you'll enjoy reading . . . " instead of "everyone will enjoy reading . . . "; say "I want you to see . . . " instead of "I want people to see. . . ."

Refer directly to commonalities between you and the audience; for example, "We are all children of immigrants" or "We all want to see our team in the playoffs." Refer to shared experiences and goals; for example, "We all want, we all need a more responsive PTA."

Recognize audience feedback and refer to it in your speech. Say, for example, "I can see from your expressions that we're all anxious to get to our immediate problem."

Forcefulness/Power

Forceful or powerful language will help you achieve your purpose, whether it be informative or persuasive. Forceful language enables you to direct the audience's attention, thoughts, and feelings.

Eliminate Weakeners Delete phrases that weaken your sentences. Among the major weakeners are uncertainty expressions and weak modifiers. *Uncertainty expressions* such as *I'm not sure of this but, perhaps it might,* or *maybe it works this way* communicate a lack of commitment and conviction and will make your audience wonder if you're worth listening to. *Weak modifiers* such as *It works pretty well, It's kind of like . . . ,* or *It may be the one we want* make you seem unsure and indefinite about what you are saying.

Cut out any unnecessary phrases that reduce the impact of your meaning. Instead of saying "There are lots of things we can do to help," say "We can do lots of things to help." Instead of saying "I'm sorry to be so graphic, but Senator Bingsley's proposal . . . ," say "We need to be graphic. Senator Bingsley's proposal. . . ." Instead of saying "It should be observed in this connection that, all things considered, money is not productive of happiness," say "Money does not bring happiness." Consider the suggestions in Table 22.2 for achieving more powerful language. These suggestions are not limited in application to public speaking; they relate as well to interpersonal and small group communication.

Vary Intensity as Appropriate Much as you can vary your voice in intensity, you can also phrase your ideas with different degrees of stylistic intensity. You can, for example, refer to an action as "failing to support our position" or as "stabbing us in the back"; you can say that a new proposal will "endanger our goals" or "destroy us completely"; you can refer to a child's behavior as "playful," "creative," or "destructive." Vary your language to express different degrees of intensity—from mild through neutral to extremely intense.

TABLE 22-2 SUGGESTIONS FOR MORE POWERFUL SPEECH

SUGGESTIONS	EXAMPLES	COMMENTS
Avoid hesitations.	I *er* want to say that *ah* this one is *er* the best, *you know.*	Hesitations make you sound unprepared and uncertain.
Avoid too many intensifiers.	*Really*, this was *the greatest;* it was *truly phenomenal.*	Too many intensifiers make your speeches all sound the same, and do not allow for intensifying what should be emphasized.
Avoid tag questions.	That's a great proposal, *don't you think?* I'll review the report now, *okay?*	Tag questions ask for another's agreement and therefore signal your need for approval and your own uncertainty or lack of conviction.
Avoid self-critical statements.	*I'm not very good at this* or *This is my first speech.*	Self-critical statements signal a lack of confidence and make public your inadequacies.
Avoid slang and vulgar expressions.	"!!#//°°°," *No problem.*	Slang and vulgarity signal a low social class and hence little power.

Avoid Bromides and Clichés *Bromides* are sentences that are worn out because of constant usage. Here are some examples.

- She's as pretty as a picture.
- Honesty is the best policy.
- If I can't do it well, I won't do it at all.
- I don't understand modern art, but I know what I like.

When we hear them, we recognize them as unoriginal and uninspired.

Clichés are phrases that have lost their novelty and part of their meaning through overuse. Clichés call attention to themselves because of their overuse. Here are some clichés to avoid:

the whole ball of wax	by hook or by crook
in this day and age	sweet as sugar
happy as a lark	tell it like it is
free as a bird	in the pink
no sooner said than done	tried and true
with bated breath	for all intents and purposes
it goes without saying	few and far between
he's a quick study	over the hill

"*This piece is brimming with clichés. Clichés are a dime a dozen!*
If I've told you once, I've told you a thousand times—be original!
Now get out there and burn the midnight oil—
it's better late than never!"

Courtesy Randy Hall.

no news is good news   mind over matter

the life of the party   keep your shirt on

a horse of a different color down in the mouth

REMEMBER: **Choose your words to achieve an effective public speaking style. Focus on:**

1. *Clarity:* be economical; be specific; use guide phrases; keep modified and modifiers together; use short, familiar, and high-frequency terms; use repetition, restatement, and internal summaries; avoid misusing the commonly confused words

2. *Vividness:* use active verbs; use strong verbs; use figures of speech; use imagery (especially, visual, auditory, and tactile imagery)

3. *Appropriateness:* speak on the appropriate level of formality; avoid unfamiliar, foreign and technical terms, jargon, and acronyms; avoid slang and vulgar terms; avoid offensive expressions

4. *Personal style:* use personal pronouns; ask questions; create immediacy

5. *Forcefulness:* eliminate weakeners; vary intensity as appropriate; avoid bromides and clichés

PHRASING SENTENCES

Give the same careful consideration that you give to words to your sentences as well. Some guidelines follow.

Use Short Sentences Short sentences are more forceful and economical. They are easier to comprehend, they are easier to remember. Listeners do not have the time or the inclination to unravel long and complex sentences. Help them to listen more efficiently. Use short rather than long sentences.

Use Direct Sentences Direct sentences are easier to understand. They are also more forceful. Instead of saying, "I want to tell you of the three main reasons why we should not adopt Program A," say "We should not adopt Program A. There are three main reasons."

Use Active Sentences Active sentences are easier to understand. They also make your speech seem livelier and more vivid. Instead of saying "The lower court's decision was reversed by the Supreme Court," say "The Supreme Court reversed the lower court's decision." Instead of saying "The proposal was favored by management," say "Management favored the proposal."

Use Positive Sentences Positive sentences are easier to comprehend and remember. Notice how sentences (a) and (c) are easier to understand than sentences (b) and (d).

a. The committee rejected the proposal.
b. The committee did not accept the proposal.
c. This committee works outside the normal company hierarchy.
d. This committee does not work within the normal company hierarchy.

Vary the Types of Sentences The advice to use short, direct, active, and positive sentences is valid most of the time. Yet too many sentences of the same type or length will make your speech sound boring. Use variety while following (generally) the preceding advice.

Here are a few special types of sentences that should prove useful, especially for adding variety, vividness, and forcefulness to your speech.

Parallel Sentences. Phrase your ideas in parallel (similar, matching) style for ease of comprehension and memory. Note the parallelism in (a) and (c) and its absence in (b) and (d).

a. The professor prepared the lecture, graded the examination, and read the notices.
b. The professor prepared the lecture, the examination was graded, and she read the notices.
c. Love needs two people to flourish. Jealousy needs but one.
d. Love needs two people. Just one can create jealousy.

Antithetical Sentences. Antithetical sentences juxtapose contrasting ideas in parallel fashion. John Kennedy used antithetical sentences when he said:

How would you adjust your style if your next speech was to be given to an audience such as that pictured here? What if it was to be given to a small group of, say, five or six?

If a free society cannot help the many who are poor, it cannot save the few who are rich.

In his inaugural speech, President Kennedy phrased one of his most often quoted lines in antithetical structure.

Ask not what your country can do for you; ask what you can do for your country.

Periodic Sentences. In periodic sentences, you reserve the key word until the end of the sentence. In fact, the sentence is not grammatically complete until you say this last word. For example, in "Looking longingly into his eyes, the old woman fainted," the sentence doesn't make sense until the last word is spoken.

REMEMBER: to construct your sentences to achieve clarity and forcefulness:

1. use short rather than long sentences
2. use direct rather than indirect sentences
3. use active rather than passive sentences
4. use positive rather than negative sentences
5. vary the types and lengths of sentences, making use of such constructions as parallel, antithetical, and periodic sentences

MAKING YOUR SPEECH EASY TO REMEMBER

How can you, as a public speaker, help your listeners to remember your speech? If your aim is to communicate information and argument to a listener, then surely part of your job is to ensure that your listeners remember what you say.

There is much that you can do to assist your listeners in remembering your speech. The following are a few of the major techniques you might use.

Stress Interest and Relevance Make your speech interesting and relevant. We learn easier and remember better that which is interesting and relevant to our own lives. The reasons for this are simple: we give this type of material much greater attention. We allow ourselves fewer lapses in attention. Almost automatically we relate this new information to our own lives and to what we already know. This association of the new with the old helps us to remember the information.

Another reason is that we think more about material that we find interesting and relevant. This "active rehearsal" significantly aids all kinds of memorization. We would have little trouble remembering the address for a job interview that promises $1250 per week to start, nor would we easily forget the amount of money being offered. We would, however, have difficulty learning a complex set of numbers if they bore no relevance to our immediate lives.

Create Connections In trying to get someone to remember anything, *associate* it with what is already known. If a new theory resembles a theory the audience is familiar with, mention this and then point out its differences. If feedback in communication works like feedback in a thermostat (with which the audience is already familiar), mention that.

Pattern Your Messages Things are much more easily remembered if they are presented in a pattern, if they are organized in some way. Consider this experiment. College students tried to memorize a list of words shown to them one at a time. Without any pattern, they had great difficulty. One group, however, was told that they should organize the words alphabetically. Each word began with a different letter. In recalling the list, the experimenters advised, they should go through the alphabet, recalling first the A word, then the B word, and so on. Not surprisingly, the group working with a pattern, in this case the alphabet, did significantly better. The pattern or organizational scheme helped the students to structure the information. This structure aided their ability to remember the words. Use this insight and likewise assist the listeners to remember what you say in the speech.

The organizational guides considered in the discussion of organization and outlining (Units 9 to 12) help you to present the listeners with patterns to aid their memory. Time sequences and spatial sequences, for example, are obvious examples of using known organizational patterns to assist memory. As a speaker, be careful when the main points of the speech do not fit into some clear pattern. If they do not, take special care to ensure that they are remembered. Try repetition and restatement, a summary visual aid of the main points, or some slides presenting the main ideas or arguments.

Mnemonic Devices. A widely used memory system is the *mnemonic device*. (Mnemosyne was the Greek goddess of memory, from whose name comes *mnemonic*.) For example, if I were to ask how many days there are in November, you might go through the mnemonic rhyme, "Thirty days have September, April, June, and November."

A useful mnemonic device is the *mediated associate*. I remember the spelling distinction between *angle* and *angel* by recalling that the sequence *el* goes up physically, as do angels. I remember the 12 cranial nerves from college physiology because of the sentence "*On old Olympus towering top a fine and gentle vision stands high*." The initial letters in this sentence remind me of the first letter of each of the cranial nerves. Similarly, I remember the seven primary colors (red, orange, yellow, green, blue, indigo, and violet) by the name "Roy G. Biv." As you can see, this technique can get very corny. Be careful in using these devices; use them sparingly and use them with some originality.

Focus Audience Attention The best way to focus the listeners' attention is to tell them to focus their attention. Simply say, "I want you to focus on three points that I will make in this speech. First, . . . " Then repeat at least once again (but preferably two or three times) these very same points. With experience in public speaking, you will be able to do this with just the right combination of subtlety and directness.

REMEMBER: Following the principles of style and memory will make your speech easier to remember:

1. make your material interesting and relevant to your audience
2. connect what the audience already knows with what you are talking about
3. give your listeners an organization or pattern to help them follow and remember your ideas
4. focus your listeners' attention on the main points of your speech

CRITICALLY SPEAKING

1. Why is clarity even more important in a public speech than it is in a written composition or book?
2. Can you identify some situations where a speaker might wish to make her or his message ambiguous?
3. Under what conditions might slang prove effective in a public speech?
4. How might unfamiliar, foreign, or technical terms actually increase the speaker's likelihood of persuading certain audiences in certain situations?
5. Listen to a good network anchorperson. How forceful or powerful is her or his language? Can you identify specific examples of powerful and powerless language?
6. How many powerful and powerless aspects are part of your general conversational style? What is the one stylistic aspect you might target for change? How will you go about effecting this change?

7. Listen carefully to the sentences used by an effective speaker or lecturer. Does this person follow the advice given here for phrasing sentences?

8. What other suggestions might you offer for making your speech easy to remember?

PRACTICALLY SPEAKING

22.1 QUALIFYING AND QUANTIFYING STATEMENTS

Read each of the following sentences and respond to the questions with specific numbers.

1. His mother is tall. How tall is she?
2. My geography instructor, Mr. Higgins, is fat. How fat is he?
3. That novel was a best-seller last year. How many copies did it sell?
4. For a physician, he doesn't make much money. How much did he make last year?
5. She watches a lot of television. How many hours per week does she watch?
6. College professors put in a lot of time preparing for a new course. How many hours would go into the preparation of a new course—from beginning to prepare the course syllabus to the preparation of the final lecture?
7. Her father is very old. How old is her father?
8. The student is a fast reader. How many words per minute can the student read?
9. He talks very slowly. How many words does he speak per minute?
10. The van Gogh painting was sold at auction for a record price. How much did it sell for?

Share your responses with others. From these responses it should be clear that general descriptions (old, tall, fat) are perceived differently by different people. If you want to create the same meaning (or at least similar meanings) in the minds of your many listeners, it is essential to be specific.

22.2 PRACTICING INCLUSIVENESS

The objectives of this brief exercise are (1) to sensitize you to some of the ways language is used to exclude others and (2) to provide some practice in rephrasing thoughts into inclusive language. The examples that follow are all drawn from sexist language, language that discriminates against women.

Each of the following terms—although technically used to refer to all people—actually refer to only one sex while excluding the other. What alternatives can you offer for each of these terms? What advantages/disadvantages do these alternative terms have as compared with the terms given here.

man	mankind
countryman	manmade
the common man	cave man
manpower	repairman
doorman	policeman
fireman	stewardess
waitress	salesman
mailman	actress

Rewrite each of the following sentences—which purposely recall the popular stereotypes—using more inclusive language so that they do not limit the referent to one sex and so that they punch holes in these limiting and discriminating stereotypes. In eliminating the stereotypes do be sure to retain the intended meaning, however. What advantages or disadvantages do you see in the rewritten versions?

1. You really should get a second doctor's opinion. Just see what he says.
2. Johnny went to school today and met his kindergarten teacher. I wonder who she is.
3. Everyone needs to examine his own conscience.
4. No one can tell what his ultimate fortune will be.
5. The effective communicator is a selective self-discloser; he discloses to some people some of the time.
6. I wonder who the new chairman will be.
7. The effective waitress knows when her customers need her.
8. Advertisers don't care what the intellectual thinks; they want to know what the man-in-the-street thinks.
9. What do you think the ideal communicator should be like? How should he talk? How should he gesture?
10. The history of man is largely one of technology replacing his manual labor.

22.3   REPHRASING CLICHÉS

Clichés are expressions whose meaning has become worn out from excessive usage. Many clichés are also idioms, expressions whose meanings are not easily deduced from the individual words but which must be understood as a single linguistic unit, much like a single word. Thus, in using clichés you betray a lack of originality and, when they are idioms, can easily create special problems for non-native speakers of the language. The clichés and idioms listed below will provide a useful opportunity to practice your abilities to use language effectively. Rephrase each of these clichés/idioms, so that they are—following the guidelines for language given in this unit—clear, vivid, appropriate, personal, and forceful.

■ It's a blessing in disguise.
■ You have to take the bitter with the sweet.

- Her problem was that she burnt the candle at both ends.
- What can I add? That's the way the cookie crumbles.
- He meant well but he drove everyone up the wall.
- So, I told her: either fish or cut bait.
- He just has to get his act together.
- She has a heart of gold.
- I talked and talked but it was in one ear and out the other.
- Lighten up; keep your shirt on.
- He let it slip through his fingers.
- That Stephen King movie will make your hair stand on end.
- Well, it's easy being a Monday-morning quarterback.
- Don't put all your eggs in one basket.
- It's just water over the dam.
- He ran out with his tail between his legs.
- They gave the detective a real snow job.
- It was fun but it wasn't what it was cracked up to be.
- I was so excited I had my heart in my mouth.
- Wow, you're touchy. You get up on the wrong side of the bed?

U N I T 23

Characteristics of Delivery

UNIT OUTLINE

Methods of Delivery

Characteristics of Effective Delivery

Using Notes

Critically Speaking

Practically Speaking

UNIT OBJECTIVES

After completing this unit, you should be able to:

1. Define the four methods of delivery in public speaking and explain their advantages and disadvantages

2. Explain the characteristics of effective delivery

3. Explain the principles that should govern the public speaker's appearance

4. Explain at least three general guidelines for using notes during the public speaking transaction

*I*f you are like my own students, delivery probably creates more anxiety for you than any other aspect of public speaking. Few speakers worry about organization or audience analysis or style. Many worry about delivery, so you have a lot of company.

In this unit the general methods and principles that govern effectiveness in delivery will be reviewed. You can then adapt them to your own personality. In the next unit, specific suggestions for effective delivery are offered.

METHODS OF DELIVERY

Speakers vary widely in their methods of delivery: some speak "off-the-cuff," with no apparent preparation; others read their speeches from manuscript; some memorize their speeches word for word; others construct a detailed outline and actualize the speech itself at the moment of delivery. Speakers use all four of these general methods of delivery: impromptu, manuscript, memorized, and extemporaneous. Each has advantages and disadvantages.

Speaking Impromptu

When you speak impromptu you speak without any specific preparation. You and the topic meet for the first time and immediately the speech begins.

On some occasions you will not be able to avoid speaking impromptu. In a classroom, after someone has spoken, you might comment on the speaker and the speech you just heard—this requires a brief impromptu speech of evaluation. In asking or answering questions in an interview situation you are giving impromptu speeches, albeit extremely short ones. At meetings, you may find yourself explaining a proposal or defending a plan of action. These too are impromptu speeches. The ability to speak impromptu effectively depends on your general public speaking ability. The more proficient a speaker you are, the better you will be able to function impromptu.

Advantages. If used properly, the impromptu experience has much merit. It is an excellent training exercise in the different aspects of public speaking. For example, in impromptu speaking you can practice maintaining eye contact, responding to audience feedback, or gesturing. You gain practice in organizing your ideas and in developing examples, arguments, and appeals almost instantly.

Disadvantages. Perhaps the major disadvantage is that it focuses on appearances. The aim is often to *appear* to give an effective and well-thought-out speech. Another disadvantage is that it does not permit attention to the details of public speaking such as research, style, and organizational strategies. Because of this inadequacy, the audience is likely to get bored. This in turn may make you, as a speaker, feel more awkward and uncomfortable.

Speaking from Manuscript

In the manuscript method, you read the entire speech. When you require exact timing and wording, the manuscript method may be your safest choice. It could be disastrous if a political leader did not speak from manuscript on sensitive issues. An ambiguous word, phrase, or sentence that proved insulting or belligerent could cause serious problems. With a manuscript speech, you can do an in-depth analysis of style, content, organization, and all other elements of the speech. In fact, the great advantage of the manuscript speech is that an entire staff of speech experts and advisers can review it. They can offer suggestions as to potential problems, how to resolve them, and so on. Manuscript delivery allows you to say *exactly* what you and perhaps a host of speech writers and advisers wish to say.

Advantages. The major advantage of a manuscript speech is that you can control the timing precisely. This is particularly important when delivering a recorded speech (on television, for example). You don't want your conclusion cut off so the fifty-ninth rerun of "The Odd Couple" can go on as scheduled. Also, there is no danger of forgetting, no danger of being unable to find the right word. Everything is there for you on paper, so, you probably will be less anxious. Another advantage is that you can distribute copies and are less likely to be misquoted.

Disadvantages. The most obvious disadvantage is that it takes lots of time to write out a speech word for word. Another disadvantage is that it is difficult to read a speech and sound natural and nonmechanical. Reading material from the printed page with liveliness and naturalness is itself a skill that is difficult to achieve without considerable practice. Audiences do not like speakers to read their speeches. They prefer speakers who speak with them.

Reading a manuscript makes it difficult (even impossible) to take in and respond to feedback from your listeners. With a manuscript you are committed to the speech word for word and cannot make adjustments on the basis of feedback.

When the manuscript is on a stationary lectern, as it most often is, it is impossible to move around. You have to stay in one place. The speech controls your movement or, rather, your lack of movement.

Speaking from Memory

The memorized method involves writing out the speech word for word and committing it to memory. The speech is then usually "acted out." Like the manuscript method, the memorized method is useful when exact timing and exact wording is crucial. In politically sensitive cases or in cases where media impose restrictions, the memorized method may be useful.

Advantages. The memorized method allows you to devote careful attention to style. As in the manuscript speech, you can carefully review the exact word, phrase, or sentence and eliminate any potential problems in advance. One of the reasons the memorized delivery is popular is that it has all the advantages of the manuscript method; at the same time, however, it allows you freedom to move about and otherwise concentrate on delivery.

Disadvantages. The great disadvantage is that you might forget your speech. In a memorized speech each sentence cues the recall of the following sentence. Thus, when you forget one sentence, you may forget the rest of the speech. This danger, along with the natural nervousness that speakers feel, makes this method a poor choice in most situations.

The memorized method is even more time-consuming than the manuscript method since it involves additional time for memorization. When you recognize that you may easily forget the speech, even after spending hours memorizing it, it hardly seems worth the effort.

The memorized method does not allow for ease in adjusting to feedback. In fact, there is less opportunity to adjust to listener feedback than in the manuscript method. And if you are not going to adjust to feedback, you lose the main advantage of face-to-face contact.

Speaking Extemporaneously

Extemporaneous delivery involves thorough preparation and a commitment to memory of the main ideas and their order. It may also involve a commitment to memory of the first and last few sentences of the speech. There is, however, no commitment to exact wording for the major parts of the speech.

Advantages. The extemporaneous method is useful in most speaking situations. Good college lecturers use the extemporaneous method. They prepare thoroughly and know what they want to say and in what order they want to say it, but they have no commitment to exact wording.

This method allows you to respond easily to feedback. Should a point need clarification, you can elaborate on it when it will be most effective. This method makes it easy to be natural because you are being yourself. It is the method that comes closest to conversation or, as some theorists have put it, enlarged conversation. With the extemporaneous method, you can move about and interact with the audience.

Disadvantages. The major disadvantage is that you may stumble and grope for words. If you have rehearsed the speech a number of times, however, this is not likely to happen. Another disadvantage is that you cannot give the speech the attention to style that you can with other methods. You can get around this disadvantage too by memorizing those phrases you want to say exactly. There is nothing in the extemporaneous method that prevents your committing to memory selected phrases, sentences, or quotations.

Guidelines for Speaking Extemporaneously

Having stated a clear preference for the extemporaneous method, I do suggest that you memorize three parts of such a speech. Memorize your opening lines (perhaps the first few sentences) and your closing lines (perhaps the last few sentences). Also memorize the major propositions and the order in which you will present them.

Memorizing the opening and closing lines will help you to focus your complete attention on the audience and will also put you more at ease. Once you know exactly what you will say in opening and closing the speech, you will feel more in control. Second, memorize the main ideas so you will not have to refer to notes—you will feel in control of the speech and the speech-making situation. After all, if you expect your audience to remember these points, surely you should remember them as well.

REMEMBER: the four methods of delivery:

1. *Impromptu:* speaking without preparation; useful in training certain aspects of public speaking
2. *Manuscript:* reading from a written text; useful when exact timing and wording are essential
3. *Memorized:* acting out a memorized text; useful when exact timing and wording are required and when eye contact and movement are essential
4. *Extemporaneous:* speaking after thorough preparation and memorization of the main ideas (in order); useful in most public speaking situations

CHARACTERISTICS OF EFFECTIVE DELIVERY

Strive for a delivery that is natural, reinforces the message, is appropriate, is varied, and is conversational.

Effective Delivery Is Natural

Listeners will enjoy and believe you more if you speak naturally, as if you were conversing with a small group of people. Don't allow your delivery to call attention to itself. Your ultimate aim should be to deliver the speech so naturally that the audience won't even notice your delivery. This will take some practice but you can do it. When voice or bodily action are so prominent that they are distracting, the audience concentrates on the delivery and will fail to attend to your speech.

Effective Delivery Reinforces the Message

Use your voice and bodily movement to reinforce your content, your point of view, your purpose. Effective delivery should aid instant intelligibility. Your main objective is to make your ideas understandable to an audience. A voice that listeners have to strain to hear, a decrease in volume at the ends of sentences, and slurred diction will hinder comprehension.

Throughout our discussions of public speaking it was noted that everything about you communicates. You cannot prevent yourself from sending messages to others. The way in which you dress is no exception. In fact, your attire will figure significantly in the way your audience assesses your credibility, something the shopper in the cartoon realizes. It will influence the extent to which they will give you attention. In short, it will influence your effectiveness in all forms of persuasive and informative speaking.

Unfortunately, there are no universal rules. There are no rules that will apply to all situations for all speakers. Thus, only general guidelines are offered. Modify and tailor these for yourself and for each unique situation.

- *avoid extremes:* don't allow your clothes to detract attention from what you are saying
- *dress comfortably:* be both physically and psychologically comfortable with your appearance so that you can concentrate your energies on what you are saying

"I'm looking for a tie that says, 'Hey, I can handle the job, Mr. Harrison, if you'll just give me the chance.'"

Reprinted by permission: Tribune Media Services.

■ *dress appropriately:* your appearance should be consistent with the specific public speaking occasion

Effective Delivery Is Varied

Listening to a speech is hard work. Flexible and varied delivery relieves this difficulty. Be especially careful to avoid monotonous and predictable patterns.

Monotonous Patterns Speakers who are monotonous keep their voices at the same pitch, volume, and rate throughout the speech. The monotonous speaker maintains one level from the introduction to the conclusion. Like the drone of a motor, it easily puts the audience to sleep. Vary your pitch levels, your volume, and your rate of speaking.

Speakers who are monotonous in their bodily action are static; they stay in exactly the same position throughout the speech. This monotonous speaker doesn't move the proverbial muscle and ends the speech in exactly the same position as she or he started it. Use your body to express your ideas, to communicate to the audience what is going on in your head.

Predictable Patterns A predictable vocal pattern is one in which, for example, the volume levels vary but always in the same pattern. Through repetition, the pattern soon becomes predictable. For example, each sentence may begin at a loud volume and then decline to a barely audible volume at the sentence end. In bodily action, the predictable speaker repeatedly uses the same movements or gestures. For example, a speaker may scan the audience from left to right to left to right throughout the entire speech. If the audience can predict the pattern of your voice or your bodily action, then it will almost surely be ineffective. It will draw their attention away from what you are saying to this patterned and predictable delivery.

Effective Delivery Is Conversational

Although more formal than conversation, delivery in public speaking should have some of the most important features of conversation. These qualities are immediacy, eye contact, expressiveness, and responsiveness to feedback.

Immediacy Create a clear connection between yourself and each member of the audience. Make your listeners feel that you are talking directly and individually to each of them. You can communicate immediacy both verbally and nonverbally. Here are a few ways to help you communicate immediacy:

- join yourself to the audience with terms such as *we, us,* and *our*
- be especially responsive to audience feedback
- maintain appropriate eye contact with the audience members
- maintain a physical closeness that reinforces a psychological closeness
- stand with a direct and open body posture

Eye Contact When you maintaining eye contact (in addition to communicating immediacy), you make the public speaking interaction more conversational. Look directly into their eyes. Make a special effort to make eye contact, to lock eyes with different audience members for short periods.

Expressiveness When you are expressive you communicate genuine involvement in the public speaking situation. You can communicate this quality of expressiveness, of involvement, in several ways.

- express responsibility for your own thoughts and feelings

TIPS FROM PROFESSIONAL SPEAKERS

Engage your audience by reaching out to them. As you speak, think that all who sit in front of you are your friends, with whom you will share something useful, valuable, or at least sufficiently attractive to absorb their attention for a few moments. If you are successful, you will have imparted a message that will be understood, retained, and even acted on.

Jack Valenti, president of the Motion Picture Association of America and former speech writer to President Lyndon Johnson. *Speak Up with Confidence: How to Prepare, Learn, and Deliver Effective Speech* (New York: William Morrow, 1982), pp. 75–76.

- vary your vocal rate, pitch, volume, and rhythm to communicate involvement and interest in the audience and in the topic
- allow your facial muscles and your entire body to reflect and echo this inner involvement
- use gestures to communicate involvement—too few gestures may signal disinterest, too many may communicate uneasiness, awkwardness, or anxiety

Responsiveness to Feedback The most defining feature of conversation is responsiveness to feedback. As a speaker, read carefully the feedback signals being sent by the audience, then respond to these signals with verbal, vocal, and bodily adjustments. For example, respond to audience feedback signals communicating lack of comprehension or inability to hear with added explanation or increased volume.

REMEMBER: that effective delivery:

1. is natural (appears genuine and does not call attention to itself)
2. reinforces the message (aids audience comprehension)
3. is varied (monotony and predictable patterns of voice and bodily action are avoided)
4. is conversational (possesses some of the essential qualities of effective conversation: immediacy, eye contact, expressiveness, and responsiveness to feedback)

USING NOTES

For many speeches it may be helpful to use notes. A few simple guidelines may help you avoid some of the common errors made in using notes.

Keep Notes to a Minimum

The fewer notes you take with you, the better off you will be. The reason so many speakers bring notes with them is that they want to avoid the face-to-face interaction required. With experience, however, you should find this face-to-face interaction the best part of the public speaking experience.

Resist the normal temptation to bring with you the entire speech outline. You may rely on it too heavily and lose the direct contact with the audience. Instead, compose a delivery outline (pp. 246–247), using only key words. Bring this to the lectern with you—one side of a 3" × 5" index card or at most an 8½" by 11" page should be sufficient. This will relieve anxiety over the possibility of your forgetting your speech. It will not be extensive enough, however, to prevent you from maintaining direct contact with your audience.

Use Notes with "Open Subtlety"

Do not make them more obvious than necessary, but at the same time don't try to hide them from the audience. Do not gesture with your notes and thus make them more obvious than they need be. At the same time, do not turn away from the audience to steal a glance at them either. Use them openly and honestly but gracefully, with "open subtlety." To do this effectively, you'll have to know your notes intimately. Rehearse at least twice with the same notes that you will take with you to the speaker's stand.

Here a student practices the characteristics of effective delivery. What characteristics of effective delivery do you want to improve most? What characteristics do you feel you have effectively mastered?

Do Not Allow Your Notes to Prevent Directness

When referring to your notes, pause to examine them. Then regain eye contact with the audience and continue your speech. Do not read from your notes, just take cues from them. The one exception to this is an extensive quotation or complex set of statistics that you have to read; then, almost immediately, resume direct eye contact with the audience.

REMEMBER: Notes should assist (not hinder) communicating your message, so:

1. use few notes—the fewer the better
2. use notes with "open subtlety," neither obviously nor secretly; be so familiar with your notes that you will be able to concentrate on your audience
3. do not allow your notes to interfere with maintaining direct contact with your audience

CRITICALLY SPEAKING

1. With which method of delivery would you feel the least apprehension? Why?
2. What are your personal reactions to someone who gives an impromptu speech? From manuscript? From memory? Extemporaneously?
3. What other aspects of effective delivery would you include here?
4. What public figure's style of delivery comes closest to your ideal?
5. Most public speaking textbooks advocate a conversational style of delivery. Are there situations in which a more formal, less conversational style might be more effective?
6. Can you offer any additional advice on using notes?
7. What is the single most common error that speakers make in using their notes? What advice would you offer them?

PRACTICALLY SPEAKING

23.1   DEVELOPING THE IMPROMPTU SPEECH

The following experience may prove useful as an exercise in delivery. Students should be given three index cards each. Each student should write an impromptu speech topic on each of the cards. The cards should be collected and placed face down on a table. A speaker is chosen through some random process and selects two cards, reads the topics, selects one of them and takes approximately one minute to prepare a two- to three-minute impromptu speech.

A few guidelines may prove helpful.

1. Do not apologize. Everyone will have difficulty with this assignment, so there is no need to emphasize any problems you may have.

2. Do not express verbally or nonverbally any displeasure or any negative responses to the experience, the topic, the audience, or even to yourself. Approach the entire task with a positive attitude and a positive appearance. It will help make the experience more enjoyable for both you and your audience.

3. When you select the topic, jot down two or three subtopics that you will cover and perhaps two or three bits of supporting material that you will use in amplifying these two or three subtopics.

4. Develop your conclusion. It will probably be best to use a simple summary conclusion in which you restate your main topic and the subordinate topics that you discussed.

5. Develop an introduction. Here it will probably be best simply to identify your topic and orient the audience by telling them the two or three subtopics that you will cover.

The topics to be used for impromptu speaking should be familiar but not clichés. They should be worthwhile and substantive, not trivial. They should be neither too simplistic nor too complex. Here are some sample topics that may be used in lieu of the procedure suggested above where students write ideas on index cards.

The values of a college education	My favorite television show
What makes someone attractive	My favorite sport
How to meet another person	My favorite meal
What is love	My favorite character from literature
What is friendship	Unusual pastimes
How to resolve conflict	An important moment from history
How to communicate with your family	A current national concern
What is success	My hero
What makes a person happy	What I hate most
Places to visit	The type of person I dislike
Things to do	What to do on a Saturday night
An ideal day	How not to be a good student
An ideal relationship	How to survive in college
An ideal occupation	How to say "I love you"
An ideal lover	How to hurt someone you love
An unusual pet	Body language
Tough decisions	Contemporary music
My favorite movie	

Effective Speech Delivery

■ ■ ■ ■

UNIT OBJECTIVES

After completing this unit, you should be able to:

1. Explain the major problems associated with each of these aspects of voice: *volume, rate, pitch, articulation and pronunciation,* and *pauses*

2. Explain how the public speaker may deal with the aspects of bodily action most effectively: *eye contact, facial expression, posture, gestures, movement,* and *proxemics*

3. Identify the goals of rehearsal as these concern voice and bodily action

4. Explain the suggested rehearsal procedures

5. Explain the long-term delivery improvement program

W hat specifically can you do to improve your delivery, your voice, and your bodily action? This unit answers that obvious and important question and also offers some suggestions for rehearsing your speech and for undertaking a long-term improvement program.

VOICE

Five dimensions of voice are significant to the public speaker: volume, rate, pitch, articulation and pronunciation, and pauses. Your manipulation of these elements will enable you to control your voice to maximum advantage.

Volume

Volume refers to the relative intensity of the voice. *Loudness*, on the other hand, refers to the perception of that relative intensity. In an adequately controlled voice, volume will vary according to a number of factors. For example, the distance between speaker and listener, the competing noise, and the emphasis the speaker wishes to give an idea will all influence volume.

The problems with volume are easy to identify, though they are difficult to recognize in ourselves. One obvious problem is a voice that is too soft. When speech is so soft that listeners have to strain to hear, they will soon tire of expending so much energy. On the other hand, a voice that is too loud will prove disturbing because it intrudes on our psychological space. However, it may be of interest to note that a voice louder than normal communicates assertiveness (Page and Balloun, 1978) and will lead people to pay greater attention to you (Robinson and McArthur, 1982). On the negative side, it can also communicate aggressiveness and give others the impression that you would be difficult to get along with.

The most common problem is too little variation. A related problem is a volume pattern that, although varied, varies in an easily predictable pattern.

Fading away at the ends of sentences is particularly disturbing. Here the speaker uses a volume that is appropriate, but ends sentences speaking the last few words at an extremely low volume. Be particularly careful when finishing sentences; make sure the audience is able to hear these at an appropriate volume.

Rate

Rate refers to the speed at which you speak. We normally measure rate in the number of words or syllables spoken per minute—about 160 to 170 words per minute seems average for speaking as well as for reading aloud.

The problems of rate are speaking too fast or too slow, or with too little variation or too predictable a pattern. If you talk too fast you deprive your listeners of time they need to understand and digest what you are saying. If the rate is extreme, the listeners will simply not spend the time and energy needed to understand your speech.

If your rate is too slow it will encourage your listeners to wander to matters unrelated to your speech. Be careful, therefore, not to bore the audience by presenting information at too slow a rate; yet do not give them information at a pace that is too rapid for listeners to absorb. Strike a happy medium. Speak at a pace that engages the listeners and allows them time for reflection but without boring them.

Like volume, rate variations may be underused or totally absent. If you speak at the same rate throughout the entire speech, you are not making use of one of your most important speech assets. Use variations in rate to call a listener's attention to certain points and to add variety. If you speak of the dull routine of an assemblyline worker in a rapid and varied pace and of the wonder of a circus in a pace with absolutely no variation, you are surely misusing this important vocal dimension. Again, if you are interested in and conscious of what you are saying, your rate variations should flow naturally and effectively. Too predictable a rate pattern is sometimes as bad as no variation at all. If the audience can predict—consciously or unconsciously—your rate pattern, you are in a vocal rut. You are not communicating ideas but words that you have memorized.

Pitch

Pitch refers to the relative highness or lowness of your voice as perceived by your listener. More technically, pitch results from the rate which your vocal folds vibrate. If they vibrate rapidly, listeners will perceive your voice as having a high pitch. If they vibrate slowly, they will perceive it as having a low pitch.

Pitch changes often signal changes in the meanings of many sentences. The most obvious is the difference between a statement and a question. Thus, the difference between the declarative sentence, "So this is the proposal you want me to support" and

---

TIPS FROM PROFESSIONAL SPEAKERS

Speaking a little faster than usual certainly beats talking too slow. Fast-paced talking requires keener listening and will make the audience pay more attention. It also gives them the subliminal message that this speech is not going to go on all day and all night. You don't want to sound like an auctioneer, but pick up the pace a little more than your regular conversational speech. Talking too fast is the biggest complaint I get—especially from the elderly. But the majority like the machine-gun fire approach that I use, so I just make sure I slow down for older audiences. (But make sure that when you do slow down, you don't talk down!)

Another benefit of a fast-paced dialogue is that when you do slow down, or stop dead, the audience is alerted to the fact that "this must be important." It's a great way to emphasize.

Don Aslett, writer and professional speaker. *Is There a Speech Inside You?* (Cincinnati, Ohio: Writer's Digest Books, 1989), p. 70.

the question "So this is the proposal you want me to support?" is inflection or pitch. This, of course, is obvious. But note also that, depending on where the inflectional change is placed, the meaning of the sentence changes drastically. Consider the following sentences, where the higher pitch is symbolized by italics:

■ Is *this* the proposal you want me to support?
■ Is this the *proposal* you want me to support?
■ Is this the proposal you want *me* to support?
■ Is this the proposal you want me to *support*?

They are all questions, but note that they all differ in the question they ask.

The obvious problems of pitch are pitch levels that are too high, too low, and too patterned. Neither of the first two problems is common in speakers with otherwise normal voices. You can correct a pitch pattern that is too predictable or monotonous with practice. With practice, pitch changes will come naturally from the sense of what you are saying. Because each sentence is somewhat different from every other sentence, there should be a normal variation—a variation that results not from some predetermined pattern but rather from the meanings you wish to convey to the audience.

REMEMBER: to combat the major voice problems:

1. volume—an overly soft or overly loud voice, an unvaried volume level, and fading away at ends of sentences
2. rate—too rapid or too slow a rate, too little variation, and too predictable a rate pattern
3. pitch—an overly high or low pitch, a pitch pattern that is monotonous, and a pitch pattern that is predictable

■■■■ ARTICULATION AND PRONUNCIATION

Articulation and pronunciation are similar in that they both refer to enunciation, the way in which we produce sounds and words. They differ, however, in a technical sense. *Articulation* refers to the movements the speech organs make as they modify and interrupt the air stream you send from the lungs. Different movements of these speech organs (for example, the tongue, lips, teeth, palate, and vocal cords) produce different sounds. *Pronunciation* refers to the production of syllables or words according to some accepted standard, identified in any good dictionary.

Our concern here is not with technical distinctions, but with identifying and correcting some of the most common problems associated with faulty articulation and pronunciation.

Articulation Problems

The three major articulation problems are omission, substitution, and addition of sounds or syllables.

Errors of Omission Omitting sounds or even syllables is a major articulation problem but is one we can easily overcome with concentration and practice. Here are some examples:

Not This	This
gov-a-ment	gov-ern-ment
hi-stry	hi-story
wanna	want to
fishin	fishing
studyin	studying
a-lum-num	a-lum-i-num
hon-orble	hon-or-able
comp-ny	comp-a-ny
vul-ner-bil-ity	vul-ner-a-bil-ity

Errors of Substitution Substituting an incorrect sound for the correct one is another easily corrected problem. Among the most popular are substituting *d* for *t* and *d* for *th*. Here are a few examples:

Not This	This
wader	waiter
dese	these
ax	ask
undoubtebly	undoubtedly
beder	better

Other types of substitution errors include these:

Not This	This
ekcetera	etcetera
ramark	remark
lenth	length

Errors of Addition When we make errors of addition, we add sounds where they do not belong. Some examples include:

Not This	This
acrost	across
athalete	athlete
Americer	America
idear	idea
filim	film
lore	law

If you make any of these errors, you can easily correct them by following these steps:

- become conscious of your own articulation patterns (and the specific errors you might be making)
- listen carefully to the articulation of prominent speakers (for example, broadcasters)
- practice the correct patterns until they become part of your normal speech behavior

Pronunciation Problems

Among the most popular pronunciation problems are accented the wrong syllable and pronouncing sounds that should remain silent.

Errors of Accent Here are some common examples of words accenting incorrectly:

Not This	This
New Orleáns	*New Órleans*
ínsurance	*insúrance*
orátor	*órator*

Errors of Pronouncing Silent Sounds For some words, the acceptable pronunciation is *not* to pronounce certain sounds, as in the following examples:

Not This	This
often	*offen*
homage	*omage*
Illinois	*Illinoi*
evening	*evning*
burgalar	*burglar*
athalete	*athlete*
airaplane	*airplane*

The best way to deal with pronunciation problems is to look up any words whose pronunciation you are not sure of in a good dictionary. Learn to read the pronunciation key for your dictionary, and make it a practice to look up words you hear others use that seem to be pronounced incorrectly or that you wish to use yourself but are not sure how to pronounce.

REMEMBER: **the major problems in articulation and pronunciation:**
1. **errors of omission**
2. **errors of substitution**
3. **errors of addition**

"You've been swallowing too many pebbles while practicing your diction, Demosthenes—now don't go in the water!"

Courtesy saro.

4. errors of accent
5. errors of pronouncing silent sounds

PAUSES

Pauses come in two basic types: filled and unfilled. *Filled pauses* are pauses in the stream of speech that we fill with vocalizations such as *-er, -um, -ah,* and the like. Even expressions such as *well* and *you know,* when used just to fill up silence, are called filled pauses. These pauses are ineffective and weaken the strength of your message. They will make you appear hesitant, unprepared, and unsure of yourself.

Unfilled pauses are silences interjected into the normally fluent stream of speech. Unfilled pauses can be especially effective if used correctly. Here are just a few examples of places where unfilled pauses—silences of a few seconds—should prove effective.

1. Pause at transitional points. This will signal that you are moving from one part of the speech to another or from one idea to another. It will help the listeners separate the main issues you are discussing.

2. Pause at the end of an important assertion. This will allow the audience time to think about the significance of what you are saying.

3. Pause after asking a rhetorical question. This will provide the necessary time so the audience can think of how they would answer the question.

4. Pause before an important idea. This will help signal that what comes next is especially significant.

In addition, pauses are helpful before beginning your speech and after you have concluded your speech. Do not start speaking as soon as you get to the front of the room; rather, pause to scan the audience and to gather your thoughts. Also, do not leave the podium as you speak your last word; pause to allow your speech to sink in and avoid giving the audience the impression that you are anxious to leave them.

Like most good things, pauses can be overdone. Used in moderation, however, they can be powerful aids to comprehension and persuasion.

REMEMBER: Pauses may serve a number of significant functions:

1. to signal a transition between the major parts of the speech, or between major propositions or items of supporting material

2. to allow the audience time to think

3. to allow the audience to ponder a rhetorical question

4. to signal the approach of a particularly important idea

BODILY ACTION

Your body is a powerful instrument in your speech. You speak with your body as well as with your mouth. The total effect of the speech depends not only on what you say but also on the way you present it. It depends on your movements, gestures, and facial expressions as well as your words.

Six aspects of bodily action are especially important in public speaking: eye contact, facial expression, posture, gestures, movement, and proxemics.

Eye Contact

The most important single aspect of bodily communication is eye contact. The two major problems with eye contact are not enough eye contact and eye contact that does not cover the audience fairly. Speakers who do not maintain enough eye contact appear distant, unconcerned, and less trustworthy than speakers who look directly at their audience. And, of course, without eye contact, you will not be able to secure that all-important audience feedback.

Maintain eye contact with the entire audience. Involve all listeners in the public speaking transaction. Communicate equally with the members on the left and on the right, in both the back and the front.

Use eye contact to secure audience feedback. Are they interested? Bored? Puzzled? In agreement? In disagreement? Use your eyes to communicate your commit-

What aspects of bodily action do you feel you need to improve? How will you go about improving these aspects?

ment to and interest in what you're saying. Communicate your confidence and commitment by making direct eye contact; avoid staring blankly through your audience or glancing over their heads, at the floor, or out the window.

Facial Expression

Facial expressions are especially important in communicating emotions—your anger and fear, boredom and excitement, doubt and surprise. If you feel committed to and believe in your thesis, you will probably display your meanings appropriately and effectively.

TIPS FROM PROFESSIONAL SPEAKERS

Your eyes make the first electrical connection with your audience. They turn on the current. The current is strengthened by an animated smile. Don't just look *at* people; look into their eyes. Give them, in turn, a few moments to take you in with *their* eyes before they have to put their ears to work.

Dorothy Sarnoff, speech consultant and trainer and developer of the "Speech Dynamics and Cosmetics" course. *Speech Can Change Your Life* (New York: Dell, 1970), p. 213.

Nervousness and anxiety, however, may at times prevent you from relaxing enough so that your emotions come through. With time and practice, however, you will relax, and the emotions you feel will reveal themselves appropriately and automatically.

Posture

When delivering your speech, stand straight but not stiff. Try to communicate a command of the situation without communicating the discomfort that is actually quite common for beginning speakers.

Avoid the common mistakes of posture: avoid putting your hands in your pockets, avoid leaning on the desk, the podium, or the chalkboard. With practice you will come to feel more at ease and will communicate this by the way you stand before the audience.

Gestures

Gestures in public speaking help illustrate your verbal messages. We do this regularly in conversation. For example, when saying "Come here," you probably move your head, hands, arms, and perhaps your entire body to motion the listener in your direction—your body as well as your verbal message say "Come here."

Avoid using your hands to preen, for example, fixing your hair or adjusting your clothing. Avoid fidgeting with your watch, ring, or jewelry. Avoid keeping your hands in your pockets or clasped in front or behind your back.

Effective bodily action is spontaneous and natural to you as the speaker, to your audience, and to your speech. If they seem planned or rehearsed, they'll appear phony and insincere. As a general rule, don't do anything with your hands that doesn't feel right for *you*; the audience will recognize them as unnatural. If you feel relaxed and comfortable with yourself and your audience, you will generate natural bodily action without conscious and studied attention.

Movement

Movement refers here to your large bodily movements. It helps to move around a bit. It keeps both the audience and you more alert. Even when speaking behind a lectern, you can give the illusion of movement. You can step back or forward or flex your upper body so it appears that you are moving more than you are.

Avoid these three problems of movement: too little, too much, and too patterned movement. Speakers who move too little often appear strapped to the podium, afraid of the audience, or too disinterested to involve themselves fully. With too much movement, the audience begins to concentrate on the movement itself, wondering where the speaker will wind up next. With too patterned a movement, the audience may become bored—too steady and predictable a rhythm quickly becomes tiring. The audience will often view the speaker as nonspontaneous and uninvolved.

Use gross movements to emphasize transitions and to emphasize the introduction of a new and important assertion. Thus, when making a transition, you might take a step forward to signal that something new is coming. Similarly, this type of movement may signal the introduction of an important assumption, bit of evidence, or closely reasoned argument.

Proxemics

Proxemics refers to the way you use space in communication. In public speaking the space between you and your listeners and among the listeners themselves is often a crucial factor. If you stand too close to the audience, they might feel uncomfortable, as if their personal space is being violated. If you stand too far away from your audience, you might be perceived as uninvolved, uninterested, and uncomfortable. Watch where your instructor and other speakers stand and adjust your own position accordingly.

REMEMBER: these general guidelines to effective use of bodily action:

1. maintain eye contact with your entire audience
2. think and feel what you are saying, and allow your facial expressions to convey these feelings
3. use your posture to communicate your command of the public speaking experience
4. gesture naturally—neither too much nor too little
5. move around a bit, avoiding too little, too much, and too patterned a movement
6. position yourself neither too close nor too far away from your audience, and try to keep audience members relatively close to each other

REHEARSAL: PRACTICING AND IMPROVING DELIVERY

Effective public speaking delivery does not come naturally—it takes practice. Learn now how to use your practice time most effectively and efficiently.

The goal of practice is to develop a delivery that will help you achieve the purposes of your speech. Rehearsal should enable you to see how the speech will flow as a whole and to make any changes and improvements you think necessary. Through practice you will learn the speech effectively and determine how best to present it to your audience. The following procedures should assist you in using your time most effectively.

Rehearse the Speech as a Whole Rehearse the speech from beginning to end. Do not rehearse the speech in parts. Rehearse it from getting out of your seat through the introduction, body, and conclusion, to returning to your seat. Be sure to rehearse the speech with all the examples and illustrations (and audiovisual aids if any) included. This will enable you to connect the parts of the speech and to see how they interact with each other.

Time the Speech Time the speech during each rehearsal. Make the necessary adjustments on the basis of this timing.

Approximate the Actual Speech Situation Rehearse the speech under conditions as close as possible to those under which you will deliver it. If possible, rehearse the speech in the same room in which you will present it. If this is impossible, try to simulate the actual conditions as close as you can—in your living room or even bathroom. If possible, rehearse the speech in front of a few supportive listeners. It is always helpful (but especially for your beginning speeches) that your listeners be supportive rather than too critical. Merely having listeners present during your rehearsal will further simulate the conditions under which you will eventually speak. Get together with two or three other students in an empty classroom where you can each serve as speaker and listener.

See Yourself as a Speaker Rehearse the speech in front of a full-length mirror. This will enable you to see yourself and to see how you will appear to the audience. This may be extremely difficult at first, and you may have to force yourself to watch. After a few attempts, however, you will begin to see the value of this experience. Practice your eye contact, your movements, and your gestures in front of the mirror.

Incorporate Changes and Make Delivery Notes Make any changes in the speech that seem appropriate between rehearsals. Do not interrupt your rehearsal to make notes or changes. If you do, you may never experience the entire speech from beginning to end. While making these changes, note too any words whose pronunciation or articulation you wish to check. Also, insert pause notations ("slow down" warnings, and other delivery suggestions) into your outline.

If possible, record your speech (ideally, on videotape) so you can hear exactly what your listeners will hear: your volume, rate, pitch, articulation and pronunciation, and pauses. You will thus be in a better position to improve these qualities.

Rehearse Often Rehearse the speech as often as seems necessary. Two useful guides are: (1) rehearse the speech at least three or four times, less than this is sure to be too little; (2) rehearse the speech as long as your rehearsals result in improvements in the speech or in your delivery.

A Long-Term Delivery Improvement Program

Presented here is a general improvement program that should be of value in dealing with long-term improvements. In reviewing these suggestions remember that your goal is to deliver a public speech with a conversational quality. You want to communicate your confidence, your enthusiasm, and your sincere concern for your listeners.

Approach your long-term delivery program with positive thinking. This will help a great deal in setting up an attitude that will help you become a truly effective public speaker. Tell yourself that you can do it and that you will do it.

1. Seek feedback from someone whose opinion and insight you respect. Your public speaking instructor may be a logical choice, but someone majoring in communication might also be appropriate. Get an honest and thorough appraisal of both your voice and your bodily action.

2. Learn to hear, see, and feel the differences between effective and ineffective patterns. Learn to hear, for example, the patterned nature of your pitch or

your too-loud volume. An audio recorder will be very helpful. Learn to feel your rigid posture or your lack of arm and hand gestures. Once you have perceived these differences, concentrate on learning more effective patterns. Practice a few minutes each day. Avoid becoming too conscious of any source of ineffectiveness. Just try to increase your awareness and work on one problem at a time. Do not try to change all your patterns at once.

3. Seek additional feedback on the changes. Make certain that listeners see and hear the new patterns you are practicing as more effective. Remember that you hear yourself through air transmission as well as through bone conduction. Others hear you only through air transmission, so what you hear and what others hear will be different. Similarly, there are great differences between what you can see and feel of your own bodily action and what others can see and feel.

4. For voice improvement, consult a book for practice exercises and for additional information on the nature of volume, rate, pitch, and quality.

5. If any of these difficulties persist, see a professional. For voice problems, see a speech clinician. Most campuses have a speech clinic. You can easily avail yourself of their services. For bodily action difficulties, talk with your public speaking instructor.

Seek professional help if you are psychologically uncomfortable with any aspect of your voice or your bodily action. It may be that all you have to do is to hear yourself or see yourself on a videotape—as others see and hear you—to convince yourself that you sound and look just fine. Regardless of what is causing this discomfort, however, if you are uncomfortable, do something about it. In a college community there is more assistance available to you at no cost than you will ever experience again. Make use of it.

REMEMBER: Rehearsal is essential to improvement, therefore:

1. establish your rehearsal goals: time the speech; perfect your volume, rate, and pitch; check your articulation and pronunciation; incorporate pauses and other delivery notes at appropriate places; and perfect your bodily action

2. follow these tested rehearsal procedures: rehearse the speech as a whole, time the speech at each rehearsal, approximate the actual speech situation, see yourself as a speaker, incorporate changes and delivery notes, and rehearse often

3. undertake a long-term delivery program: seek feedback; learn to hear, see, and feel the different patterns; seek additional feedback on changes; consult additional sources for more detailed information; seek professional assistance for persistent problems

CRITICALLY SPEAKING

1. How would you describe your own speaking voice in terms of volume, rate, pitch, and quality? Which aspects are you pleased with? Which aspects do you feel need work?

2. What voice problems do you hear most often in your college instructors? How might these be remedied?

3. What happens in the minds of listeners when speakers fail to pause sufficiently? What happens when speakers pause too often or for too long a time?

4. How would you describe the bodily action of talk show hosts like Phil Donahue, Oprah Winfrey, Jay Leno, Sally Jesse Raphaël, or Geraldo Rivera? How would you describe your own bodily action when speaking?

5. Can eye contact or facial expressions ever be used too extensively and actually work against the speaker? How?

6. Have you discovered any useful rehearsal suggestions that might be of value to others?

PRACTICALLY SPEAKING

24.1   COMMUNICATING VOCALLY BUT NONVERBALLY

This exercise is designed to give you practice in communicating effectively with your voice and body. In this exercise a subject recites the alphabet attempting to communicate each of the following emotions:

anger	nervousness
fear	pride
happiness	sadness
jealousy	satisfaction
love	sympathy

The subject may begin the alphabet at any point and may omit and repeat sounds, but the subject may use only the names of the letters of the alphabet to communicate these feelings.

The subject should first number the emotions in random order so that he or she will have a set order to follow that is not known to the audience, whose task it will be to guess the emotions expressed.

As a variation, have the subject go through the entire list of emotions twice: once facing the audience and employing any nonverbal signals desired, and once with his or her back to the audience without employing any additional signals. Are there differences in the number of correct guesses depending on which method is used? Why?

After the exercise is completed, consider some or all of the following questions:

1. What vocal cues are used to communicate the various emotions?

2. Are some cues useful for communicating some emotions and not useful (or even detrimental) for communicating others? Explain.

3. What bodily cues are useful in communicating these various emotions?

4. Are some bodily cues useful for communicating some emotions and not useful for others? Explain.

5. Are there significant gender differences for effectively communicating these emotions? That is, should men and women use different cues in communicating these emotions?

24.2 COMMUNICATING BY HANDSHAKE

The purpose of this exercise is to identify some of the meanings communicated by the handshake and some of the nonverbal behaviors that accompany different types of handshakes, and to heighten awareness of the messages our own handshakes may communicate to others.

Divide the class into groups of four persons.

Before reading any further, all four members should shake hands so that each member shakes hands with each other member at least once.

Designate two members as observers and two as performers (A and B). Performer A will serve as the principal subject or "actor," while Performer B will serve as the "recipient" of the handshake message. The two observers should watch the interaction carefully and then record their observations.

The procedures are as follows: Performer A should read the list of feeling states provided below and shake hands with Performer B while role-playing each of these feeling states. Performer B should note mentally how he or she felt about each handshake.

After all five feeling states have been portrayed, Performer B becomes the "actor" and Performer A becomes the "recipient." The procedure is then repeated. Next, the observers become performers and the procedure is again repeated until each person has served as actor, recipient, and observer.

After all interactions have been completed, the observers' reactions should be discussed along with the feedback from the recipients.

Feeling States

1. I'm feeling nervous and uncomfortable in this setting.
2. I'm totally in control of myself and of the situation; I feel confident and perfectly at ease.
3. I feel down, depressed; I have a low self-concept and generally think of myself as inadequate.
4. I like you and I want you to like me.
5. I want you to think of me as friendly, outgoing, and an all-around good person.

■ PART FIVE CHECKLISTS

Performance Checklist: Evaluating Your Style and Delivery

YES   **NO**   Have you:

☐   ☐   1. Used language that is appropriate in terms of directness, level of abstraction, objectivity, formality, and accuracy?

☐   ☐   2. Used an oral rather than a written style?

☐   ☐   3. Followed the principles of relevance, brevity, spontaneity, tastefulness, and appropriateness in using humor?

☐   ☐   4. Chosen words that are clear? Vivid? Appropriate? Personal? Forceful?

☐   ☐   5. Phrased your sentences so they are short, direct, active, positive, and varied in type?

☐   ☐   6. Built in aids to make your speech easy to remember such as stressing relevance, creating associations, patterning the message, and focusing audience attention?

☐   ☐   7. Rehearsed a method of delivery (impromptu, manuscript, memory, or extemporaneous) appropriate to the occasion?

☐   ☐   8. Achieved a delivery that is natural? Reinforces the message? Varied? Conversational?

☐   ☐   9. Rehearsed using notes effectively—with "open subtlety"?

☐   ☐   10. Practiced the speech using vocal volume, rate, pitch, and pauses to reinforce your message? Avoided the common voice problems?

☐   ☐   11. Avoided the common pronunciation and articulation errors?

☐   ☐   12. Rehearsed bodily action so that it reinforces your message? Eye contact? Facial expressions? Posture? Gestures? Movement? Proxemics?

Critical Thinking Checklist: Thinking Critically About Style and Delivery

YES	NO	Do you:
☐	☐	1. Analyze language choices in terms of directness, abstraction, objectivity, and formality, and use language that is most appropriate to your message and audience (Unit 21)?
☐	☐	2. Distinguish between oral and written language and use the language most appropriate to the specific communication task (Unit 21)?
☐	☐	3. Express ideas clearly—with economy, specific terms, guide phrases, short and familiar terms, and appropriate repetition and restatement (Unit 22)?
☐	☐	4. Express ideas so that they are easy for listeners to remember (for example, stress relevance, create associations, pattern your messages, and focus audience attention) (Unit 22)?
☐	☐	5. Deliver a message with appropriate voice and bodily action (Units 23 and 24)?

Appendix:
Thinking Critically
About Speeches

Here are four very different speeches, all models of excellence. Two speeches are by college students:

- Joey Callow's (Reynolds and Schnoor, 1991) is an informative speech dealing with micromachines
- Shelley Schnathorst's (Boaz and Brey, 1988) is a persuasive speech dealing with the need for regulating medical devices

Two speeches are by professional speakers:

- Martin Luther King, Jr.'s "I Have a Dream," one of the best-known speeches of our time, focuses on civil rights
- William J. Banach's (1991) "Are You Too Busy to Think?" focuses on critical thinking and the need to raise questions even about widely held assumptions

Along with each speech is a series of questions to provide some initial structure for thinking critically about speeches. The questions are numbered to make it easier to refer to these in small group or general class discussions. The questions focus on a variety of critical thinking skills:

- **Identification** or **discovery** questions ask you to examine a portion of the speech and identify the means used by the speaker to accomplish some aim; for example, How did the speaker gain attention? What thought pattern did the speaker use? What forms of reasoning did the speaker rely on?

- **Evaluation** questions are both specific and general. **Specific evaluation** questions ask that you examine a particular section and evaluate how effectively the speaker handled a task; for example, How effectively did the speaker support an argument? How effective was the orientation? Did the speaker effectively relate the topic to the specific audience? **General evaluation** questions ask you to make an overall assessment of the speech; for example, Did the speaker accomplish his or her aim? Was the speech an effective one?

- **Problem-solving** or **application** questions ask that you place yourself in the role of the speaker and consider how you would deal with specific issues; for example, If this speech was addressed to your class, what changes would the speaker have to make in the examples used? Would the organizational pattern the speaker used prove effective with your class?

473

The following suggestions will help you get the most out of your reading-thinking:

1. First, read the speech all the way through, ignoring the questions
2. After you have read through the entire speech, quickly read through the questions to give yourself a broad overview of the areas focused on
3. Read the speech in brief sections and respond to the questions keyed to these sections
4. Think too about these general issues:
   a. What principle is the speaker following or violating?
   b. How might the speaker have accomplished his or her aim more effectively? What could the speaker have done better?
   c. What adjustments or changes would the speaker have had to make if he or she was speaking to other audiences, say, for example, to your class?
   d. What rhetorical devices or techniques can you identify that might prove useful to you as a public speaker?

Use these speeches as learning tools, as models. What can you learn from these speeches that will help you in your own public speaking?

Informative Speech

Joey Callow, *Miami University*

One of the primary functions of the introduction is to gain attention and to focus it on the topic of the speech. (1) What method did Callow use to gain attention? (2) How effectively was this done?

Remember the old saying, "Little things mean a lot?" The one that's become associated with the cheapest presents? [laughter] Or the hugs and handshakes of friends instead of sweaters and Swatches on our birthday? [laughter] Well, no more, for today little things do mean a lot. In fact some little things mean a multibillion dollar industry in the next few years. Things capable of repairing electrical circuits, creating safer nuclear power plants, and changing medicine and medical technology as we know it today. Little things called micromachines. Miniaturized mechanical devices such as heaters, springs, tongs, (unintelligible) even electrical motors built to the size of one-fifth the width of a human hair. According to Dr. George Hazelring of the National Science Foundation, micromachines have people walking around bug-eyed thinking about what the future holds. The electronics revolution of the '70s and '80s can be copied—and even surpassed—by the micromechanical revolution of the 1990s and beyond. Little things do mean a great deal. And it's time for us to put our eyes back in our sockets and turn to the microscope [laughter]

The second major function is to create a speaker-audience-topic connection. (3) Did the speaker do this?

(4) How would you evaluate this topic if the speech were given in your class? (5) Is it worthwhile? Appropriate to your class? Sufficiently narrow in scope?

to explore this fascinating world of micromachines. First we're going to simply look at the basis and excitement surrounding these devices. Second, focus on some commercial applications of micromachines that are already prevalent in our daily lives. Finally, turn our microscope into a time machine and view some slides to see what the future holds for all of us. Only then will we truly realize the revolution that is underway and grasp the big picture created by these little machines.

Basically, micromachines are simply machines built at the microscopic level. [laughter] In our quest to change cumbersome computers into portable pc's, engineers have discovered a technology which makes common, everyday devices to sizes of 15/100 microns of a micro—or 1/10 of a millimeter at best. At such measurements, micromachines operate and function though they may be invisible to the naked eye.

Machines such as mechanical gears, built with a special process using silicon, so small individual red blood cells can fit between these mechanical teeth. A larger, but still simple pair of tongs, barely big enough to grasp onto a human hair, will be the standard. What makes these micromachines even more impressive, according to *Popular Mechanics*, July 1988, is that each micromachine can cost less than 1/10 of a cent to produce. In actuality, thousands of micromachines can fit into a square inch and cost only a few dollars.

Adding to the excitement surrounding these micromachines is the development of a micromotor, tiny turbines run by static electricity. While rubbing a rubber comb on wool seems insignificant to us, according to Ken Gabriel of AT&T Laboratories right here in Hofield, New Jersey, at the micro level it is enough power to run simple circuitry, start the rotary engine that will spin at half the speed of sound, and it will be in 1/10 of a millisecond. With their size, cost, and new power source, micromachines are creating a whole new line of products with a varying degree of functions, and will allow operations to take place on scales that until recently were not possible.

Perhaps the idea of living with invisible machines sounds, well, ominous, complicated. But all of us have already been affected by these amazing devices. Micromachines have done many commercial applications— medical equipment, automotive operations, and nuclear power plants. According to Kirk Peterson, executive vice-president of (unintelligible) of Fremont, California, mil-

The third major function is to orient the audience. (6) What method does Callow use to accomplish this orientation? How effectively does Callow accomplish this?

(7) What is the thesis of this speech? Would this thesis be appropriate for your class as an audience? Does Callow explicitly identify his thesis or does he leave it only implied?

(8) What is the specific purpose? Is this purpose sufficiently narrow for a speech of this length? (9) Did the speaker accomplish his purpose (assume you were a member of the audience)?

(10) What are the major propositions of this speech? How effectively are they derived from the thesis? Are they effectively highlighted?

(11) What organizational pattern does Callow use? Is this effective? Would you have used the same pattern for your class?

(12) Were the sources used sufficient to support the propositions the speaker advances? What types of source material would you have liked to see used more extensively?

(13) What types of supporting materials would you have used?

(14) What means does Callow use to involve his audience? How does he relate his speech directly to the needs and wants of his audience?

(15) How does Callow try to communicate an excitement about micromachines? How effectively does he do this?

(16) Does Callow use language effectively? Is his language clear? Personal? Vivid? Forceful? Immediate? Can you supply examples to support your conclusions about Callow's use of language? Would you offer any suggestions for using language more effectively?

(17) How effectively did Callow use humor? Is the humor relevant, brief, spontaneous in appearance, tasteful, and appropriate? Do you have any suggestions for making Callow's humor more effective?

lions of micromachines are in use everywhere, in blood pressure measuring devices, in air intake systems, and electronically fuel-injected cars. In both cases, the micromachines serve as sensors, measuring changes in air pressure that causes either the mercury, the column, or the gas intake in your engine, to function accordingly. The automobile industry is not stopping there. They're adapting these same micromachines in the new air bag systems as well. According to July 7, 1988 *New York Times,* it's the micromachines that will automatically determine when the air bags open whenever there is a specific drop in acceleration. And as is the case with the air bag system, protect the driver from serious injuries. When I spoke to Dr. George Hazenbake of the National Science Foundation, he explained to me how German scientists are adapting these same micromachines to create safer nuclear power plants. They separate lighter forms of uranium used in creating nuclear power from the heavier forms of the element that only causes destabilization at the reactor core. Surprisingly enough, micromachines that we've never seen are monitoring, aiding, and protecting the personal health and safety of millions of people that take their blood pressure, drive new cars, and (unintelligible). And yet these micromachines are the most basic types available. Static electric motors as a new power source are instigating the more important movable micromechanical revolution in the next 12 months alone, especially in the personal, industrial, and medical fields. Because of their relative cost, micromachines will have a major impact on the personal housegoods, from watches that cost less than a penny to produce, to major household appliances reduced in both size and cost. Rodney Brooks, of MIT's Artificial Intelligence Laboratory, is working on a micromechanical vacuum, about 4 to 6 inches in length, and all the power of today's larger appliance. Until you drop it on the floor and the independent machine seeks and vacuums. [laughter] Sort of like a giant, silvery, mechanical roach that can roam around your house without your knowledge, yet with more of a fairly useful purpose. [laughter] Well while we're not asking for further roaches to stay underground, according to Neal Flynn, presenter of the microbotic workshop in November 1987, these micromachines have some industrial applications as well. According to Flynn, underground electrical cables, that can sometimes take days to find and fix, can be sought out and repaired by our friends in only a few hours. The microrobot measures current using its mechanical legs. When it reaches the break, it extends its body across the fault, reestablishing the connection and literally becoming a piece of that electric wire.

But however impressive these applications in personal households and industries may seem, perhaps the most important application is coming in the medical field in the next year. Hundreds of micromachines can fit into a capsule the size of an aspirin and can be simply swallowed—no incision, and no (unintelligible). Once inside the body, they can be programmed to come up anywhere they're needed—insulin regulators and nitroglycerine patches, for diabetes and heart patients will be fixed internally, as needed when a micromachine performs the appropriate functions. The November 30, 1987, *Newsweek* points out that tiny scissors with electronic eyes just like an electronic pac-man, will travel through your arteries, [laughter] chomping away cholesterol and other forms of impurities that cause heart attacks and other problems. With the help of a computer mouse-like hook-up doctors can perform surgical techniques more accurately than any fiberoptic technologies medically. With the help of those electronic eyes, doctors will actually be inside the body, cutting away polyps from the colon, (unintelligible) and removing cancerous tumors from the brain. The silicon that I mentioned earlier, that all micromachines are made of, is also inert to all biological systems. Translated into common terms, just as a microrobot can extend itself to repair an electrical wire, micromachines can extend themselves to repair ulcers of the stomach, broken arterial walls, or even tissues of the human heart with no adverse effects on the rest of the body. Long hospital stays and large hospital bills are a thing of the past. Micromachines work just as effectively by lying in the soft (unintelligible) for a few hours, giving new meaning to the doctor's phrase "Take two pills and call me in the morning." [laughter] Medical technology as we know it today will be completely transformed by our micromechanical applications.

From measuring of blood pressure to cleaning out the buttresses, from preventing injuries from automobiles, to deaths from heart attacks and cancer, micromachines are only beginning to establish themselves as the most important development of the 1990s and beyond. After examining their basis, focusing on some commercial applications,

(18) Does Callow establish the credibility of his sources? (19) What is the most important dimension of credibility for sources such as Callow uses, that is, competence, moral character, or charisma?

(20) Did Callow establish his own credibility? How? For example, does he establish his competence, moral character, or charisma? (21) Which is the most important aspect of credibility in this situation?

This speech is not titled. (22) What would you title it?

(23) How effectively does Callow follow the principles of informative speaking? (24) Does he limit the amount of information he presents? (25) Does he stress relevance and usefulness? (26) Does he present information on the appropriate level (use your own class as the target audience in answering this question)? (27) Does he relate new information to old? (28) Does he present information through several senses? (29) Does he vary the level of abstraction appropriately?

One of the two major functions of the conclusion (in an informative speech) is to summarize the thesis or major points of the speech. (30) Does Callow do this effectively? The other function is to bring the speech to a definite close. (31) Does Callow do this effectively?

(32) What is your overall evaluation of this speech? That is, if this speech were given in your class what grade would you give it? (33) What is the major

strength of this speech as you see it? (34) What is the major weakness? How might this weakness have been corrected?

and viewing some slides of what the future holds for all of us, it seems clear that these little things will soon be having a big, big impact. Because little things can mean a lot.

This speech won as best informative speech in the 1989 National Forensic Association's Individual Events Tournament. It is reprinted from *1989 Championship Debates and Speeches*, © 1989 American Forensic Association, ed. Christina L. Reynolds and Larry G. Schnoor (Fargo, ND: North Dakota State University, 1991), pp. 70–72. Reprinted by permission of the American Forensic Association.

Persuasive Speech

Shelley Schnathorst, *University of Northern Iowa*

*I*n Roman times the Latin phrase "caveat emptor" or "let the buyer beware" was an appropriate warning to the citizens of that time. In the United States today we pride ourselves on a system which protects consumers from dangerous products. And while we understand that we still have responsibilities in our own protection, we have come to trust the safety of the products we must use. But for thousands of people each year that trust is misplaced. They are the ones who use medical devices ranging from x-rays to incubators and pacemakers to prostheses.

There are over 1,600 different types of medical devices in use today by virtually every patient who enters a doctor's office for tests or a hospital for operations. Although the range of medical devices may seem broad, they are all subject to the medical regulatory system.

The Food and Drug Administration, or the FDA, has been given responsibility to approve medical devices. Yet Representative Henry Waxman of California stated on May 4th of 1987 that "only a handful have actually been so approved." Because most devices have not gone through rigorous approval processes, they present enormous hazards to us. In testifying before the House of Representatives on May 5th of last year, Stephen Ferguson, President of one of the world's largest manufacturers of medical devices stated, "Everyone in this room will someday want one of the devices we have under development, as the best available choice for yourselves or someone you know." So that we can improve the safety of

Of all the speeches included here this is the most difficult. It deals, in a relatively sophisticated way, with a topic about which most people know very little. (1) If this speech were given in your class, would you consider this too complex? If so, what would you do to make it simpler and easier to understand?

(2) What type of introduction did Schnathorst use? Does this introduction gain your attention? Establish a speaker-audience-topic connection? Orient the audience?

(3) Does Schnathorst avoid the common faults of introductions: apology, hollow promises, pretending, prefacing?

(4) In what way does Schnathorst establish the importance of the topic? How would you have done this?

those choices, we need to look at the importance of regulating medical devices, flaws in current regulations, and finally workable solutions to insure that we are adequately protected.

Adequate regulation is essential for two reasons. First and foremost, medical devices are often critical to the health and survival of individuals. By definition, a medical device is any instrument or apparatus intended to prevent, diagnose, or treat a human illness or disorder. And of course, when we seek the help of a doctor or a hospital, we hope that the devices they use will make us better, and we trust that they will not make us worse. Yet sometimes devices that are considered life supporting become life threatening.

John Villforth an FDA administrator reported in a May 1986 *FDA Consumer* that a heart resuscitation unit failed when the machine, like many of its type, had no warning device to indicate that the batteries powering units were defective. In addition, a July 2, 1987 segment of "20/20" reported that investigators discovered a flaw in the Therac 25, a radiation machine used in the treatment of cancer. Each of the three patients interviewed complained of being burned by the machine. After the loss of two lives, investigations led to the discovery of a computer program error which had given some patients forty-five times the amount of radiation requested. As amateurs in health care, we cannot be expected to have a clear understanding of every medical device and its hazards. Yet, our lives are at stake.

A second reason for adequate regulation was described by Representative Waxman, who is chairman of the House Subcommittee on Medical Devices. He stated that unlike a consumer product such as a child's toy, or even a Toyota, which can be recalled, it is more difficult to deal with medical devices for often times they have been implanted into a human body. Consider the case of Constance Walters, who testified in a video tape before House hearings. To correct a curvature in her spine, she had an operation in which a medical device called a Weiss spring was implanted into her back in February of last year. By April she was experiencing tremendous pain. The Weiss spring which had never been submitted for testing snapped inside her. As Walters said, "It is worse now, I can't be anybody. Do something so that someone else's life is not totally ruined like this."

(5) What is the thesis of this speech? Would this thesis be appropriate for your class?

(6) What is the general purpose? What is the specific purpose? Would the specific purpose be appropriate if this speech was given in your class? Was the specific purpose sufficiently narrow in scope? Did the speaker accomplish her aim?

(7) What organizational pattern is used in this speech? Is this pattern effective given the speaker's purpose? (8) Does Schnathorst use primacy or recency? (9) Climax or anticlimax order? Were the orders selected effective in achieving the speaker's purpose?

How effectively does Schnathorst apply the principles of persuasion? (10) Does she use the credibility principle? (11) The audience participation principle? (12) The inoculation principle? (13) The magnitude of change principle?

(14) What forms of reasoning does the speaker use? Specific instances? Analogy? Causes and effects? Sign? Is the reasoning sound? Does the evidence pass the tests for validity?

(15) What kinds of motivational appeals are used here? Are these effective?

(16) How effectively are the statistics used in this speech? (17) What other forms of supporting material are used? Are these effective in supporting Schnathorst's thesis? (18) Would you have preferred other types of supporting materials? Why?

(19) Are transitions used effectively? Where might more transitions be used? (20) What about internal summaries? How effective is this internal summary?

According to Waxman, the best solution is to have a system that provides reasonable assurance that devices are both safe and effective. Well, there is a law intended to provide such an assurance. However, that law, the Medical Device Amendment of 1976, is flawed itself.

In his May 4, 1987 testimony, Dr. Sidney Wolf, Director of the Public Citizen Health Research Group, outlined three specific flaws in current regulation. First, legislation requires that most devices meet FDA performance standards. The catch is the FDA has never devised any standards, and thus cannot regulate the devices.

In the absence of standards, the FDA relies upon Article (510K) of the Medical Device Amendment. (510K) allows a manufacturer to introduce a new device on the market simply by claiming it is substantially equivalent to devices on the market in 1976. There is no need to claim that the devices are any better than the devices in 1976, and the claims that are made go untested. Dr. Wolf stated that this second flaw is perhaps the biggest loophole in the law.

In fact, Representative Waxman noted that well over ninety-eight percent of the new medical devices that enter the market each year do so by claiming substantial equivalence rather than going through pre-market safety tests and reviews. What this means is that Americans continue to serve as guinea pigs for new medical devices. Constance Walters was a guinea pig, for the Weiss spring had never been submitted for testing.

Now the question that some of you may be asking is how common is such a problem. The third flaw in this system insures that we will never know the answer, for complete, systematic reporting of defects is not required. Now the law requires that manufacturers report defects directly to the FDA. But, hospitals, doctors, distributors, those who actually work with the devices are not mandated to report the defects to anyone. And for the information that is reported, a General Accounting Office study published in December of 1986 found that there is a funneling effect. They examined what happened to nearly 1,200 reports of medical device problems and found that because of the informality of the process and lack of required reporting, less than one percent of those problems ever reached FDA files.

Failure to develop standards, reliance on an equivalent standard instead, and finally incomplete reporting all combine to create inadequate protection. It is protection which Tama and James Jackson wish they had had when their firstborn baby, a baby boy, developed jaundice. The baby was placed in an illuminated hospital incubator which rid the child's body of the yellow coloration. The next day the incubator was empty. Their baby was found in intensive care with a fever of 106 degrees. The next morning, the Jackson's firstborn died. The cause of death, the incubator. With a broken thermostat and alarm and a defective on-off switch, the incubator literally became an oven. To prevent such horrors, immediate action needs to be taken. As is evident, current regulation must be modified.

(21) The example of the Jackson baby is a good example of mixing the levels of abstraction considered in Unit 21. How effective is this example in supporting Schnathorst's thesis?

First, the FDA should be required to develop the standards called for twelve years ago, so that the design of the device will be safe to begin with. For none of the examples that I have provided is an isolated malfunction, but rather a flaw in the design itself.

(22) Does Schnathorst establish her credibility? How? Is this sufficient? What suggestions would you offer for increasing speaker credibility?

Second, establishing design standards will close the (510K) loophole, and products won't be approved only because they are equivalent to devices in 1976. For as you well know, since 1976, improvements in medical technologies have occurred. Therefore, we should demand that such technologies be incorporated into new medical devices.

(23) Would you characterize the language of the speech as direct or indirect? Abstract or concrete? Objective or subjective? Formal or informal? Accurate or inaccurate? What specific elements can you identify to support your conclusions?

Third, reporting of defects should be mandated. Not just by manufacturers, but of course by doctors, hospitals, and distributors. This again should be standardized format of reporting. Now this proposal will work, for when reports of problems do reach the FDA they have been proven to be quite effective in protecting our interest. For example, when the FDA received reports of faulty sleep apnea monitors which help children prone to sudden infant death syndrome, they [were] able to respond quite quickly. The FDA received reports that faulty monitors had electrocuted one child and burned several others. With this information, the FDA was able to issue safety alerts to health care professionals, home users, sleep apnea support groups, and of course the manufacturers who could improve the device.

(24) Is the language used clear? Vivid? Appropriate to the audience (assume an audience like your class members) and topic? Personal? Forceful?

Currently, there is a bill before the House Subcommittee on Health, Environment and Energy. Although not yet in its final form, this bill will insure that necessary alterations be made in FDA regulations. It is this bill, HR 2595, which you should encourage your legislators to support.

(25) What do you remember most after reading this speech? What do you think you will remember from this speech next week? Next month? (26) What public speaking principle might you derive on the basis of what you remember now and what you think you'll remember later from this speech?

(27) What type of conclusion did Schnathorst use? Was this effective? (28) How effective was the quotation from Helen Keller? Did it effectively bring the speech to a crisp and definite close?

(29) What is your overall evaluation of this speech? That is, if this speech were given in your class, what grade would you give it? (30) What is the major strength of this speech as you see it? (31) What is the major weakness? How might this weakness have been corrected?

This is probably one of the most famous speeches of the twentieth century. Before reading the speech, examine what you know about this speech. What did you hear about it? Did you read it in elementary or high school or college? In what context? What image do you have of this speech?

One of the standards often used in evaluating speeches is that of universality—that is, to what extent does the speech address issues that are important for all time and for all people. This standard is

Again, although we cannot be expected to know everything about every medical device, there are times that we or someone we know will be using one. Therefore we need to trust the proverb, "let the buyer beware," and become more informed about such devices.

The 1976 bill was well-intentioned. However, after a decade of talk and no action, it is time that Congress with our assistance take serious steps in regulating this multi-billion dollar medical device industry. With timely action we can discover and correct what otherwise might be a fatal flaw. But we must act. For as Helen Keller once wrote, "Science may have found a cure for most evils, but it has found no remedy for the worst of them all, the apathy of human beings."

I Have a Dream

Martin Luther King, Jr.*

I am happy to join with you today in what will go down in history as the greatest demonstration for freedom in the history of our nation.

Five score years ago, a great American, in whose symbolic shadow we stand today, signed the Emancipation Proclamation. This momentous decree came as a great beacon light of hope to millions of Negro slaves, who had been seared in the flames of withering injustice. It came as a joyous daybreak to end the long night of their captivity.

But one-hundred years later, the Negro is still not free. One-hundred years later, the life of the Negro is still sadly crippled by the manacles of segregation and the

*Martin Luther King, Jr. (1929–1968), Baptist minister and civil rights leader, won the Nobel Prize in 1964 for his nonviolent struggle for racial equality. The following speech was delivered on August 28, 1963, at the Lincoln Memorial in Washington, D.C., to some 200,000 blacks and whites holding a demonstration. Some ten civil rights leaders—after meeting with President Kennedy—addressed the crowd. It was generally agreed that King's speech was the highlight of the demonstration.

chains of discrimination. One-hundred years later, the Negro lives on a lonely island of poverty in the midst of a vast ocean of material prosperity. One-hundred years later, the Negro is still languished in the corners of American society and finds himself an exile in his own land. So we have come here today to dramatize a shameful condition.

In a sense we've come to our nation's capital to cash a check. When the architects of our republic wrote the magnificent words of the Constitution and the Declaration of Independence, they were signing a promissory note to which every American was to fall heir. This note was a promise that all men—yes, black men as well as white men—would be guaranteed the unalienable rights of life, liberty, and the pursuit of happiness.

It is obvious today that America has defaulted on this promissory note insofar as her citizens of color are concerned. Instead of honoring this sacred obligation, America has given the Negro people a bad check; a check which has come back marked "insufficient funds." But we refuse to believe that the bank of justice is bankrupt. We refuse to believe that there are insufficient funds in the great vaults of opportunity of this nation. So we've come to cash this check—a check that will give us upon demand the riches of freedom and the security of justice. We have also come to this hallowed spot to remind America of the fierce urgency of *now*. This is no time to engage in the luxury of cooling off or to take the tranquilizing drug of gradualism. *Now is the time* to make real the promises of Democracy. *Now is the time* to rise from the dark and desolate valley of segregation to the sunlight of racial justice. *Now is the time* to lift our nation from the quicksands of racial injustice to the solid rock of brotherhood. *Now is the time* to make justice a reality for all of God's children.

It would be fatal for the nation to overlook the urgency of the moment. This sweltering summer of the Negro's legitimate discontent will not pass until there is an invigorating autumn of freedom and equality. Nineteen-sixty-three is not an end, but a beginning. Those who hope that the Negro needed to blow off steam and will now be content will have a rude awakening if the nation returns to business as usual. There will be neither rest nor tranquility in America until the Negro is granted his citizenship rights. The whirlwinds of revolt will con-

much like the standard used in evaluating great literature. As you read this speech, keep this standard in mind. (1) How would you evaluate this speech using the standard of universality?

Speeches are addressed to specific audiences and are judged largely on the basis of how effectively the speaker adapts the topic and purpose to that specific audience. Yet, there are often other audiences that the speaker hopes to address. (2) To whom was King speaking? That is, who did King see as his primary audience? What other audiences was King addressing?

Notice that in this speech there is neither an elaborate orientation nor are there any lengthy attention-getting devices used in the introduction. (3) Given the circumstances of this speech (see footnote to speech), were King's rhetorical choices effective?

(4) How effective is this metaphor of the "check" and "promissory note"? Would this metaphor work if members of your class were the intended listeners?

(5) Given the times and what you know of Martin Luther King's reputation during this time in history, how would you estimate King's credibility prior to the speech (his intrinsic credibility)? (6) Did King do anything in the speech to further establish his credibility (extrinsic credibility)? (7) How would you describe King's terminal credibility to his immediate audience after the speech?
(8) What is the thesis of this speech? Was this thesis appropriate given the general climate of the times, the specific occasion, the immediate audience, and King's purpose?

(9) What is the general purpose of this speech? The specific purpose? (10) What response did King want from his immediate audience? What response did King want from the black community? From the white community? From the country at large?

(11) What kinds of reasoning can you identify in this speech? Was the reasoning logical? Effective?

(12) What kinds of motivational appeals does King use? Are these generally effective? (13) What to you is the single most effective motivational appeal?

(14) What organizational pattern did King use in this speech? Was this pattern effective? (15) Was this speech organized on the basis of primacy or recency? (16) Was a climax or an anticlimax order used? Were these orders effective? What specific evidence can you cite to support your conclusions?

tinue to shake the foundations of our nation until the bright day of justice emerges.

But that is something that I must say to my people who stand on the warm threshold which leads into the palace of justice. In the process of gaining our rightful place we must not be guilty of wrongful deeds. Let us not seek to satisfy our thirst for freedom by drinking from the cup of bitterness and hatred.

We must forever conduct our struggle on the high plane of dignity and discipline. We must not allow our creative protest to degenerate into physical violence. Again and again we must rise to the majestic heights of meeting physical force with soul force. The marvelous new militancy which has engulfed the Negro community must not lead us to a distrust of all white people, for many of our white brothers, as evidenced by their presence here today, have come to realize that their destiny is tied up with our destiny. And they have come to realize that their freedom is inextricably bound to our freedom. We cannot walk alone.

And as we walk we must make the pledge that we shall always march ahead. We cannot turn back. There are those who ask the devotees of civil rights, "When will you be satisfied?" We can never be satisfied as long as the Negro is the victim of the unspeakable horrors of police brutality. We can never be satisfied as long as our bodies, heavy with the fatigue of travel, cannot gain lodging in the motels of the highways and the hotels of the cities. We cannot be satisfied as long as the Negro's basic mobility is from a smaller ghetto to a larger one. We can never be satisfied as long as our children are stripped of their selfhood and robbed of their dignity by signs stating "For Whites Only." We cannot be satisfied as long as a Negro in Mississippi cannot vote and a Negro in New York believes he has nothing for which to vote. No, no, we are not satisfied, and we will not be satisfied until justice rolls down like waters and righteousness like a mighty stream.

I am not unmindful that some of you have come here out of great trials and tribulations. Some of you have come fresh from narrow jail cells. Some of you have come from areas where your quest for freedom left you battered by the storms of persecution and staggered by the winds of police brutality. You have been the veterans of creative suffering. Continue to work with the faith that unearned suffering is redemptive.

Go back to Mississippi, go back to Alabama, go back to South Carolina, go back to Georgia, go back to Louisiana, go back to the slums and ghettos of our northern cities knowing that somehow this situation can and will be changed. Let us not wallow in the valley of despair.

I say to you today, my friends, so even though we face the difficulties of today and tomorrow, I still have a dream. It is a dream deeply rooted in the American dream.

I have a dream that one day this nation will rise up and live out the true meaning of its creed: "We hold these truths to be self-evident; that all men are created equal."

I have a dream that one day on the red hills of Georgia the sons of former slaves and the sons of former slaveowners will be able to sit down together at the table of brotherhood; I have a dream—

That one day even the state of Mississippi, a state sweltering with the heat of injustice, sweltering with the heat of oppression, will be transformed into an oasis of freedom and justice; I have a dream—

That my four little children will one day live in a nation where they will not be judged by the color of their skin but by the content of their character; I have a dream today.

I have a dream that one day down in Alabama, with its vicious racists, with its governor having his lips dripping with the words of interposition and nullification, one day right there in Alabama little black boys and black girls will be able to join hands with little white boys and white girls as sisters and brothers; I have a dream today.

I have a dream that one day every valley shall be exalted, every hill and mountain shall be made low, and rough places will be made plane and crooked places will be made straight, and the glory of the Lord shall be revealed, and all flesh shall see it together.

This is our hope. This is the faith that I go back to the South with. With this faith we will be able to hew out of the mountain of despair a stone of hope. With this faith we will be able to transform the jangling discords of our nation into a beautiful symphony of brotherhood. With this faith we will be able to work together, to pray together, to struggle together, to go to jail together, to stand up for freedom together, knowing that we will be free one day.

(17) How effective are the specific examples that King uses throughout the speech? (18) What other kinds of supporting materials does King use?

(19) How effective is the repetition of "I have a dream"?

This speech is regarded by many as a model of stylistic excellence. Examine the language used. (20) How effective is it? (21) What stylistic elements make it effective? Do some stylistic elements detract from its effectiveness? Explain.

(22) How would you characterize this speech on an oral-written style continuum? What specific phrases can you point to in support of your conclusion?

Each speaker has his or her own style. Another speaker's style—especially a speaker as unique as King—cannot easily be adapted. (23) What aspects of King's style would be inappropriate for you to adapt into your own speaking? (24) What aspects would be appropriate? On what basis do you make this distinction?

This will be the day. . . . This will be the day when all of God's children will be able to sing with new meaning "My country 'tis of thee, sweet land of liberty, of thee I sing. Land where my fathers died, land of the pilgrim's pride, from every mountainside, let freedom ring," and if America is to be a great nation—this must become true.

So let freedom ring—from the prodigious hilltops of New Hampshire, let freedom ring; from the mighty mountains of New York, let freedom ring—from the heightening Alleghenies of Pennsylvania!

Let freedom ring from the snowcapped Rockies of Colorado.

Let freedom ring from the curvaceous slopes of California!

But not only that; let freedom ring from Stone Mountain of Georgia!

Let freedom ring from Lookout Mountain of Tennessee!

Let freedom ring from every hill and mole hill of Mississippi. From every mountainside, let freedom ring, and when this happens. . . .

When we allow freedom to ring, when we let it ring from every village and every hamlet, from every state and every city, we will be able to speed up that day when all of God's children, black men and white men, Jews and Gentiles, Protestants and Catholics, will be able to join hands and sing in the words of the old Negro spiritual, "Free at last! free at last! thank God almighty, we are free at last!"

Source: Copyright © 1963 by Martin Luther King, Jr., copyright renewed 1991 by Coretta Scot King. Reprinted by arrangement with the Heirs of the Estate of Martin Luther King, Jr., c/o Joan Daves Agency as agent for the proprietor.

Are You Too Busy to Think?

CHANGE COMES FROM THE QUESTIONS WE ASK

William J. Banach

My business is creating strategic advantage. I help people envision preferred futures and develop plans for getting there. My clients tend to be ahead of the curve. Here's why: They understand that thinking is the first step to being a step ahead.

But most people don't have time to think. They're too busy working!

(25) What type of conclusion did King use? Was this effective?

(26) What one feature of this entire speech do you find most effective? (27) What one feature do you find least effective?

(28) What do you remember most after reading this speech? (29) What public speaking principle might you derive on the basis of what you remember from this speech?

(1) How effectively does Banach involve his audience? (Remember that the audience consists of members of the Association of Wisconsin School Administrators.)

Strange, isn't it?

How many times have you heard people say that they do their best thinking in the car. But when they pull into the parking lot, they turn off the car and shut down their thinking . . . so they can "get to work."

Perhaps that's why there are too few new ideas. Perhaps that's why much of what we do looks like much of what we've done.

Here's your chance to rebel. Take time to think . . . right now. Shut the door. Get comfortable. Read the rest of this article. Then stare out the window. Indulge yourself in 20 minutes of thinking—30 if you're radical.

To get started, use Banach's Woodpecker Questions. These are questions for which we have an answer, but we're really not sure it's correct. (The classic is: "Do woodpeckers get headaches?" Scientists tell us the woodpecker's brain is wrapped in a huge mucous pad, so the bird can bang away all day and never get headaches. So, while the answer to the question is "no," we're not really sure.)

Woodpecker Question 1: Why do we use textbooks? We think we know the answer, but are we really sure?

Information is doubling every 2½ years—every 900 days! By the time today's kindergartner moves through the grades to graduation, the body of information will quadruple!

Now, add the data above to this: It takes about 10 years to get a textbook into print. From the time the author conceives ideas, develops thoughts, writes, edits, hooks up with a publisher, rewrites, and engages in myriad other steps, a decade passes. Next, a school district curriculum review committee spends two years evaluating the book before making a recommendation (which then passes through the administrative hierarchy before approval by the school board). Finally, the school district adopts a brand new 12-year old book . . . and students use it for five to seven years, sometimes more.

In this scenario, the student at the end of the line is using a 19-year old book (10 + 2 + 7). This leads to a dead duck question: How can a student keep current by reading a 19-year old book? (We have an answer to dead duck questions *and* we're sure it's right; e.g., "Do dead ducks quack?")

Woodpecker Question 2: Why do schools have to be places? Twenty percent of Americans work at home. The percentage is destined to increase.

(2) Does Banach gain attention in his introduction? How? (3) Does Banach continue to use attention-gaining devices throughout his speech? (4) Does Banach establish a speaker-audience-topic relationship? How? (5) Does Banach orient or preview his speech for his listeners? How?

(6) Does Banach avoid the major pitfalls of introductions? Does he apologize or pretend? Make hollow promises? Preface his introduction?

(7) What is the thesis of this speech? How is it presented in the speech? For example, is it explicitly stated? Implied? (8) Is this thesis appropriate to the speaker's audience?

(9) What is the general purpose of the speech? The specific purpose? (10) Do you think the speaker accomplishes his purpose? On what do you base your conclusion?

(11) Does this example of the delay in textbooks and the inevitability of their being outdated convince you that textbooks are in fact outdated? (12) How might you verify Banach's claim?

(13) How effective was the Woodpecker theme? Would it be effective with your class as an audience?

Many of these home-based workers have computers, fax machines and sophisticated telephone equipment. Long distance they look and sound like "real" companies. And who else has access to the technology which makes home-based employment possible? The children of these workers.

So, why should students be transported to a place. They can get their lesson on video, from the best instructors in the world. Why should students spend time in an ill-equipped lab? They can do computer simulations. Why should they write out their lessons long hand? They can use word processors and fax their lessons to school.

During the 1990s we will repackage education. Learning will take place in the home, in the community, at school and in between. And by the dawning of the new century we will have dramatic new designs for the delivery of schooling.

"What about socialization?" asks Brontosaurus Skepticus. "Students won't learn how to interact with one another." The fact is there isn't much socializing at school. A lot of kids don't know a lot of kids. Think about it. In a high school there are typically five or six 55-minute periods with five minutes for passing from one class to the next. How do you socialize when you have to rush from one place to another and be quiet once you get there? (Woodpecker Question 2a!)

Woodpecker Question 3: Why don't we teach to the test? Obviously, it wouldn't be fair . . . or so we have learned.

But, if you think about it, education is one of the few arenas where participants often don't know what's expected of them . . . until it's too late.

In every sport, the objective is clear and the evaluation criteria are known before the game begins. Basketball players know they have to get the ball through the hoop more frequently than members of the other team. In baseball, the objective is to score more runs; in football, more points.

Other professions know the objectives in advance. For example, in medicine everyone works to heal the patient. In fact, the patient is part of the process. He/she knows in advance of any treatment which procedures will be performed, the expected outcomes, and his/her role in the process.

But in education the objectives aren't clear. Most school districts can't tell students and their parents what

(14) Does Banach establish his credibility (competence, moral character, and charisma)? How? Which dimensions does Banach stress? (15) Are these attempts sufficient? Are they effective?

(16) Do any of these "Woodpecker Questions" lead you to question your own educational experiences? Why?

(17) What are the major propositions of this speech? How effectively are they highlighted?

(18) How effectively does Banach demonstrate the inability of groups to solve problems? Are you ready to accept Banach's conclusion? What additional data would you need?

(19) How would you evaluate Banach's use of language? Is the language direct or indirect? High or low in abstraction? Objective or subjective? Formal or informal? Accurate or inaccurate? What specific examples can you give to support your conclusions about the language of this speech?

to expect from a twelve-year investment. (Sorry, Brontosaurus Skepticus, we haven't explained what we mean by "a quality education for every child" . . . nor have we defined "skills for the changing world of work" or "producing learners who will be fully functioning members of a multifaceted society.")

Perhaps we should start by spelling out what we want students to learn. Then we should tell them the objectives and expectations up front. We should also make clear their responsibility in the process. Maybe that's all that blocks effective teacher-student-parent partnerships. Maybe that's all that is keeping some students from saying, "*Now* I understand."

Woodpecker Question 4: Why can't groups come up with solutions? Pick an answer: (a) They don't have all the data. (b) There are usually too many people in the group. (c) Group members don't get along. (d) None of the above.

The correct answer is d, none of the above. Groups can't come up with solutions because solutions—real solutions!—are situational and personal.

Groups are good at identifying issues and obstacles, but they can't accommodate specific situations, local politics and delicate interrelationships. During group process, people tend to get side tracked thinking about how they can survive the problem at home . . . or giving silent thanks that, in the end, it will be Bob or Mary who will have to handle the flak and deal with the fallout.

Getting everybody to agree that there is a problem is not a problem. In fact, every group can come to consensus on the dimensions of the problem and agree on a problem-solving model. But groups can't develop—let alone implement!—a common solution, and that's why groups always reach the point where "it's time to go home and do something."

Good administrators learn from group process, combine new information with what they know, bounce ideas off people "back home," and develop a solution.

This approach does not preclude citizen involvement or building decision-making teams. In fact, wise leaders involve people in things that affect their destiny. But realize that groups cannot take responsibility, and that's why there is often a gap between what they propose and what works. It is the job of the person in charge to accommodate the variables and develop localized solutions that have a chance. (This is why we have "ring lead-

(20) Would you characterize the style of the speech as "oral" or "written?" What specific language elements can you use to support your conclusion?

(21) Is the language used generally clear? Vivid? Appropriate to the speaker, audience, and topic? Personal? Forceful? What specific elements can you point to in support of your conclusion?

(22) Which of the propositions do you think would be the most powerful for his audience of administrators? Which would be the most powerful to your class as an audience?

(23) Considering that Banach is addressing school administrators, is this proposition about the defensiveness of educators well positioned? Would you have used it earlier or at about this point? Why?

(24) What organizational pattern is used? Was this effective?

(25) How would you describe the internal organization of the speech? For example, did the speaker use primary or recency? Was this a wise decision in your opinion? (26) Did the speaker use climax or anticlimax order? Was this a wise decision?

(27) What types of supporting material does the speaker use? Examples and illustrations? Definitions? Testimony? Statistics? Are these effectively used?

(28) What are the major forms of reasoning used? From specific instances? Analogy? Causes and effects? Sign? Is the reasoning sound? Does the reasoning pass the logical tests?

(29) What types of motivational appeals does the speaker use? Are these effective (given the speaker's audience)?

(30) How effective was the speaker's use of questions throughout the speech?

(31) What type of conclusion does Banach use? Does it effectively summarize and bring the speech to a definite close?

ers" and "team captains." Eventually, someone has to take responsibility.)

Woodpecker Question 5: Why are educators so defensive? Well, reading scores are down and violence is up; teachers aren't dedicated and administrators don't care. There are all kinds of reasons to be defensive and cover the flanks. But this is a dead duck question with lame duck answers. The reality is that educators have been assigned both blame and responsibility for society's problems. Most critics follow what's wrong with society (crime, drugs, violence, ill-prepared workers, etc.) by saying: "The schools have to improve!" (Notice that they don't say schools are a reflection of society and *we* are society so *we* must improve *our* schools.)

Nothing new here. America's educational system has taken responsibility in the past. Think about it. The industrial era required workers who were obedient, could handle routine work, didn't have to think too much and understood the importance of being on time. Look at the schools. They stressed discipline, drill and practice, not questioning your elders and being in your seat ". . . by the time the bell rings." Our schools produced the workforce industrial America demanded.

How well did the schools do? (Dead duck question!) American productivity reached new highs. Our quality of life surpassed anything forecasters imagined. U.S. graduate schools enrolled more foreign students than the graduate schools of all other nations combined. And our system of public education was envied throughout the world.

Now we are six decades into the Information Age. No one is sure of the future, and, hence, there is a lot of finger-pointing—people seeking to blame someone for the instability characterizing their lives. And guess what institution is front and center?

We demand more from our public schools than any other institution (with the possible exception of marriage). And they have produced what we have demanded.

But now the rules have changed. Knowledge is capital. There are new alliances in an international economy. Competition is being redefined, and so is work. We live in a period of turbulence, and during such times we tend to grab for the familiar and cling to the past.

But, our new age dictates a renaissance in education. Schools must accommodate the change in our society. They must become sensitive to marketplace forces, tailored to customer needs, and future focused. The changes ahead will redefine our concept of school. They also provide promise for an even better system of public education.

Get involved in the transformation. Start by asking questions. Think about the answers. Share the thoughts. Lead the revitalization wherever you are.

Need more?

Why do teachers have to be people? Okay, why do they have to be people trained as teachers?

Why do we set up evaluation systems that make schools look bad?

Why are our schools structured like the factories of the Industrial Age that ended 50 years ago?

Why do we spend so much time on squeaking wheels while ignoring the things that hum along?

Why is everything "bolted on" to the curriculum instead of integrated in?

Why do we lecture all the time?

Change comes from the questions we ask. Questions allow us to think, thinking allows us to make connections, connections produce understanding . . . and that's what leads to strategic advantage and preferred tomorrows.

Before you go back to work, think about it.

Banach is executive director, the Institute for Future Studies, Macomb Community College. The speech was delivered to the Association of Wisconsin School Administrators, Milwaukee, Wisconsin (October 25, 1990). The speech is reprinted from *Vital Speeches of the Day* (March 15, 1991):351–352.

(32) Does Banach avoid the common faults of conclusions? Does he apologize? Introduce new material? Dilute his position in any way? Drag out the conclusion?

(33) What is your overall evaluation of this speech? That is, if this speech were given in your class, what grade would you give it? (34) What is the major strength of this speech as you see it? (35) What is the major weakness? How might this weakness have been corrected?

(36) How effective do you think the speech title is? What titles do you think would work better? Why? What would be an absolutely inappropriate title? Why?

Bibliography

Adams, Dennis M., and Hamm, Mary E. (1990). *Cooperative Learning: Critical Thinking and Collaboration Across the Curriculum.* Springfield, IL: Charles C. Thomas.

Adams, Linda, with Lenz, Elinor. (1989). *Be Your Best.* New York: Putnam.

Addeo, Edmond G., and Burger, Robert E. (1973). *Egospeak: Why No One Listens to You.* New York: Bantam.

Adler, Mortimer J. (1983). *How to Speak, How to Listen.* New York: Macmillan.

Adler, Ronald B. (1977). *Confidence in Communication: A Guide to Assertive and Social Skills.* New York: Holt, Rinehart and Winston.

Ailes, Roger (1988). *You Are the Message.* New York: Doubleday.

Akinnaso, F. Niyi (1982). On the Differences between Spoken and Written Language. *Language and Speech* 25, part 2, 97–125.

Albrecht, Karl (1980). *Brain Power: Learn to Improve Your Thinking Skills.* Englewood Cliffs, NJ: Prentice-Hall [Spectrum].

Alisky, Marvin (1985). *Vital Speeches of the Day* 51 (January 15).

Allen, Mike, and Preiss, Raymond W. (1990). Using Meta-analysis to Evaluate Curriculum: An Examination of Selected College Textbooks. *Communication Education* 38 (April):103–116.

Allen, Steve (1991). *Dumbth and 81 Ways to Make Americans Smarter.* Buffalo, NY: Prometheus Books.

American Psychiatric Association (1980). *Diagnostic and Statistical Manual,* 3d ed. Washington, DC: American Psychiatric Association.

Archambault, David (1992). *Vital Speeches of the Day* (June 1):491–493.

Argyle, Michael (1988). *Bodily Communication,* 2d ed. New York: Methuen.

Arnold, Carroll C., and Bowers, John Waite, eds. (1984). *Handbook of Rhetorical and Communication Theory.* Boston: Allyn & Bacon.

Aronson, Elliot (1980). *The Social Animal,* 3d ed. San Francisco: Freeman.

Asch, Solomon (1946). Forming Impressions of Personality. *Journal of Abnormal and Social Psychology* 41: 258–290.

Authier, Jerry, and Gustafson, Kay (1982). Microtraining: Focusing on Specific Skills. In Marshall, Eldon K., Kurtz, P. David, and Associates. *Interpersonal Helping Skills*: A Guide to Training Methods, Programs, and Resources. San Francisco: Jossey-Bass, pp. 93–130.

Aylesworth, Thomas G., and Aylesworth, Virginia L. (1978). *If You Don't Invade My Intimate Zone or Clean Up My Water Hold, I'll Breathe in Your Face, Blow on Your Neck, and Be Late For Your Party.* New York: Condor.

Ayres, Joe (1986). Perceptions of Speaking Ability: An Explanation for Stage Fright. *Communication Education* 35:275–287.

Ayres, Joe, and Miller, Janice (1986). *Effective Public Speaking,* 2d ed. Dubuque, IA: Brown.

Backrack, Henry M. (1976). Empathy. *Archives of General Psychiatry* 33:35–38.

Banach, William J. (1991). Are You Too Busy to Think? *Vital Speeches of the Day* 62 (March 15):351–352.

Barker, Larry, Edwards, R., Gaines, C., Gladney, K., and Holley, F. (1980). An Investigation of Proportional Time Spent in Various Communication Activities by College Students. *Journal of Applied Communication Research* 8:101–109.

Barna, LaRay M. (1985). Stumbling Blocks in Intercultural Communication. In Samovar, Larry A., and Porter, Richard E., eds. *Intercultural Communication: A Reader,* 4th ed. Belmont, CA: Wadsworth, pp. 330–338.

Barnlund, Dean C. (1970). A Transactional Model of Communication. In Akin, J., Goldberg, A., Myers, G., and Stewart, J., comps. *Language Behavior: A Book of Readings in Communication.* The Hague: Mouton.

Barnlund, Dean C. (1975). Communicative Styles in Two Cultures: Japan and the United States. In Kendon, A., Harris, R. M., and Key, M. R., eds. *Organization of Behavior in Face-to-Face Interaction.* The Hague: Mouton.

Baron, Robert A., and Byrne, Donn (1984). *Social Psychology: Understanding Human Interaction,* 4th ed. Boston: Allyn & Bacon.

Beck, Aaron (1988). *Love Is Never Enough.* New York: HarperCollins.

Beier, Ernst (1974). How We Send Emotional Messages. *Psychology Today* 8 (October): 53–56.

Bennis, Warren, and Nanus, Burt (1985). *Leaders: The Strategies for Taking Charge.* New York: Harper & Row.

Berger, Charles R., and Chaffee, Steven H., eds. (1987). *Handbook of Communication Science.* Newbury Park, CA: Sage.

Bettinghaus, Erwin P., and Cody, Michael J. (1987). *Persuasive Communication,* 4th ed. New York: Holt, Rinehart & Winston.

Blankenship, Jane (1968). *A Sense of Style: An Introduction to Style for the Public Speaker.* Belmont, CA: Dickenson.

Blumstein, Philip, and Schwartz, Pepper (1983). *American Couples: Money, Work, Sex.* New York: Morrow.

Boaz, John K., and Brey, James R., eds. (1987). *1987 Championship Debates and Speeches.* Normal, IL: American Forensic Association.

Boaz, John K., and Brey, James R., eds. (1988). *1988 Championship Debates and Speeches.* Normal, IL: American Forensic Association.

Bochner, Arthur, and Kelly, Clifford (1974). Interpersonal Competence: Rationale, Philosophy, and Implementation of a Conceptual Framework. *Communication Education* 23:279–301.

Bok, Sissela (1978). *Lying: Moral Choice in Public and Private Life.* New York: Pantheon.

Bok, Sissela (1983). *Secrets.* New York: Vintage Books.

Borisoff, Deborah, and Merrill, Lisa (1985). *The Power to Communicate: Gender Differences as Barriers.* Prospect Heights, IL: Waveland Press.

Boster, Frank, and Mongeau, Peter (1984). Fear Arousing Persuasive Messages. In Bostrom, Robert, ed. *Communication Yearbook 8.* Newbury Park, CA: Sage, pp. 330–377.

Boyd, Stephen D., and Renz, Mary Ann (1985). *Organization and Outlining: A Workbook for Students in a Basic Speech Course.* New York: Macmillan.

Bradac, James J., Bowers, John Waite, and Courtright, John A. (1979). Three Language Variables in Communication Research: Intensity, Immediacy, and Diversity. *Human Communication Research* 5:256–269.

Bradley, Bert E. (1991). *Fundamentals of Speech Communication: The Credibility of Ideas,* 6th ed. Dubuque, IA: Brown.

Brody, Jane F. (1991). How to Foster Self-Esteem. *New York Times Magazine.* (April 28), p. 15.

Brougher, Toni (1982). *A Way With Words.* Chicago: Nelson-Hall.

Buchsbaum, S. J. (1991). *Vital Speeches of the Day* (December 15):150–155.

Buchstein, Frederick (1988). *Vital Speeches of the Day* (June 15):534–536.

Buckley, Reid (1988). *Speaking in Public*. New York: Harper & Row.

Burgoon, Judee K., Buller, David B., and Woodall, W. Gill (1989). *Nonverbal Communication: The Unspoken Dialogue*. New York: Harper & Row.

Buscaglia, Leo (1988). Leo Buscaglia's Golden Rules of Love. *Women's Day* (June 29).

Butcher, Willard C. (1987). *Vital Speeches of the Day* (September 1):680.

Chisholm, Shirley (1978). *Vital Speeches of the Day* 44 (August 15).

Cialdini, Robert T. (1984). *Influence: How and Why People Agree to Things*. New York: Morrow.

Cialdini, Robert T., and Ascani, K. (1976). Test of a Concession Procedure for Inducing Verbal, Behavioral, and Further Compliance with a Request to Give Blood. *Journal of Applied Psychology* 61:295–300.

Clark, Herbert (1974). The Power of Positive Speaking. *Psychology Today* 8:102.

Clement, Donald A., and Frandsen, Kenneth D. (1976). On Conceptual and Empirical Treatments of Feedback in Human Communication. *Communication Monographs* 43:11–28.

Condon, John C., and Yousef, Fathi (1975). *An Introduction to Intercultural Communication*. Indianapolis: Bobbs-Merrill.

D'Angelo, Frank J. (1980). *Process and Thought in Composition*, 2d ed. (1980). Cambridge, MA: Winthrop.

DeJong, W. (1979). An Examination of Self-Perception Mediation of the Foot-in-the-Door Effect. *Journal of Personality and Social Psychology* 37:2221–2239.

Delattre, Edwin (1988). *Vital Speeches of the Day* (May 15):467.

DeVito, Joseph A. (1965). Comprehension Factors in Oral and Written Discourse of Skilled Communicators. *Communication Monographs* 32 (1965):124–128.

DeVito, Joseph A. (1969). Some Psycholinguistic Aspects of Active and Passive Sentences. *Quarterly Journal of Speech* 55:401–406.

DeVito, Joseph A. (1970). *The Psychology of Speech and Language: An Introduction to Psycholinguistics*. New York: Random House.

DeVito, Joseph A. (1974). *General Semantics: Guide and Workbook*, rev. ed. DeLand, FL: Everett/Edwards.

DeVito, Joseph A. (1976). Relative Ease in Comprehending Yes/No Questions. In Blankenship, Jane, and Stelzner, Herman G., eds., *Rhetoric and Communication*. Urbana, IL: University of Illinois Press, pp. 143–154.

DeVito, Joseph A. (1986). *The Communication Handbook: A Dictionary*. New York: Harper & Row.

DeVito, Joseph A. (1989). *The Nonverbal Communication Workbook*. Prospect Heights, IL: Waveland Press.

DeVito, Joseph A. (1992). *The Interpersonal Communication Book*, 6th ed. New York: Harper-Collins.

DeVito, Joseph A. (1993). *Messages: Building Interpersonal Communication Skills*, 2d ed. New York: HarperCollins.

DeVito, Joseph A., Giattino, Jill, and Schon, T. D. (1975). *Articulation and Voice: Effective Communication*. Indianapolis: Bobbs-Merrill.

DeVito, Joseph A., and Hecht, Michael L., eds. (1990). *The Nonverbal Communication Reader*. Prospect Heights, IL: Waveland Press.

Dodd, Carley H. (1982). *Dynamics of Intercultural Communication*. Dubuque, IA: Brown.

Dodd, David H., and White, Raymond M., Jr. (1980). *Cognition: Mental Structures and Processes*. Boston: Allyn & Bacon.

Eisen, Jeffrey, with Farley, Pat (1984). *Power-Talk: How to Speak It, Think It, and Use It*. New York: Simon and Schuster.

Eisenberg, Nancy, and Strayer, Janet (1987). *Empathy and Its Development*. New York: Cambridge University Press.

Ellis, Albert, and Harper, Robert A. (1975). *A New Guide to Rational Living*. Hollywood, CA: Wilshire Books.

Ennis, Robert H. (1987). A Taxonomy of Critical Thinking Dispositions and Abilities. In Baron, Joan Boykoff, and Sternberg, Robert J., eds., *Teaching Thinking Skills: Theory and Practice*. New York: Freeman, pp. 9–26.

Faber, Adele, and Mazlish, Elaine (1980). *How to Talk So Kids Will Listen and Listen So Kids Will Talk*. New York: Avon.

Filley, Alan C. (1975). *Interpersonal Conflict Resolution*. Glenview, IL: Scott, Foresman.

Floyd, James J. (1985). *Listening: A Practical Approach*. Glenview, IL: Scott, Foresman.

Folger, Joseph P., and Poole, Marshall Scott (1984). *Working Through Conflict: A Communication Perspective*. Glenview, IL: Scott, Foresman.

Freedman, J., and Fraser, S. (1966). Compliance Without Pressure: The Foot-in-the-Door Technique. *Journal of Personality and Social Psychology* 4:195–202.

Gabor, Don (1989). *How to Talk to the People You Love*. New York: Simon and Schuster.

Garner, Alan (1981). *Conversationally Speaking*. New York: McGraw-Hill.

Gibb, Jack (1961). Defensive Communication. *Journal of Communication* 11:141–148.

Gordon, Thomas (1975). *P.E.T.: Parent Effectiveness Training*. New York: New American Library.

Goss, Blaine (1989). *The Psychology of Communication*. Prospect Heights, IL: Waveland Press.

Goss, Blaine, Thompson, M., and Olds, S. (1978). Behavioral Support for Systematic Desensitization for Communication Apprehension. *Human Communication Research* 4:158–163.

Gronbeck, Bruce E., McKerrow, Raymie E., Ehninger, Douglas, and Monroe, Alan H. (1990). *Principles and Types of Speech Communication*, 11th ed. New York: HarperCollins.

Gross, Ronald (1991). *Peak Learning*. Los Angeles: Jeremy P. Tarcher.

Guerra, Stella (1986). *Vital Speeches of the Day* (September 15):727.

Hamlin, Sonya (1988). *How to Talk So People Listen*. New York: Harper & Row.

Haney, William (1973). *Communication and Organizational Behavior: Text and Cases*, 3d ed. Homewood IL: Irwin.

Hayakawa, S. I., and Hayakawa, Alan R. (1990). *Language in Thought and Action*, 5th ed. New York: Harcourt Brace Jovanovich.

Hecht, Michael, and Ribeau, Sidney (1984). Ethnic Communication: A Comparative Analysis of Satisfying Communication. *International Journal of Intercultural Relations* 8:135–151.

Heinrich, Robert et al. (1983). *Instructional Media: The New Technologies of Instruction*. New York: Wiley.

Heldmann, Mary Lynne (1988). *When Words Hurt: How to Keep Criticism from Undermining Your Self-Esteem*. New York: Ballantine.

Henley, Nancy M. (1977). *Body Politics: Power, Sex, and Nonverbal Communication*. Englewood Cliffs, NJ: Prentice-Hall.

Hess, Ekhard H. (1975). *The Tell-Tale Eye*. New York: Van Nostrand Reinhold.

Hewitt, John, and Stokes, Randall (1975). Disclaimers. *American Sociological Review* 40:1–11.

Hickey, Neil (1989). Decade of Change, Decade of Choice. *TV Guide* 37 (December 9):29–34.

Hickson, Mark L., and Stacks, Don W. (1989). *NVC: Nonverbal Communication: Studies and Applications*, 2d ed. Dubuque, IA: Brown.

Hocker, Joyce L., and Wilmot, William W. (1991). *Interpersonal Conflict*, 3d ed. Dubuque, IA: Brown.

Infante, Dominic A. (1988). *Arguing Constructively*. Prospect Heights, IL: Waveland Press.

Infante, Dominic A., Rancer, Andrew S., and Womack, Deanna F. (1990). *Building Communication Theory*. Prospect Heights, IL: Waveland.

Jackson, William (1985). *Vital Speeches of the Day* (September 15).

Jaksa, James A., and Pritchard, Michael S. (1988). *Communication Ethics: Methods of Analysis*. Belmont, CA: Wadsworth.

Jensen, J. Vernon (1985). Perspectives on Nonverbal Intercultrual Communication. In Samovar, Larry, and Porter, Richard E., eds., *Intercultural Communication: A Reader*, 4th ed. Belmont, CA: Wadsworth, pp. 256–272.

Johnson, Geneva B. (1991). *Vital Speeches of the Day* (April 15):393–398.

Kemp, Jerrold E., and Dayton, Deane K. (1985). *Planning and Producing Instructional Media*, 5th ed. New York: Harper & Row.

Keohane, Nannerl O. (1991). *Vital Speeches of the Day* (July 15):605–608.

Kesselman-Turkel, Judi, and Peterson, Franklynn (1982). *Note-Taking Made Easy*. Chicago: Contemporary Books.

Kim, Hyun J. (1991). Influence of Language and Similarity on Initial Intercultural Attraction. In Ting-Toomey, Stella, and Korzenny, Felipe, eds., *Cross-Cultural Interpersonal Communication*. Newbury Park, CA: Sage, pp. 213–229.

Kim, Young Yun, ed. (1986). *Interethnic Communication: Current Research*. Newbury Park, CA: Sage.

Kim, Young Yun (1991). Intercultural Communication Competence. In Ting-Toomey, Stella, and Korzenny, Felipe, eds., *Cross-Cultural Interpersonal Communication*. Newbury Park, CA: Sage, pp. 259–275.

Kim, Young Yun, and Gudykunst, William B., eds. (1988). *Theories in Intercultural Communication*. Newbury Park, CA: Sage.

Kleinke, Chris L. (1978). *Self-Perception: The Psychology of Personal Awareness*. San Francisco: Freeman.

Kleinke, Chris L. (1986). *Meeting and Understanding People*. New York: Freeman.

Knapp, Mark, and Hall, Judith (1992). *Nonverbal Behavior in Human Interaction*, 3d ed. New York: Holt, Rinehart and Winston.

Kohn, Alfie (1989). Do Religious People Help More? Not So You'd Notice. *Psychology Today* (December):66–68.

Kramarae, Cheris (1981). *Women and Men Speaking*. Rowley, MA: Newbury House.

Lambdin, William (1981). *Doublespeak Dictionary*. Los Angeles: Pinnacle Books.

Lamkin, Martha (1986). *Vital Speeches of the Day* (December 15):152.

Langer, Ellen J. (1978). Rethinking the Role of Thought in Social Interaction. In Harvey, J. H., Ickes, W. J., and Kidd, R. F., eds. *New Directions in Attribution Research*, vol. 2. Hillsdale, NJ: Erlbaum, pp. 35–58.

Langer, Ellen J. (1989). *Mindfulness*. Reading, MA: Addison-Wesley.

Larson, Charles U. (1992). *Persuasion: Reception and Responsibility*, 6th ed. Belmont, CA: Wadsworth.

Leathers, Dale G. (1992). *Successful Nonverbal Communication: Principles and Applications*, 2d ed. New York: Macmillan.

Leeds, Dorothy (1988). *Powerspeak*. New York: Prentice-Hall.

Littlejohn, Stephen W. (1992). *Theories of Human Communication*, 4th ed. Belmont, CA: Wadsworth.

Littlejohn, Stephen W., and Jabusch, David M. (1987). *Persuasive Transactions*. Glenview, IL: Scott, Foresman.

Loden, Marilyn (1986). *Vital Speeches of the Day* (May 15):472–475.

Loftus, Elizabeth, and Palmer, J. C. (1974). Reconstruction of Automobile Destruction: An Example of the Interaction Between Language and Memory. *Journal of Verbal Learning and Verbal Behavior* 13:585–589.

Lunsford, Charlotte (1988). *Vital Speeches of the Day* (September 15):731.

Lurie, Alison (1983). *The Language of Clothes*. New York: Vintage.

Mackay, Harvey B. (1991). *Vital Speeches of the Day* (August 15):656–659.

MacLachlan, John (1979). What People Really Think of Fast Talkers. *Psychology Today* 13 (November):113–117.

McCarthy, Michael J. (1991). *Mastering the Information Age*. Los Angeles: Jeremy P. Tarcher.

McCroskey, James C. (1982). *An Introduction to Rhetorical Communication*, 4th ed. Englewood Cliffs, NJ: Prentice-Hall.

McGill, Michael E. (1985). *The McGill Report on Male Intimacy*. New York: Harper & Row.

McLaughlin, Margaret L. (1984). *Conversation: How Talk Is Organized*. Newbury Park, CA: Sage.

McMahon, Ed (1986). *The Art of Public Speaking*. New York: Ballantine.

McNamara, Robert (1985). *Vital Speeches of the Day* (July 1):549.

Malandro, Loretta A., Barker, Larry, and Barker, Deborah Ann (1989). *Nonverbal Communication*, 2d ed. New York: Random House.

Marien, Michael (1992). *Vital Speeches of the Day* (March 15):340–344.

Marshall, Evan (1983). *Eye Language: Understanding the Eloquent Eye*. New York: New Trend.

Martel, Myles (1989). *The Persuasive Edge*. New York: Fawcett.

Marwell, G., and Schmitt, D. R. (1967). Dimensions of Compliance-Gaining Behavior: An Empirical Analysis. *Sociometry* 39:350–364.

Matsuyama, Yukio (1992). *Vital Speeches of the Day* (May 15):461–466.

Miller, Gerald, and Parks, Malcolm (1982). Communication in Dissolving Relationships. In Duck, Steve, ed., *Personal Relationships: 4. Dissolving Personal Relationships*. New York: Academic Press.

Miller, Sherod, Wackman, Daniel, Nunnally, Elam, and Saline, Carol (1982). *Straight Talk*. New York: New American Library.

Morris, Desmond, Collett, Peter, Marsh, Peter, and O'Shaughnessy, Marie (1979). *Gestures: Their Origins and Distribution*. New York: Stein and Day.

Murphy, Richard (1958). The Speech as Literary Genre. *Quarterly Journal of Speech* 44 (April):117–127.

Naisbitt, John (1984). *Megatrends: Ten New Directions Tranforming Our Lives*. New York: Warner.

Nichols, Ralph (1961). Do We Know How to Listen? Practical Helps in a Modern Age. *Communication Education* 10:118–124.

Nichols, Ralph, and Stevens, Leonard (1957). *Are You Listening?* New York: McGraw-Hill.

Nickerson, Raymond S. (1987). Why Teach Thinking? In Baron, Joan Boykoff, and Sternberg, Robert J., eds., *Teaching Thinking Skills: Theory and Practice*. New York: Freeman, pp. 27–37.

Orski, C. Kenneth (1986). *Vital Speeches of the Day* (February 1):274.

Osborn, Alex (1957). *Applied Imagination*, rev. ed. New York: Scribners.

Page, Richard A., and Balloun, Joseph L. (1978). The Effect of Voice Volume on the Perception of Personality. *Journal of Social Psychology* 105:65–72.

Payan, Janice (1990). *Vital Speeches of the Day* (September 1):697–701.

Pearson, Judy C. (1985). *Gender and Communication*. Dubuque, IA: Brown.

Pease, Allen (1984). *Signals: How to Use Body Language for Power, Success and Love*. New York: Bantam.

Pei, Mario (1956). *Language for Everybody*. New York: Pocket Books.

Penfield, Joyce, ed. (1987). *Women and Language in Transition*. Albany: State University of New York Press.

Penn, C. Ray (1990). *Vital Speeches of the Day* (December 1):116–117.

Peterson, Russell W. (1985). *Vital Speeches of the Day* (July 1):549.

Pratkanis, Anthony, and Aronson, Elliot (1991). *Age of Propaganda: The Everyday Use and Abuse of Persuasion*. New York: Freeman.

Qubein, Nido R. (1986). *Get the Best from Yourself*. New York: Berkley.

Rankin, Paul (1929). Listening Ability. In *Proceedings of the Ohio State Educational Conference's Ninth Annual Session*.

Reed, Warren H. (1985). *Positive Listening: Learning to Hear What People Are Really Saying*. New York: Franklin Watts.

Reynolds, Christina L., and Schnoor, Larry G., eds. (1991). *1989 Championship Debates and Speeches*. Normal, IL: American Forensic Association.

Richmond, Virginia P., and McCroskey, James C. (1992). *Communication: Apprehension, Avoidance, and Effectiveness*, 3d ed. Scottsdale, AZ: Gorsuch Scarisbrick.

Richmond, Virginia, McCroskey, James, and Payne, Steven (1987). *Nonverbal Behavior in Interpersonal Realtionships*. Englewood Cliffs, NJ: Prentice-Hall.

Riggio, Ronald E. (1987). *The Charisma Quotient*. New York: Dodd, Mead.

Robinson, Janet, and McArthur, Leslie Zebrowitz (1982). Impact of Salient Vocal Qualities on Causal Attribution for a Speaker's Behavior. *Journal of Personality and Social Psychology* 43:236–247.

Rockefeller, David (1985). *Vital Speeches of the Day* (March 15):328–331.

Rosenthal, Peggy (1984). *Words and Values: Some Leading Words and Where They Lead Us*. New York: Oxford University Press.

Rosenthal, Robert, and Jacobson, L. (1968). *Pygmalion in the Classroom*. New York: Holt, Rinehart and Winston.

Rothwell, J. Dan (1982). *Telling It Like It Isn't: Language Misuse and Malpractice/What We Can Do About It*. Englewood Cliffs, NJ: Prentice-Hall.

Ruben, Brent D. (1985). Human Communication and Cross-Cultural Effectiveness. In Samovar, Larry A., and Porter, Richard E., eds. *Intercultural Communication: A Reader*, 4th ed. Belmont, CA: Wadsworth, pp. 338–346.

Rubenstein, Eric (1992). *Vital Speeches of the Day* (April 15):401–404.

Ruchlis, Hy (1990). *Clear Thinking: A Practical Introduction*. Buffalo, NY: Prometheus Books.

Ruggiero, Vincent Ryan (1987). *Vital Speeches of the Day* 53 (August 15).

Ruggiero, Vincent Ryan (1990). *The Art of Thinking: A Guide to Critical and Creative Thought*, 3d ed. New York: HarperCollins.

Samovar, Larry A., Porter, Richard E., and Jain, Nemi C. (1981). *Understanding Intercultural Communication*. Belmont, CA: Wadsworth, 1981.

Samovar, Larry A., and Porter, Richard E., eds. (1988). *Intercultural Communication: A Reader*, 5th ed. Belmont, CA: Wadsworth.

Schaefer, Charles E. (1984). *How to Talk to Children About Really Important Things*. New York: Harper & Row.

Seidler, Ann, and Bianchi, Doris (1988). *Voice and Diction Fitness: A Comprehensive Approach*. New York: Harper & Row.

Singer, Marshall R. (1987). *Intercultural Communication: A Perceptual Approach*. Englewood Cliffs, NJ: Prentice-Hall.

Spitzberg, Brian H., and Cupach, William R. (1984). *Interpersonal Communication Competence*. Newbury Park, CA: Sage.

Spitzberg, Brian H., and Cupach, William R. (1989). *Handbook of Interpersonal Competence Research*. New York: Springer-Verlag.

Spitzberg, Brian H., and Hecht, Michael L. (1984). A Component Model of Relational Competence. *Human Communication Research* 10:575–599.

Sprague, Jo, and Stuart, Douglas (1988). *The Speaker's Handbook*, 2d ed. San Diego: Harcourt Brace Jovanovich.

Stark, Peter B. (1985). *Vital Speeches of the Day* 51 (October 1).

Steil, Lyman K., Barker, Larry L., and Watson, Kittie W. (1983). *Effective Listening: Key to Your Success*. Reading, MA: Addison-Wesley.

Sternberg, Robert J. (1987). Questions and Answers About the Nature and Teaching of Thinking Skills. In Baron, Joan Boykoff, and Sternberg, Robert J., eds., *Teaching Thinking Skills: Theory and Practice*. New York: Freeman, pp. 251–259.

Swets, Paul W. (1983). *The Art of Talking so that People Will Listen*. Englewood Cliffs, NJ: Prentice-Hall [Spectrum].

Thorne, Barrie, Kramarae, Cheris, and Henley, Nancy, eds. (1983). *Language, Gender and Society*. Rowley, MA: Newbury House.

Trenholm, Sarah (1986). *Human Communication Theory*. Englewood Cliffs, NJ: Prentice-Hall.

Truax, C. (1961). *A Scale for the Measurement of Accurate Empathy*. Wisconsin Psychiatric Institute Discussion Paper No. 20. Madison, WI: Wisconsin Psychiatric Institute.

Valenti, Jack (1982). *Speaking Up with Confidence: How to Prepare, Learn, and Deliver Effective Speeches*. New York: Morrow.

Verderber, Rudolph F. (1991). *The Challenge of Effective Speaking*, 8th ed. Belmont, CA: Wadsworth.

Wade, Carole, and Tavris, Carol (1990). *Learning to Think Critically: The Case of Close Relationships*. New York: HarperCollins.

Warnick, Barbara, and Inch, Edward S. (1989). *Critical Thinking and Communication: The Use of Reason in Argument*. New York: Macmillan.

Watson, Arden K., and Dodd, Carley H. (1984). Alleviating Communication Apprehension through Rational Emotive Therapy: A Comparative Evaluation. *Communication Education* 33:257–266.

Weaver, Richard L. (1991). *Vital Speeches of the Day* (August 1):620–623.

Wells, Theodora (1980). *Keeping Your Cool Under Fire: Communicating Non-Defensively*. New York: McGraw-Hill.

Whitman, Richard F., and Timmis, John H. (1975). The Influence of Verbal Organizational Structure and Verbal Organizing Skills on Select Measures of Learning. *Human Communication Research* 1:293–301.

Williams, Andrea (1985). *Making Decisions*. New York: Zebra.

Wolf, Florence I., Marsnik, Nadine C., Tacey, William S., and Nichols, Ralph G. (1983). *Perceptive Listening*. New York: Holt, Rinehart and Winston.

Credits

Page 364: Crandall, Stock, Boston
Page 374: © Conklin, PhotoEdit
Page 384: King, Gamma-Liaison
Page 393: © Borden, PhotoEdit
Page 408: © Conklin, PhotoEdit
Page 416: Daemmrich, Stock, Boston
Page 424: © Currea, PhotoEdit
Page 436: Coletti, Stock, Boston
Page 442: Daemmrich, Stock, Boston
Page 451: Burnett, Stock, Boston
Page 454: © Neubauer, PhotoEdit
Page 463: © Ogust/The Image Works

Index